DESTROYER
COSSACK

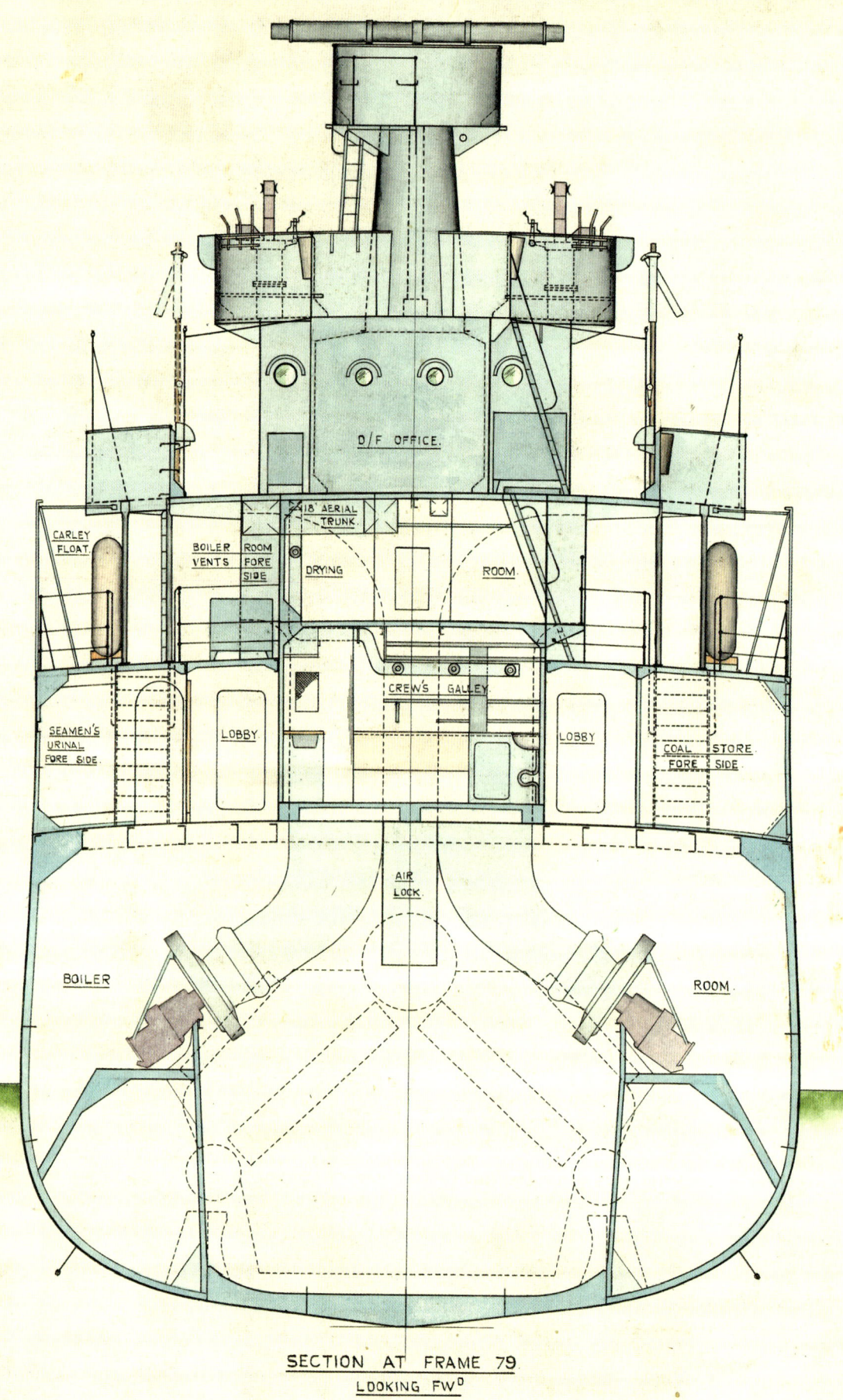

DESTROYER COSSACK

detailed in the original builders' plans

JOHN ROBERTS

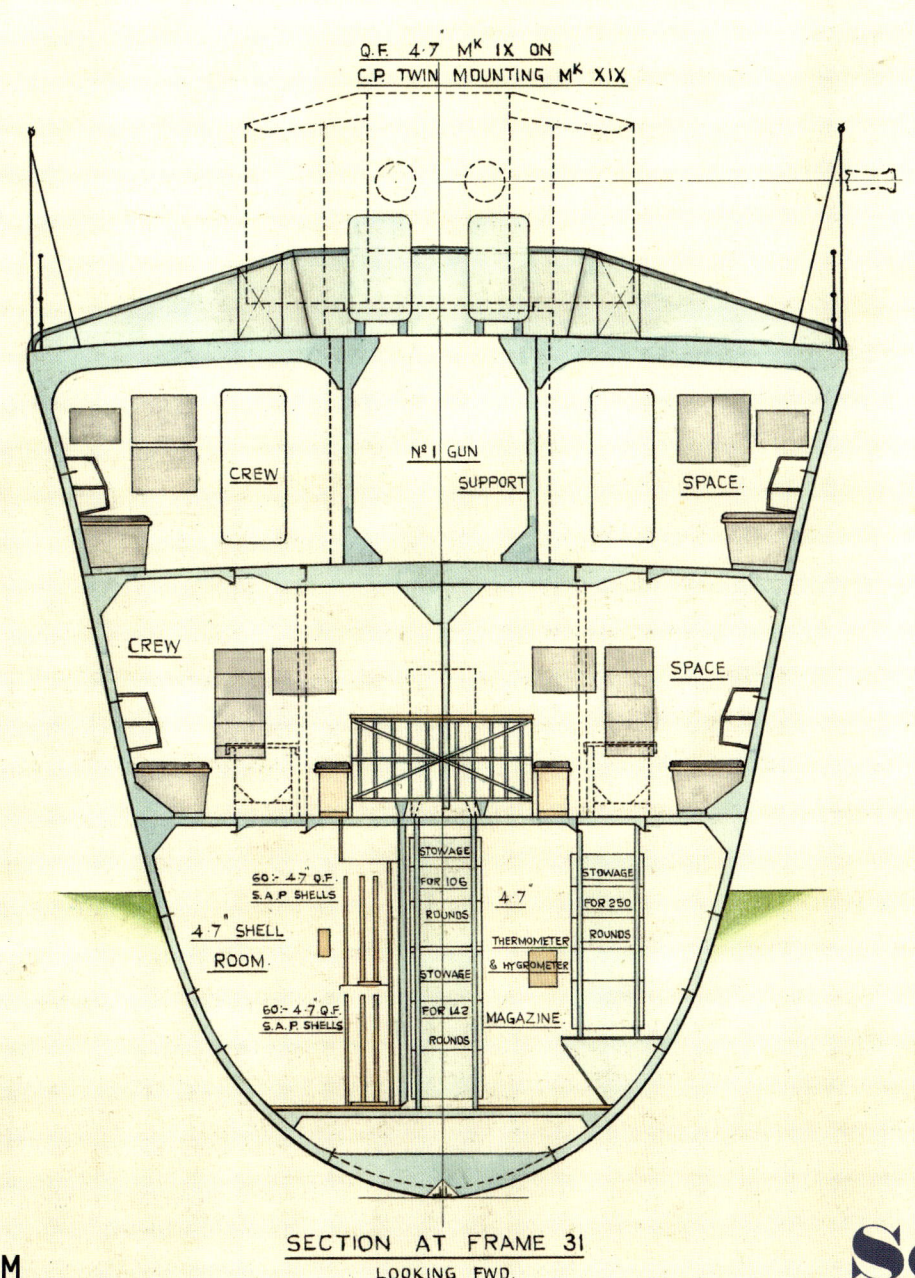

Q.F. 4.7 MK IX ON
C.P. TWIN MOUNTING MK XIX

SECTION AT FRAME 31
LOOKING FWD

NATIONAL MARITIME MUSEUM GREENWICH

Seaforth
PUBLISHING

Half title image: The badge of HMS *Cossack*. The ship's motto, *Non est utilitas equum mortem flagellant*, translates as 'It's no use flogging a dead horse'.
(Badge artwork by Stephen Dent)

Frontispiece: Sections at Frames 79 and 31 of HMS *Mohawk*, as fitted.
(© National Maritime Museum, Greenwich, London, detail from M1843)

ACKNOWLEDGMENTS

As with the book on *Repulse* this publication was reliant on the close co-operation between publisher and author and my thanks are due to both the series originator, Robert Gardiner of Seaforth Publishing, and to the book's designer, Steve Dent. My thanks are also due to the staff of the Photograph and Ship Plans Department of the National Maritime Museum at Woolwich for the assistance and friendly cooperation they have provided both at the time of the original research I undertook in relation to *Cossack* and more recently for this project. In the latter case particular thanks are due to Alex Grover. Lastly, I owe thanks to Jean, my wife, for her support and patience while I concentrated for several weeks on the present subject with little thought to other, no less important, matters.

John Roberts,
February 2020

Copyright © Seaforth Publishing 2020
Plans copyright © National Maritime Museum, Greenwich, London 2020

This edition first published in Great Britain in 2020 by
Seaforth Publishing,
An imprint of Pen & Sword Books Ltd,
47 Church Street,
Barnsley
South Yorkshire S70 2AS

www.seaforthpublishing.com
Email: info@seaforthpublishing.com

Published in association with Royal Museums Greenwich,
the group name for the National Maritime Museum,
the Royal Observatory, the Queen's House and *Cutty Sark*

British Library Cataloguing in Publication Data
A catalogue record for this book is available from the British Library

ISBN 978 1 5267 7706 5 (Hardback)
ISBN 978 1 5267 7707 2 (ePub)
ISBN 978 1 5267 7708 9 (Kindle)

All rights reserved. No part of this publication may be reproduced or transmitted in any form or by any means, electronic or mechanical, including photocopying, recording, or any information storage and retrieval system, without prior permission in writing of both the copyright owner and the above publisher.

Typeset and designed by Stephen Dent
Printed and bound in China

CONTENTS

PREFACE — 6
Abbreviations — 6

INTRODUCTION — 7
Origins — 7
Design — 9
Modifications 1936–1937 — 14
Armament — 16
Fire Control — 22
Machinery — 23
General — 23
HMS *Cossack* Career Summary — 24

FITTINGS — 26
Weather Deck Fittings — 26
HMS *Nubian*: Arrangement of Petrol System — 31

GATEFOLD PLANS — 32
HMS *Ashanti*: Expansion of Plating — 32
HMS *Cossack*: Profile, as fitted August 1938 — 35
HMCS *Haida*: Sketch of Rig, as fitted October 1943 — 41

DECKS — 42
HMS *Mohawk*: Upper, Forecastle and Bridge Decks, as fitted October 1938 — 42
HMS *Mohawk*: Lower Deck and Hold, as fitted October 1938 — 44

ARMAMENT — 46
4.7-inch Twin Mk XIX CP Mounting — 46
Main Armament Directors — 48
HMS *Cossack*: No3 Magazine and Shell Room, as fitted — 50
HMS *Cossack*: Stowage of 4.7-inch Shell Room, as fitted — 51
HMS *Cossack*: Stowage of 4.7-inch Magazine, as fitted — 52
HMS *Cossack*: Stowage of 2pdr and 0.5-inch Magazine, as fitted — 53
HMS *Cossack*: Torpedo Head Room and Torpedo Store Room, as fitted — 54
HMS *Ashanti*: Stowage of 4-inch Magazines, as fitted — 57

MACHINERY — 58
HMS *Mohawk*: General Arrangement of Main Machinery, 1938 — 58
'Tribal Class: Arrangement of Machinery in Engine Room — 60
'Tribal Class: Arrangement of Machinery in Boiler Rooms — 64

HMS *Cossack*: Water and Oil Fuel Services — 66
HMS *Cossack*: Ventilation Arrangement — 72
HMS *Cossack*: Holes in Bottom — 74
HMS *Ashanti*: Twin Barrel Steam Capstan — 76

HMS *COSSACK*: ENLARGED PROFILE AND SECTIONS, AS FITTED 1938 — 78
Stern to Frame 172 — 78
Frames 172 to 155 — 80
Frames 155 to 138 — 82
Frames 138 to 118 — 84
Frames 118 to 76 — 86
Frames 76 to 64 — 88
Frames 64 to 46 — 90
Frames 46 to 29 — 92
Frame 29 to stem — 94

COMMUNICATIONS — 96
HMS *Cossack*: Pneumatic Transmission of Messages, as fitted — 96
HMS *Nubian*: Arrangement of Main W/T Office, as fitted — 98
HMS *Nubian*: Arrangement of 2nd W/T Office, as fitted — 100
HMS *Cossack*: Echo Sounding Installation Type 753, as fitted — 102

HMS *COSSACK*: ENLARGED DECKS, AS FITTED 1938 — 103
0.5-inch Machine Gun Platform — 103
After Superstructure Deck — 104
Signal Deck and Bridge — 106
Forecastle Deck — 108
Upper Deck — 110
Lower Deck — 114
Hold — 118

LATER DEVELOPMENTS — 122
HMS *Eskimo*: Action Damage sustained on 12 July 1943 — 122
HMCS *Athabaskan*: Profile, as fitted 1943 — 124
HMS *Ashanti*: Arrangement of Steam Heating for Arcticisation, as fitted — 126

BIBLIOGRAPHY — 128

LIST OF PLANS — 128

PREFACE

Like my previous book in this series the choice of subject was dictated to a large extent by research readily available. – in this case for an old project that failed to materialise and which has lain dormant for over a quarter of a century. That material has been updated to some extent and is greatly enhanced in value by being associated with the original plans for *Cossack* and some of her sisters. Unfortunately, the National Maritimes Museum's collection of Admiralty plans included very little for the 'Tribal' class ships beyond their appearance at the time of completion during 1938–39. All the available as-fitted plans for the class are as-completed and none of these include subsequent modifications. A couple of profiles from the British-built Canadian 'Tribal's are included to show at least the basic early modifications to the class and the differences in the appearance resulting from their modified design. Some compensation is provided by including the 1935–36 design drawings for the class and several of the more interesting detailed design and as-fitted detail drawings of which there are a considerable number in the Admiralty collection. Again, very few of these relate to modification after completion. The accompanying text has, of necessity, to serve in covering alterations and additions. These are based on photographic evidence, written records and published works but are limited by available space and generally concentrate on *Cossack* so far as her alterations can be discerned from limited evidence. What would have been the best recorded information on modifications to all RN ships, the 'Ship's Books', were almost entirely destroyed in one of the civil service's over-enthusiastic weeding of records. Among the few that survive is that for *Afridi* but since she was lost in April 1940 its value in tracing wartime changes is limited. Hopefully, this book will help both now and in the future in expanding the understanding and interpretation of the details of warship design.

John Roberts,
February 2020

ABBREVIATIONS USED IN TEXT

AA	Anti-Aircraft	D of P	Director of Plans (Naval Staff)	QR	Quadruple Revolving (torpedo tubes)
ac	Alternating Current [electricity]	D of TD	Director of Tactical Division (Naval Staff)	RA(D)	Rear Admiral (Destroyers). [Senior officer of a fleet's destroyer flotillas]
ACNS	Assistant Chief of Naval Staff	EinC	Engineer in Chief		
AEW	Admiralty Experimental Works	ER	Engine Room	RDF	Radio Direction Finder [radar]
A/F	As Fitted (Plans)	FKC	Fuse Keeping Clock	RH	Right Hand
AFCC	Admiralty Fire Control Clock	GMT	Greenwich Mean Time	rpg	Rounds Per Gun
ARL	Admiralty Research Laboratory	HA/LA	High Angle/Low Angle (also used separately)	rpm	Revolutions Per Minute
BP	Bullet Proof			RU	Ready Use
BM	Breech Mechanism	HEDA	High Explosive Direct Action	SA	Semi Automatic (gun)
BR	Boiler Room	HETF	High Explosive Time Fuse	SAP	Semi Armour Piercing (shell)
CAFO	Confidential Admiralty Fleet Order	H/F	High Frequency	shp	Shaft Horse Power
Capt(D)	Captain (Destroyers). [Senior officer of a destroyer flotilla]	HF/DF	High Frequency/Direction Finder	Sqd	Squadron
		IFF	Identification Friend or Foe	TDF	Tribal Destroyer Flotilla
CNS	Chief of Naval Staff (1st Sea Lord)	lbs	Pounds (weight)	TIC	Time Interval Compensation
CRAA	Close-Range Anti-Aircraft	M/F	Medium Frequency	TIR	Time Interval Receiving
DC	Depth Charge	MG	Machine Gun	TS	Transmitting Station
dc	Direct Current [electricity]	M/G	Motor Generator	TT	Torpedo Tube
DCNS	Deputy Chief of Naval Staff	oa	Over All	VSG	Variable Speed Gear
DCT	Director Control Tower (also Depth Charge Thrower)	OF	Oil Fuel	wl	Water Line
		pdr	Pounder	wt	Water-Tight
DF	Destroyer Flotilla (and Direction Finding or Finder)	PIL	Position in Line	W/T	Wireless Transmitter (or Transmission)
		pp	Between Perpendiculars		
Div	Division	psi	Pounds per Square Inch		
DNC	Director of Naval Construction	QF	Quick Firing		
DNO	Director of Naval Ordnance				

INTRODUCTION

ORIGINS

Developed during 1935, the 'Tribal' class represented a major departure from the Admiralty's recent destroyer construction programme – the eight full flotillas and one half-flotilla of the 'A' to 'I' classes provided under the 1927 to 1935 Naval Estimates. The most outstanding differences between the 'Tribal' class and their predecessors was a shift in armament priority from the torpedo to the gun and a 35 per cent increase in standard displacement. This change in construction policy was initiated by two major considerations. The first was the construction by foreign powers of large fast destroyers with heavy armaments – in particular the Japanese *Fubuki* class (1750 tons, 6 x 5in guns, 9 x 24in torpedo tubes), twenty of which entered service during 1928–1932; and the second, a shortage of cruisers resulting from a combination of the limitations imposed by the 1930 London Naval Treaty and the political restrictions on naval expenditure due to the effects of recession and the desire for disarmament.

The 1930 Treaty stated that by the end of 1936 Britain should have no more than 50 cruisers – a number long regarded as inadequate to meet the commitments of the Royal Navy – with total tonnage not exceeding 339,000. A modest building programme of 6in-gun medium sized cruisers initiated in 1929 was disrupted in 1931 when the Japanese began the construction of the 8500-ton *Mogami* class cruisers, each armed with fifteen 155mm guns in five triple turrets. Acknowledging the fact that the existing 6in-gun designs were inadequate to face these new ships the Admiralty replied with the 9000-ton *Southampton* class (12 x 6in in four triple turrets). This increase in size directly affected the number of cruisers that could be accommodated within the existing tonnage limitation and prompted a revival of earlier investigations of designs for small fleet cruisers as direct replacements for the ageing 'C' and 'D' classes. Several outline designs designated 'P' to 'U', the majority armed with 6in guns on single open shield mountings (the one exception had two triple turrets), were prepared in 1934 for discussion of this problem. The last design in this series, 'V', was a hybrid scout vessel akin to a large destroyer leader, which resulted in its initial designation as 'V' Leader. This alternative was strongly favoured by the Naval Staff since it provided a solution to the need for numbers of ships and was considered a reasonable alternative to the small cruiser designs. In addition, by restricting displacement to 1850 tons the ships would by treaty definition come out of destroyer rather than cruiser tonnage.

These designs, and the Staff's views, were communicated for comment to the principal commanders afloat – the CinCs of the Home and Mediterranean Fleets and the China Station. Both the CinC Home Fleet (Admiral Sir W Boyle) and the CinC China (Admiral Sir F Dreyer) favoured the 'V' Leader but strong objections were raised by the CinC Mediterranean (Admiral Sir W Fisher), his second in command (Vice Admiral Roger Backhouse) and the RA(D) Mediterranean (Andrew Cunningham). The objections were extensive but, in greatly simplified form, came down to the 'Leader' being too small to adequately function as a cruiser and too big and vulnerable for destroyer duties. There was also a preference for an earlier suggestion by the Mediterranean Fleet for a slow 4.7in gun cruiser to provide fleet AA defence, a function for which the 'V' Leader was viewed as unlikely to provide the steady gun platform necessary for accurate AA fire. These objections were answered in detail by the D of TD (Captain D Boyd) in a memorandum of 1 February 1935 which pointed out that although the 'V' Leader was not ideal it was considered the best compromise to meet existing requirements and outlined the vessel's basic purpose as '… to meet our need for "numbers" of ships for certain cruiser and patrol duties (for many of which destroyers are already used, …) by the best unprotected gun carrying vessel obtainable.' He also considered that the larger numbers of 'V' Leaders would provide better AA coverage than a limited number of AA cruisers and that rather than reducing destroyer numbers it would release them for the duties they were designed for. There was also a need to build such ships in order to evaluate their suitability for cruiser, patrol and AA duties. The actions proposed by the Staff were either to:

1. Continue with existing cruiser and destroyer construction policy.
2. Build destroyers with 6 x 4.7in. (This proposal, employing three twin mountings, was investigated in November 1934 and reappeared later in the design of the 'J' class destroyers of the 1936 Programme.)
3. Include 'V' Leader in 1935 Programme.

Some consideration was given to a 2000-ton 'V' Leader, to meet the purpose of 'A ship of a size, larger than which becomes too big a target and needs protection, smaller than which is of insufficient gun power and an inadequate gun platform'. It was suggested that six such ships be included in the 1935 Programme and another six in the following year, but this would have compromised the intended cruiser programme for 1936 and caused problems with manning. On 8 February the 1st Sea Lord (Admiral Lord Chatfield) insisted that if these ships were to be built '…they must come out of Destroyer not Cruiser tonnage.' Despite this, the form for a 2000-ton ship of 35.5 knots, 395ft long and 37ft beam, was tried at the AEW in April 1935. It was later argued that the extra 150 tons would not in any case enhance the military characteristics sufficiently to justify a shift into the cruiser class, even if the treaty restrictions on tonnage were later removed. Nevertheless, the larger ship was favoured by many senior officers on the basis that it would provide for a stronger hull and improved endurance and seaworthiness. It therefore continued to be discussed, but politics, finance and necessity eventually forced the acceptance of the 1850-ton limit.

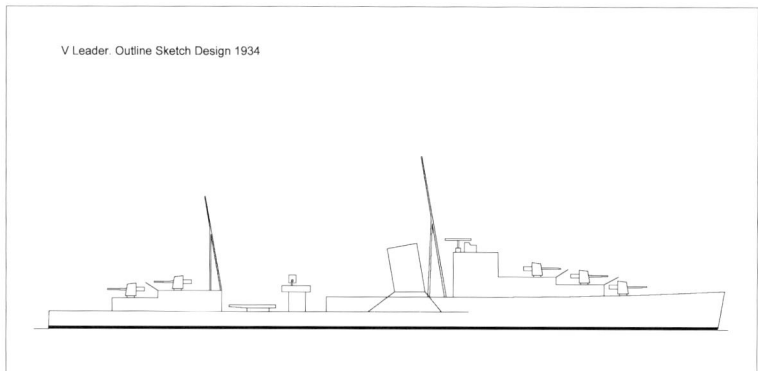

'V' LEADER PRELIMINARY OUTLINE DESIGN

The original conception for the ten-gun 'V' Leader with a triple superfiring arrangement of the forward twin 4.7in gun mountings. This layout was not liked because it increased the ship's profile and hence target. In subsequent ten-gun designs Nº3 mounting was moved to a position between the funnels, following the standard arrangement of destroyer leaders. This allowed a lowering of the bridge as well as the gun mounting. It did, however, require the acceptance of reduced ahead fire and an inconvenient ammunition supply arrangement for Nº3 mounting. The latter proved critical in the eventual acceptance of an 8-gun main armament. (Author)

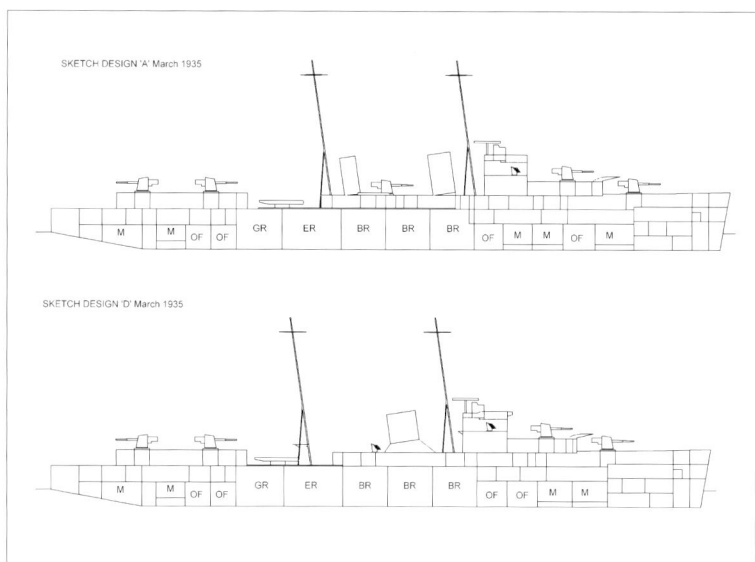

SKETCH DESIGNS 'A' AND 'D' OF MARCH 1935

The general layout of Design 'A' was repeated in Designs 'B', 'C' and 'E' which varied from each other primarily in engine power and speed. Design 'E' also exchanged Nº3 4.7in mounting for a quad pom-pom. Design 'D' sacrificed a midships mounting entirely for a speed of 37 knots, a single funnel and two more 0.5in MG mountings. The close spacing of the masts in these designs was criticised since it adversely affected W/T range. A single funnel was investigated again in about August 1935. An undated document in the 'Tribal' Class Cover refers to the submission of a sketch (not present) for a design with a single funnel and vertical masts (presumably the funnel would also have been vertical). The 0.5in were fitted en echelon abaft the funnel and the bridge moved further aft.

KEY
- **BR** Boiler Room
- **ER** Engine Room
- **GR** Gearing Room
- **M** 4.7in Magazine and Shell Room
- **OL** Oil Fuel

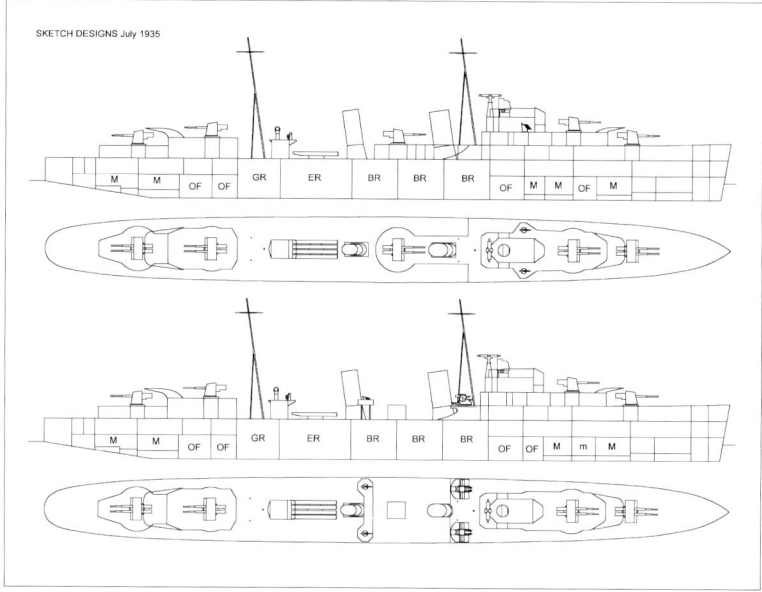

SKETCH DESIGNS OF JUNE/JULY 1935

The original of the ten-gun design (top) is dated 22 June 1935 while the eight-gun design, with sided quad pom-poms on the forecastle and the 0.5in MG located abreast the fore side of the after funnel, followed in July. The mainmast has been moved further aft and both masts have been shortened in height by 10ft.

Key as above except m = 2pdr pom-pom magazine.

SKETCH DESIGNS OF SEPTEMBER 1935

The alternative layouts for eight-gun designs with either two quad pom-poms or a single eight-barrel pom-pom. Note that the foremast has been changed to a pole mast and that the eight-barrel pom-pom alternative has a flat top to the fore funnel. There were also two outline designs showing alternative sided quad pom-pom mountings – one similar to that of July, but with the mountings slightly further forward, and one with the mountings on each side of a platform between the funnels. The original drawings in the Ships' Cover only illustrate the designs from the break of the forecastle to the mainmast so the arrangement of the bridge, in particular the location of the 0.5in MG, 18in searchlight and the pom-pom director (for the two-quad version), is assumed. The pom-pom director for the eight-barrel mounting is on the 24in searchlight/ after control platform at the base of the mainmast.

The 1930 Treaty limited standard destroyers to a maximum displacement of 1500 tons and a total overall tonnage of 150,000 of which 16 per cent (25,000 tons) were permitted to be up to 1850 tons. On 20 February 1935 the Sea Lords decided to recommend to the Board that all the available destroyer tonnage of the 1935 Programme should consist of seven 'V' Leaders of 1830 tons with eight or ten 4.7in guns. The principal reason for this decision was again given by the 1st Sea Lord as the need to make provision for meeting the latest Japanese and US destroyers. He also concluded that the question of the replacement of the 'C' and 'D' classes should return to consideration of a small fleet-cruiser – in effect agreeing with earlier comments by the DCNS (Vice Admiral C Little) and ACNS (Rear Admiral C Kennedy-Purvis) that too much was being expected from the proposed design.

For financial reasons it was intended that the 'V' Leader should replace the eight 'I' class destroyers originally approved for the 1935 Construction Programme. In March 1935 the estimated cost for seven 'V' Leaders was £3,360,000, a relatively modest increase of £110,000 on the 'I' class Flotilla and their leader. On this basis the proposed alteration to the estimates received Cabinet agreement. It was intended that this information was to remain 'confidential' until later in the year but the proposed alteration of the destroyer construction programme was overtaken by subsequent events. In the autumn of 1935, fears of war with Italy over the Abyssinian Crisis reinforced the initial moves toward re-armament that were already taking place and it was decided that the seven 'Tribal's would be additional to, instead of in lieu of, the 'I' class. The latter was ordered under the original estimates in October 1935 while the seven 'Tribal' class gained Parliamentary approval as a Supplement to the 1935 Estimates in March 1936. A further nine 'Tribal's were ordered three months later under the 1936 Estimates to meet the Naval Staff's ideal of 16 ships organised in four squadrons in similar fashion to cruisers. In October 1935, the DCNS had made the obvious suggestion of increasing the number of the 1935 Programme ships to eight but this was considered 'difficult' by Chatfield on the grounds that cost had already increased (£210,000 above the figure given to the Cabinet in March) – presumably asking for even more money from the Treasury was considered politically unwise.

OUTLINE DESIGNS, MARCH 1935

	A	B	C	D	E
Standard displacement (tons)	1870	1830	1810	1830	1846
Length (ft)	370	370	370	360	366
Shp	45,000	41,500	40,000	48,000	45,000
Speed (kts)	36	35.5	35	37	36
Gun Armament	10 x 4.7in 8 x 0.5in	10 x 4.7in 8 x 0.5in	10 x 4.7in 8 x 0.5in	8 x 4.7in 16 x 0.5in	8 x 4.7in 4 x 2pdr 8 x 0.5in

All designs had a single quad TT mounting and a beam of 36ft. The 4.7in guns were on twin mountings, the 2pdr pom-pom and 0.5in MG were on quad mountings.

DESIGN

In February 1935 the 3rd Sea Lord (Henderson) was asked to examine the possible characteristics of the proposed design as an aid to further discussion prior to preparation of Staff Requirements. Five outline designs (Table 1) were supplied by the DNC (A W Johns) on 28 March 1935. Three showed the effect of varying the ship's speed while the remaining pair served to demonstrate the reduction in size and the gains in speed or CRAA armament possible with the main armament reduced from ten to eight guns. Although design 'A' was favoured it exceeded the displacement limit set by the Board and in April the ACNS commented that the loss of 0.5 knots in design 'B' was an acceptable sacrifice given that 40 tons 'may be too dear at the price' for 36 knots. He added that under operational conditions it was unlikely that such ships would exceed 32 knots (or 30 knots when in company). He also asked for an investigation of the possibility of providing a unit machinery arrangement (alternate engine and boiler rooms).

These comments were considered at a meeting of the DNC, EinC and DNO on 3 May. The EinC stated that it would be possible, as a result of recent machinery developments, to increase the engine power of design 'B' to 43,500shp which would provide for 36 knots on 1830 tons. This was perhaps slightly optimistic given that the displacement soon increased to the maximum allowed and, with it, the engine power to 44,000shp. In the case of unit machinery, investigation by the DNC and EinC concluded that, due to the need for an additional boiler room, the machinery length would increase from 131ft to 165ft and that of the ship to 420ft giving a displacement of about 2100 tons. There would also be increased operational complexity in the machinery arrangement and, not surprisingly, the idea was dropped.

On 27 June 1935 the DNC submitted the preliminary legend (Table 2) and sketch design based on the Staff requirements. The sketch design followed the basic arrangement of the earlier sketch designs except for a re-arrangement of the after 4.7in mountings and superstructure and the provision of a new bridge design. This initiated a long design process that primarily evolved around the question of the armament, something that was not completely resolved until after construction of the ships began. Although the ten-gun armament was a primary Staff Requirement there were concerns about Nº3 mounting since its ammunition supply was not entirely satisfactory, due to its distance from the forward magazines and the consequent need to transport ammunition aft along the open deck. In addition, the mounting's arc of fire was limited to 60°–155° on each beam. The staff requirements included secondary requirements for CRAA and suggested either two quad pom-poms (sided), one quad pom-pom on the centreline and two quad 0.5in (sided) or as many quad 0.5in MG as can be fitted. The June design, with only two quad 0.5in, was, therefore, offering the minimum of close-range air defence. At the prompting of Henderson, investigation began into increasing the CRAA armament at the expense of Nº3 4.7in mounting. On 9 July the DNC submitted a sketch showing a quad pom-pom on each side at the after end of the Forecastle Deck where

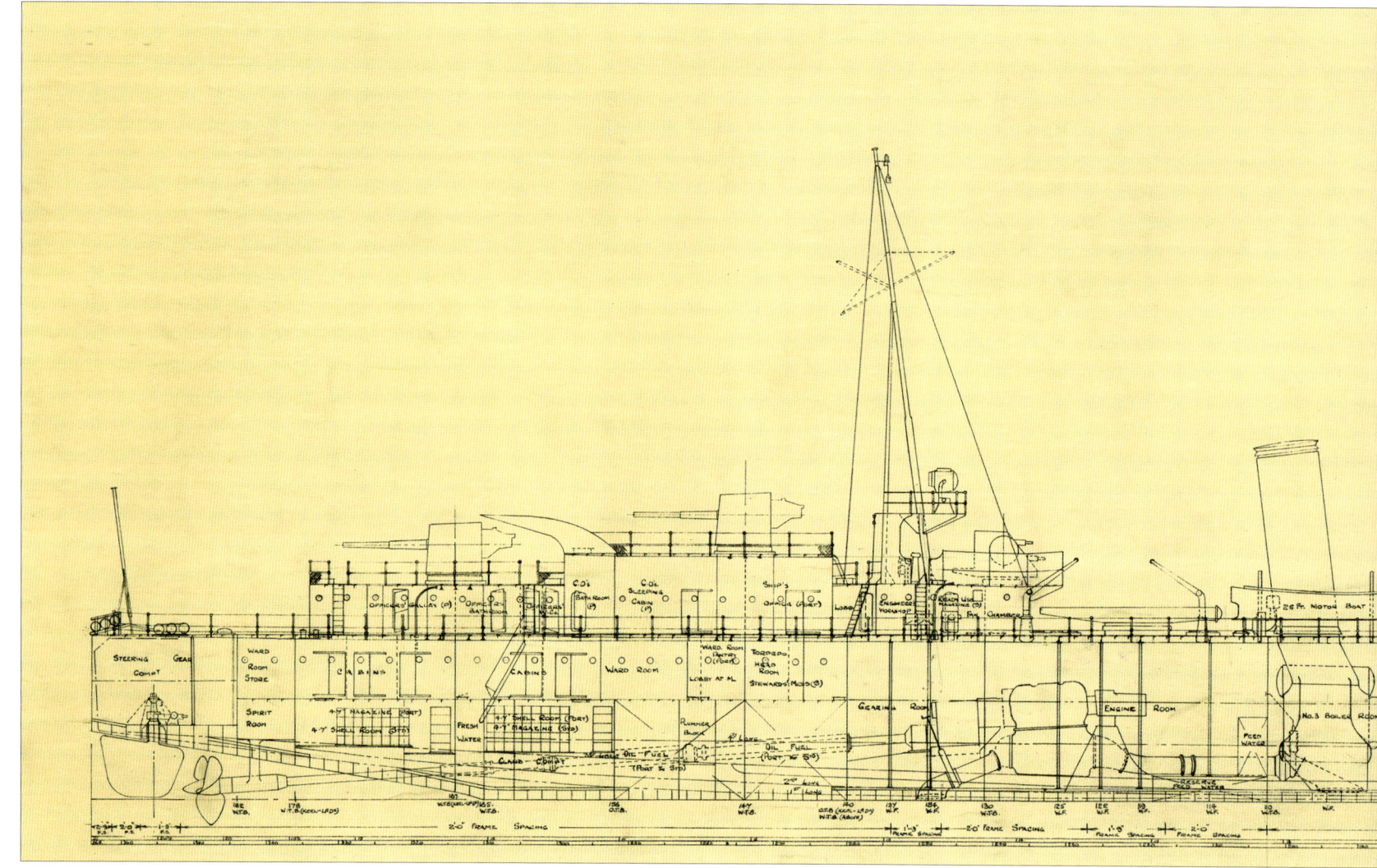

'TRIBAL' CLASS DESIGN, NOVEMBER 1935 – PROFILE

The original approved design for the 'Tribal' class with both the after 4.7in mountings on the superstructure, two quad pom-poms and a straight, slightly angled stem. Normally, a design that had reached this point did not change substantially but subsequent alterations, particularly the adoption of a raked stem, gave this and later British destroyer designs a new, sleeker appearance. Note the figures for the frame spacing – 1ft 9in forward, 2ft 0½in over the length of the boiler rooms and then 2ft for the remainder, except for closer 1ft 9in spacing below the torpedo tube mounting, mainmast and rudder post. (M1797)

LEGEND PARTICULARS OF PRELIMINARY SKETCH DESIGN, JUNE 1935

Standard displacement:	1850 tons
Length:	360ft (pp), 370ft (wl), 374ft 6in (oa)
Beam:	37ft (extreme)
Draught (mean):	9ft (standard), 11ft (deep)
Shp:	44,000
Speed:	36 knots (trial), 32.5 knots (deep)
Oil Fuel capacity:	500 tons
Endurance:	5700 miles at 15 knots.
Complement:	225
Armament:	10 x 4.7in (250rpg + 50 star-shell for ship); 8 x 0.5in MG (10,000rpg); 4 x 0.303in Lewis MG (2000rpg); 4 x 21in torpedo tubes; 6 DCs.

Weights (tons):	
General Equipment:	105
Machinery:	595
Armament:	240
Hull:	910
Total:	1850

The eight-gun version of the above design had a beam of 36ft 6in and two quad pom-poms (1800rpg). The machinery and hull weight were reduced by 3 and 4 tons respectively and the armament weight increased by 7 tons. In other respects, the particulars were the same.

DESIGN

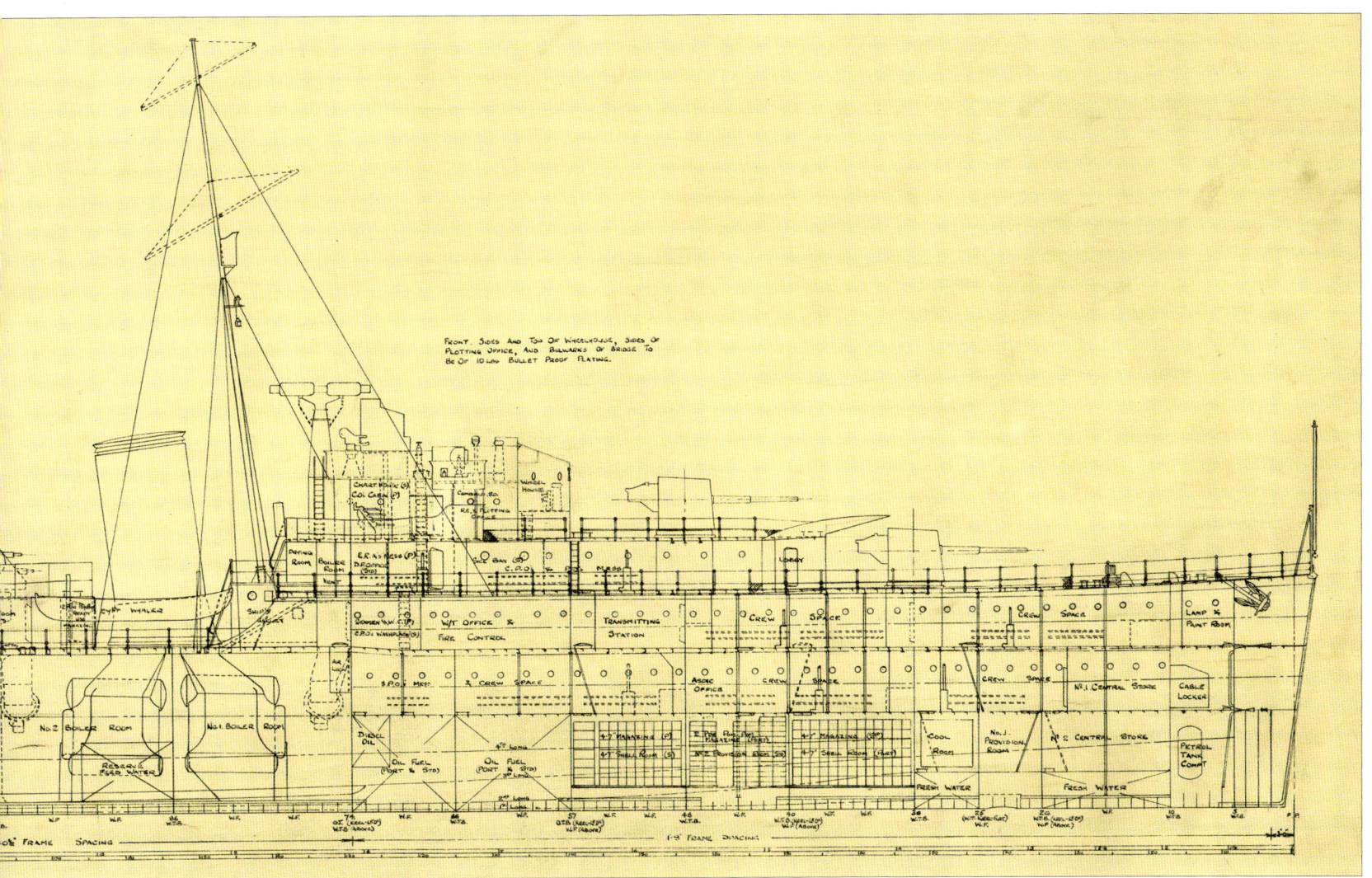

they provided good arcs of fire fore and aft and the ability to engage targets on either side simultaneously.

In subsequent discussions the 1st Sea Lord, Controller and DCNS preferred to retain the ten-gun design while the ACNS and the Naval Staff favoured the eight-gun version. It was decided that the question would have to be brought before the full Board. This met on 1 August but, while giving general approval to the ten-gun Sketch Design, deferred any decision on the armament question pending further discussion. This was resolved on 15 September when the Sea Lords decided that two quad pom-poms, with directors, should replace Nº3 4.7in mounting, Henderson being requested to initiate investigation of the best disposition of the guns and to provide information on the differences in weight should it be decided to fit an eight-barrel pom-pom instead of the two quads. Sketch designs, with two quads on the middle line, and the eight-barrel alternative were considered by the Sea Lords on 20 September. The difference in overall weight (including ammunition, hoists, general fittings, etc) was 3.1 tons in favour of the eight-barrel mounting. However, the Sea Lords approved the two-quad version for development, possibly swayed by the improved chance of survivability with two mountings and the ability to fire on both sides simultaneously. On 26 November, the DNC submitted the builder's drawings and legend (Table 3) and these received the Board stamp two days later. At the same time the Board considered the designation of the new ships since 'V' Leader was inappropriate given that their functions differed substantially from existing flotilla leaders, which were essentially destroyers of slightly increased size to provide flotilla command facilities and a fifth 4.7in gun. Most of the alternative suggestions made to date were rejected because they either indicated a false or inadequate description of the ships' purpose. It having been decided at an earlier stage that the new ships were to be given the names of ethnic groups, imitating the earlier 'Tribal' class of the Great War (themselves a departure from standard destroyer construction), the Board decided to simply call them 'Tribal Destroyers'.

Apart from the above-mentioned armament change, the design had been modified during August–November as follows:

1. Estimated standard displacement increased to 1854 tons but DNC gave assurance that economies effected during construction would bring this below the 1850-ton limit (initially achieved by reducing the quantity of central stores included in the standard displacement – see Table 3 footnote).
2. The addition of Asdic, DCs, DC throwers, D/F and 2nd W/T office (all secondary Staff Requirements) and a power-driven torpedo

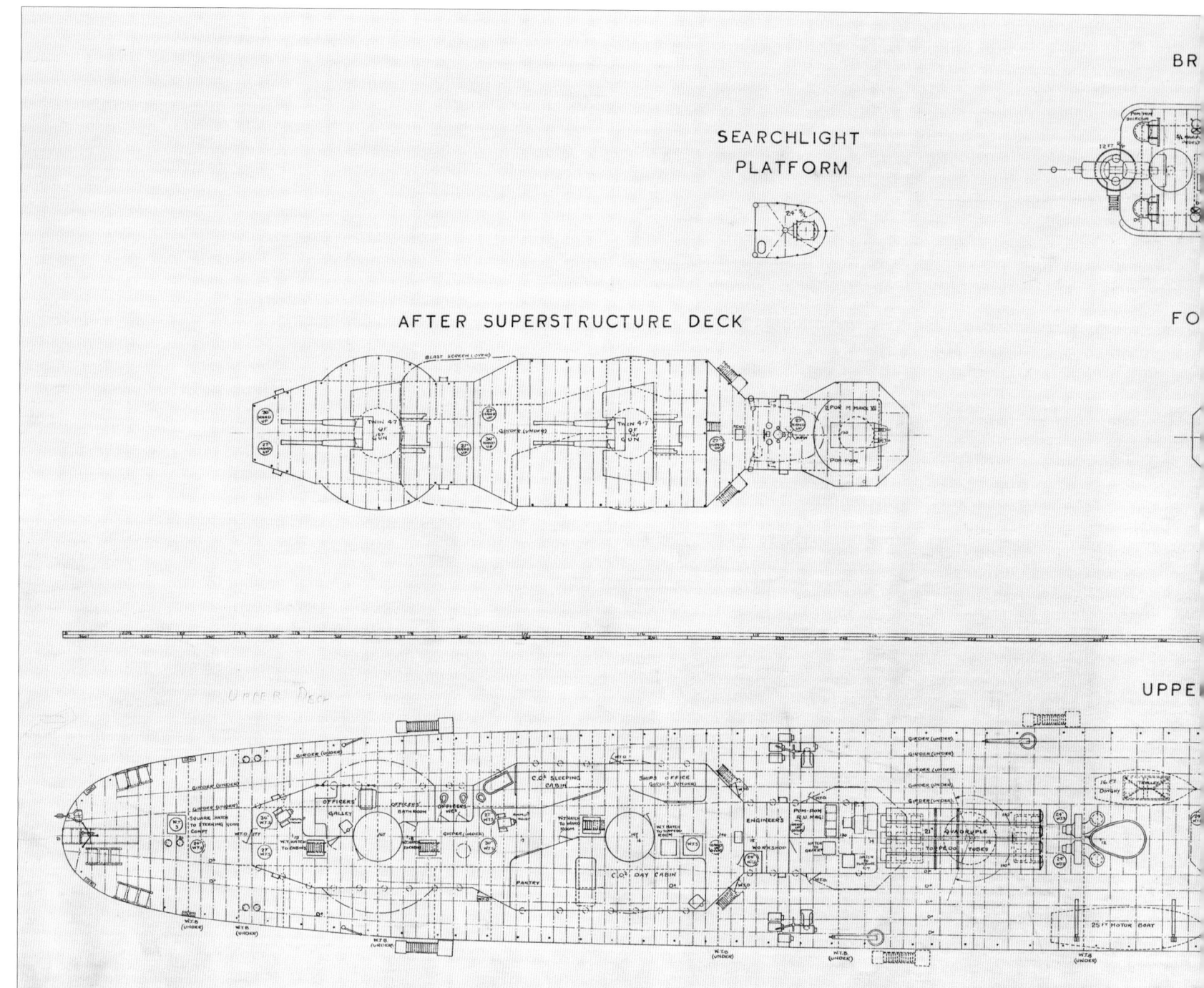

'TRIBAL' CLASS DESIGN, NOVEMBER 1935 – SUPERSTRUCTURE, FORECASTLE AND UPPER DECK

The prime reason for the subsequent rearrangement of the after superstructure (see page 22) was the congested area around the base of the mainmast and the detrimental effects of blast to the after steering position, searchlight and after pom-pom mounting from Nº3 4.7in mounting. The steering position did have a blast screen, shown on the profile but not on this drawing, but it seems unlikely that it would have been sufficiently effective. Note that at this stage the design has the depth charge throwers mounted on the Upper Deck abreast the mainmast. (M1796)

hoist. The additional weight was compensated by reducing the 4.7in rpg from 250 to 230 (180 LA, 50 HA) in the standard condition. Since the magazine and shell room capacity remained at 250rpg (200 LA and 50 HA) this was not in the spirit of the Treaty standard which required the inclusion of *all* ammunition, stores, etc required for war. Note that this should not be confused with a similar proposal in July 1935 to compensate for an increase in the weight of the 4.7in cartridge cases by altering the total 4.7in ammunition stowage from 2500 to 2300 rounds, in this case by limiting the stowage for two of the mountings to 200rpg. This idea was dropped when it was decided to reduce the main armament to eight guns.

3. Arranging the structure between the funnels to support the weight of a twin 4.7in in case it was later decided to restore it.

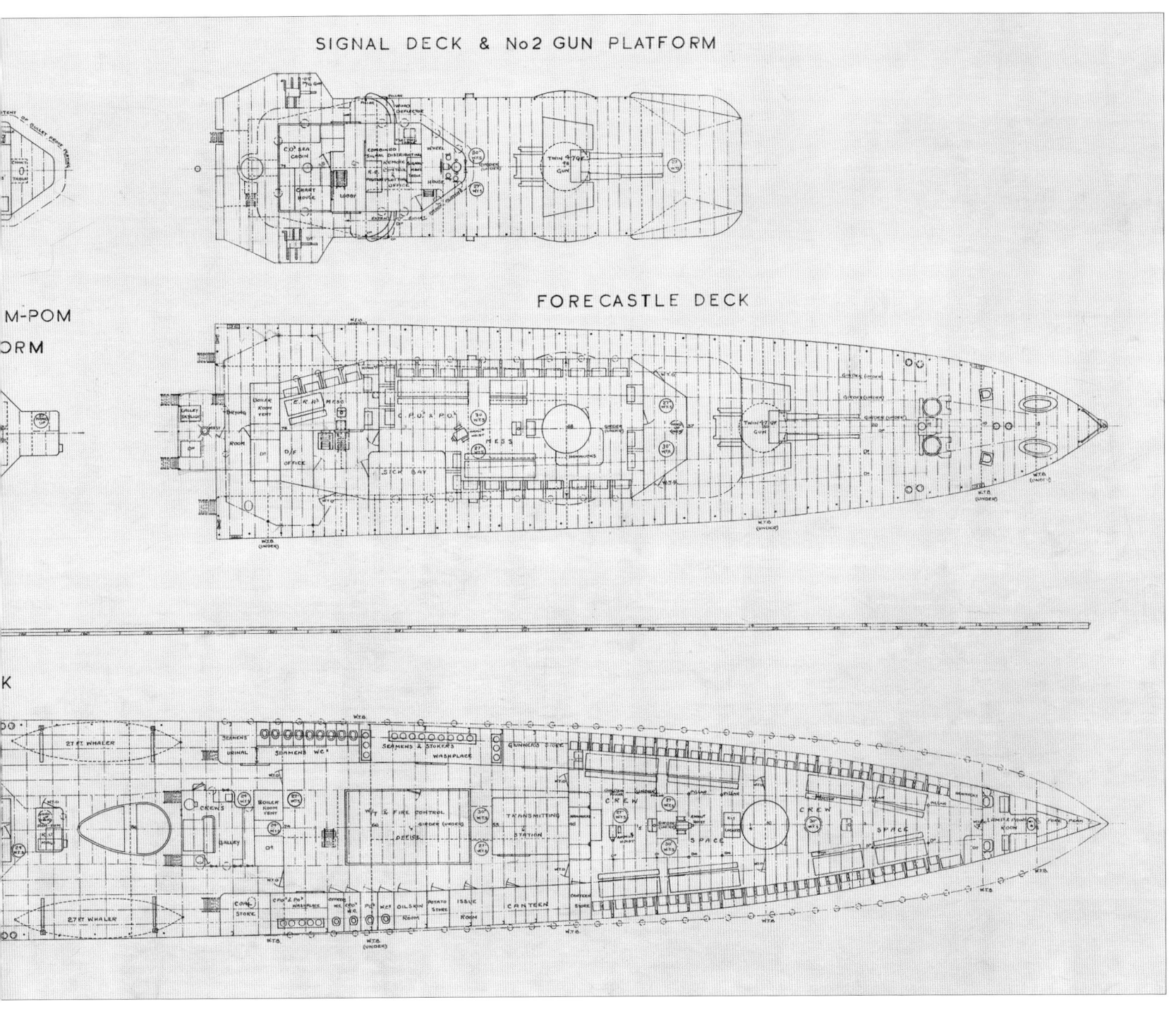

SIGNAL DECK & No 2 GUN PLATFORM

FORECASTLE DECK

4. Two pom-pom directors added, one on each side of the bridge, these being considered essential for accurate AA fire.
5. BP plating added around wheelhouse and fore end of bridge.
6. The Lewis MGs were omitted since no suitable space could be found in which to locate them.

Commenting on the design, the ACNS concluded that the Staff Requirements had been 'met in a most satisfactory manner in the face of severe treaty restrictions'. He still pressed for the later adoption of a 2000-ton design if future treaty limits permitted on the basis that this would improve hull strength, increase endurance and give greater scope for general improvements. He had also been given to believe that the silhouette, and therefore target area of what was an unprotected ship, would not be greatly increased. In the event, the new London Naval Treaty of 1936 removed all quantitative limits while the upper limit on standard displacement for the design group applicable to destroyers was raised to 3000 tons. Hence the critical problem of 'numbers of ships' that had initiated the 'V' Leader design would no longer apply once the 1930 Treaty expired on 31 December 1936.

Invitations to tender for the new ships were sent out in November. That received from Vickers Armstrongs on 9 December was accepted for the construction of two of the class, *Afridi* and *Cossack*, on 10 March 1936. Both ships were laid down on 9 June 1936 and launched on 8 June 1937, but *Cossack* completed six weeks after her

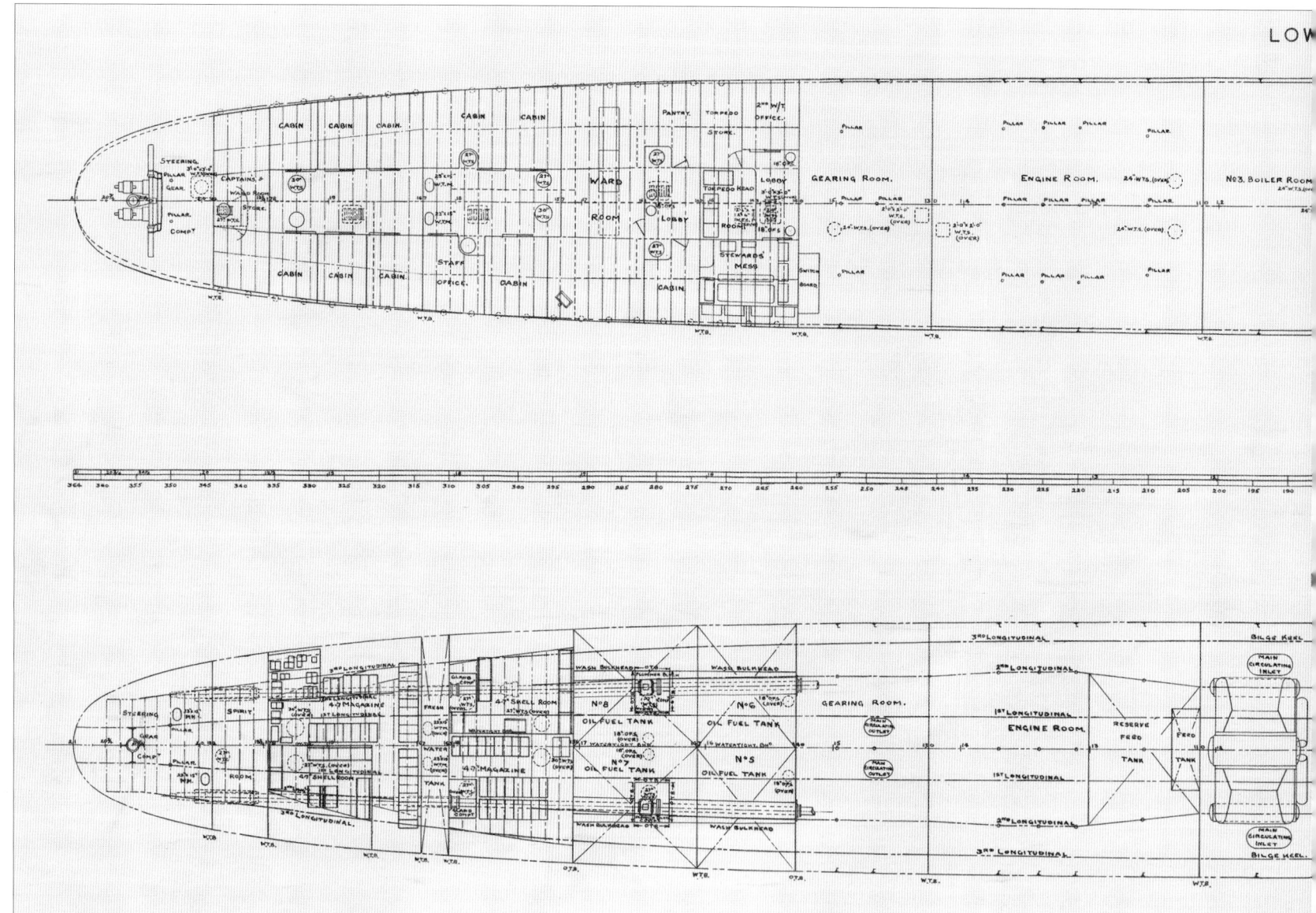

'TRIBAL' CLASS DESIGN, NOVEMBER 1935 – LOWER DECK AND HOLD

Compared with the external appearance, the post-1935 changes to the internal design are less obvious. The main alterations were made to the area abaft the engine room as a result of the relocation of Nº3 and Nº4 4.7in mountings. The officer accommodation in this area was to be substantially re-arranged, while the after fresh-water stowage in the Hold (Frames 165–167) was moved to tanks in Nº2 boiler room. At this point in the design the chain hoists for the 4.7in shell and cartridges had not been included. (M1795)

sister. Vickers Armstrongs were also to build the hulls of *Eskimo* and *Mashona* of the 1936 Programme, both under sub-contract from Parsons who built the turbine machinery.

MODIFICATIONS 1936–1937

The evolution of the design did not end in November 1935. By early 1936 it had been decided to fit power hoists for the 4.7in ammunition supply, relocate Nº4 mounting to the after end of the upper deck and move Nº3 mounting to the after end of the superstructure deck. The power hoists added a total of 22.8 tons which, together with a 2.92-ton increase in the design weight of each 4.7in mounting, raised the estimated standard displacement to 1891 tons with a possible loss in speed of 0.5 knots. It was proposed to simply wait for the actual condition of the ships to be established at the time of completion (*Cossack* was actually a close match to this design estimate).

The primary purpose of the relocation of the after 4.7in mountings was the reduction of blast effects from Nº3 mounting on the operation of after pom-pom mounting, after steering position and 24in searchlight. It also allowed the mainmast to be moved 19ft further aft which improved W/T range and reduced the congestion between Nº3 mount and the torpedo tubes. Fitting the after 4.7in mounting on the quarterdeck was not a new idea since it had been decided to do this in May 1935 but not implemented at that time due to concerns about the loss of efficiency in the ammunition supply along the Upper Deck in poor weather. This problem was substantially reduced by arranging the hoists from the after magazine and shell room to feed into a screened area at the after end of the superstructure immediately forward of Nº4 mounting.

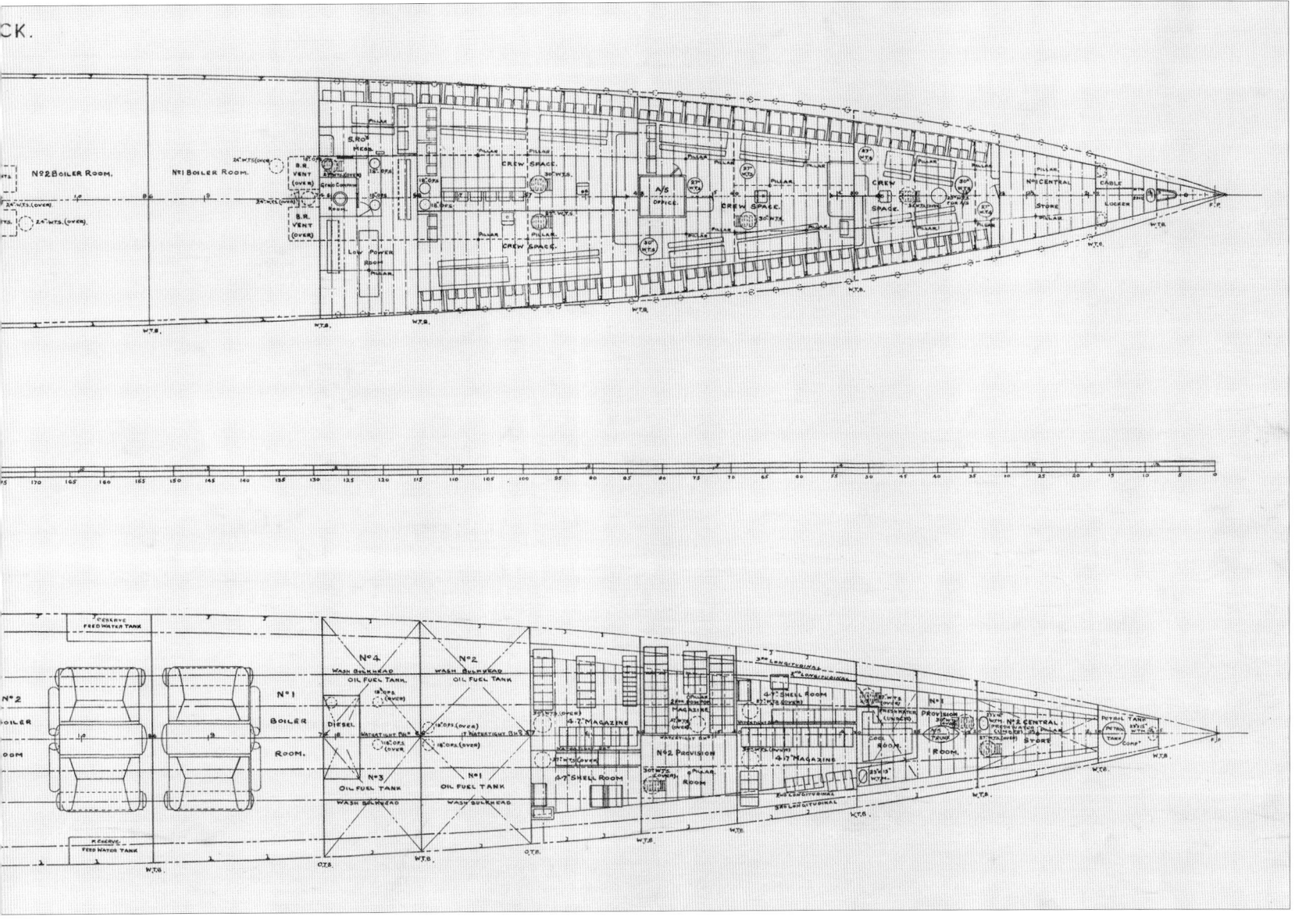

LEGEND OF PARTICULARS, 6 NOVEMBER 1935

Displacement:	1854 tons (standard), 2519 tons (deep)
Length:	355ft 6in (pp), 364ft (wl), 367ft (oa)*
Beam:	36ft 6in (extreme)
Draught (mean):	9ft (standard), 11ft 3in (deep)
Freeboard (to 9ft wl)	22ft 3in (forward), 12ft 6in (amidships), 13ft 3in (aft)
shp:	44,000
speed:	36 knots in trial condition (1950 tons), 32.5 knots (deep)
Oil Fuel Capacity:	520 tons.
Endurance:	5700 miles (clean), 5000 miles (6 months out of dock) at 15 knots
Complement:	239 (peace), 246 (war)
Armament:	8 x 4.7in; 8 x 2pdr; 8 x 0.5in MG; 4 x 21in TT; 2 x DC throwers, 1x DC rail, 20 (peace), 30 (war) DCs

*The overall length increased to 377ft with the adoption of the 'clipper' bow in early 1936.

Weights (tons):	Standard**	Deep
General Equipment:	94	174
Machinery:	585	585
Hydraulic machinery and piping:	11	11
Reserve feed water	0	40
Oil fuel	0	520
Armament:	254	279
Hull:	910	910
Total:	1854	2519

** The reductions in general equipment were due to the omission of the weights for coal, reserve lubricating oil, petrol and paraffin (all classified as 'fuel') and reductions in the weights for canteen stores, provisions, fresh water and central stores. It was proposed that a further reduction in the canteen stores would serve to lower the standard displacement to 1850 tons. The reduction in armament weight was due to the omission of 20rpg (plus practice rounds) from the 4.7in ammunition, the torpedo collision heads, the 10 'war' stowage DCs and the sub-calibre guns and their ammunition.

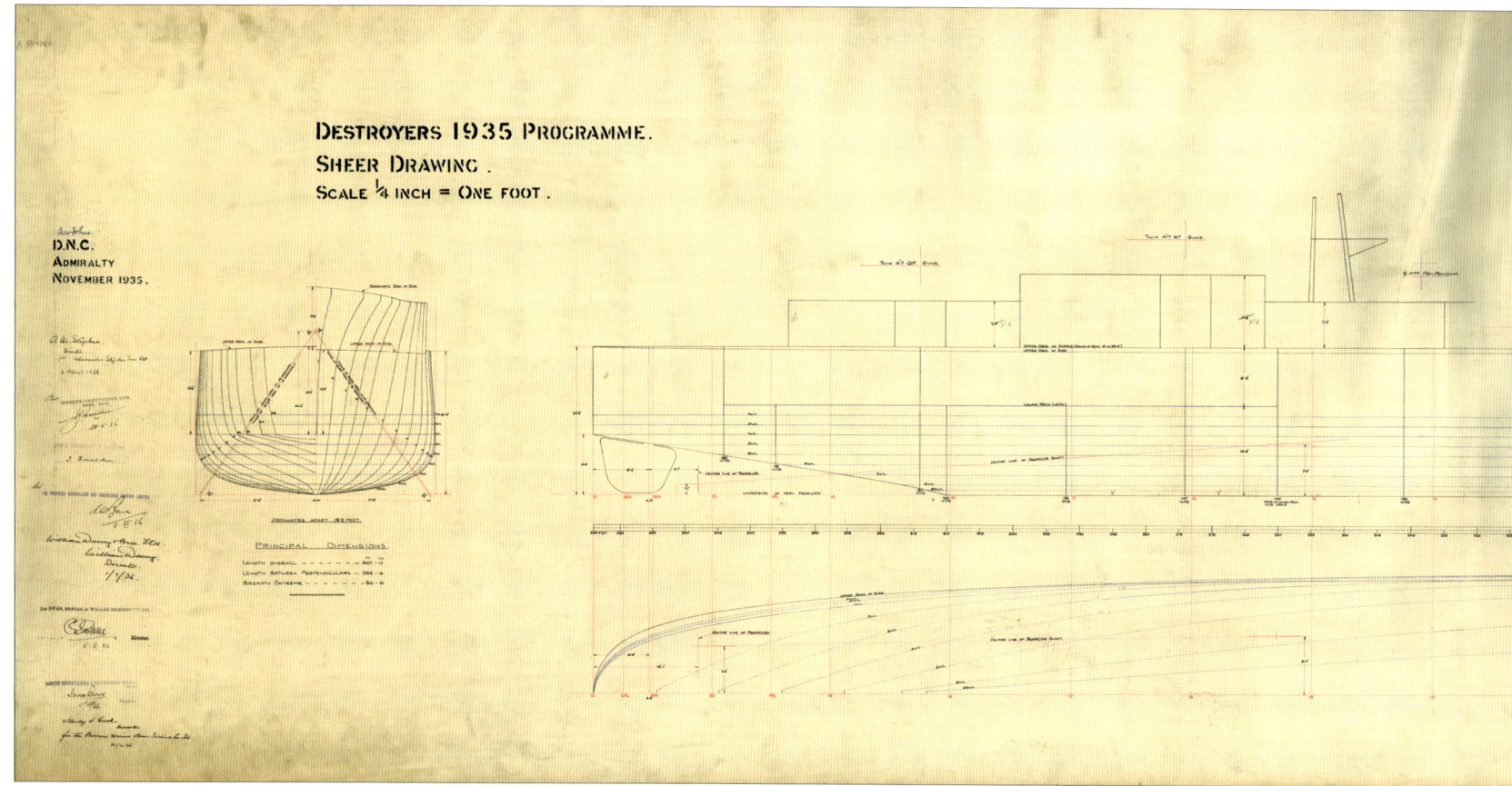

'TRIBAL' CLASS, NOVEMBER 1935 – SHEER DRAWING
The hull lines and body plan as originally prepared prior to the modification of the forward and after form early in 1936. The waterlines are spaced at 1ft 6in intervals, except for the intermediate 6½ wl between the 6 wl and the flat bottom. N°1 wl is at the designed, even-keel, load waterline (9ft). Lengthwise the hull is divided into 20 equal sections with the primary ordinates, spaced 18.2ft apart. Intermediate ordinates at 1½/ 2½/ 19½/ 20½ and 20¾ served to more closely define the greater extent of the change in form at the fore and after ends. (M1792)

Consideration was also given to fitting either the pom-pom or the torpedo tube mounting on the quarterdeck. The former was dismissed on the grounds that it would restrict the arcs of fire of both the pom-pom and N°4 mounting, and the latter because the resultant layout was impractical.

Also under consideration in early 1936 was the modification of the hull form at the after and forward ends. The former related to providing more clearance to the propellers to reduce vibration and allow for larger propellers should they be required. The latter related to a possible improvement of seaworthiness by replacing the straight, 7.5° forward sloping, stem with a clipper form which would extend the forecastle and increase the flare at the bows. Model experiments with the hull forms were carried out at the AEW during February–March 1936. These indicated a slight advantage for the modified bow, but it was pointed out that tank tests for sea conditions were artificial and could not reproduce the considerable variations likely to be encountered at sea. Nevertheless, the alterations were made, which increased the overall length by 10ft, moved the forefoot aft by about 2ft 10in and increased the freeboard forward to 23ft. Further experiments resulted in the provision of a breakwater on the forecastle – an item not fitted in destroyers prior to the 'I' and 'Tribal' classes.

At some stage during 1936–37 the pom-pom directors on the bridge were replaced with searchlight sights and moved down to the wings of the Flag Deck where they in turn replaced the quad 0.5in MG mountings. Later, in September 1937, it was decided to omit the quad pom-pom mounting between the funnels due to a shortage in their supply. It was intended that these mountings should be fitted when available, but they were never installed in any of the ships of the class. The omitted 0.5in MG mountings were restored to extensions on each side of the empty pom-pom platform as a 'temporary' measure. The pom-pom directors were also omitted (also likely due to shortage in supply), the space they vacated allowing for the reinstatement of the Lewis MG, which were provided with pedestals in the wings of the Flag Deck.

ARMAMENT
In November 1934 the functions of the class were described as 'Patrol work, shadowing, screening, close support of destroyer flotillas and, in

HMS *COSSACK*: BULLET PROOF PLATING, AS FITTED
This drawing indicates the extent and dimensions of the bullet proof plating applied to the bridge and wheelhouse as defence against strafing attacks by aircraft and, to a lesser extent, splinters. Plates 21–24 are part of the side screens abreast the bridge at Signal Deck level. 'Non-magnetic' plating refers to plating manufactured of austenitic stainless steel which, fairly obviously, has the odd property for steel of being non-magnetic. It was used to limit interference with the magnetic compasses in the wheelhouse and on the bridge. (M1831)

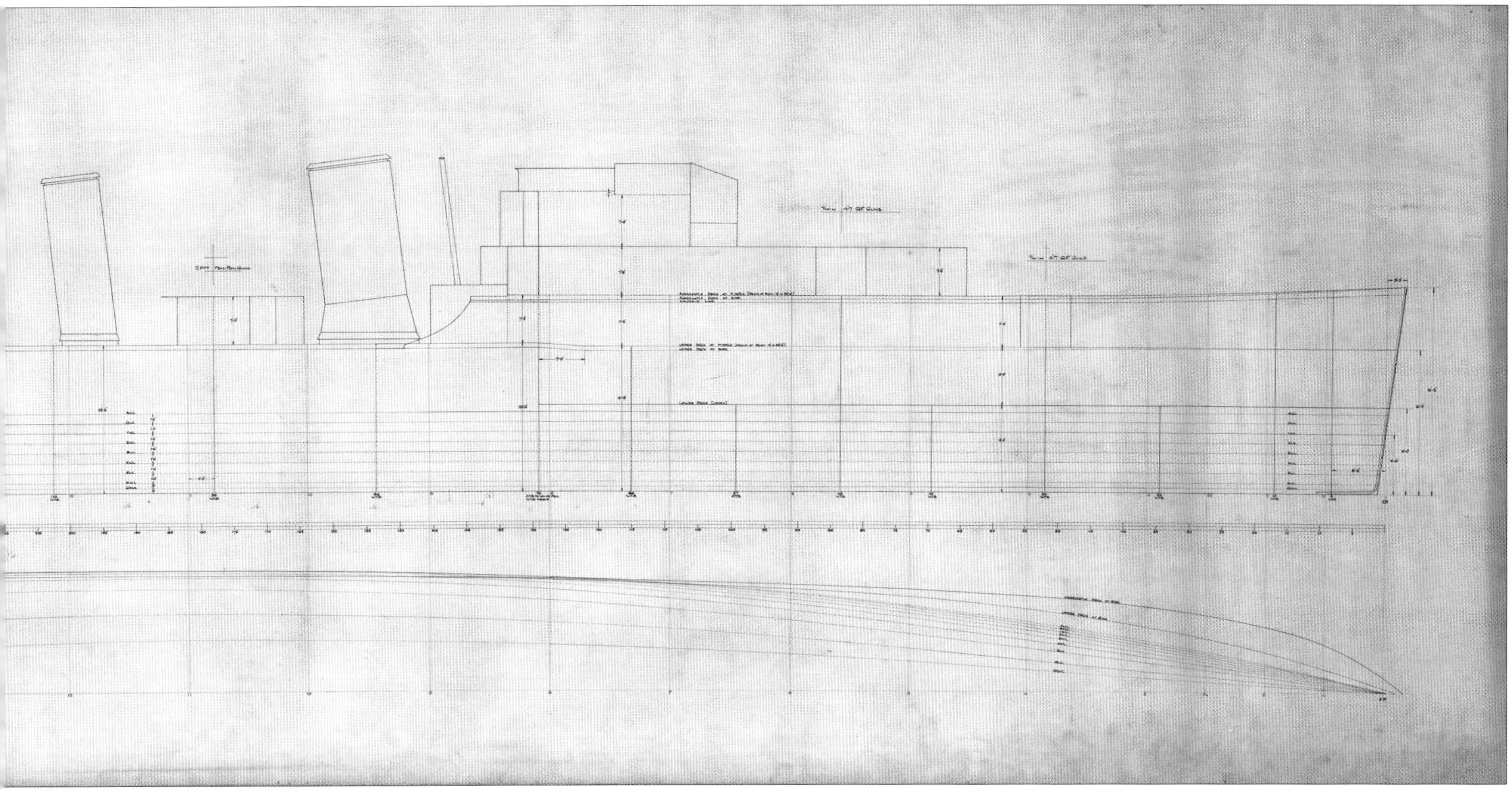

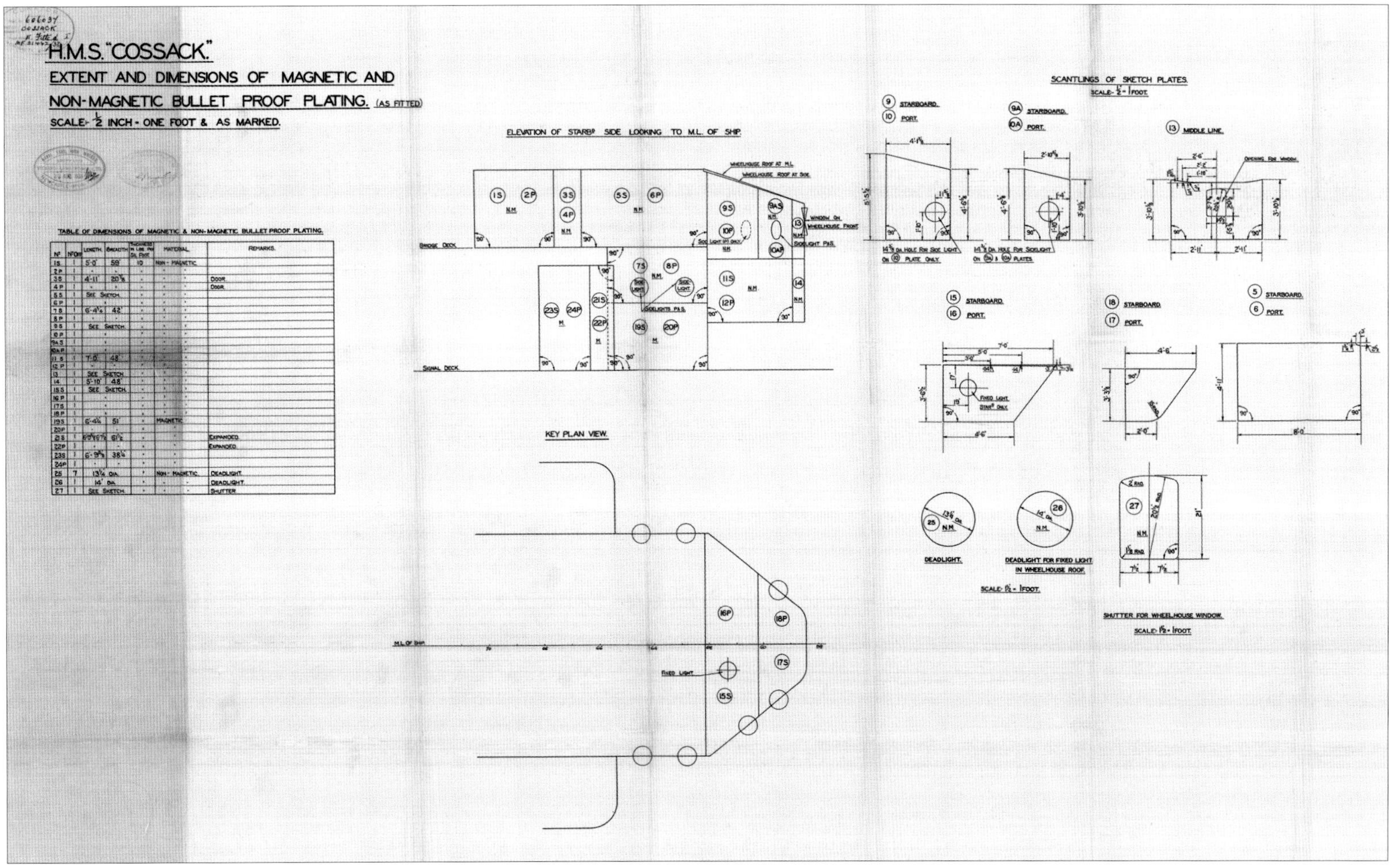

ARMAMENT

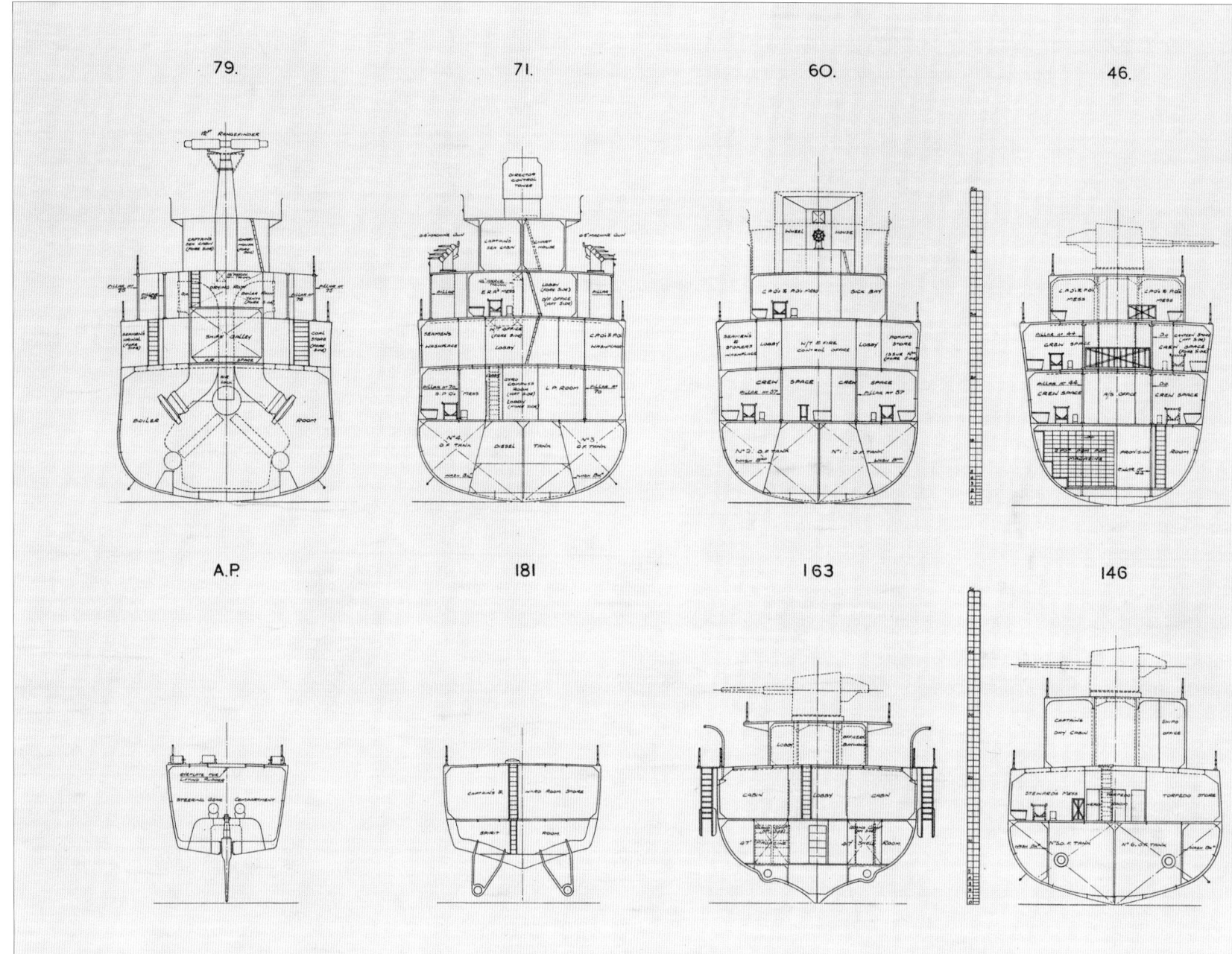

conjunction with cruisers, reconnaissance and escort duties. It is further required, although not as a primary function, that … a V leader be able to contribute to the AA defence of the fleet, convoys and harbours. A powerful gun armament and good communications are of the first importance for these duties which also require numbers of ships.'

The ships of the 'Tribal' class were the first British destroyers to carry twin rather than single mounted main armament guns and the first to have their mountings power operated. The 4.7in QF Mk XII gun was a standard weapon, being a slightly modified version of the Mk IX gun mounted in destroyers since the 'A' class of the 1927 Programme. It fired a 50lb projectile employing a separate charge in a brass case, the separate ammunition being employed to make handling and loading easier. The Mk XIX mounting was powered hydraulically from off-mounting Hele-Shaw pumps driven by small steam turbines.

The double pump unit for the forward mountings was located in No 1 boiler room and that for the after mountings in the gearing room. Training and elevation were driven by on-mounting VSG swash-plate motors and ramming by a piston driven chain-rammer. The power drive provided train and elevation speeds of 10°/sec. Alternative manual operation was available for elevation, training and ramming in the event of power failure. The prototype mounting was tried in the newly completed destroyer *Hereward* during January–March 1937.

The mountings' elevation of 40°, although more than adequate for the ships' primary purpose of surface action, was insufficient for its secondary function as an AA weapon except against torpedo bombers since they attacked at low level. Against high level bombers the target could only be engaged for a short period. In mid-1935 the Naval Staff calculated that a 184mph bomber heading *directly* towards the firing ship at the following heights could be engaged for a maximum of

ARMAMENT

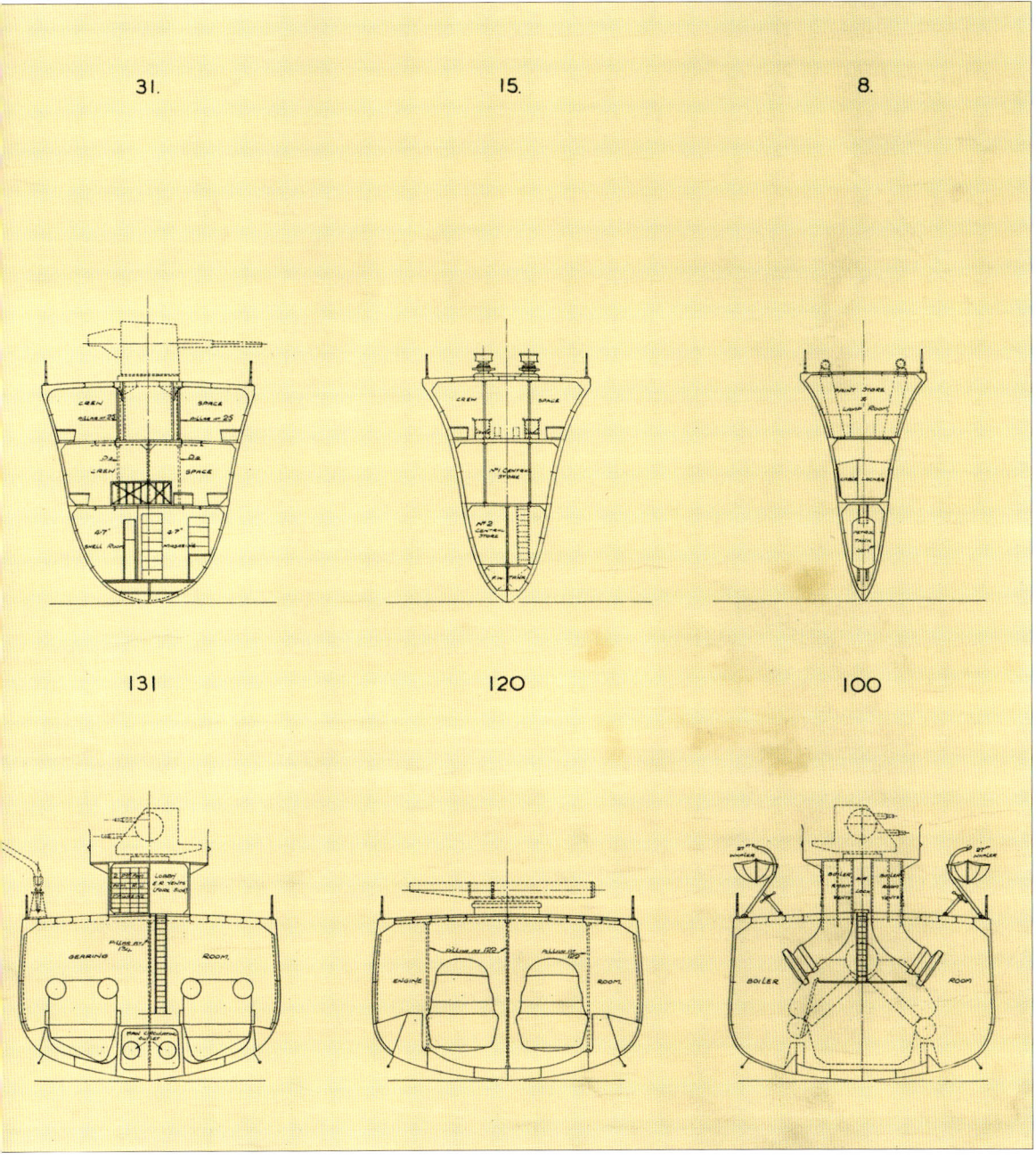

'TRIBAL' CLASS DESIGN, NOVEMBER 1935 – SECTIONS

Apart from the introduction of changes between 1935 and 1938 these sections serve as a useful addition to the as-fitted sections of the *Cossack*. Normally as-fitted drawings follow the pattern set by the design drawings, which is particularly noticeable in the case of sections since they generally follow the same frame positions as those employed in the design. However, *Cossack*'s as-fitted sections not only occur at different frame locations (with the sole exception of 46), but they are also fewer in number – 9 rather than 14. Consequently, there is additional 'section' information to be found here such as the 4.7in magazine and shell room at Frame 31, the wheelhouse at Frame 60 and the diesel tank and DCT at Frame 71.

The Admiralty design drawings were commonly circulated to the builders to be copied and returned. This process is clearly illustrated by the Sheer Drawing (page 16) where several of the firms that built ships of the class have signed and, in most cases, dated the drawing before passing it on. (M1798)

120 seconds (5000ft), 96 seconds (8000ft), 78 seconds (10,000ft) and 45 seconds (12,000ft) – this at a time when the development of a medium calibre HA/LA mounting and fire control system for small, lively ships was acknowledged as both necessary and unlikely to be fulfilled in the near future. During a DNO meeting in April 1935 it was pointed out that accepting a speed of 10°/sec would effectively make accurate AA fire impossible if the ship was rolling badly. The requests and demands for improvements in AA defence to be found in contemporary documents leave little doubt that the problem of defending ships against aircraft, although not its full extent, was understood both at the Admiralty and in the fleet. However, the damaging effects of retrenchment meant that doing something about it was going to take some time.

Given that the AA requirement was intended solely for long range defence of the fleet, convoys and harbours, the ship's self-defence against aircraft was reliant on its CRAA guns and its manoeuvrability. This was especially the case against dive-bombers for which the 4.7in mounting was effectively useless, either for self-defence or protecting other ships. This was one of the primary reasons for the substitution of two quad pom-poms for the fifth 4.7in gun mounting. The single mounting that was fitted had limited value due to the blind arcs created by its position and the lack of a director – an item the naval staff had considered 'vitally important' for accurate AA fire. The other CRAA weapon, the quad 0.5in MG, although possessing a formidable rate of fire, was close to useless due to its firing solid bullets rather than explosive shell and the difficulties of keeping it on target.

A primary Staff Requirement was a torpedo armament for close action at night or in conditions of low visibility. Since this involved rapid response to any threat or opportunity, it was important that the torpedo tubes be readily available to fire on either side. Given that the

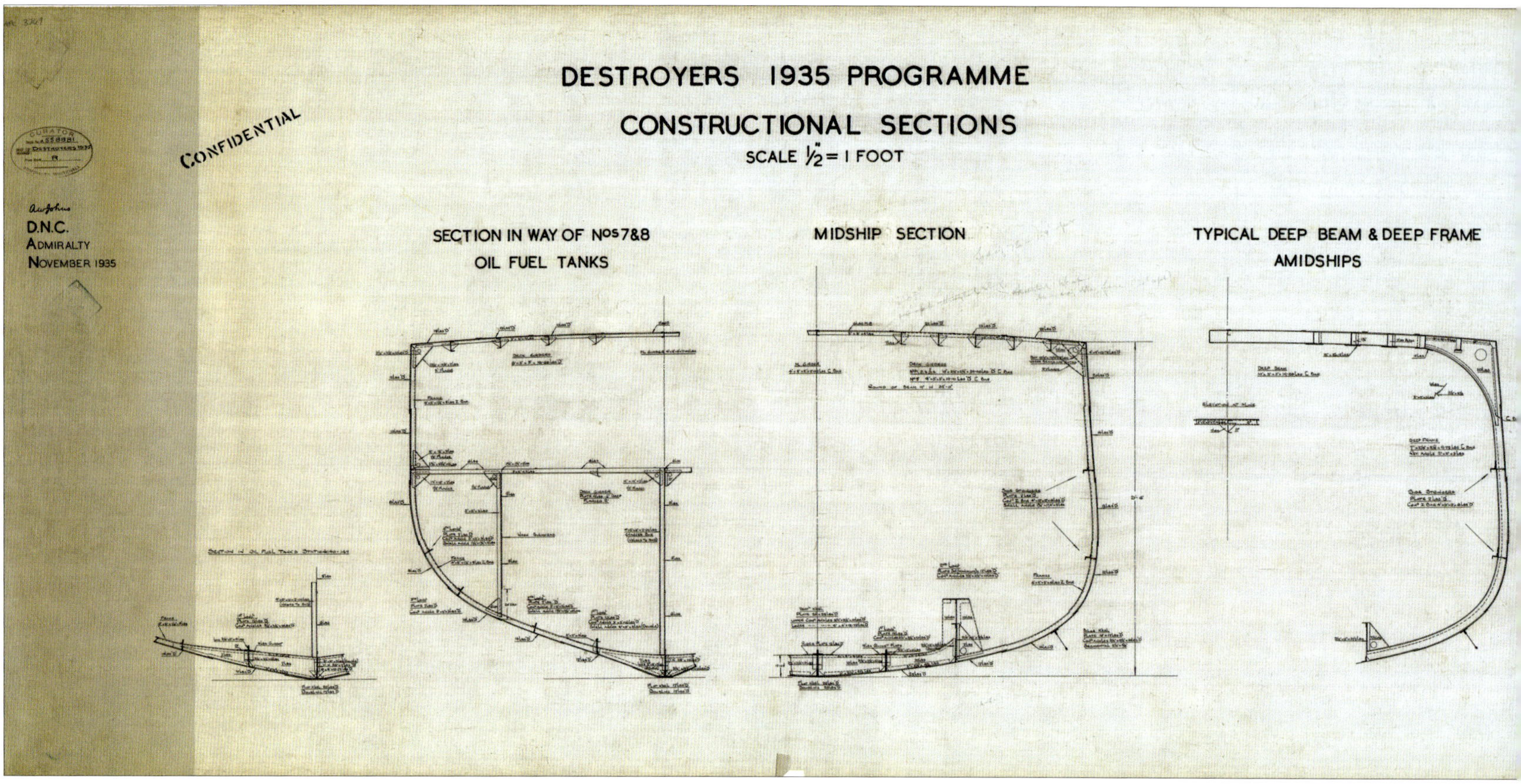

'TRIBAL' CLASS DESIGN, NOVEMBER 1935 – CONSTRUCTIONAL SECTIONS

These sections in combination with the relevant parts of the Specification Book served as a guide to the builders for the expected arrangement and material of the ship's structure. The builders did have some leeway in interpretation to suit their own methods and to accommodate equipment and fittings but no deviation of importance could be made without the approval of either the Admiralty overseer or, in more serious cases, reference to the DNC's department. The 'Tribal' class were the last British destroyers to employ transverse framing, subsequent classes adopting longitudinal framing. (M1791)

number of tubes that could be provided was limited the Staff suggested the following alternatives:

a) A triple tube each side.
b) Fixed tubes each side, if possible three, fitted either in nests or singly as convenient for construction.
c) A quintuple centre line mount arranged to fire two torpedoes one way and three the other.
d) A normal quintuple mounting, if possible, with power training operated from the bridge.

FLY TO SHEER DRAWING, MARCH 1936

The alteration of the form of bow and stern early in 1936 was specified by this fly to the November 1935 Sheer Drawing. While this is limited to the changes at the ends of the ship, the body plan is given in full and enhanced by a table of offsets. Oddly, the body plan also shows, in light pencil, an arrangement that extends the forecastle to the full length of the ship, increases the sheer of the forecastle at the fore end and provides vertical sides in place of a tumblehome. This does not appear to match any other RN ship design of the time and would seem to be speculative, but for what purpose is unknown. (M1793)

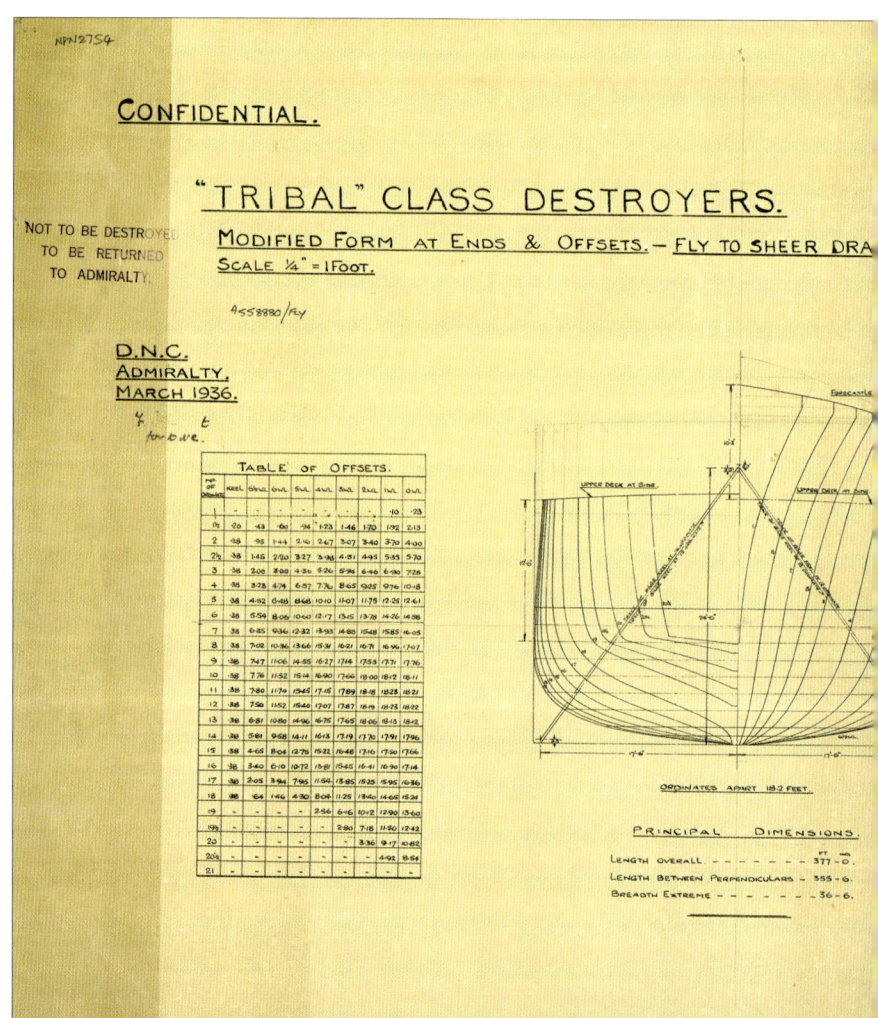

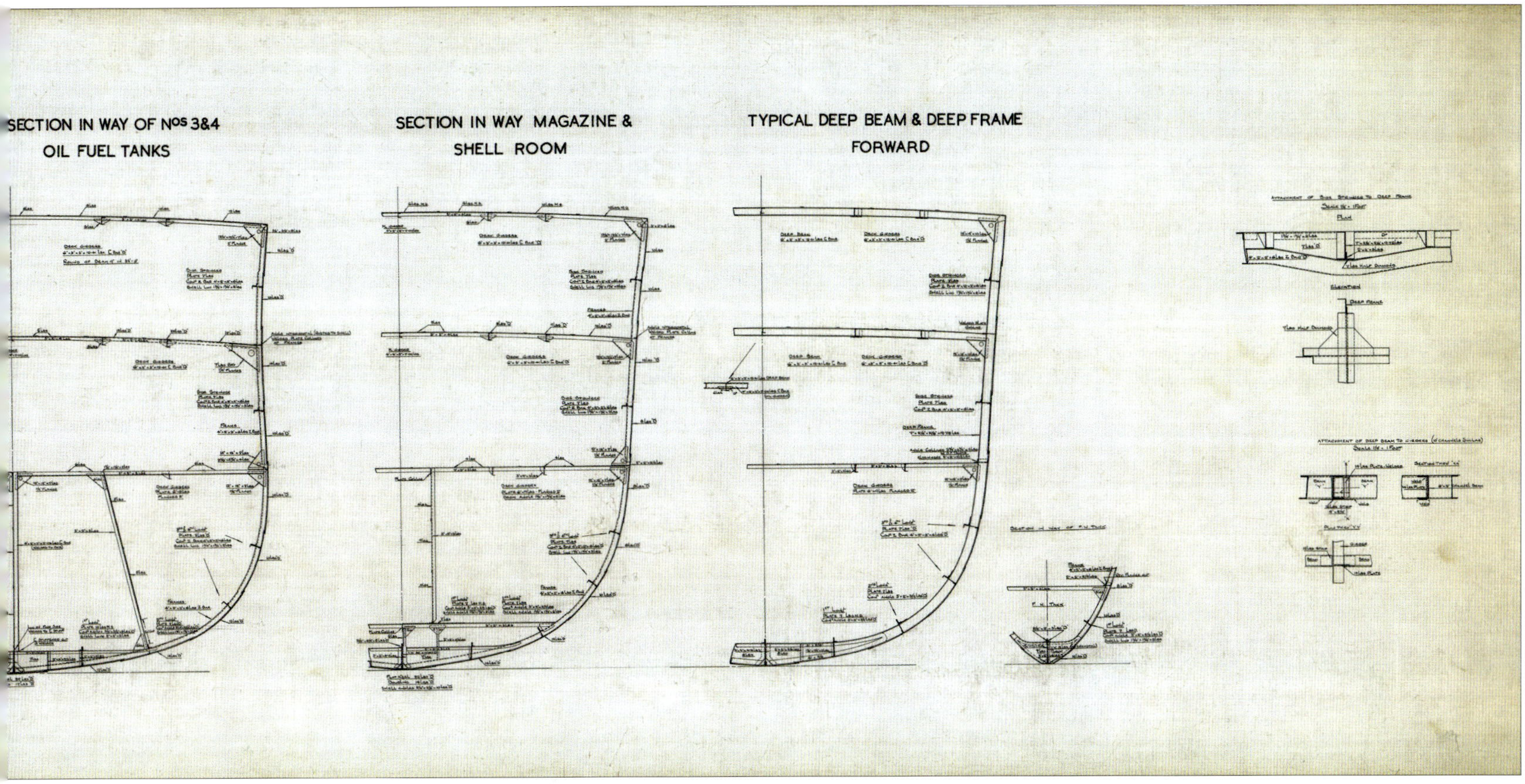
SECTION IN WAY OF Nos 3&4
OIL FUEL TANKS
SECTION IN WAY MAGAZINE &
SHELL ROOM
TYPICAL DEEP BEAM & DEEP FRAME
FORWARD

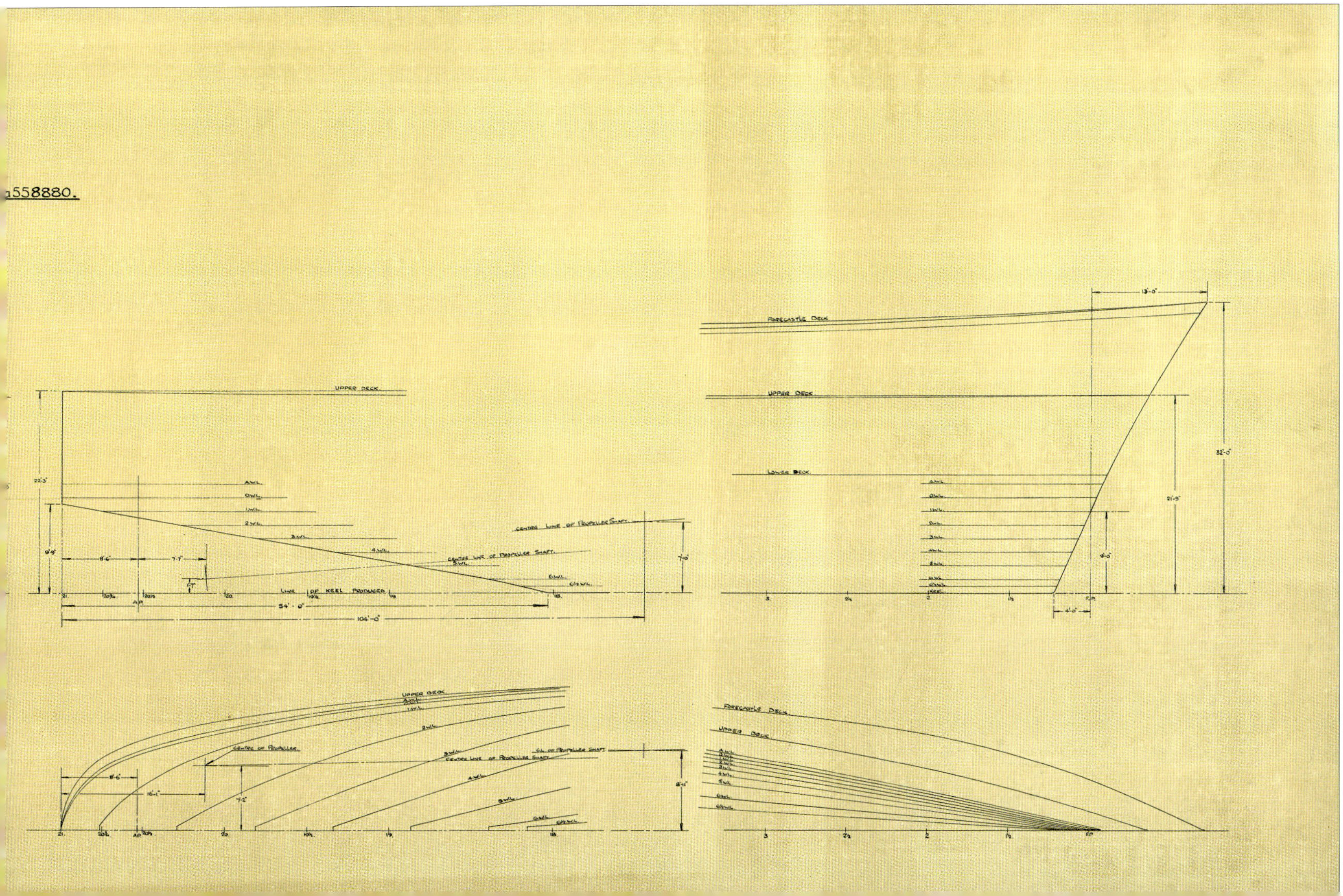
558880.
UPPER DECK
FORECASTLE DECK
LOWER DECK
CENTRE LINE OF PROPELLER SHAFT
LINE OF KEEL PRODUCED

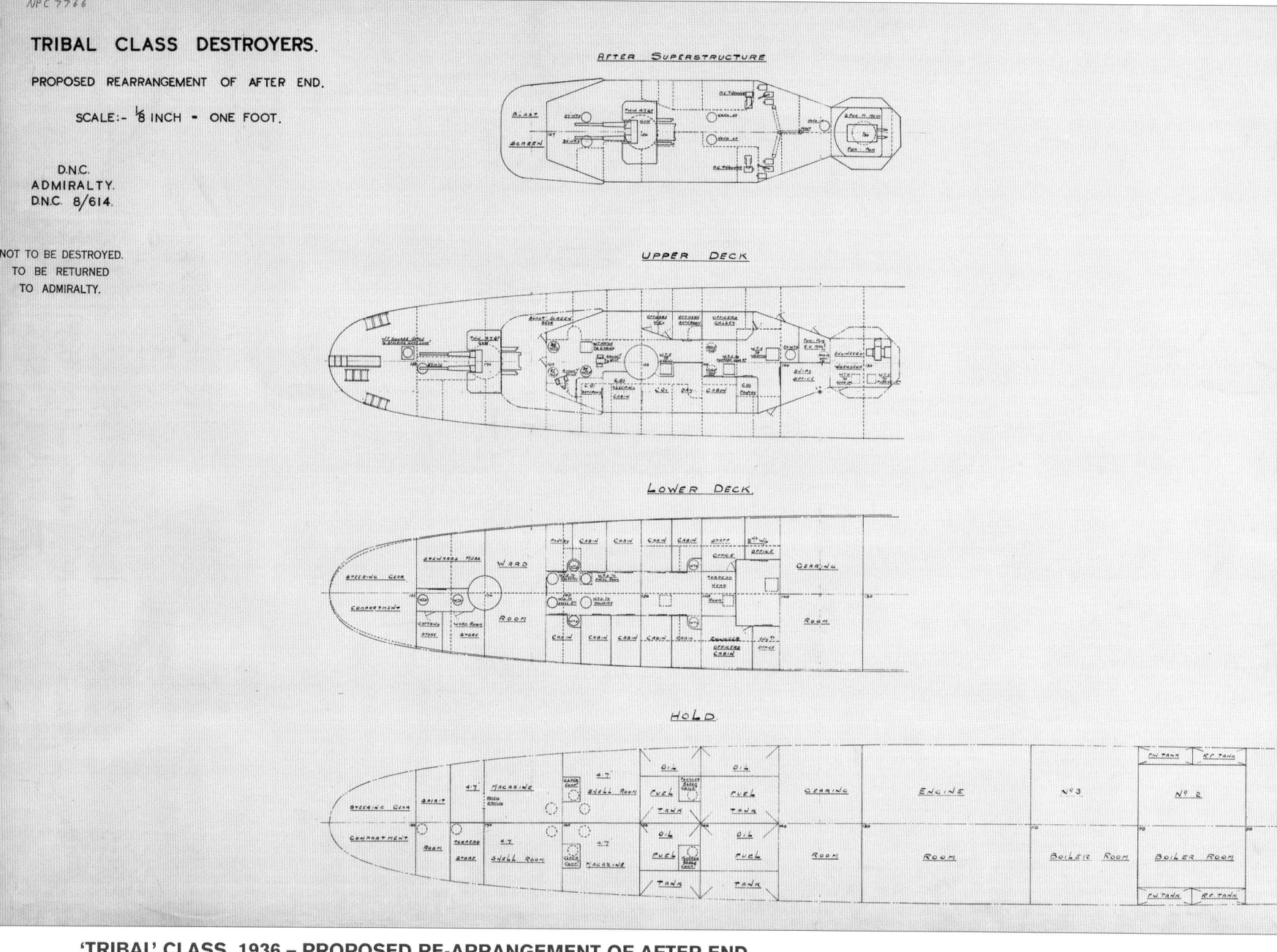

'TRIBAL' CLASS, 1936 – PROPOSED RE-ARRANGEMENT OF AFTER END

The modified design of the after end of the 'Tribal' class resulting from the decision to relocate the two after 4.7in gun mountings. These alterations are close to those of the ships as built apart from some minor changes to the officer accommodation on the Lower Deck, and the torpedo store in the Hold which ended up as a baggage room. The 4.7in ammunition supply is still shown as provided by whip hoists and hand-ups – the after end of the superstructure was moved forward 4ft when power hoists were adopted. (M1800)

The choice was d) but with a quad rather than quintuple mounting to reduce weight. The Mk IX became the first power trained torpedo tube mounting in British service. Like the 4.7in mountings, this employed a hydraulic VSG motor but in this case the pump was driven by an electric motor and all of the power equipment was fitted on the mounting.

FIRE CONTROL

As with earlier destroyers, a DCT, containing a Type H gyro gun-sight, the primary control personnel and their instruments, was fitted on the bridge. Abaft this was a rangefinder/director Mk II which served solely as a rangefinder position in surface action but became an independent director for AA control. Target bearing and range data from these positions were transmitted to the TS on the Upper Deck where it was processed through an AFCC for surface control or a FKC for AA control, the corrected elevation and bearing information being sent to elevation and training receivers at the guns. The FKC also sent fuse setting data to fuse receivers on each side of the gun mounting platforms. Previous destroyers also had a rangefinder separate from the DCT but not in combination with an AA director, this being the first such installation in a destroyer; the prototype Mk I had been fitted for trial in the sloop *Fleetwood*.

HMS *COSSACK*, PARTICULARS 1938

Builder:	Vickers-Armstrongs (High Walker Yard, Newcastle-upon-Tyne)
Ordered:	10 March 1936
Laid down:	9 June 1936
Launched:	8 June 1937
Completed:	10 June 1938
Commissioned:	14 June 1938
Displacement:	1890 tons (standard), 2540 tons (deep)
Length:	355ft 6in (pp), 364ft (wl), 377ft (oa)
Beam:	36ft 6in (extreme)
Draught (standard):	9ft 1in (mean), 8ft 5in (forward), 9ft 9in (aft)
Draught (deep):	11ft 4in (mean)
Freeboard:	23ft 7in (forward), 12ft 5in (amidships), 12ft 6in (aft) to top of deck at side (in standard condition, with trim by the stern as above)
Machinery:	Two sets of Parsons single-reduction geared turbines; 44,000shp = 36 knots at 350rpm in trial condition (1940 tons), 32.75 knots (deep). Three Admiralty 3-drum water tube boilers (max working pressure 300psi at 620°F)
Oil Fuel:	542.28 tons (capacity), 515.16 tons (95%)
Diesel fuel:	12.72 tons (capacity), 12.08 tons (95%)
Endurance:	Clean with 95% fuel. 1110 miles at 33 knots (max authorised speed[1]), 5600 miles at 12 knots (economic speed).
Armament:	8 x 4.7in QF Mk XII guns on 4 twin CP Mk XIX mountings. 250rpg (230 at standard displacement); 40(LA) and 13(HA) rpg practice + 50 star shell for ship.
	4 x 2pdr pom-poms Mk VIII on quad Mk VII mounting, 1800rpg + 84rpg practice
	8 x 0.5in Mk III MG on two quad Mk III mountings, 2500rpg
	1 x 21in QR Mk IX TT mounting, 4 x Mk IX/IX* torpedoes.
	2 x DC throwers, 1 x DC rail; 20 (peace), 30 (war) Type 'D' DCs
Small arms:	60 rifles, 10 revolvers
Complement:	236 (berthing provided for 253)

Weights[2]

	Deep
General equipment:	179.19
Machinery:	576.73
Armament;	276.15
RFW	39.9
Oil Fuel	515.16
Diesel Fuel	12.08
Hull and fittings	940.58
Total	2539.79

Stability:[3]

	Light	Half-Oil	Deep
Displacement (tons)	1869	2261	2525
Mean draught (ft)	9.04	10.38	11.28
GM (ft)	2.9	2.8	2.67
Angle of maximum, stability	34°	40°	41.5°
Angle at which stability vanishes	59°	68.5°	75°

Footnotes

1. The maximum speed allowed except in emergencies or when running full speed trials.
2. Based on *Cossack*'s D284 Form of July 1938 (Ship's Cover).
3. These are the figures based on the inclining of *Afridi* on 16 February 1938. Given that *Cossack* and *Afridi* were built alongside each other by the same contractor it seems highly unlikely that there was any substantial difference between the two, especially given that it was common practice to base the stability of an entire class on the inclining of one or two ships. The *Zulu* was also inclined and produced much the same results. Based on these experiments the accepted standard displacement for the entire class was 1870 tons.

MACHINERY

The machinery arrangement followed standard destroyer practice with three Admiralty three-drum boilers and two sets of Parsons single-reduction geared turbines driving two shafts. The only differences of note were the increased power (44,000shp compared with 34,000shp in the 'G' to 'I' classes) and the subdivision of the engine room into engine and gearing rooms, both a reflection of the increased size of the 'Tribals'. Three boiler rooms had been standard since the 'E' class.

Unlike larger ships, steam trials were limited to the basic 6-hour high-power acceptance trial at a nominal trial displacement (1940 tons). For speed trials at other powers and at deep displacement, representative trials were made with selected ships of the class. Only *Afridi*, *Ashanti*, *Mohawk*, *Punjabi* and *Zulu* ran high-power trials at deep displacement and (except for *Afridi*) a progressive series in the light and half-oil conditions. During acceptance trials *Cossack* developed a mean of 45,214shp and 36.7 knots with 371.2rpm during her measured mile runs at a displacement of 1970 tons. The average measured mile speed for all sixteen ships of the class was 36.9 knots. Four achieved over 37 knots, the fastest being *Ashanti* at 37.58 knots with 44,940shp. The average figures for the five ships that carried out deep trials were 35 knots at 44,610shp but these were carried out in close to half-oil condition rather than at deep displacement.

GENERAL

The ships of the class saw extensive war service and suffered severely from being placed in harm's way. Twelve of the original sixteen ships were lost – five to torpedoes (one from a destroyer, one from an aircraft and three from submarines), five to bombs, one to shore batteries and one to accidental collision. The high incidence of loss to aircraft and the lack of any losses to surface gun action is notable, although it should be said that the vessel sunk by an aerial torpedo

COSSACK'S SISTERS

RN

1935 Programme: *Afridi, Gurkha, Maori, Mohawk, Nubian, Zulu*

1936 Programme: *Ashanti, Bedouin, Eskimo, Mashona, Matabele, Punjabi, Sikh, Somali, Tartar*

RAN

Arunta, Bataan, Warramunga

RCN

Athabaskan (a 2nd RCN 'Tribal' of this name was completed in 1948, the first having been lost in 1944), *Cayuga, Haida, Huron, Iroquois, Micmac, Nootka*.

(*Bedouin*) had already been disabled by the guns of Italian cruisers. For the most part the ships did operate as divisions rather than flotillas and were successful in their primary role of surface action on the few occasions that the opportunity presented itself. They did not achieve much in AA defence, but then no destroyer with a pre-war armament did. In July 1935, the ACNS had pretty much predicted the limited value of the existing CRAA weapons in a destroyer by stating that defence against air attack (especially by dive-bombers) was more likely to depend on rapid manoeuvring than the 'dubious value of a pom-pom'. During her two-year war career *Cossack* suffered multiple instances of damage from enemy action, weather and accidents as can be seen in the accompanying list of refits, repairs and modifications.

HMS *COSSACK* CAREER SUMMARY

When the first of the class entered service during 1938–39 they became the 1st and 2nd 'Tribal Destroyer Flotillas' (note that at this time there was also a 1st and a 2nd Destroyer Flotilla consisting of the 'G' and 'H' classes respectively). This rather unhandy designation was abandoned in April 1939 when the 'Tribal' class became the 4th and 6th Destroyer Flotillas, the ships having been reclassified as simply destroyers. On 14 June 1938 the *Cossack* commissioned at Portsmouth for service in the Mediterranean Fleet as the leader of the 8th Div of the 1st TDF. Following equipment and torpedo trials she sailed from Portland and arriving at Malta on 12 July where she joined the *Afridi*, Capt(D) of the 1st TDF and leader of the 7th Division. The rest of the Flotilla arrived during October–December, *Maori, Nubian* and *Zulu* joining the 8th Division and *Gurkha, Mohawk* and *Sikh* the 7th Division. The other eight ships of the class joined the Home Fleet as the 2nd TDF between December 1938 and March 1939.

Following the outbreak of war, *Cossack* was employed briefly in patrol and convoy escort operations before returning to the UK in October to join the Home Fleet. Here she returned to escort and patrol work – primarily screening the convoy route between Norway and Scotland. On 18 January she took over as flotilla leader for two months while *Afridi* was undergoing repairs. It was during this time that she came to international attention when her 'temporary' commander, Capt(D) Phillip Vian, in contravention of international law, took her into Norwegian territorial waters in order to release 299 merchant navy prisoners from the German supply ship *Altmark*. Protests from the Norwegian and German Governments were somewhat overridden by the popularity of the event at home and, later, the German invasion of Norway.

On 13 April during the 2nd Battle of Narvik the *Cossack* was hit by seven 128mm shells and received extensive splinter damage from two others – one detonated alongside, on impact with the water, and the other on striking a backstay of the forward funnel. One of the hits detonated in Nº2 boiler room, cutting a main steam pipe and the telemotor pipes of the steering gear. Superheated steam killed the personnel in Nº2 boiler room and Nº3 boiler room had to be abandoned due to steam entering through splinter holes in its forward bulkhead. The loss of steam and steering caused the ship to run aground. It took 13 hours to get her re-floated and several days of temporary repairs before she was fit to sail to Scapa where she arrived on 27 April. Repairs were carried out by Thornycroft during May–June, on completion of which she became the leader of the 4th DF replacing *Afridi*, which had been lost in May. *Afridi* had served as leader of the Flotilla since 1938 and had long close association with *Cossack*, they having been laid-down side-by-side on the same day in 1936.

For the remainder of 1940 and the early months of 1941 *Cossack* resumed the routine duties of screening the fleet and the ships laying the Northern Barrage, escorting convoys (primarily between Pentland Firth and Cape Wrath), general patrols and the occasional sweep of the Norwegian coast. From May to October 1941 she was almost entirely employed in the escort of military convoys in the Eastern Atlantic and supply convoys for Malta. Among the more interesting events of this period were an action in company with *Ashanti, Maori* and *Sikh* against a small German convoy off Egersund, Norway, during the night of 13/14 October 1940. *Cossack* torpedoed and sank one ship (netlayer *Genua*) and was damaged by a shell hit in her stern. She was also involved in the *Bismarck* action during the night of 26/27 May 1941 when, with *Maori, Sikh, Zulu* and the Polish destroyer *Piorun*, she shadowed and harassed the damaged German battleship. The weather was poor and several attempts to torpedo the *Bismarck* failed, but the destroyers only suffered light splinter damage from near misses – which in the case of *Cossack* removed her main W/T aerials. In July 1941 *Cossack* detached to Force H with several other Home Fleet Ships (Force X). The primary purpose was to provide additional support in forthcoming operations to supply stores and personnel to Malta, *Cossack* serving as part of the escort for Operations Substance (21–24 July) and Halberd (25–28 September) and diversionary support for Operation Style (1 August).

At 16.00 on 22 October 1941 *Cossack* sailed from Gibraltar as senior escort of the homeward bound convoy HG75. In the evening of the following day she was stationed astern of the convoy, zigzagging at 13 knots. At 22.38, in position 35.36N/10.04W, she was hit on the port side abreast 'B' mounting by a torpedo fired by *U563*. The explosion, possibly involving some of the forward magazines, destroyed a large section of the ship's fore end and wrecked the bridge, leaving whatever structure had survived before the break of the forecastle sloping steeply down into the sea. The explosion started a fire at the after end of the bridge which ignited the ready-use ammunition for

COSSACK, REFITS, REPAIRS AND MODIFICATIONS 1938–1941

5–18 September 1938: Malta

Docked Nº4 Dock, for minor repairs to fore peak and starboard side resulting from double collision with *Barham* on 17 August during refuelling exercise at sea.

December 1938

Pendant No changed from L03 to F03.

14–26 April 1939: Malta

Annual refit. Docked Nº2 Dock 17–18 April.

9 November 1939–10 January and 13–19 January 1940: Robb, Leith

Damage repairs following collision on 7 November with SS *Bothwick* off May Island, Firth of Forth while escorting convoy HN1. Shortly after completion returned for further repairs following collision on 13 January with cable ship *Royal Scot* in Firth of Forth.

3 May–15 June 1940: Thornycroft, Woolston

Refit and action damage repairs following 2nd Battle of Narvik.

Twin 4in Mk XIX HA/LA mounting fitted in place of Nº3 4.7in mounting. Fitted with temporary system of HA control for control of 4in mounting.

Nº3 4.7in magazine and shell room converted to 4in magazines (fixed ammunition).

Upper (c10ft) of mainmast removed and W/T yard lowered.

28 August–13 October 1940: Rosyth

Refit and repairs to weather damage. Cracks in side plating, 2in to 3in long at break of forecastle (Station 84 Upper Deck level) repaired and location strengthened (problem also found in *Zulu* and *Sikh*).

15 October–4 November 1940: Rosyth

Damage repairs to stern and rudder following shell hit sustained in action against enemy convoy off Norway on 13/14 October 1940.

30 December 1940–3 January 1941: Scapa Flow

Temporary repairs to weather damage by HMS *Tyne* and floating dock at Scapa prior to full repair by Thornycroft.

8 January–24 February 1941: Thornycroft, Woolston

Refit and repair of damage to bottom plating (corrugated keel and garboard strake between Stations 10 and 40) and leaks in RFW tanks due to use of high speed in rough weather on passage to Iceland.

Additional stiffening fitted to outer bottom abreast keel between Stations 25 and 40.

Fitted Type 286M RDF with fixed aerial at top of foremast (radar detection limited to forward bearing of 50 degrees on each side).

Height of after funnel reduced by 4ft.

March 1941: HMS *Tyne*, Scapa Flow

Repairs to minor but extensive shock damage caused by a nearby mine explosion during passage of Irish Sea, SW of Isle of Man, on 3 March.

3 May–15 June 1941: Thornycroft, Woolston

Refit

Fitted 2 x 2pdr single pom-poms, one each side in the wings of the Flag Deck.

Modifications where precise date is unknown

25ft motor boats converted from petrol to diesel. Petrol tank in bow removed.

Degaussing gear fitted (probably during May–June 1940 refit).

Modification of FKC and fitting of new fuse setting gear for HA control of twin 4in mounting (probably during refits at Rosyth August–November 1940). This replaced temporary system fitted in May–June 1940.

---

the single 2pdr pom-poms fitted on the Signal Deck and the coal stowed in a bunker on the starboard side of the Upper Deck. At the time of the attack only Nº1 and Nº2 boilers were in operation, Nº3 being at one-hour notice. Fuel supply to the boilers was lost, Nº1 boiler room began to flood with oil fuel from the forward tanks due to damage to its forward bulkhead and Nº2 was flooding with water; both rooms were abandoned. Attempts to get pumps running to put out the fire failed and at about 23.00 it was decided to abandon ship due to concerns that the fire would spread to the oil fuel in Nº1 boiler room or to the forward magazines (the extent of damage forward could not be seen). The survivors were picked up by the destroyer *Legion* and the Free French sloop *Commandant Duboc*.

Having realised that the flooded fore end presented no danger of magazine explosion, it was concluded that salvage might be possible if the fire, which died down after it had consumed the 2pdr ammunition, could be put out. The corvette *Carnation* managed to get alongside aft and at 01.00 the ship was re-boarded and the fire extinguished (except for the coal bunker which continued to smoulder for some time). Initial efforts were made to reduce topweight, including firing three of the torpedoes (the fourth misfired). Attempts to get the machinery running during the morning of the 24th failed due to difficulties with feed water supply, although the ship was run astern at slow speed for a short period and the steam ejector worked long enough to reduce the level of flood water in Nº2 boiler room. Also, on this morning *Cossack* fired her guns for the last time, briefly engaging an approaching German aircraft with her twin 4in and quad pom-pom mountings.

In the meantime, the tug *Thames* had been dispatched from Gibraltar escorted by the corvette *Jonquil* but, having failed to find *Cossack* in her reported position, did not turn up until the afternoon of the 25th. To make matters worse she was not equipped with a portable salvage pump. *Cossack* was taken in tow, stern first by *Thames* at 14.15 but the drag of the wrecked fore end limited speed to 2 knots. On the 26th the weather began to worsen so the ship was abandoned for the night. In the morning it was concluded that re-boarding the ship was impractical since she was further down by the bows and the sea was sweeping over the Upper Deck. The working of the hull almost certainly caused the forward boiler room bulkheads to give way and at 10.43 on 27 October she trimmed down bow first, raised her stern vertically and sank in position 52.12N/08.17W. She lies, with her captain and 153 men of her crew, at a depth of 1500 fathoms – one other man was killed but did not go down with the ship and, of the 32 men wounded or injured, four later died of their wounds.

(Times given above are GMT)

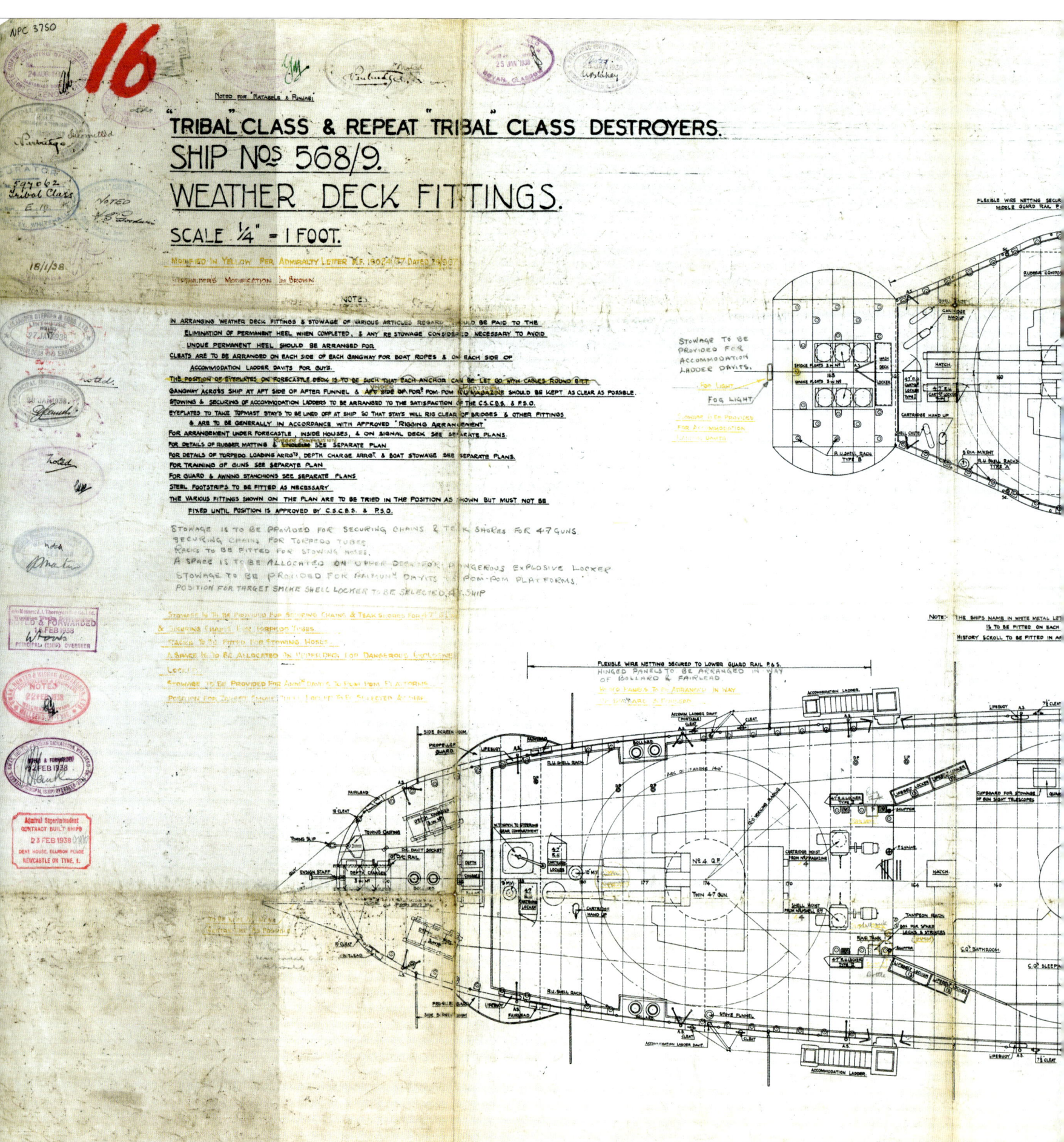

'TRIBAL' CLASS WEATHER DECK FITTINGS, 1937

Caption and key overleaf.

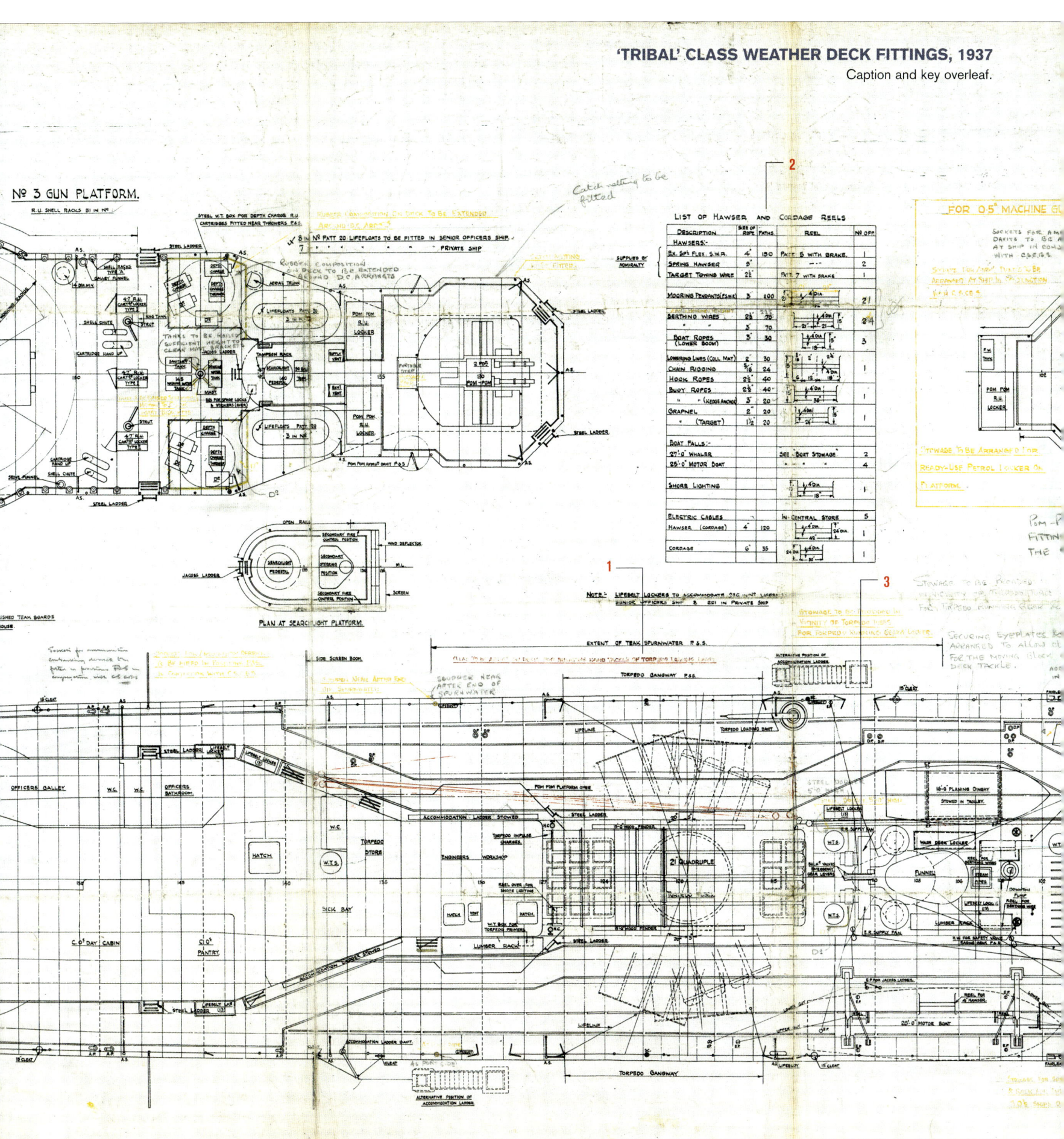

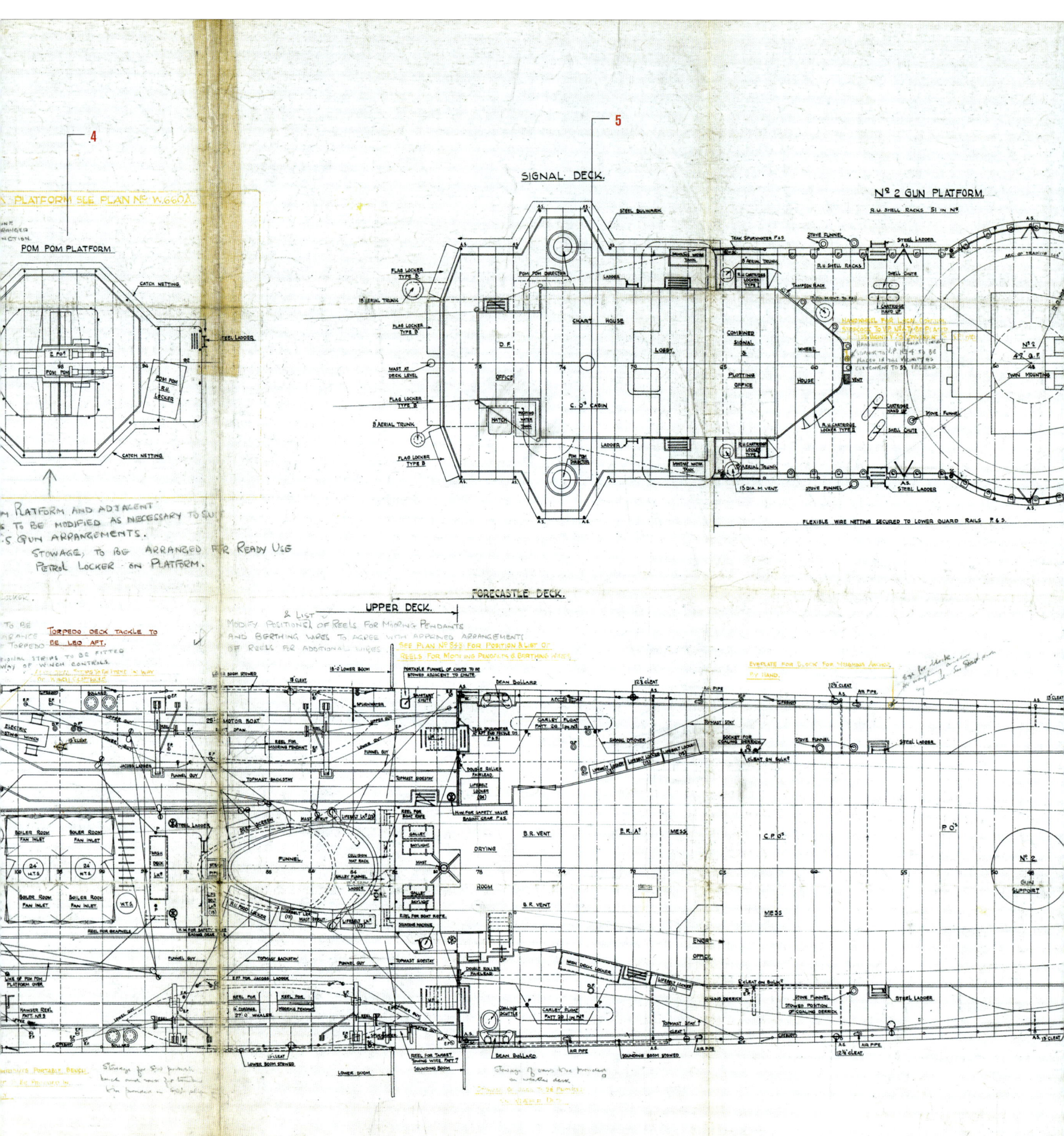

'TRIBAL' CLASS WEATHER DECK FITTINGS, 1937

The origin of this drawing is a little obscure although its purpose in serving as a guide to the builders for the deck fittings is clear. It seems probable that the original drawing was drafted at the Admiralty but, given the specific mention under the title of 'Ship Numbers 568/9', it would seem that this is a copy of the original and specific to Scotts' of Greenock since these are the yard numbers of the two 'Tribal' class ships that they built (*Matabele* and *Punjabi*), noting that such numbers were unique to the shipbuilding firms concerned. The odd thing about the plan is that, following modification, it was circulated to all the builders of the class as evidenced by the stamps down the left-hand side – dated sequentially over the period Jan–Feb 1938.

The drawing has a considerable amount of annotation some of which is unlikely to be readable. This is particularly the case with that in yellow ('modifications made as a result of Admiralty letter dated 29 Sep 1937') but much of this text has been re-written alongside the original in pencil which may help. In general, the fittings shown do not vary substantially from those actually fitted in *Cossack* but there are a number of minor variations in detail and some additional information to be found for those who wish to compare this with the as-fitted deck plans. (M1832)

1. **Torpedo hand tackle.** This item of text appears to state 'gear to be arranged on deck for belaying hand tackle of torpedo loading davit'. It refers to the tackle added to the drawing between Frames 114 and 139 to port of the torpedo tube mounting. This replaced the block and tackle which ran from Frames 89 to 114 to port of the funnels linking the hoisting winch with the torpedo davit (see also page 30). Although this modification is referred to below the title as a 'shipbuilder's modification in brown' it actually appears to be in red. It also appears to have been drawn in coloured pencil which has been partially erased by wear.

2. **The Table of Hawser and Cordage Reels** provides a complete list of all the reels required to be fitted and includes their purpose, dimensions and intended rope type and capacity, providing somewhat greater detail of these fittings than is available in the as-fitted plans.

3. **The emergency valve gear levers** provided a means of closing the main steam valves between the boiler rooms and engine room from the Upper Deck. This served as a back-up to the primary means of closing the valves located in the engine room. These levers are not shown in the as-fitted plans due either to a simple omission from those plans or the provision of some other form of secondary operation.

4. **Quad pom-pom mounting.** One of the primary advantages of this plan is the depiction of the original intention of fitting a quad pom-pom mounting between the funnels. It was not fitted due to the limited supply of such mountings, which had only recently been introduced. Despite the intention to fit them when available, no second mounting was ever supplied to any of the class. The fly showing the modified arrangement of the platform is on page 30.

5. **The pom-pom directors** were moved from the bridge to the wings of the Flag Deck where they replaced the 0.5in MG mountings provided in the original design. Like the second quad pom-pom these were not fitted in the ships as completed. As they could only cover one side of the ship, both would have been required to control the after quad pom-pom unless a new position covering both sides could be found for a single director.

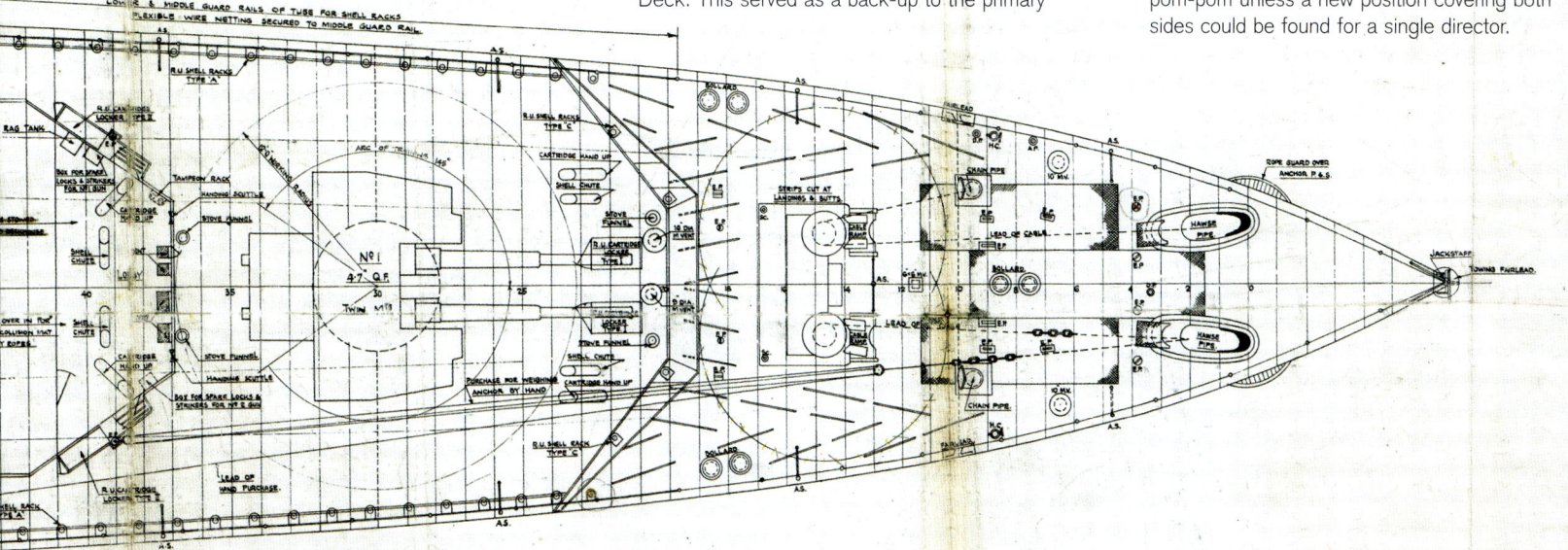

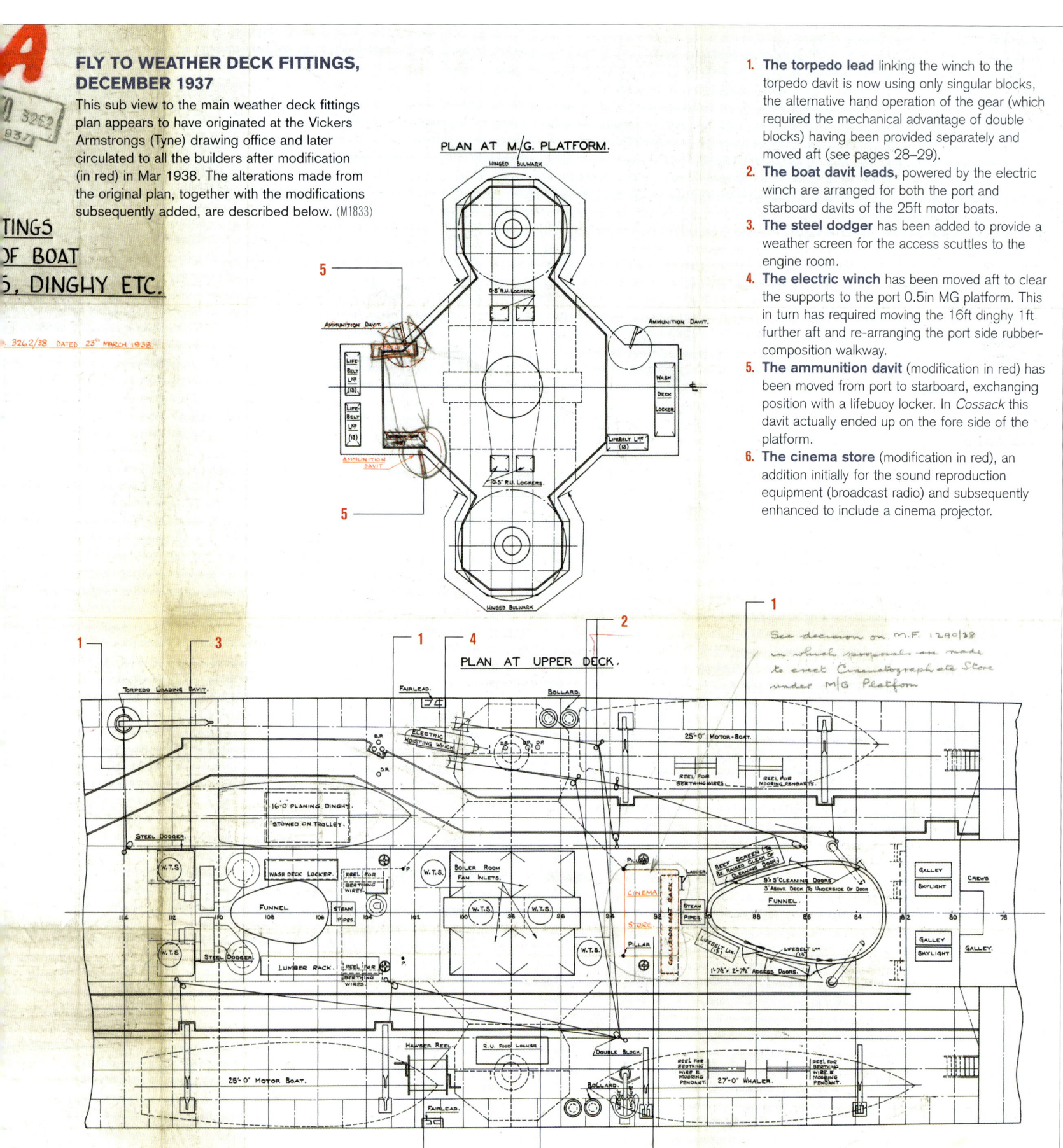

FLY TO WEATHER DECK FITTINGS, DECEMBER 1937

This sub view to the main weather deck fittings plan appears to have originated at the Vickers Armstrongs (Tyne) drawing office and later circulated to all the builders after modification (in red) in Mar 1938. The alterations made from the original plan, together with the modifications subsequently added, are described below. (M1833)

1. **The torpedo lead** linking the winch to the torpedo davit is now using only singular blocks, the alternative hand operation of the gear (which required the mechanical advantage of double blocks) having been provided separately and moved aft (see pages 28–29).
2. **The boat davit leads,** powered by the electric winch are arranged for both the port and starboard davits of the 25ft motor boats.
3. **The steel dodger** has been added to provide a weather screen for the access scuttles to the engine room.
4. **The electric winch** has been moved aft to clear the supports to the port 0.5in MG platform. This in turn has required moving the 16ft dinghy 1ft further aft and re-arranging the port side rubber-composition walkway.
5. **The ammunition davit** (modification in red) has been moved from port to starboard, exchanging position with a lifebuoy locker. In *Cossack* this davit actually ended up on the fore side of the platform.
6. **The cinema store** (modification in red), an addition initially for the sound reproduction equipment (broadcast radio) and subsequently enhanced to include a cinema projector.

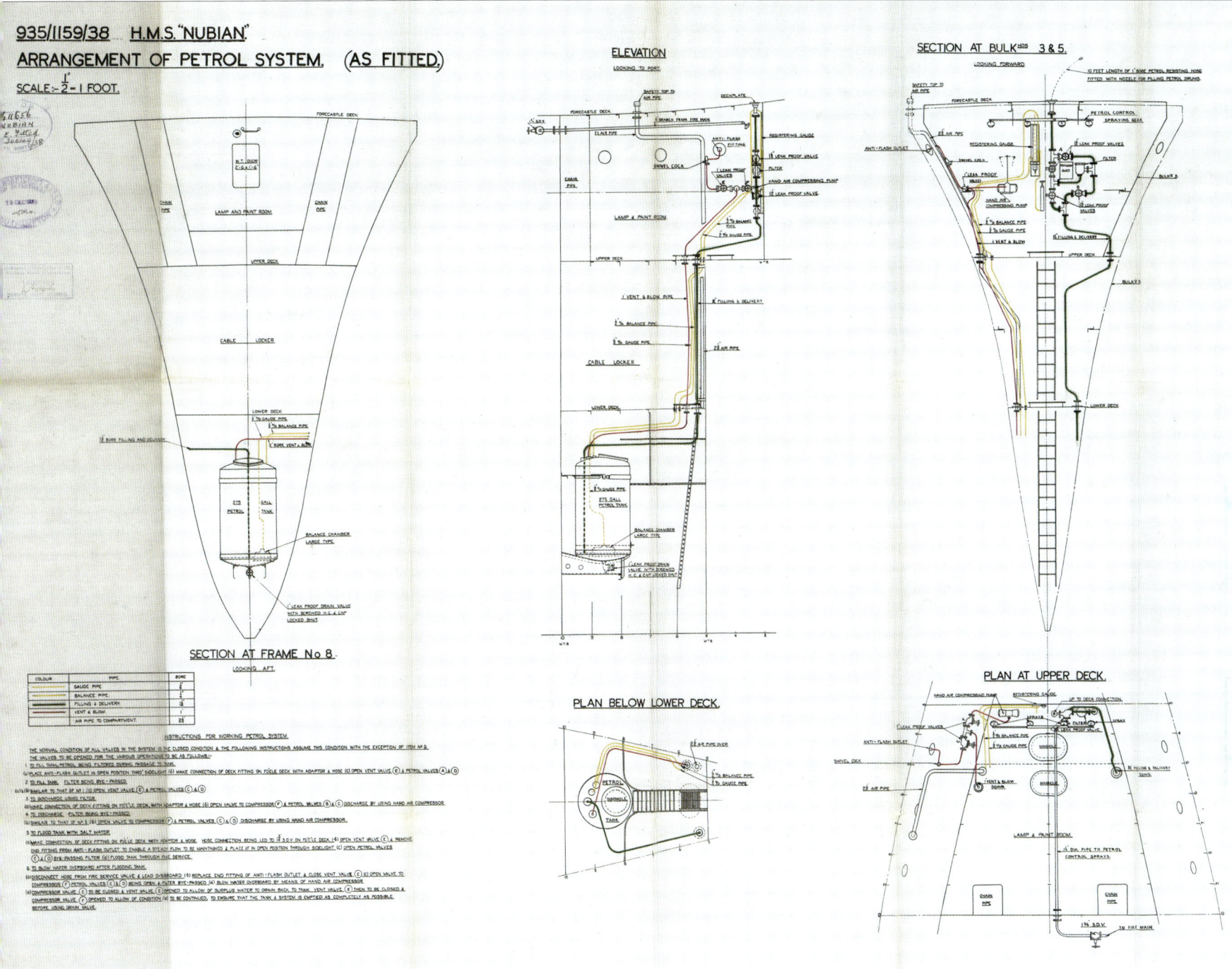

HMS *NUBIAN*: ARRANGEMENT OF PETROL SYSTEM, AS FITTED 1938

Although specific to *Nubian*, the arrangement shown here for the stowage of fuel for the ship's motor-boats was the same in all 16 of the original 'Tribal' class. Because of the volatile nature of petrol, particularly the highly explosive air/vapour mixture that might be generated by spillage, it was given the same level of security as that for magazines. The compartment was kept locked, no device (steel, electrical or inflammable) apart from magazine safety lamps was allowed into the compartment and any personnel entering had to wear rubber footwear. Nobody could enter the compartment until the engineer officer of the ship was satisfied that it was safe to do so. The location of the tank in the fore end, also for reasons of safety, was a standard arrangement throughout the ships of the fleet apart from aircraft carriers. Note that the cable locker had a separate enclosure within the compartment shown here as the 'cable locker' – the actual locker can be clearly seen in the profile of *Cossack*. Diesel engine boats later replaced the petrol driven ones and the tanks, and the danger they represented, were removed (noting that it is possible that the *Cossack*, although no longer carrying petrol, may not have had the redundant tank removed prior to her loss).

The tank was filled, via the green pipe, from the deck plate on the forecastle. This pipe also served for supply, the petrol being forced back up to the deck plate by pumping air into the top of the tank, via the red pipe, using the hand pump in the lamp and paint room on the lower deck. A hose connected to the deck plate was then used to fill petrol cans for transport aft to the boats. The red pipe could also serve as a vent to the tank. The air vent with a safety top on the forecastle deck served as a vent to the compartment containing the tank. (M1812)

EXPANSION OF SHELL PLATING AND UPPER AND FORCASTLE DECK PLATING

These are a combination of the shell expansion for *Ashanti* and the deck plating of *Cossack*. This has been adopted because *Cossack* does not have a surviving shell expansion and, while *Ashanti*'s plan covers both shell and deck plating, *Cossack*'s deck plans have the advantage of having the structure under the deck coloured blue and therefore easily distinguishable from the deck plating and structure above the deck. In general, these plans are applicable to all 16 ships of the original 'Tribal' class. (M1807 and M1808)

Plating is designated by its nominal weight in lbs/ft², this, and not measured thickness, being the standard form in which plates were specified and ordered. Bars across plate joints refer to the number of rivet rows – one bar for single riveting, two for double riveting and so on. The 'S' shape with a vertical bar through it along the deck edges in the deck plans indicates that there is a joint in the side plating at these points. The areas with shaded edges indicate the fitting of doubling plates to compensate for holes (such as the circulating intakes and outlets in the shell plating) or to provide additional support (such as the areas round the bases of the 4.7in gun mountings or the heels of davits, bollards, etc). Note that the 'S' shape with a double bar across it, under the doubling of the 4.7in mountings, indicates a double riveted edge butt (the doubling plate serving as a strap). The majority of doubling plates are external with the main exception of the inner flat keel and the compensation plate around the opening for the Asdic dome. Note that some of the doubling plates on the shell plating are one side only – this is indicated by (p) or (s).

The garboard (A) strake from Frames 12 to 174 and the sheer (G) strake from Frames 88 to 160 have their butts offset at port and starboard by one or two frame spaces. The butts to port are indicated as such by broken line (noting that the edges of the butt straps are shown in broken line on both sides except where the starboard straps are external). Apart from the sheer strake between Frames 74 and 138, all the butts above the waterline are lapped while below the waterline all the butts have straps. The longitudinal laps (landings) of the deck plating are joggled while the shell plating is arranged as in/out strakes with the frames joggled to fit.

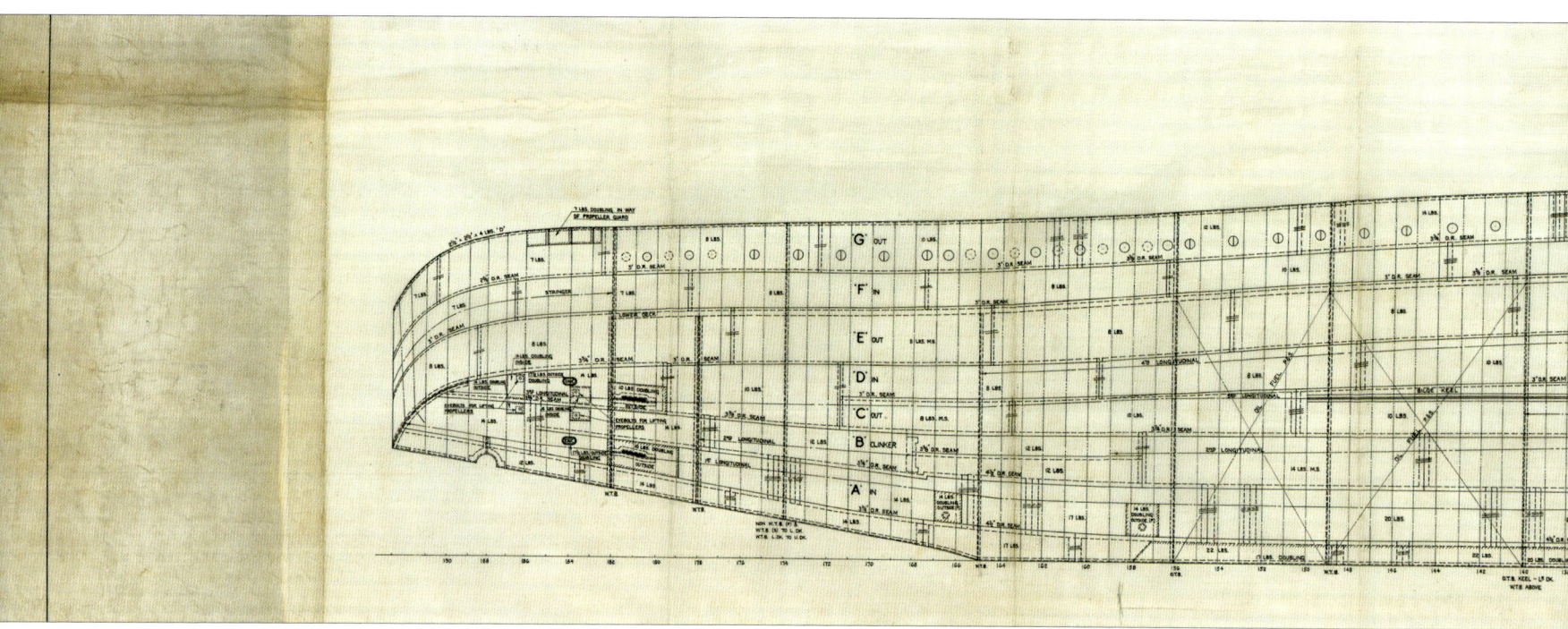

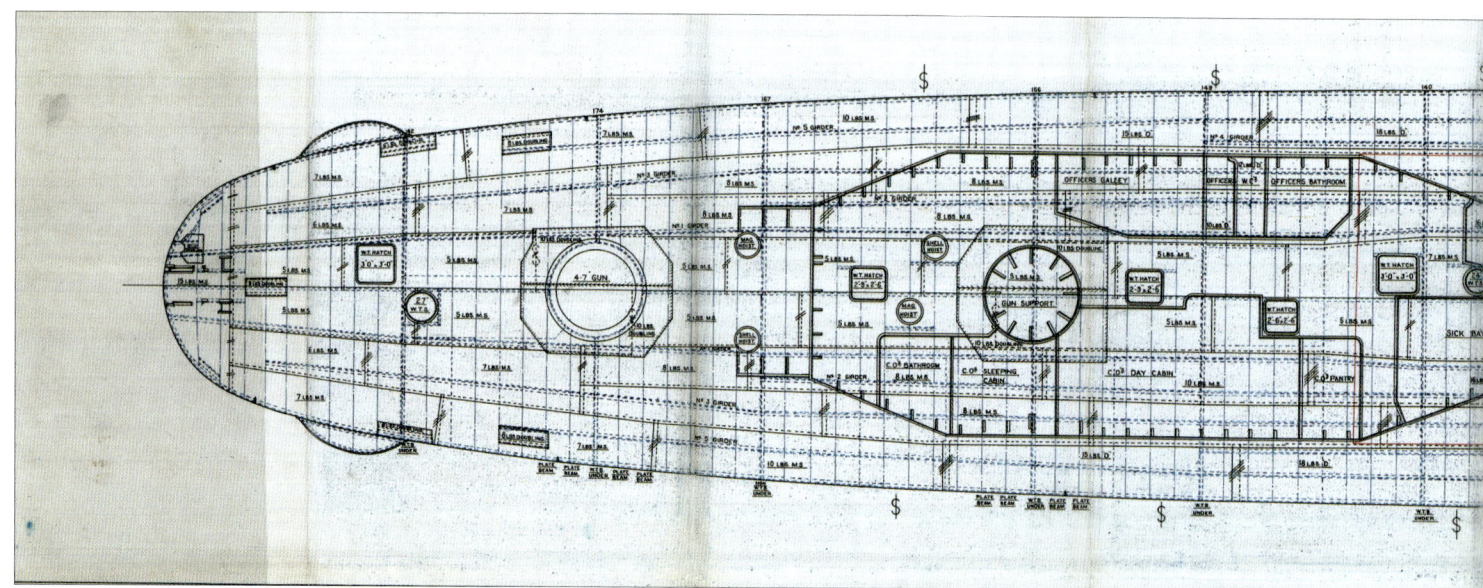

H.M.S. "COSSACK"

PROFILE (AS FITTED)
SCALE:- ¼ INCH = 1 FOOT

ABBREVIATIONS USED ON THE PLANS

AP	After Perpendicular/ Admiralty Pattern/ Air Pipe	LUB^N	Lubrication	T/S	Transmitting Station
A/S	Anti-Submarine	M/A	Motor Alternator	UJ	Universal Joint
AS	Awning Stanchion	M/G	Motor Generator/ Machine Gun	VP	Voice Pipe
ASA	Ammunition, Small Arms (ammunition boxes)	ML	Metal Lined (ammunition box)	WC	Water Closet
BI	Bearing Indicator	MV/MUSH	Mushroom Vent	WF	Web Frame
BR	Boiler Room	NAT	Natural (vent)	WT	Water-Tight
CE	Composition Exploding	NAT EXH^T	Natural Exhaust (vent)	W/T	Wireless Transmitter
CIRC	Circulating	NUC	Not Under Command (signals)	WTB	Water-Tight Bulkhead
CL	Centre Line	NWTM	Non water-tight manhole	WTH	Water-Tight Hatch
CPO	Chief Petty Officer	OF	Oil Fuel	WTM	Water-Tight Manhole
CO	Commanding Officer	OFF	Oil Fuel Filling (connection)	WTS	Water-Tight Scuttle
cwt	Hundred weight (112 lbs)	OTB	Oil-Tight Bulkhead	WTSV	Water-Tight Shut Valve (also given as 'WTS' valve)
DC	Depth Charge	OTS	Oil-Tight Scuttle		
DCT	Depth Charge Thrower	P	Port/Pillar		
D/F	Direction Finder	PATT	Pattern		
DP	Deck Plate	PDR	Pounder		
EL	Electric Light	PL	Punkah Louvre		
EP	Eye Plate	P & S	Port and Starboard		
ER	Engine Room/ Electric Radiator	PO	Petty Officer		
ERA	Engine Room Artificer	PRACT	Practice (ammunition)		
FD	Forced Draught (fan)	QF	Quick Firing		
FL	Forced Lubrication	QR	Quadruple Revolving (torpedo tube)		
FP	Forward Perpendicular	RF	Reserve Feed (water)		
FW	Fresh Water	RU	Ready Use		
HA	High Angle	S	Starboard		
HB	Hammock Berth	SAP	Semi Armour-Piercing (shell)		
HC	Hose Connection	SD Valve/SDV	Screw Down Valve		
HEDA	High Explosive, Direct Action (shell/fuse)	SFP	Special Fleet Practice (torpedoes)		
HETF	High Explosive, Time Fuse (shell/fuse)	SPO	Steward Petty Officer		
HW	Hot Water/ Hand Wheel	TIT	Tube Impulse Torpedo		
LA	Low Angle				
LKR/LK^R	Locker				
LP	Low Power				
LUB	Lubricating (oil)				

Abbreviations

'D'	D steel
DR	Double Riveted
MS	Mild Steel
QR	Quadruple Riveted
SR	Single Riveted
TR	Triple Riveted
WF	Web Frame
WTH	Water-Tight Hatch

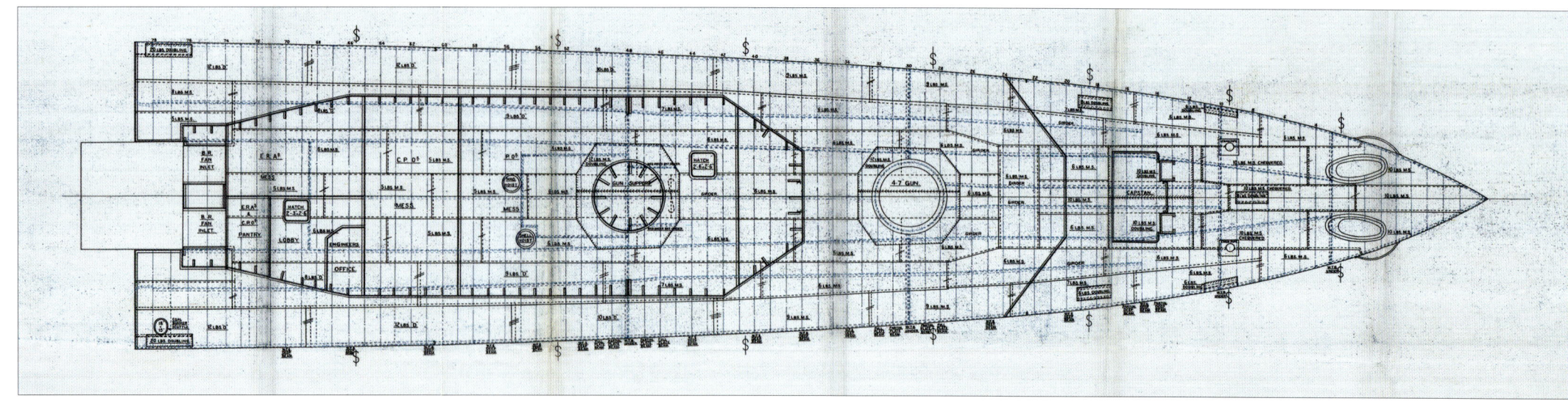

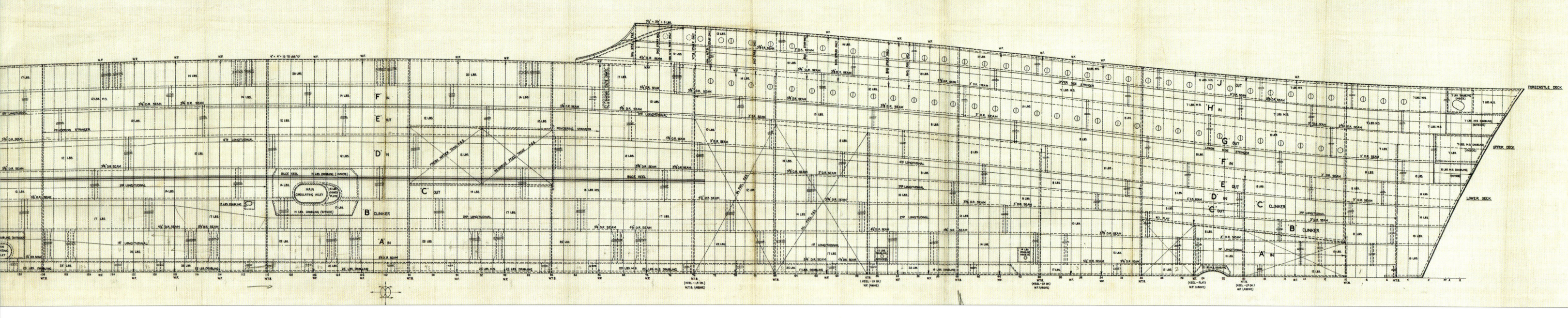

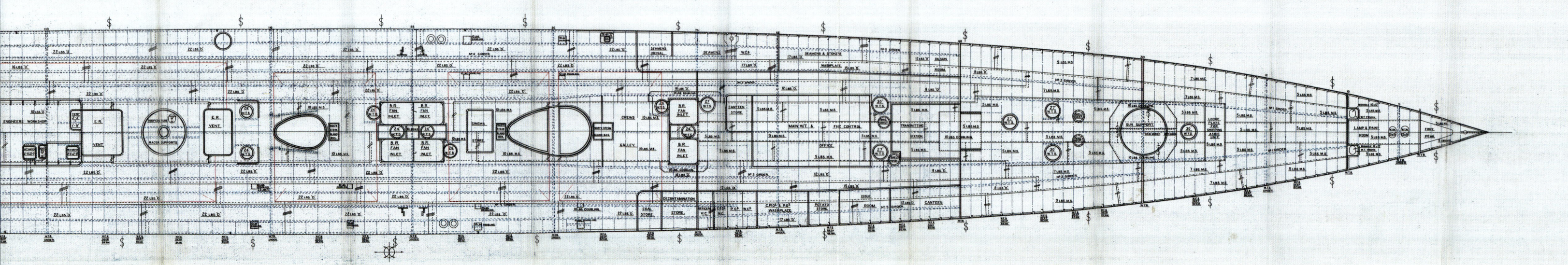

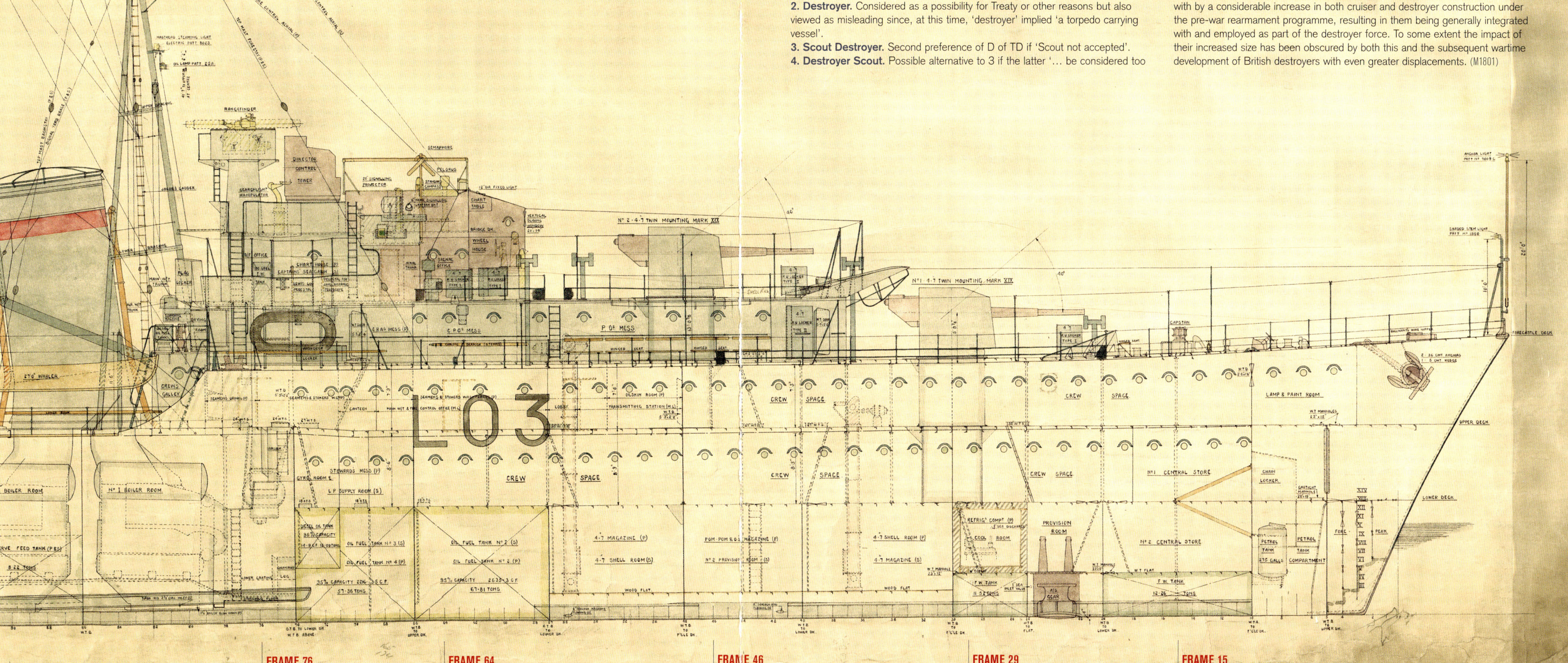

HMS *COSSACK*: PROFILE, AS FITTED AUGUST 1938

A glance at the 1935 design profile (pages 10–11) could easily be mistaken for a standard 'A' to 'I' class destroyer or one of their leaders – which is not the case in this view due almost entirely to the adoption of the clipper bow. A more detailed study soon reveals a considerable number of differences between the 'Tribal's and their predecessors and points to the fact that they were not originally regarded as destroyers at all. The original designation as 'V Leader' merely served as a convenient way of setting them apart from both destroyers and cruisers. Unfortunately, the use of the word 'leader' carried with it an implication of a function that did not exist. This was first pointed out by the D of P in April 1935 in stating that 'The name "V" leader is unsatisfactory as these craft are not going to lead flotillas.' However, he also proposed that since they were being arranged to fit within the limits of the destroyer category the use of that term with a suitable addition 'such as "large destroyer", "patrol destroyers" or even "Tribal class destroyers",...' might serve. Suggested designations made up to June 1935, and the comments upon them recorded by the D of TD were as follows:

1. **Scout.** Preferred by D of TD although emphasising the scouting rather than the fighting roles.
2. **Destroyer.** Considered as a possibility for Treaty or other reasons but also viewed as misleading since, at this time, 'destroyer' implied 'a torpedo carrying vessel'.
3. **Scout Destroyer.** Second preference of D of TD if 'Scout not accepted'.
4. **Destroyer Scout.** Possible alternative to 3 if the latter '… be considered too provocative to France, whose *Fantasques* might be taken as the "Scouts" to be destroyed.'
5. **Patrol or Support Destroyer.** 'Have a somewhat defensive sound'.
6. **Cruiser Destroyer.** While intending to indicate the combination of functions, it also falsely implied destruction of cruisers. The use of the term 'cruiser' in the title was also objected to.
7. **Heavy/ Large/ Super Destroyer.** Of these 'heavy destroyer' was preferred by D of TD but he considered that they all present an '… impression of size, which is inconsistent with the normal conception of "destroyer".'
8. **Tribal Destroyer.** 'They would be known as "Tribals", a good name within the Service, but not lending itself to a definition of a type, nor to the naming of squadrons.'

[The quoted sections above are from ADM1/9376. The numbered list is paraphrased from the same document with the exception of the direct quotes.]

Other names considered included 'Chaser', 'Corvette' and 'Gunvessel'. That finally chosen was '8' but it only survived officially until 1939 when the ships were re-designated as 'Destroyers'. The change in designation reflected the fact that the problems the class had been intended to resolve had been more-or-less dealt with by a considerable increase in both cruiser and destroyer construction under the pre-war rearmament programme, resulting in them being generally integrated with and employed as part of the destroyer force. To some extent the impact of their increased size has been obscured by both this and the subsequent wartime development of British destroyers with even greater displacements. (M1801)

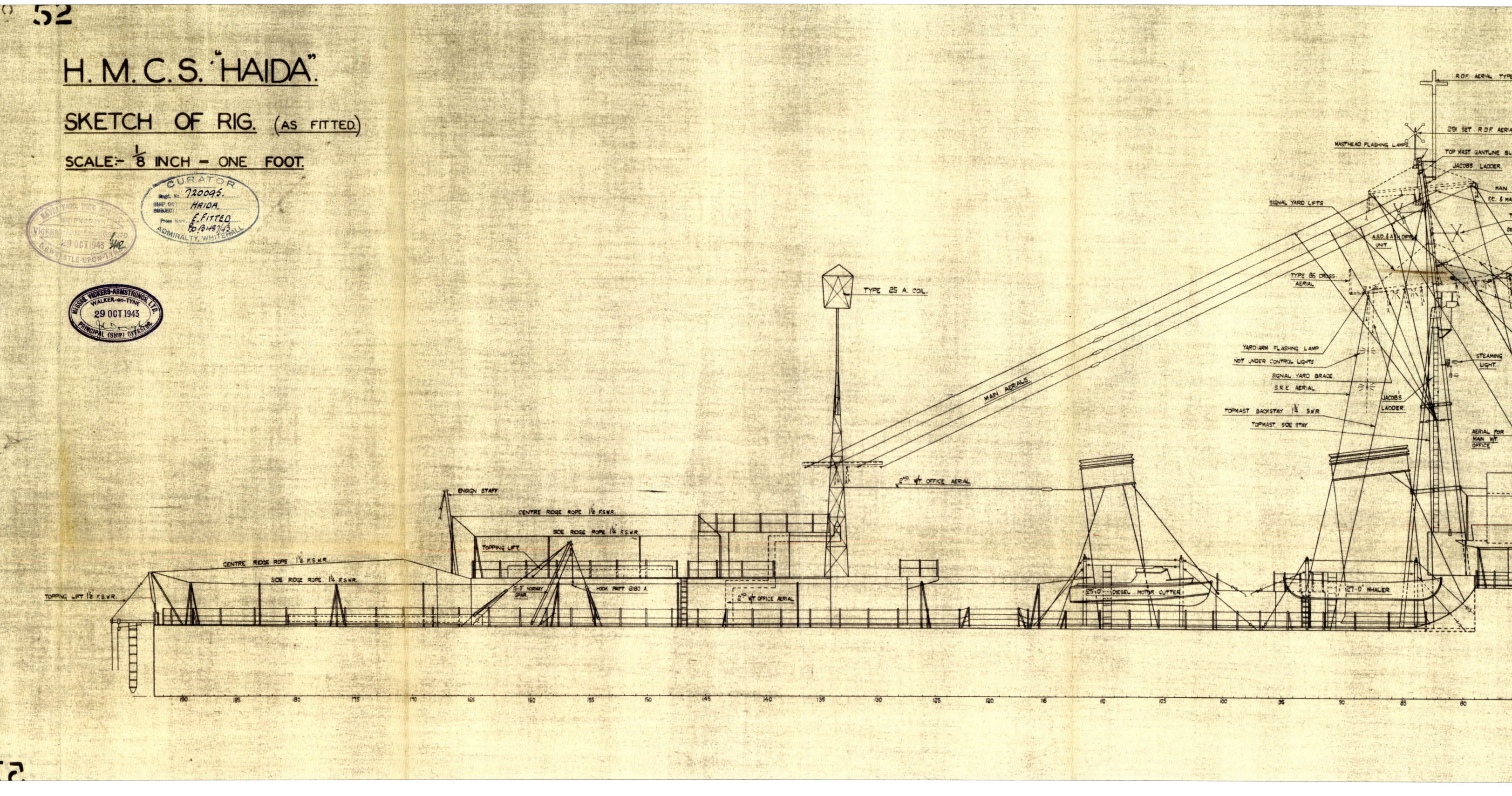

HMCS *Haida*: SKETCH OF RIG, AS FITTED OCTOBER 1943

Completed in September 1943, *Haida*, like three of her Canadian sisters and *Cossack*, was constructed, at the High Walker Yard of Vickers Armstrongs on the Tyne. Unlike *Cossack*, all four of these Canadian vessels were in fact contracted to Parsons, who supplied the machinery and sub-contracted the hulls.

This plan concentrates on the ship's rig and, unlike many such drawings, does not include anything but a very basic outline of the ship. It does, however, benefit from combining the running and standing rigging with the W/T and Radar aerial outfit. There are some aspects of the latter that do not appear to be accurately represented – possibly a misunderstanding on the part of the draughtsman resulting from the secrecy surrounding radar equipment. The only serious error is the indication of the vertical pole at the head of the foremast as 'RDF aerial Type 285' – although the ship did have Type 285, its aerial consisted of a Yagi array (not shown) mounted directly above the rangefinder director. The ship did have a pole at the masthead but it probably carried a Type 86M aerial for radio communication with fighter aircraft. Another Type 86M aerial is indicated as fitted at the starboard end of the signal yard but it was not unusual for ships to have more than one Type 86 aerial. Other anomalies are created by the aerials for the ship's Type 242 and Type 253 radars, interrogator and transponder respectively for the Mk III IFF, in that some are indicated by the set number and others by the aerial designation. The aerial fitted to the foremast below the W/T yard, labelled 'ASD & ASH dipole unit' is probably just the ASD (associated with both Types 242 and 253) while that projecting forward and labelled as the Type 253 is the ASH aerial for that set (note that both ASD and ASH were wire frame double cones not simple crosses as shown here). Another IFF aerial, just above the signal yard, is designated by both aerial and radar set as the ASM aerial for the Type 242.

There is only one search radar aerial – that for the Type 291 combined air/surface warning set on a short pole mounted on the aft side of the foremast head. The lattice mainmast carries the S25A frame aerial for the FH4 HF/DF but the MF/DF aerial, which the ship carried on the fore side of the bridge, has been omitted from the drawing. The '4T transmitter aerial', between the bridge and starboard end of W/T yard, is for the Type 49 W/T, the 'SRE aerial' running from the SRE store to the starboard end of the signal yard is for the reception of radio broadcasts, while the 'sense aerial', between the bridge and the port end of the signal yard, served to correct the signal orientation of the MF/DF.

During a refit at Devonport in early 1944 *Haida* was fitted with surface warning radar Type 271 at the fore end of the after superstructure. The aerial was enclosed in a raised lantern type structure with the associated IFF aerial (ASS for Type 242M) fitted on its roof. During a more extensive refit at Halifax in Oct–Dec 1944 and some additions to the radar fit at Devonport in January 1945, her foremast was replaced with a lattice structure, the FH4 aerial re-located to the head of the fore topmast and the Type 291 aerial moved aft to the position previously occupied by the HF/DF aerial. The Type 271 and associated structure was removed, supplanted by a Type 293 air/surface/target indication radar with its cheese aerial mounted on a platform at the top of the lattice foremast. (M1820)

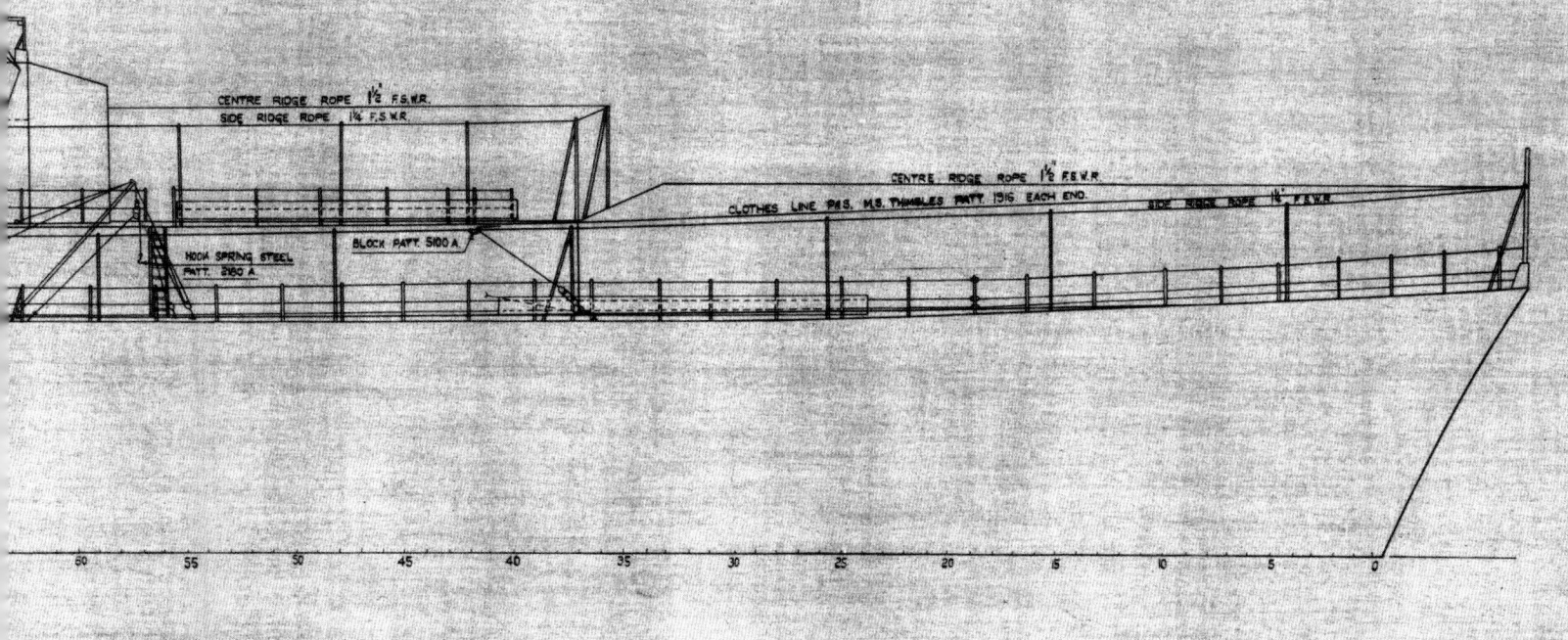

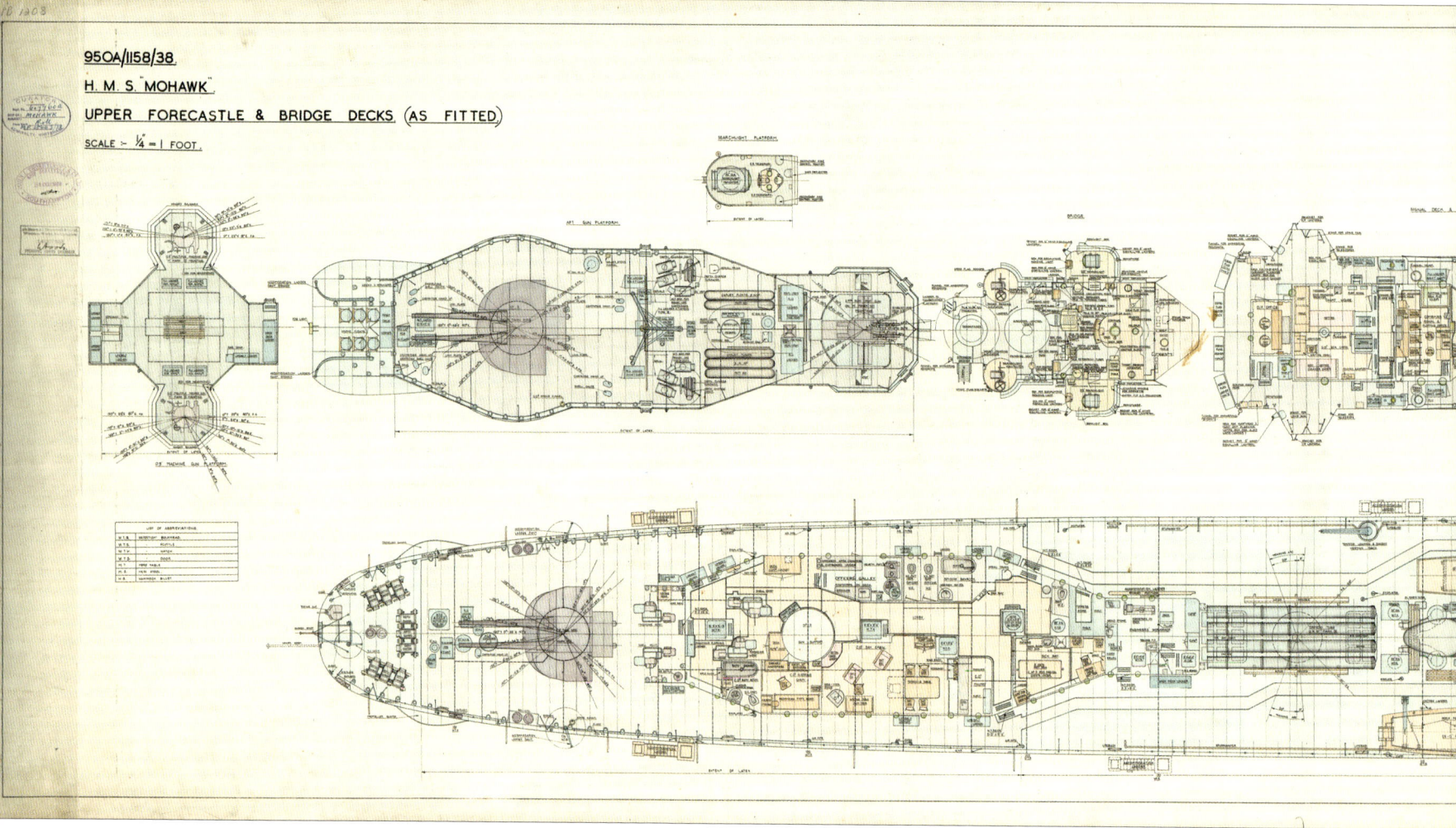

HMS *MOHAWK*: UPPER, FORECASTLE AND BRIDGE DECKS, AS FITTED OCTOBER 1938

These as-fitted plans, and those on the following pages, serve as a comparison with those of *Cossack* reproduced in enlarged form on pages 103–121. They have been included primarily because the originals are in excellent condition and are of exceptional quality – a testament to the skill of the draughtsmen of Thornycroft. Although essentially the same as the plans for *Cossack*, the individual fittings are, in most cases more detailed, and comparing these features on the plans of the two ships is a worthwhile exercise. The main exception to the latter is the depiction of the main machinery – very nicely produced but lacking much of the finer detail in the *Cossack* as-fitted set. Note that the limits on depression and elevation of the guns of all mountings are indicated at the related limits of training (something not included in the *Cossack* as-fitted). In the plans above there are some minor differences in the location of fittings between *Mohawk* and *Cossack* – particularly noticeable in the arrangement of the lockers, seats and davits on the 0.5in MG platform. *Mohawk* also shows some additional detail, such as the siren platform on the after funnel and the masts being shown to their full extent. (M1842)

HMS *MOHAWK*: SECTIONS AT FRAMES 71 AND 60 LOOKING FORWARD

When preparing the as-fitted plans it was usual for the builders to follow the layout of the design GAs prepared by the DNC's Dept. This was particularly noticeable in the case of the sections where the same locations were normally used in both cases. This is true for *Mohawk* with fourteen sections that match those used in the design drawing. The as-fitted sections for *Cossack* on the other hand were not only positioned, in all but one case, differently but reduced in number to nine. Some of those for *Mohawk* are only slightly offset from those of *Cossack* but several are without a *Cossack* equivalent – six of these are reproduced within these pages, two opposite, two on page 45 and one each on pages 79 and 94. Some of the items that serve to enhance the detail in *Cossack*'s sections include:

1. **VF lantern locker** below the starboard 20in searchlight provided stowage for flashing signal lights which, in operation, were fitted to brackets on the foremast and on the screens of the wing extensions to the Signal Deck (see *Mohawk* plan view and *Cossack* profile).
2. **Power unit** for the pneumatic message gear.
3. **M/G units** in the low power room.
4. **Back-up batteries** in case of failure of the M/G units.
5. **Diesel fuel tank** fitted between angled wash bulkheads of the OF tanks from Frames 71 to 74.
6. **The wheelhouse** interior showing the wheel, ER telegraphs, compass and the helmsman's window.
7. **The main W/T office** in somewhat greater detail than that in Frame 64 of *Cossack*.
8. **The heating stoves** for the mess spaces. Note that the portable section of the stove funnel above the signal deck on the starboard side has been omitted.

(Detail from M1843)

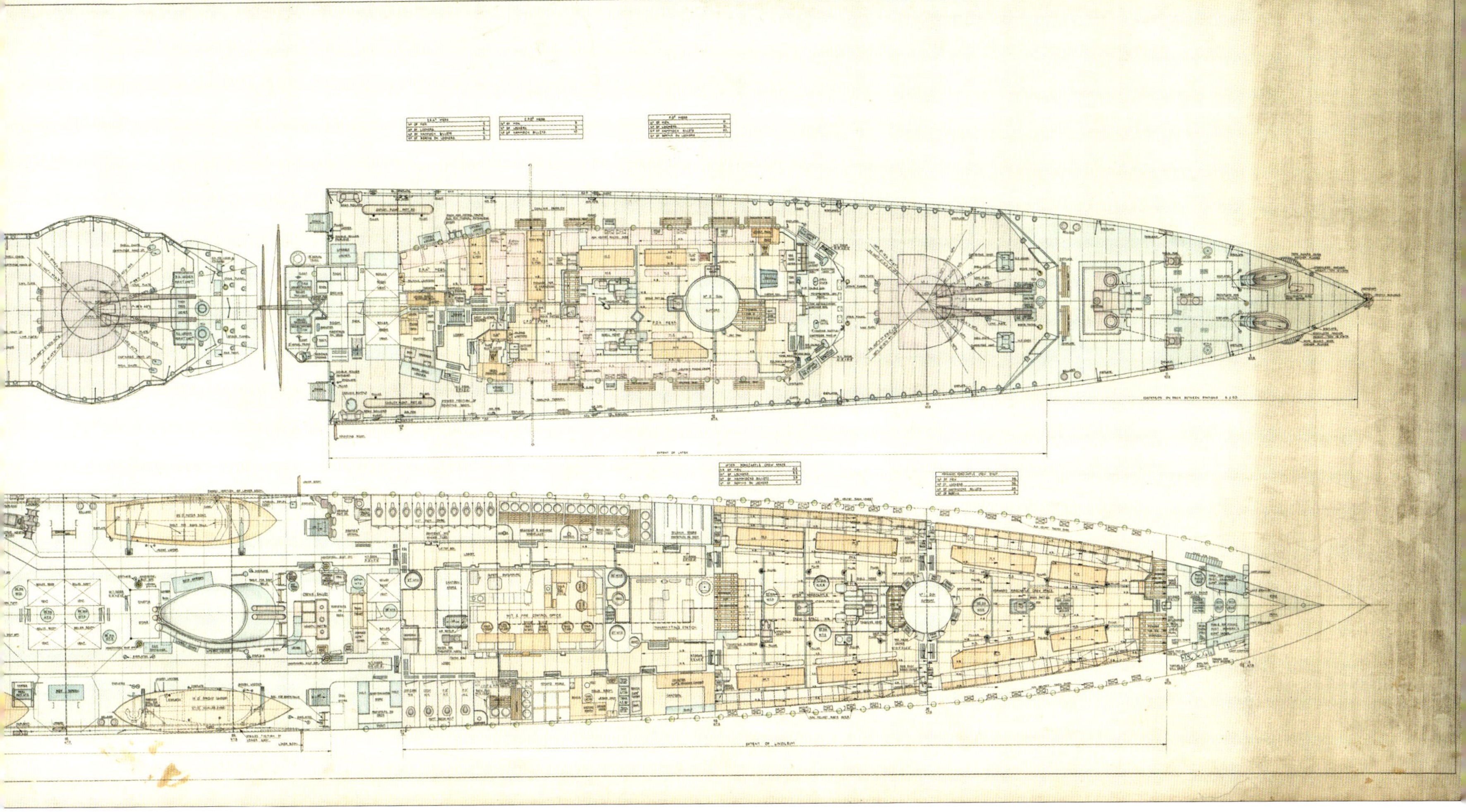

HMS MOHAWK: UPPER, FORECASTLE AND BRIDGE DECKS, AS FITTED OCTOBER 1938

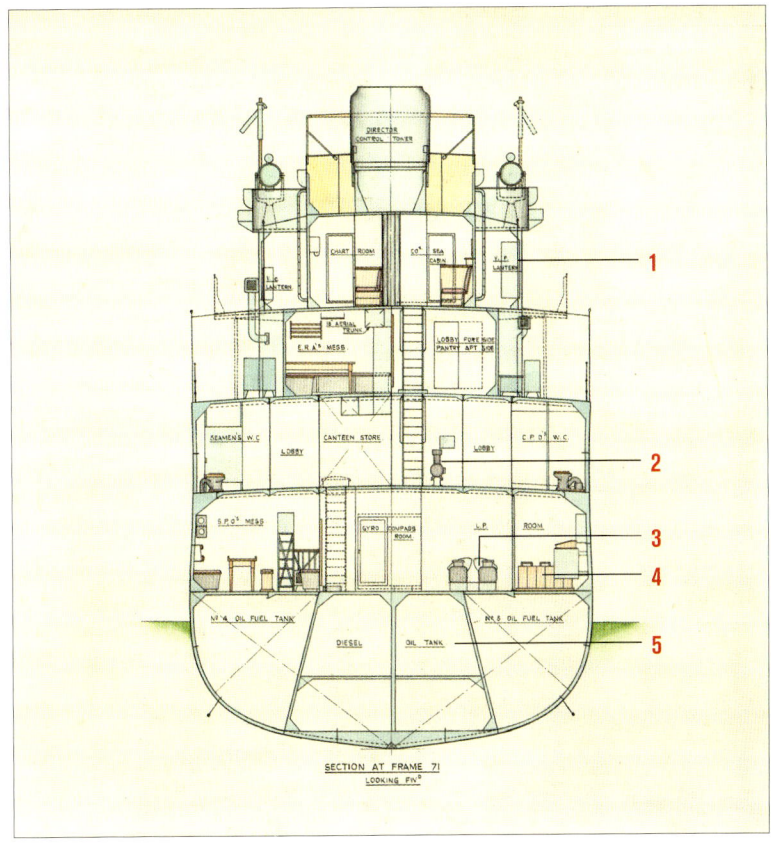

SECTION AT FRAME 71
LOOKING FWD

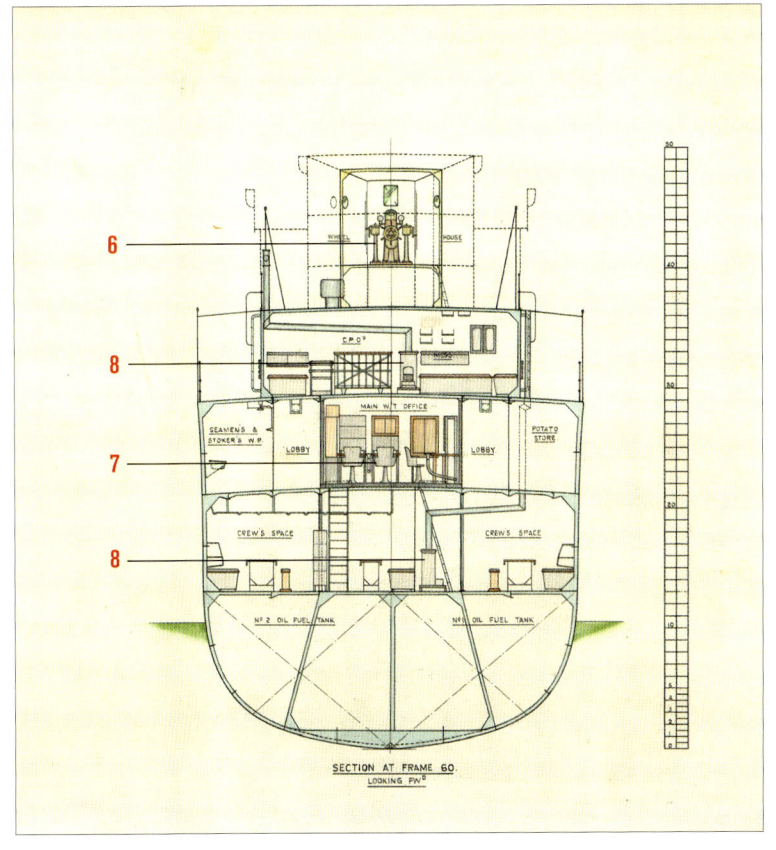

SECTION AT FRAME 60
LOOKING FWD

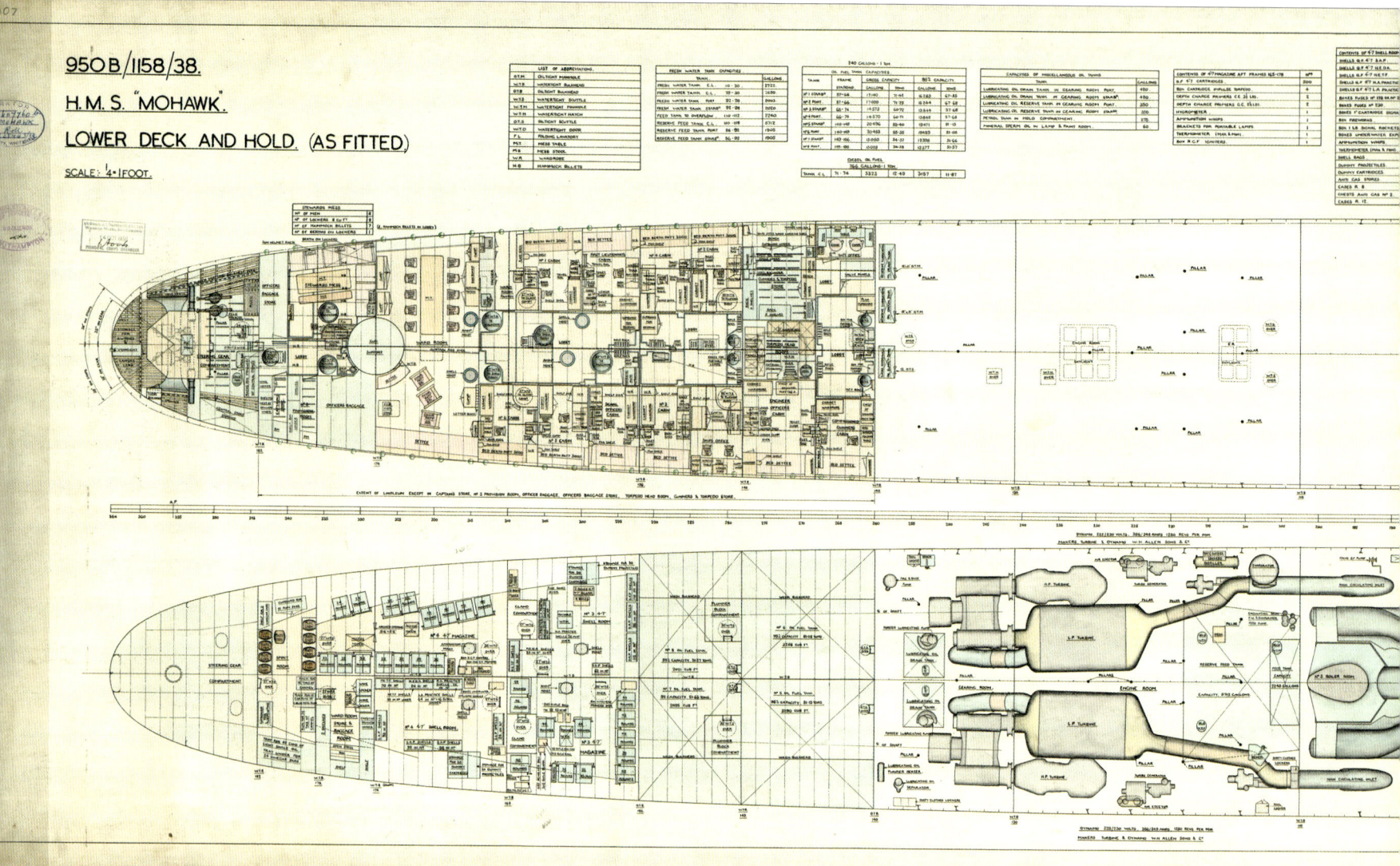

HMS *MOHAWK*: LOWER DECK AND HOLD, AS FITTED OCTOBER 1938

In comparison with the as-fitted plans for *Cossack*, those for *Mohawk* show a substantially different approach in the depiction of the machinery compartments – a reflection of the preferences of the builders. The Lower Deck includes only details near the deck head – air locks, skylights, scuttles, the tanks on the after bulkhead of the gearing room and the deck support pillars. *Cossack* on the other hand shows the main machinery at this level while in *Mohawk* it is shown at Hold level. The Hold in *Cossack* includes only some auxiliaries and the machinery foundations – the latter being completely omitted in the plans for *Mohawk*.

The tables along the top of this plan follow the pattern in *Cossack*'s Hold as-fitted plan. There are, however, some additions – a list of abbreviations at far left and contents lists for the torpedo head room and the gunner's and torpedo store (in three sections) on the far right. There are also some small tables to port of the plan views on this and the previous pages indicating the crew accommodation, lockers and hammock berths adjacent to the relevant mess spaces. Similar information is provided on *Cossack*'s as-fitted plans but in a different and a more detailed form. (M1841)

HMS *MOHAWK*: SECTIONS AT FRAMES 146 AND 100 LOOKING AFT

The section at Frame 146, which has no equivalent in those for *Cossack*, is just aft of the mainmast so only its struts are shown. Apart from accommodation spaces, it includes the Torpedo Head Room and Torpedo Store (the contents of which are listed on the plan above) and two of the ship's eight oil-fuel tanks. The second section, at Nº3 Boiler Room, adds detail to the nearest equivalent in the *Cossack* set (Frame 98), in particular a view of the after funnel.

1. **The engineer officer's cabin** shows a knee-hole desk, with a ledger rack above it, on the port side a chest of drawers, with a cabinet wardrobe beyond it and on the starboard side a bed settee, with a wardrobe beyond.
2. **RU 4.7in cartridge lockers,** the two shorter ones are Type I and the middle one Type II.
3. **Diesel oil tank** for the officer's galley in the after superstructure.
4. **Life belt lockers** (p&s).
5. **The after oil-fuel tanks** had vertical wash bulkheads unlike those in the fore tanks which were set at an angle.
6. **The fore davit** of the starboard 25ft motor boat.
7. **Wire-hawser reel.**
8. **The ship's syrens** (p&s) with their access platform below.
9. **Cordage reels** fitted to the supports of the 0.5in MG platform.
10. **The electric hoisting winch** which served primarily for handling torpedoes and lifting the 25ft motor boats.

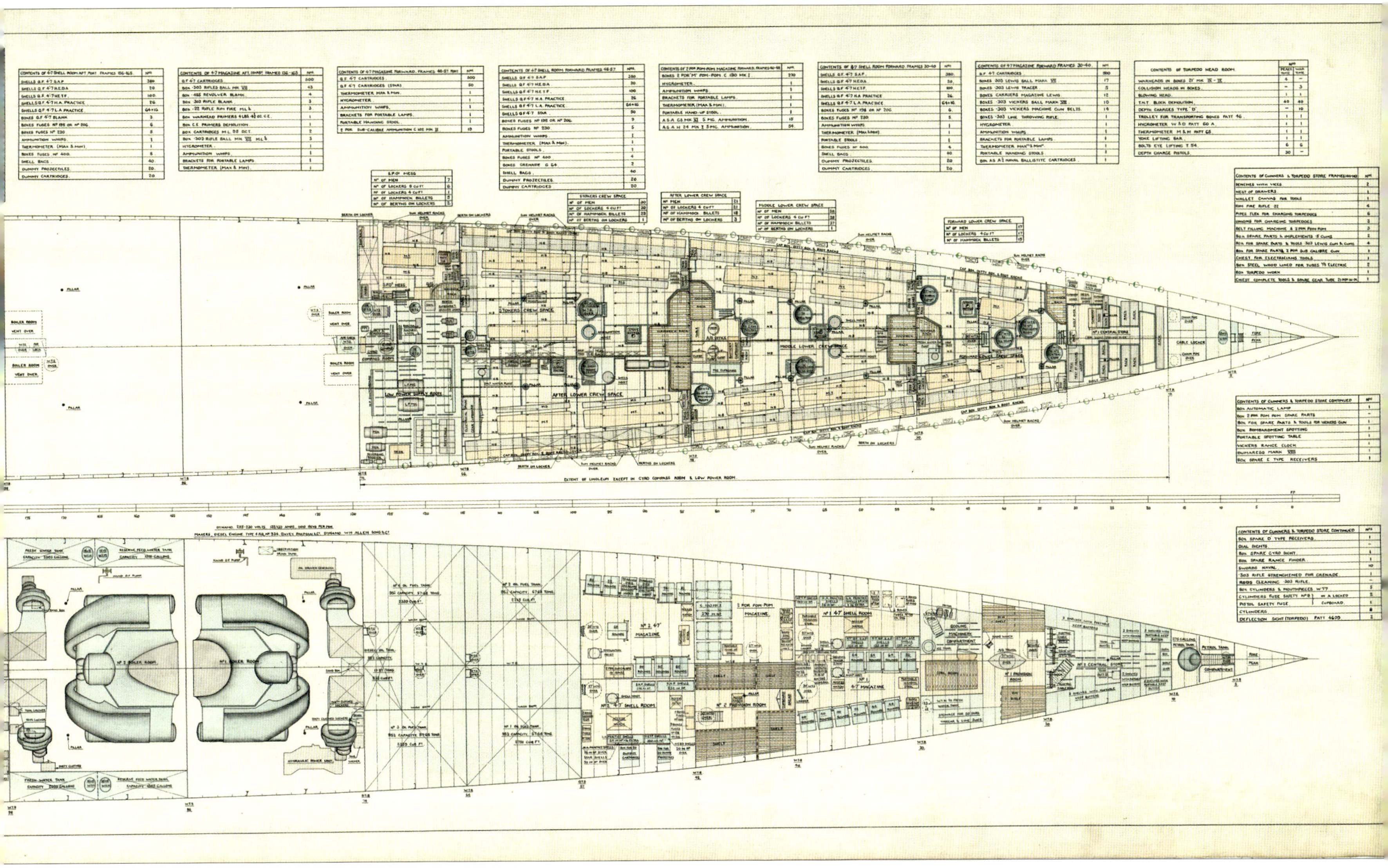

HMS MOHAWK: LOWER DECK AND HOLD, AS FITTED OCTOBER 1938

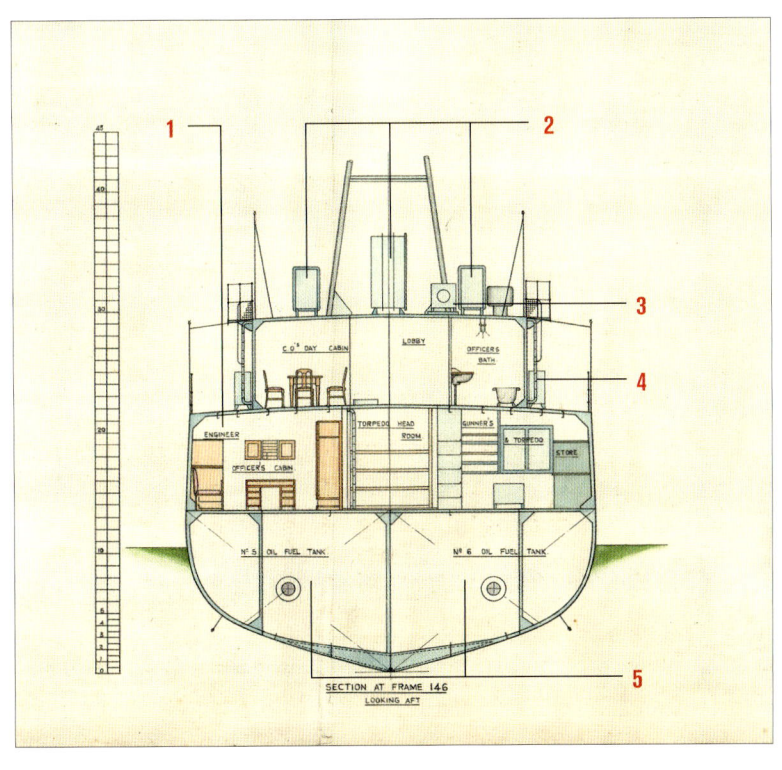

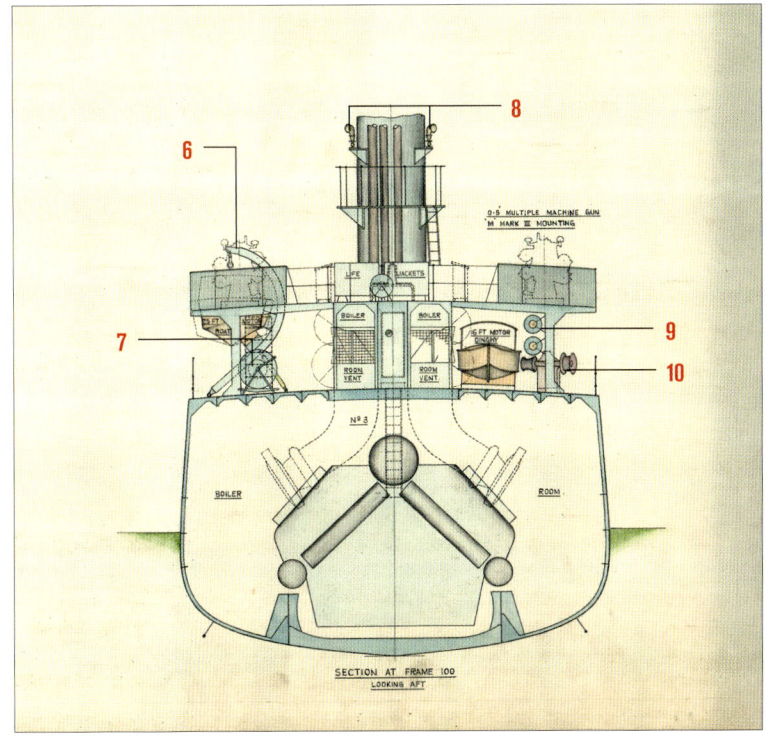

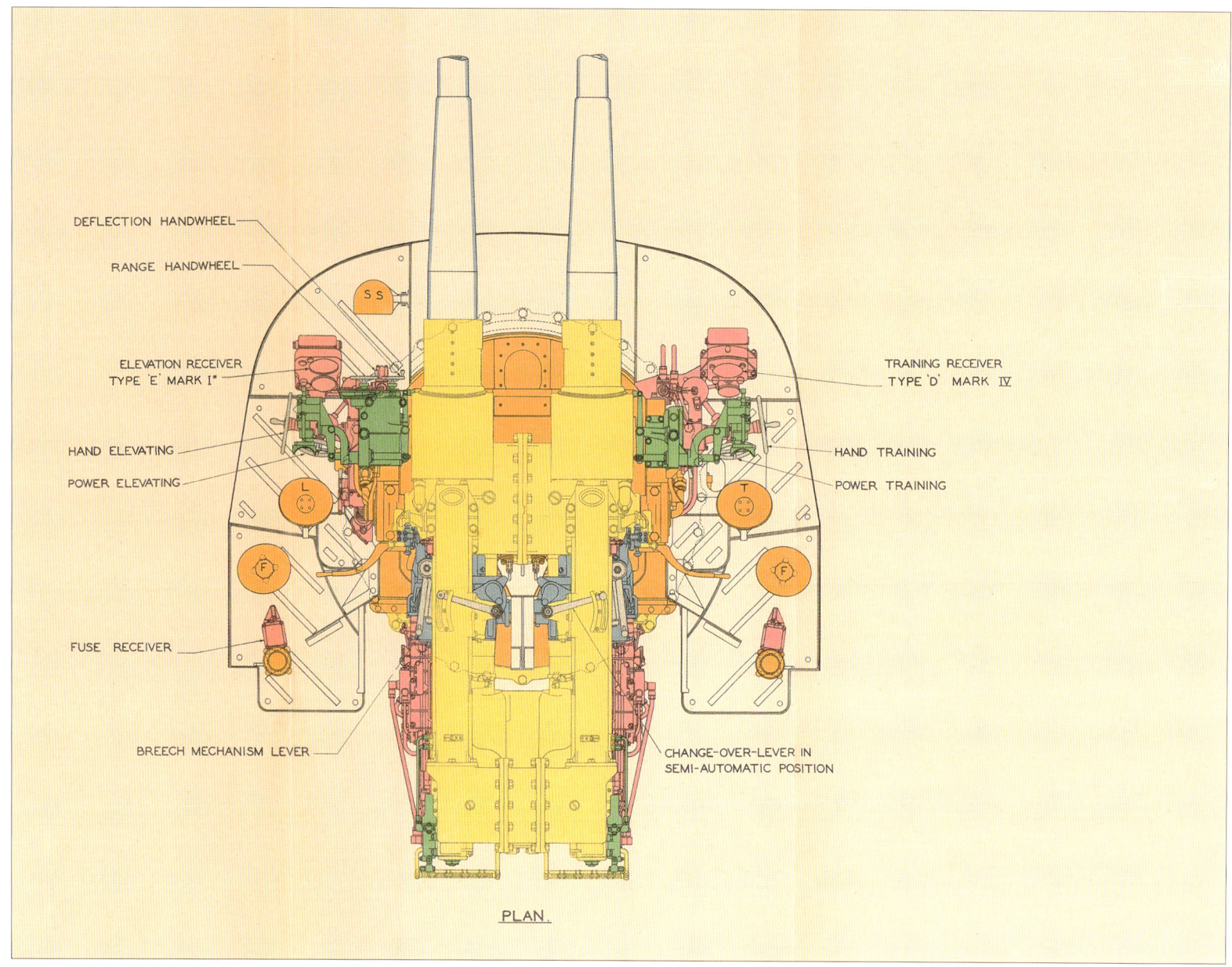

GENERAL ARRANGEMENT OF 4.7-INCH TWIN Mk XIX CP MOUNTING

The gun's crew for this mounting consisted of ten men. The arrangement in LA fire being gun-layer (L), trainer (T), sight-setter (SS) and, for each gun, a breech-worker, tray-worker and two ammunition supply numbers. The sight-setter also served as the communication number. When employed in AA mode the arrangement was the same except that the sight-setter and one of the supply numbers were employed as fuse-setters and located at the seats (F). Primary control was from the directors with the layer and trainer simply following the pointers on their receivers, the guns being fired from the director. In quarters or gun-layers control the gun-layer and trainer used their monocular telescope sights which were adjusted for range and deflection by the sight-setter. The guns could also be fired locally either by the gun-layer's foot-pedal (which could fire the guns alternately or simultaneously) or by the breech-workers from firing levers fitted on each gun. It should be noted that methods of firing and methods of control were independent of each other and there were multiple variations in which the system could be worked to cover both breakdowns and engaging more than one target. In SA firing the firing pin was withdrawn and cocked, the breech opened and the empty cartridge case ejected automatically during run out. In QF firing these operations were initiated manually by the breech lever (indicated in grey on top of the breech ring) once the gun came to rest. The items hanging down from the rear of the counter-balance weight are heavy rope nets to arrest the cartridge cases ejected from the guns. The loading trays were hinged on tubes attached to the gun cradles so they could be swung in or out. The two supply numbers for each gun (one for the cartridge and one for the shell) laid the ammunition in the tray when in the out position and the tray-worker pushed it into the ramming position, operated the ram and withdrew the tray. For LA fire the SA system could achieve 12 rpg/min but the mounting was less efficient in AA fire. Practice firings in 1938 gave an average of 3.5 rpg/min. However, these were affected by limited practice with new weapons and suffered from failures in both drill and material. At the time it was considered that a 'reasonable possibility of' 6 rpg/min could be anticipated in HA fire. (S5725)

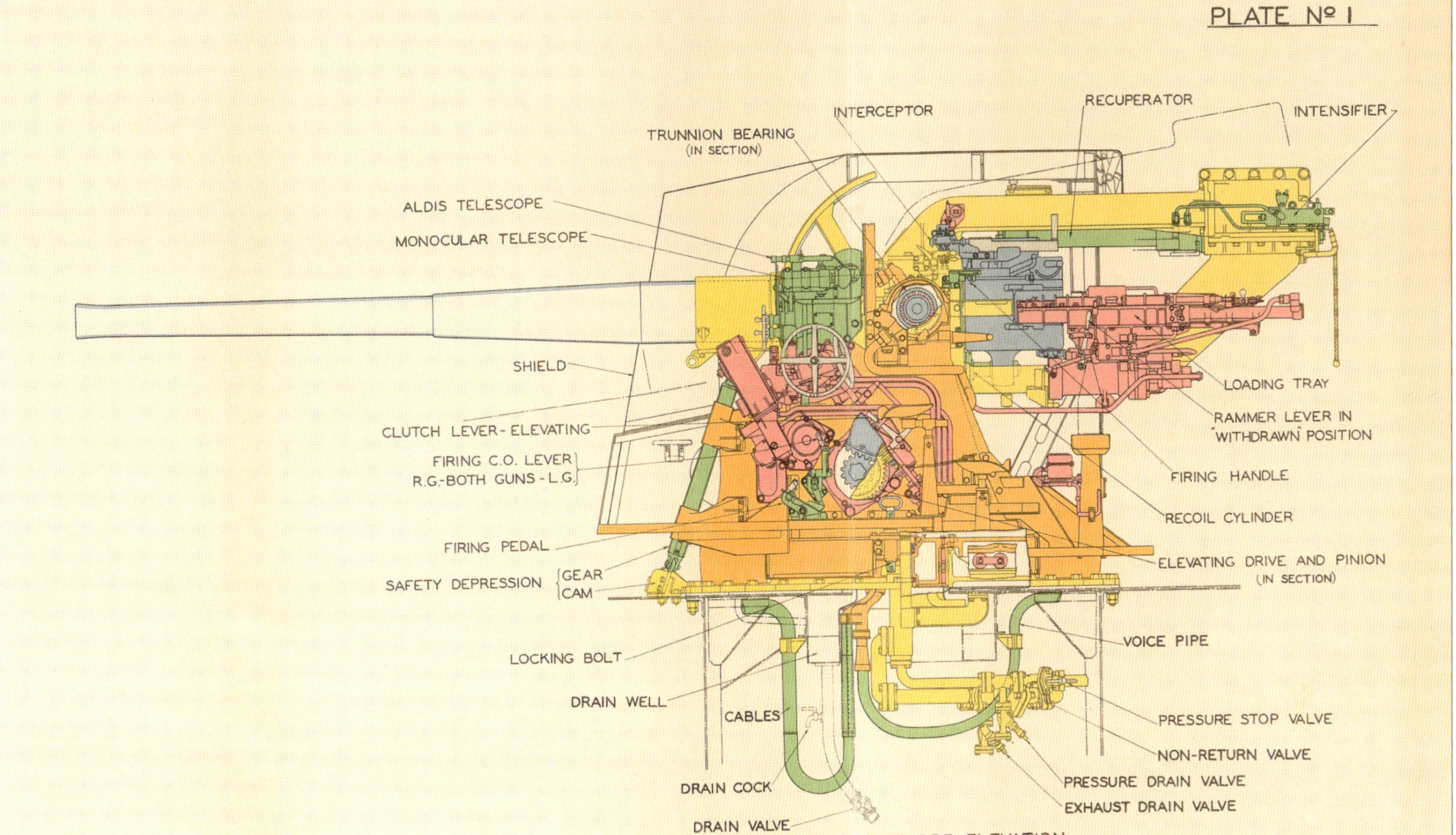

4.7-INCH TWIN MK XIX CP MOUNTING

PLATE No. 1

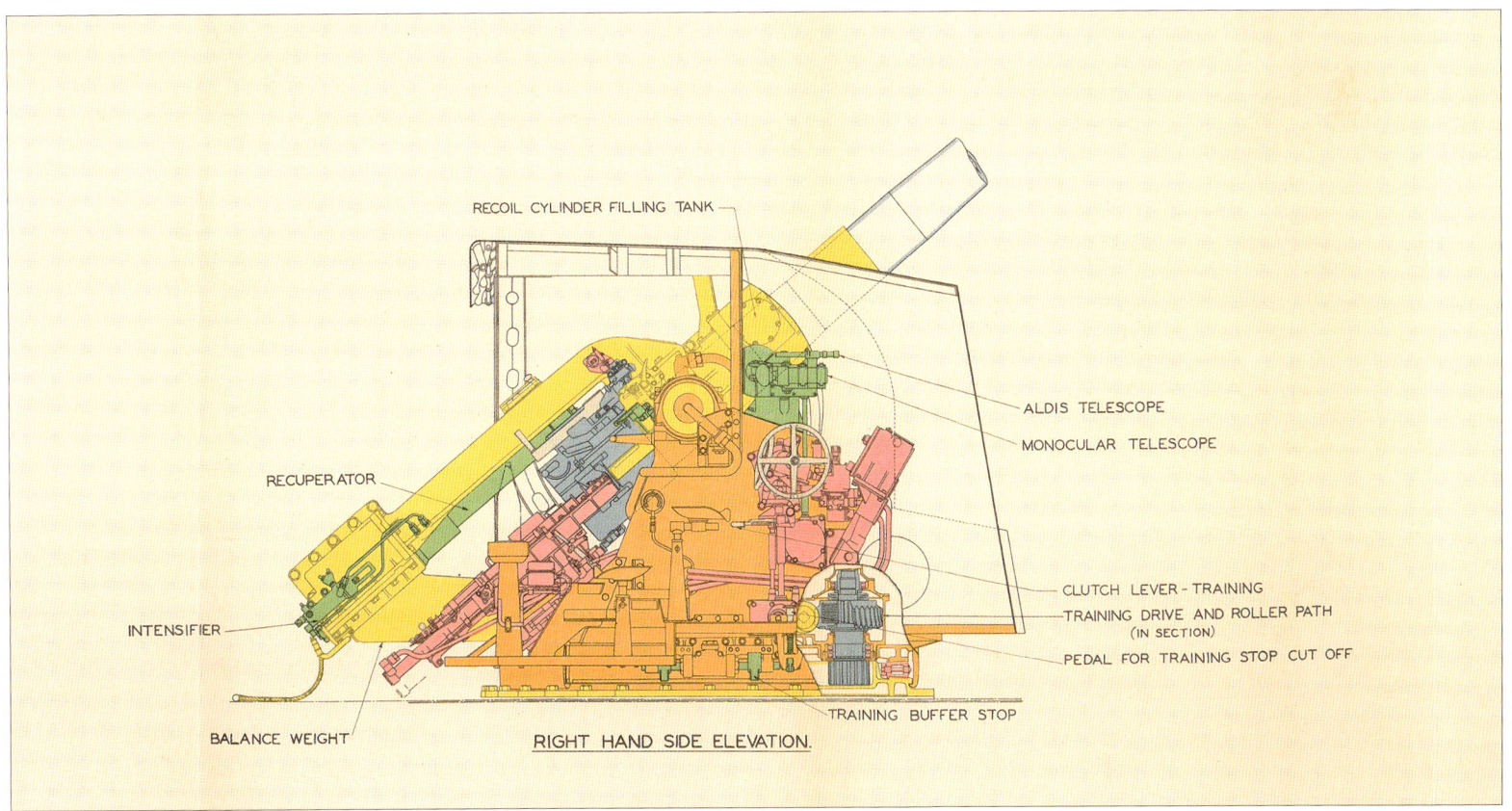

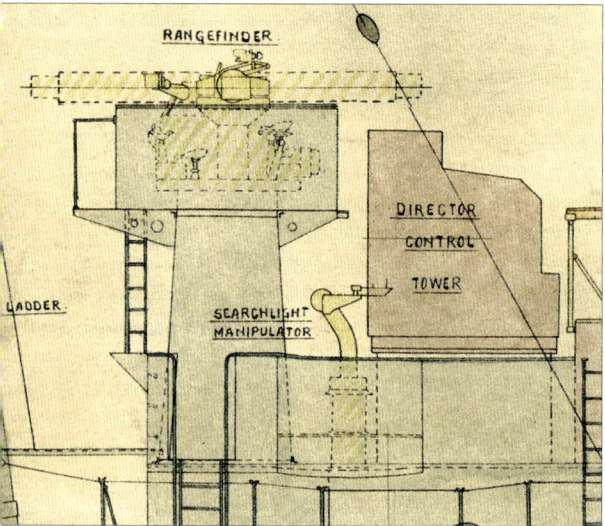

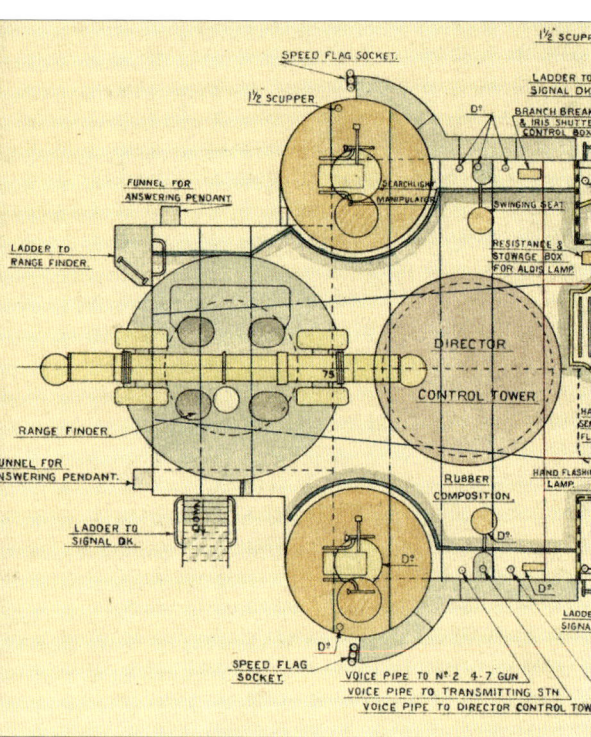

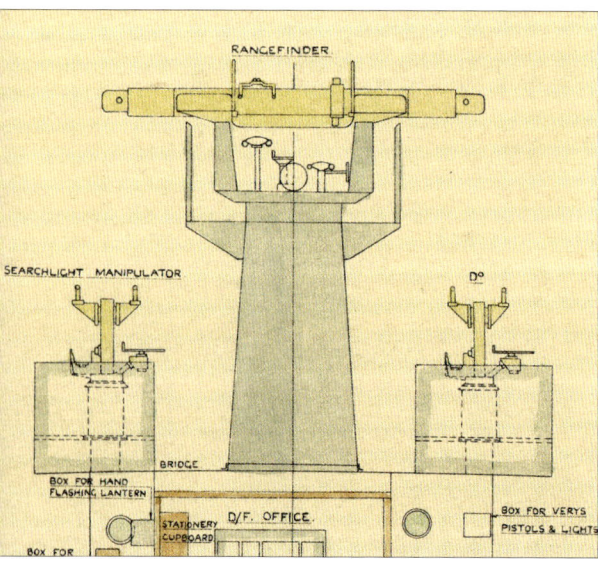

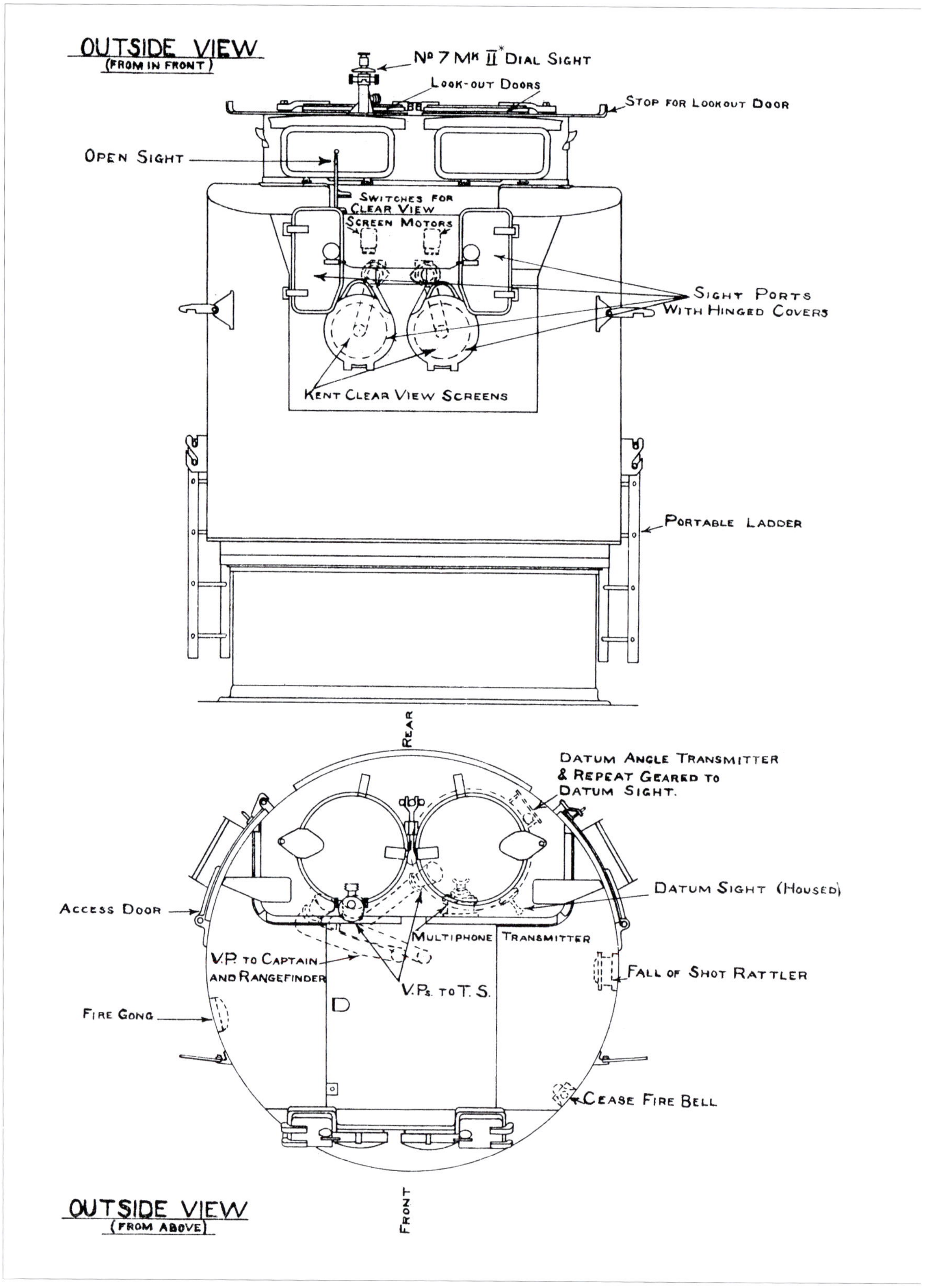

MAIN ARMAMENT DIRECTORS

Three views (left) from the as-fitted drawings of *Cossack* showing the primary director positions at the aft end of the bridge. Behind the DCT is the Rangefinder/Director Mk II which accommodated the sights for HA control and a 12ft UK3 coincidence rangefinder on an anti-vibration mounting which served for both HA and LA control. Manufactured by Barr and Stroud, the director had a total weight of 3350lbs and the rangefinder 785lbs. In HA fire the crew consisted of four men – control officer, range-taker, layer and trainer; in LA fire only the trainer and range-taker were required. In the section view the low seat on the right is that of the range-taker, the high seat on the left for the control officer, both behind the rangefinder. The trainer and layer were positioned in front of the rangefinder to left and right respectively. (Details from M1801, 1805 and 1806)

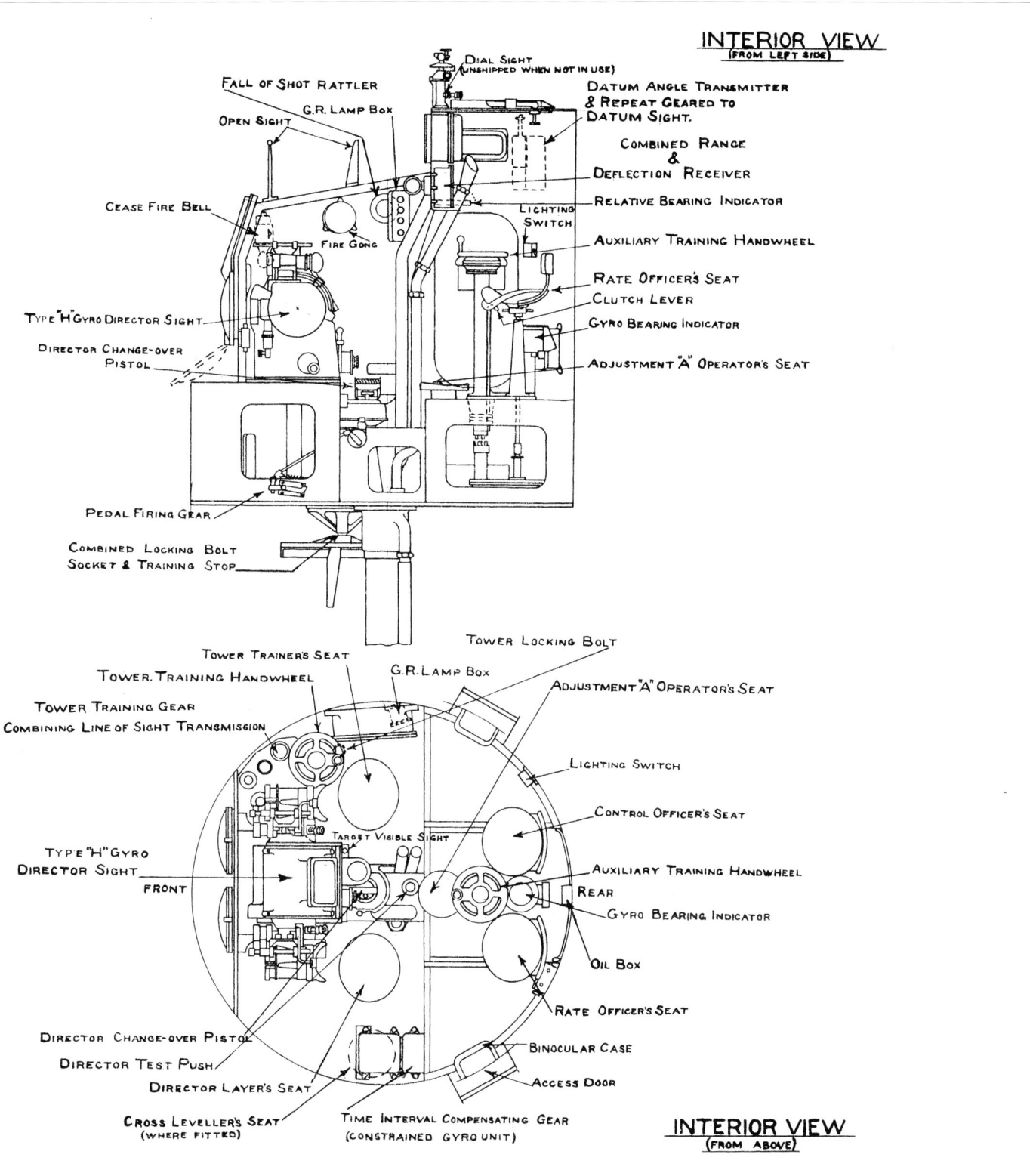

THE DIRECTOR CONTROL TOWER

This GA is for the DCT of the 'E' class destroyers but the design was essentially the same for all flotillas from the 'C' to the 'K' class. The tower had a revolving weight of approximately 4250lbs (without personnel), had a nominal rotation speed of 9°/sec and, from the 'E' class onward, was constructed of bullet proof plating. The stabilised Gyro Sight Type H Mk II* (manufactured by Vickers and first fitted in the 'F' class) provided observation through the Kent clear-view screens at the front of the tower. Unstabilised binocular sights, sighting through rectangular ports, were clamped to the top of the Gyro Sight housing, for use when the gyro sight was out of action. The control officer could communicate with the bridge and rangefinder by voice pipe and, together with the rate officer, to the TS by both voice pipe and telephone. The destroyer DCTs of the 'Tribal's were unique in being provided with a portable 80cm FT35 rangefinder for PIL purposes (obtaining range to accompanying ship in concentration firing) which could be fitted on top of the DCT. (Plate from CB1925, Part 12)

HMS COSSACK: Nº3 MAGAZINE AND SHELL ROOM, AS FITTED

Although they varied in detail, the four magazine/shell room groups were essentially similar, differing mainly in shape and in the distribution of their primary contents to accommodate the structural arrangements. Since shells were heavier than cartridges, the shell rooms and magazines alternated their port/starboard positions to balance the distribution of weight. Each shell room contained the same number of SAP, HE, practice and dummy shell while Nº2 shell room also accommodated 50 star-shell since it supplied the mounting designated for this function. The shell rooms also provided stowage for boxed HE shell fuses, primarily those for the HETF shell which were supplied plugged. The HEDA, SAP and star-shell were supplied with their fuses fitted, the fuse for the SAP being Nº501. Although the HE shell outfit was pre-determined as consisting of 10rpg HEDA and 50rpg HETF the difference was purely a case of which fuse was fitted. The stowage of boxed fuses was in fact sufficient to refuse the HEDA shell with time fuses, and to fit all the plugged shell with direct action fuses. The 4.7in gun could also be supplied with smoke shell for shore bombardment but, since these are not listed, it would seem they were only provided when operationally required.

Each magazine contained 500 cartridges with the exception of Nº2 which for some reason had 503. In addition, Nº2 had 56 cartridges for the star-shell which again was in excess of the shell carried, and all the 2pdr sub-calibre ammunition for the ship. Note that 500 cartridges were sufficient only for the main SAP and HE shell and that no additions were provided for the practice projectiles, provision presumably being made to quickly replace any cartridges used for practice firing. Some ammunition stores for the torpedo and depth charge armament were located close to their point of use in Nº3 and 4 magazines while space for the small-arms ammunition was provided in Nº1 and 3 magazines.

The 'gland compartments' to port and starboard are trunks between the Lower Deck and Hold, giving access to the propeller shaft stuffing-boxes. The shafts are shown in broken line since they are below the magazine/shell room flat. They should, however, be shown in full within the gland compartment since the flat did not continue across this space. Access to the trunk was via the circular scuttles in the Lower Deck but for safety reasons no access was possible from the gland compartments to the magazine/shell room. (detail from M1804)

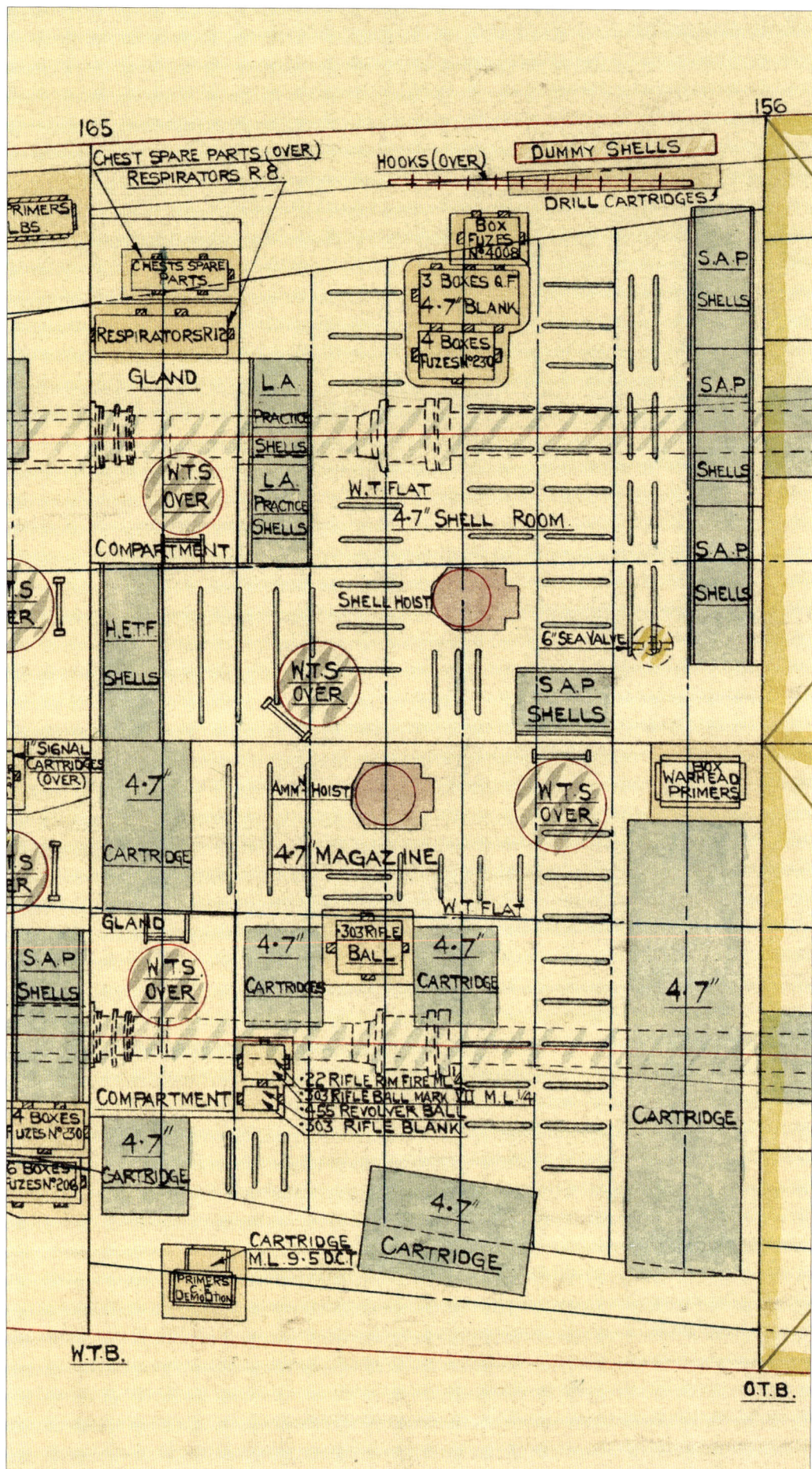

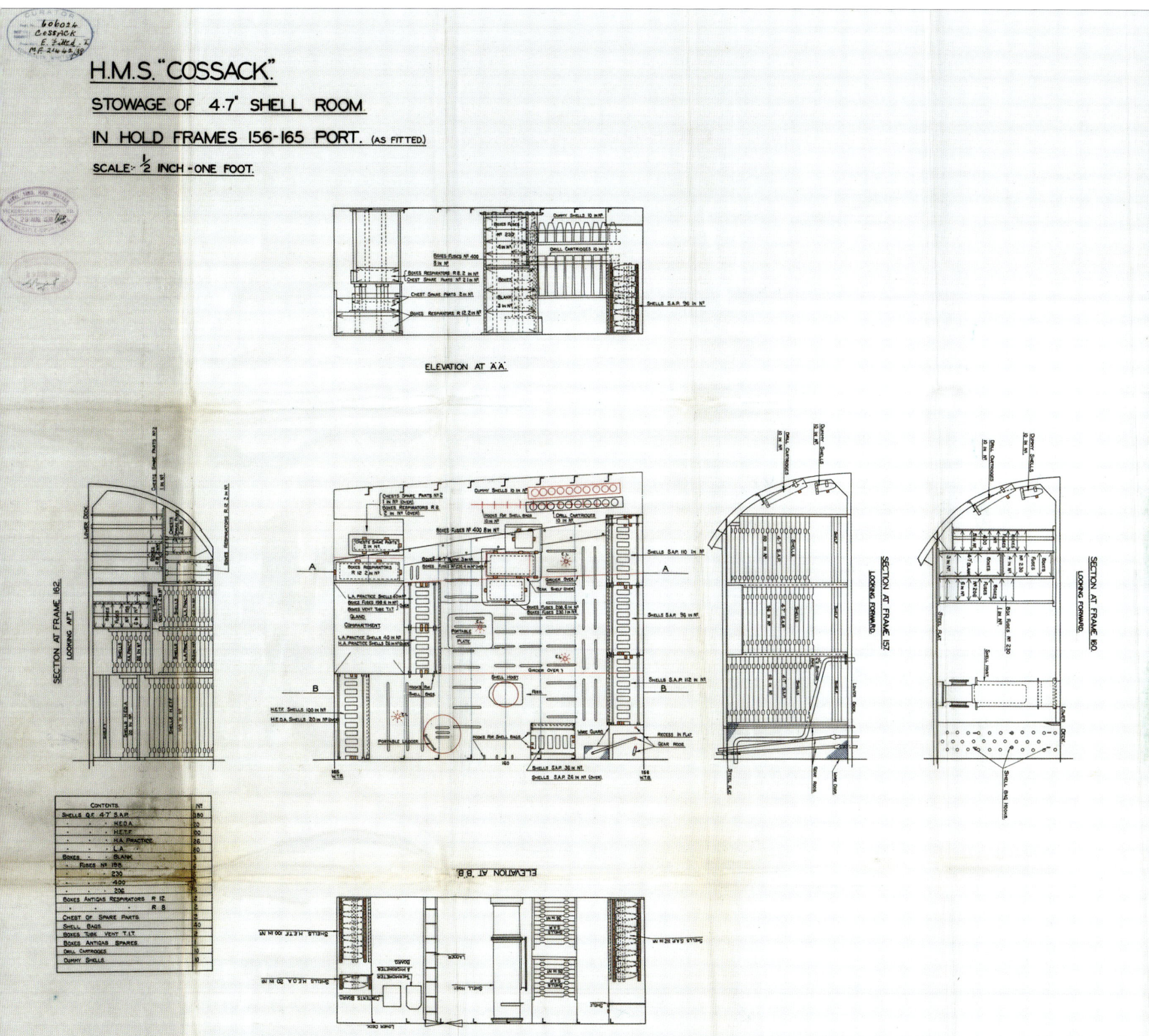

HMS *COSSACK*: STOWAGE OF N°3 4.7-INCH SHELL ROOM

The shells were stacked on top of each other in racks and securely retained by wood battens which were removed from the top down as the shell were transferred to the hoists. The exceptions are the vertically stowed, dummy shell and cartridges for loading practice. The fuses in the contents list are the planned outfit rather than those actually provided since N°206 was not supplied to the 'Tribal' class until late 1939/1940. N°206 was to supersede N°198 as the primary (HETF) AA time fuse but both were used in conjunction for some time as a result of the limited supply of N°206. The HE shell was standard and could accept several fuse types which, apart from N°198 and N°206, included N°230 DA for bombardment and N°400 for short-range AA barrage fire. The same fuses were used for the appropriate practice shell and the N°198 for the star-shell. Note the 'portable plate' in the flat at the centre of the plan view gave access to the after coupling of the port propeller shaft. This was bolted down and was almost certainly only accessed, if necessary, when the ship was in dockyard hands and de-ammunitioned. The strips on the flat are anti-slip bars. (M1826)

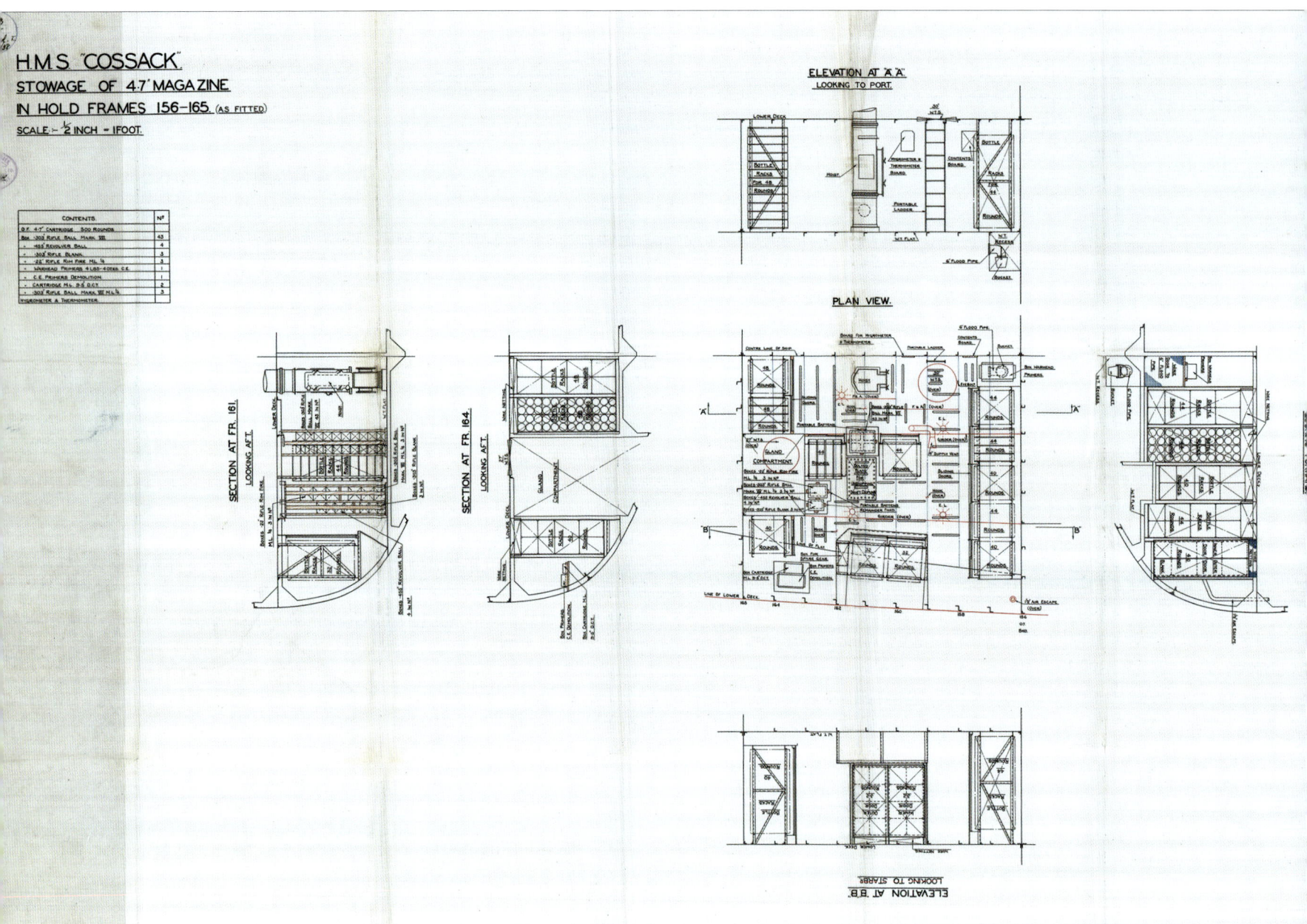

HMS COSSACK: STOWAGE OF Nº3 4.7-INCH MAGAZINE

The cartridge cases were stowed in bottle racks – metal frames with fixed tubes for the cartridges fitted behind sliding doors. Each tube incorporated a retaining clip to hold the cartridge in place. Apart from the 500 brass-cased 4.7in charges, this magazine stored the primers for the torpedo warheads and demolition charges, the firing cartridges for the depth-charge throwers and the ammunition for the ship's outfit of rifles and revolvers. The latter consisted of sixty 0.303in, four 0.22in and one line-throwing rifle, ten 0.455in revolvers and three signal cartridge pistols. Note that 'portable cover' for access to the starboard propeller coupling is orientated differently from that to port to fit with the compartment contents. (M1825)

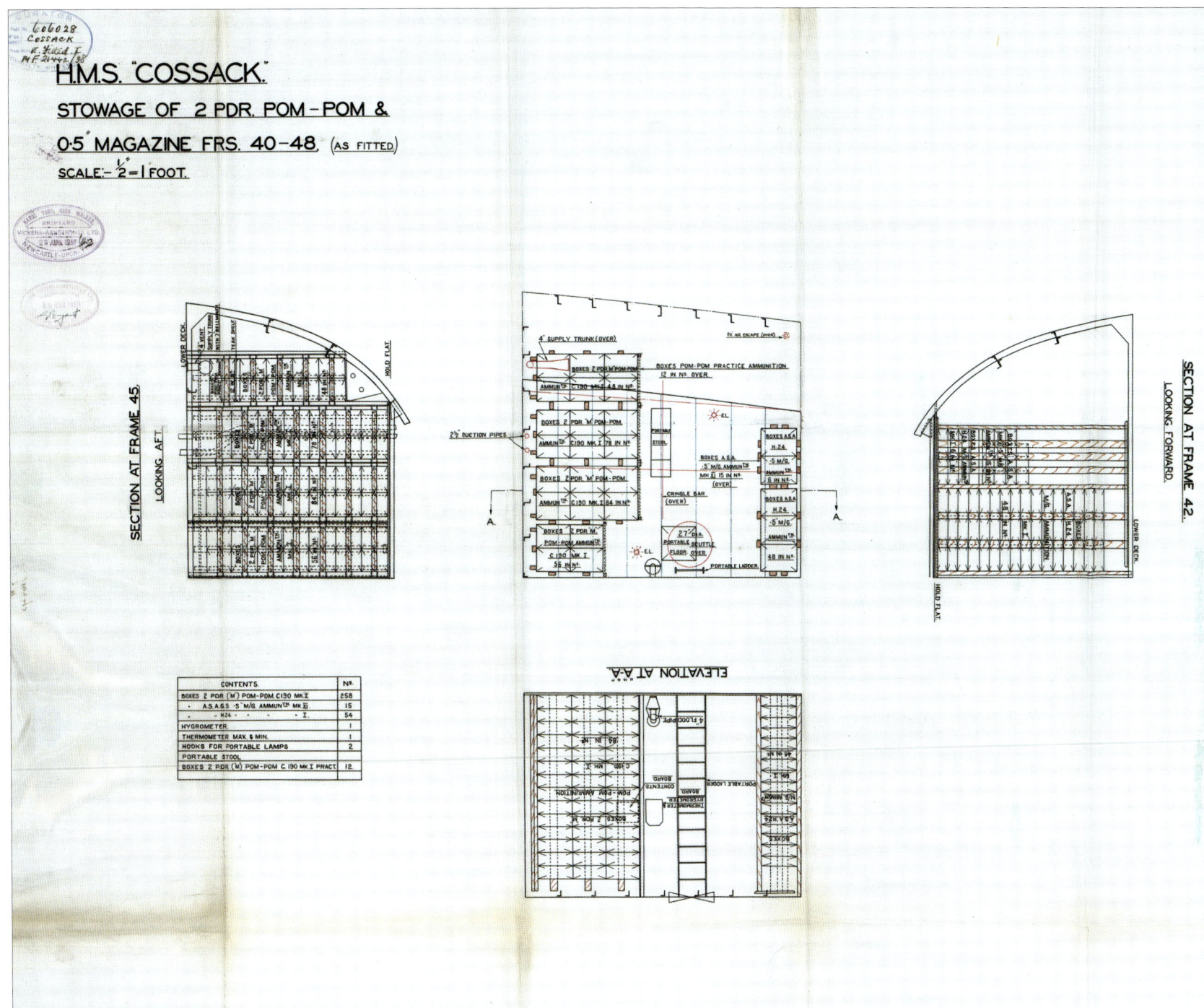

HMS COSSACK: STOWAGE OF 2PDR POM-POM AND 0.5-INCH MAGAZINE

This compartment was in the hold between Nº1 4.7in shell room and Nº2 4.7in magazine. Its considerable distance from the mountings it supplied must have been somewhat inconvenient since both the pom-pom and the 0.5in MG could, in any sustained air attack, consume their on-mounting and ready-use ammunition supply very quickly. The 2pdr pom-pom ammunition was stowed in C190 steel boxes each containing two 14-round articulated belts, each of which weighted about 45lbs. Eight belts linked together were required for each ammunition tray on the quad pom-pom mounting. Note that the number of boxes listed in the table (258) does not match those shown in the drawings (266). The nominal 2pdr outfit was 7200 rounds but 258 boxes were sufficient for 7258 and 266 boxes (as indicated on the drawing) for 7448. The former might be explained as a slight deviation from the nominal but the latter would seem excessive. Some of this might be explained as either spare boxes or another example of weight adjustments to stores to keep the recorded displacement closer to the design/treaty limit. The 12 boxes for practice projectiles match the nominal outfit of 336 rounds. The 0.5in MG ammunition was stowed in tin plate boxes each containing 100 rounds in articulated belts, three such boxes being fitted in each of the H24 wood boxes shown in the plan. (M1827)

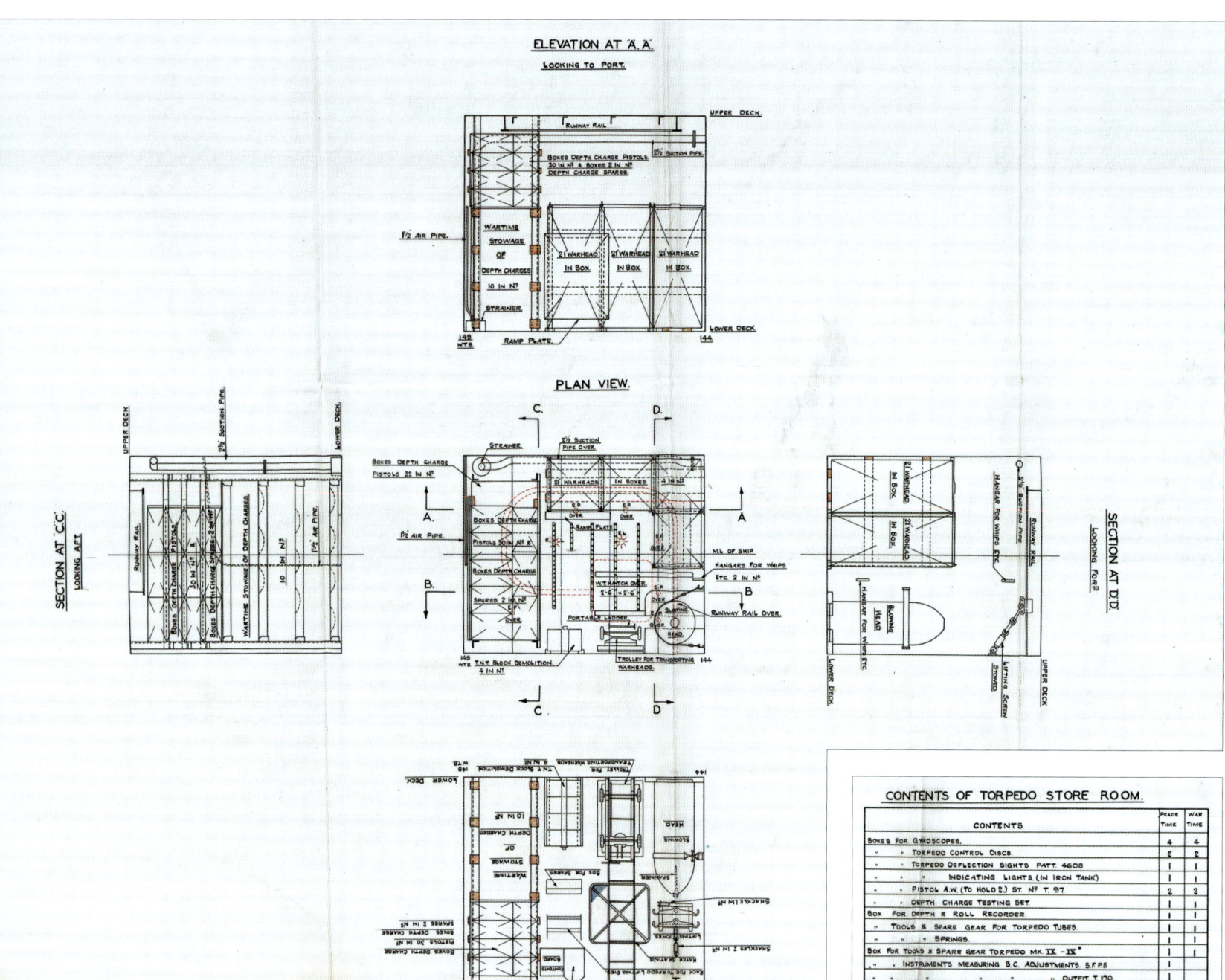

HMS COSSACK: TORPEDO HEAD ROOM AND TORPEDO STORE ROOM

The Torpedo Head Room was located on the Lower Deck amidships between Frames 144 and 149. In peacetime it contained the four warheads of the ship's 21in Mk IX torpedoes. In wartime these heads were fitted to the torpedo bodies in the torpedo tubes. The single 'blowing head' was for torpedo practice, the head serving to bring the torpedo to the surface for recovery at the end of its run. For practice, old marks of torpedo, designated SFP (Special Fleet Practice), were supplied from shore bases. In war the ship also carried three collision heads (presumably in the spaces vacated by the warheads) which served for more realistic practice against ship targets, the head being designed to absorb the force of impact and avoid damage to the target. The room also stored 10 depth-charges in wartime – additional to the 20 on the Upper Deck and after superstructure. Other stores included torpedo handling gear, demolition charges and the depth-charge pistols (30 plus 2 spares).

The Torpedo Store Room was on the Upper Deck in the port side of the after superstructure between Frames 134 and 137. It accommodated torpedo and torpedo tube spares and maintenance tools together with control instruments. The full contents are given in the list above. (M1828)

HMS COSSACK: TORPEDO HEAD ROOM AND TORPEDO STORE ROOM, AS FITTED

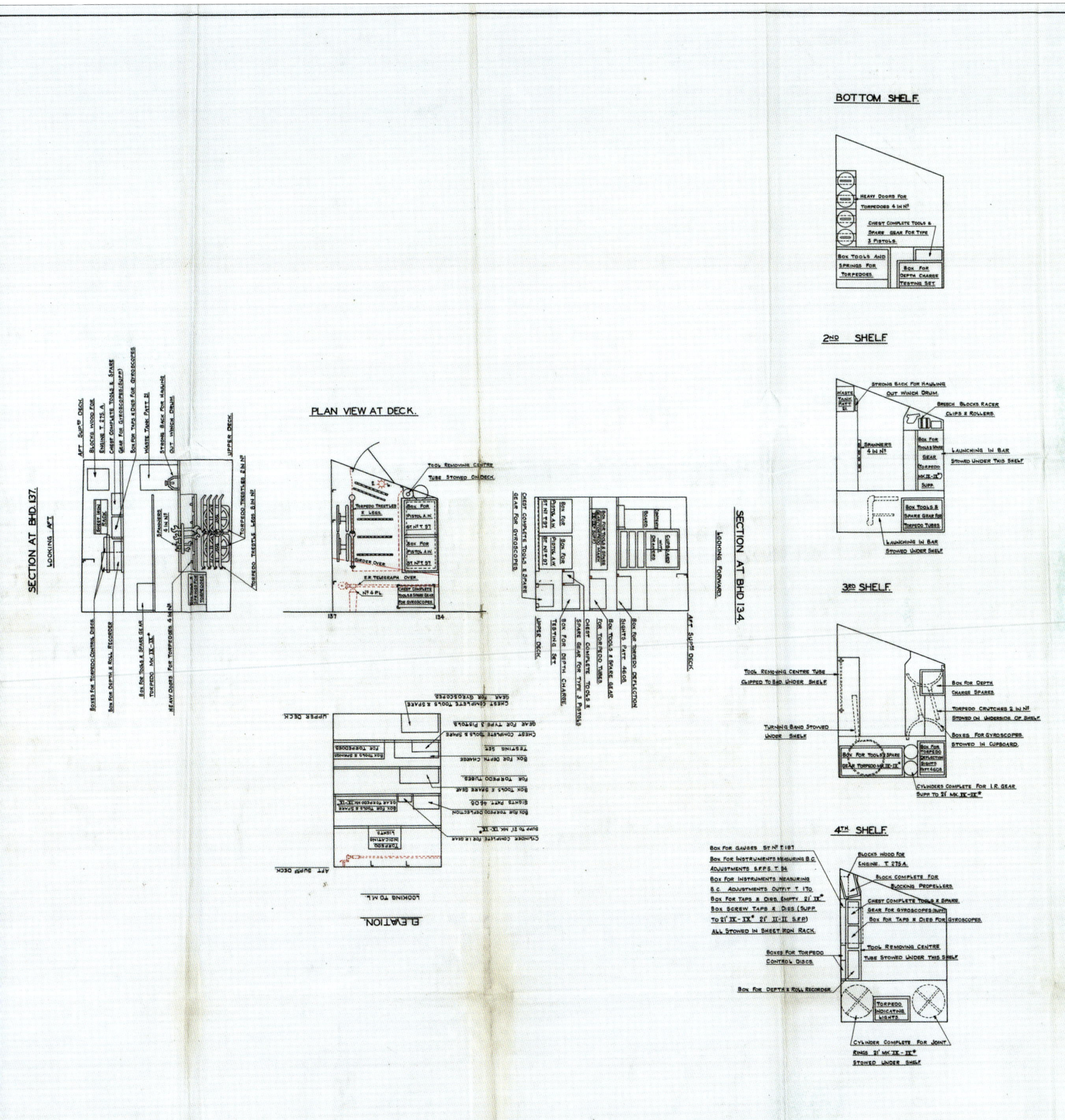

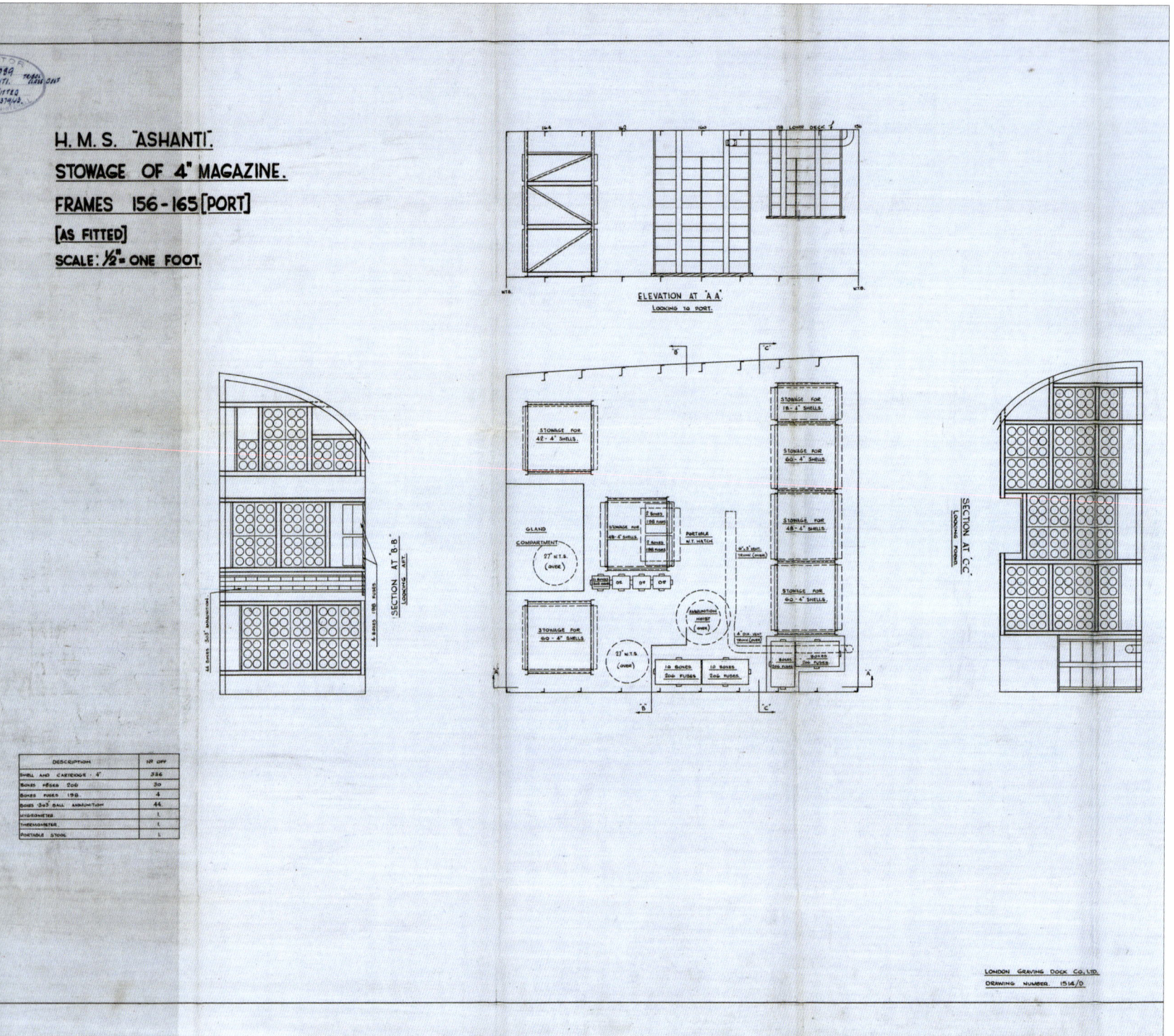

HMS ASHANTI: STOWAGE OF 4-INCH MAGAZINE (PORT), AS FITTED 1941

Although the AA capabilities of destroyers were viewed pre-war with some pessimism, early war experience made it clear that this problem was even worse than anticipated. Emergency additions were soon introduced to deal to a limited extent with this problem but they involved some sacrifice in existing armaments. In the case of the 'Tribal' class this involved the loss of No3 4.7in mounting in favour of a twin 4in Mk XIX HA/LA mounting. The *Cossack* was one of the first of the class so fitted, in May–June 1940. This plan, and that on the next page, show the modifications made, during Nov 1940–Aug 1941, to No3 4.7in magazine and shell room of *Ashanti* to accommodate the 4in ammunition. Although this would have been the same for all the pre-war 'Tribal' class ships (unfortunately there are no similar plans for *Cossack*), the ammunition outfit shown here is at variance with that first intended. This room has stowage for 336 rounds, that to starboard 340 (or 342 according to the figures on the plan) – a total of 676 or 678. A CAFO of Feb 1941 specified the outfits for the 4in ammunition to be carried by the 'Tribal' class as 564 rounds of which 468 were to be stowed in the magazines and 96 in ready-use lockers. The total was made up of 490 HETF (No206 fuse), 50 star-shell (No198 fuse) and 24 practice (No206 fuse). However, it is possible that more stowage was provided than actually required by the nominal outfit. (M1829)

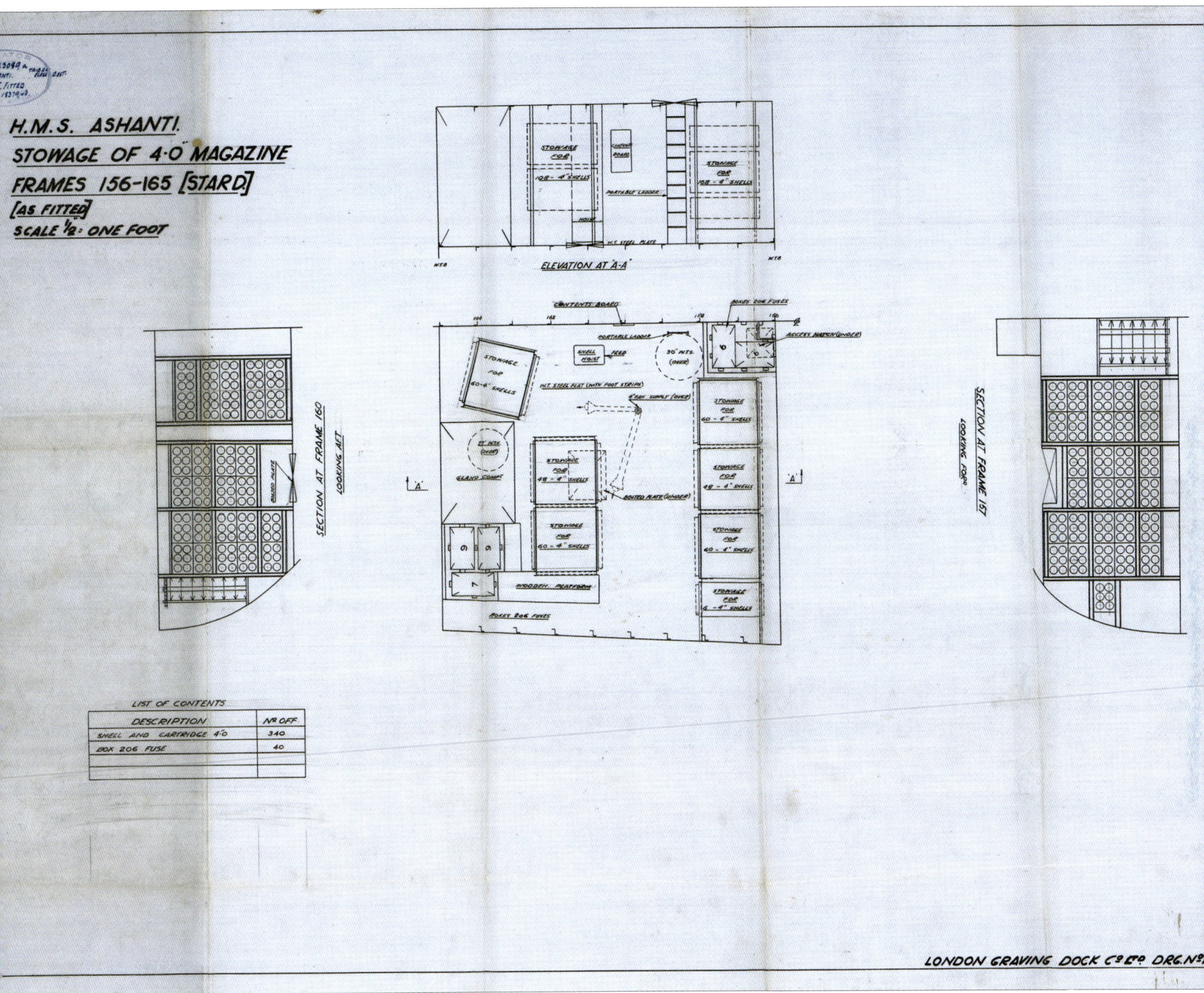

HMS *Ashanti*: STOWAGE OF 4-INCH MAGAZINE (STARBOARD), AS FITTED 1941

This magazine is essentially similar to that to port. The projectiles and their cartridges were supplied 'fixed' (*ie* as a single unit) and stowed in bottle racks like the 4.7in cartridges. The power hoists were retained in their original positions but were either modified or replaced to fit the greater length and smaller diameter of the 4in ammunition. It is unclear why the hoist to starboard is depicted differently from that to port, although it is possible that the former is actually a hand-up rather than a power hoist (perhaps a temporary installation due to limited supply).

The ammunition for the remaining six 4.7in guns was, as before, 190 SAP and 60 HE rpg except that, as the star-shell function had been transferred to the 4in guns, the 50 star-shell in Nº2 shell room were landed and replaced with 50 HETF shell. This information, derived from the same CAFO mentioned on the previous page, implied there were no HE shell fused DA but it seems unlikely that no DA fuses were available in the shell rooms should they be required. (M1830)

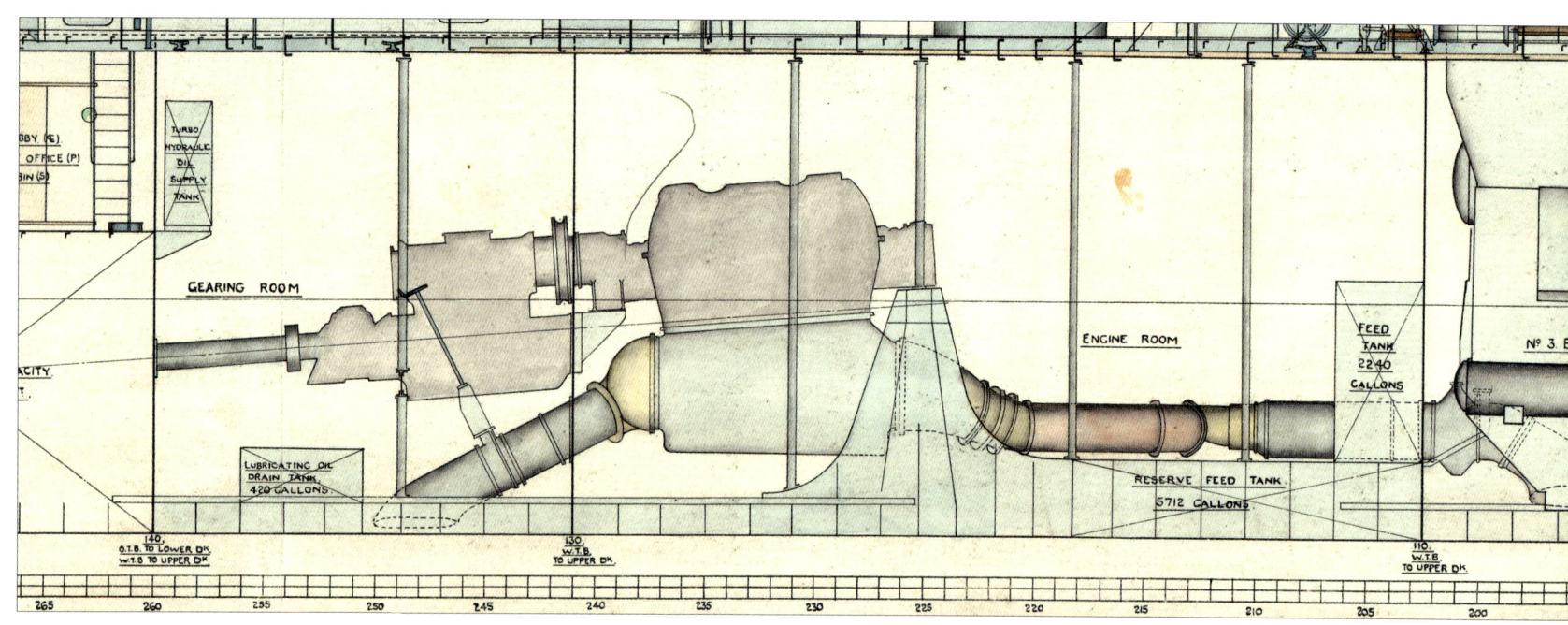

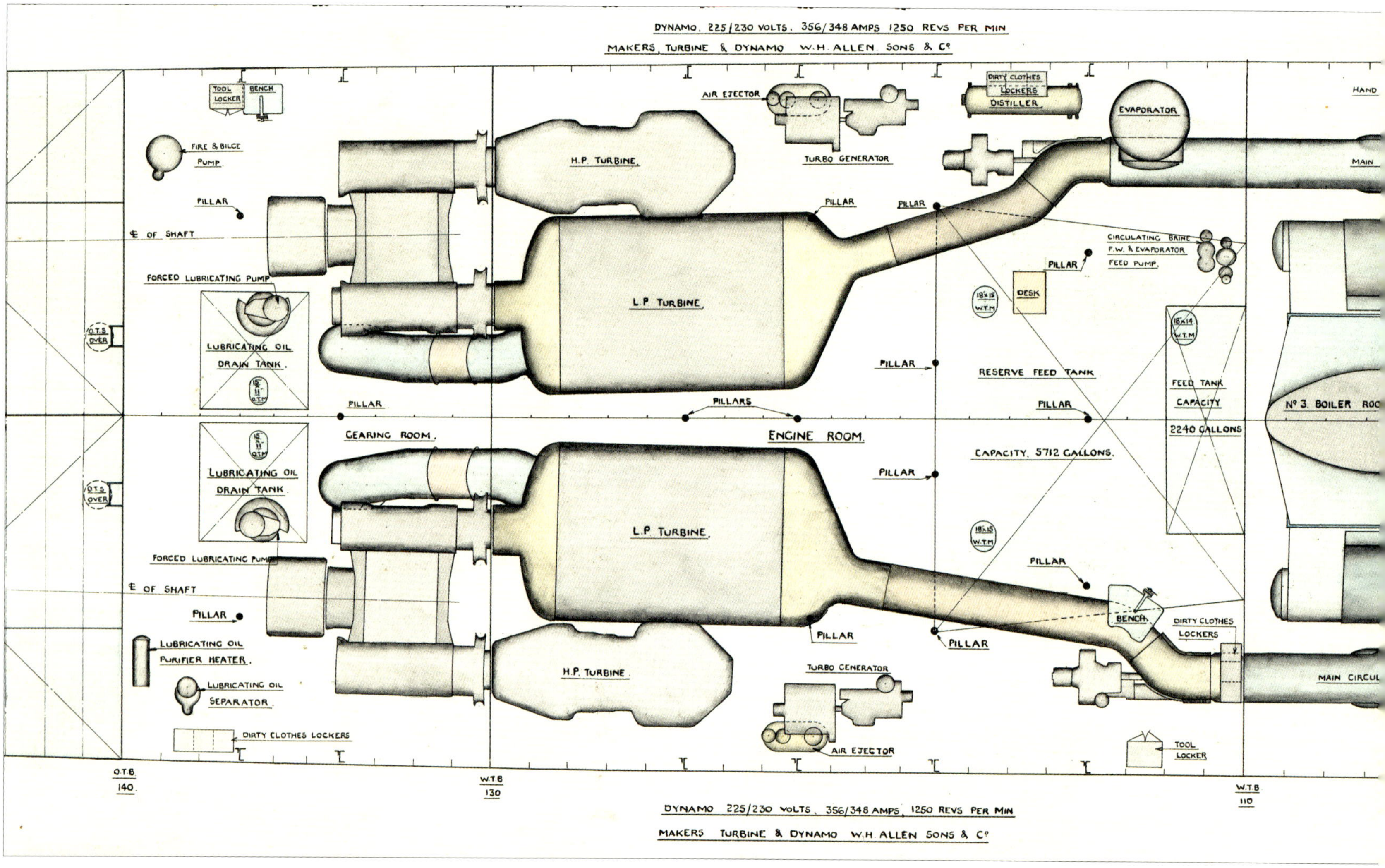

HMS *MOHAWK*: GENERAL ARRANGEMENT OF MAIN MACHINERY, 1938

The as-fitted drawings of *Mohawk* provide a very clear representation of the locations of the main and auxiliary machinery in the engine and boiler rooms since, with the exception of a few lockers, only the primary items are shown, almost all the accompanying fittings – such as platforms, support structure, valves and the propeller shafts, etc – having been omitted. With the exception of some minor auxiliaries, the port and starboard arrangement of the machinery in the engine and

HMS MOHAWK: GENERAL ARRANGEMENT OF MAIN MACHINERY, 1938

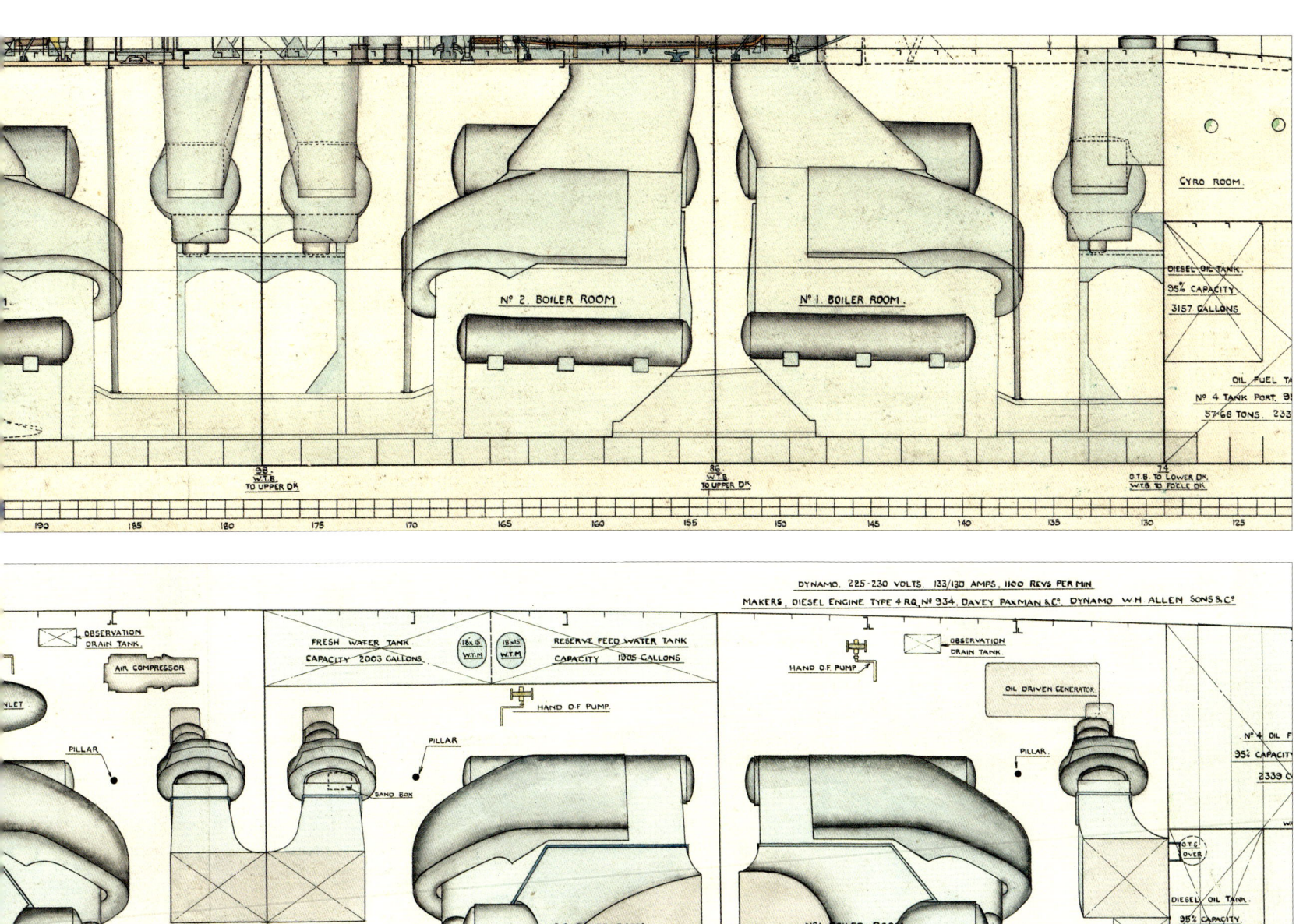

gearing rooms is the same apart from them being mirror images of each other. The three boiler rooms are also generally similar in layout except for the water tanks located in Nº2 boiler room and the different fore-and-aft orientation of the boilers.

(Detail from M1841 and M1840)

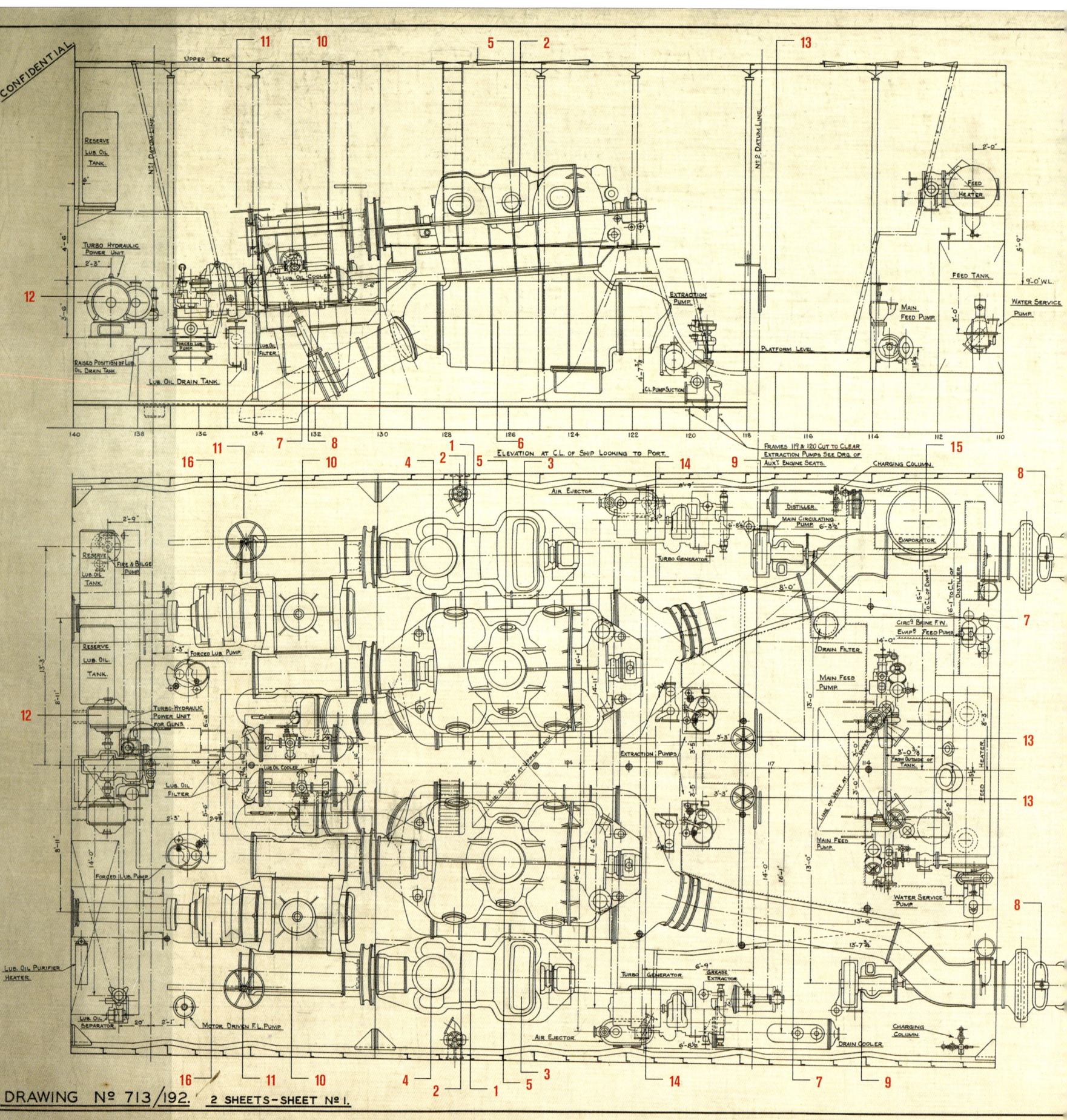

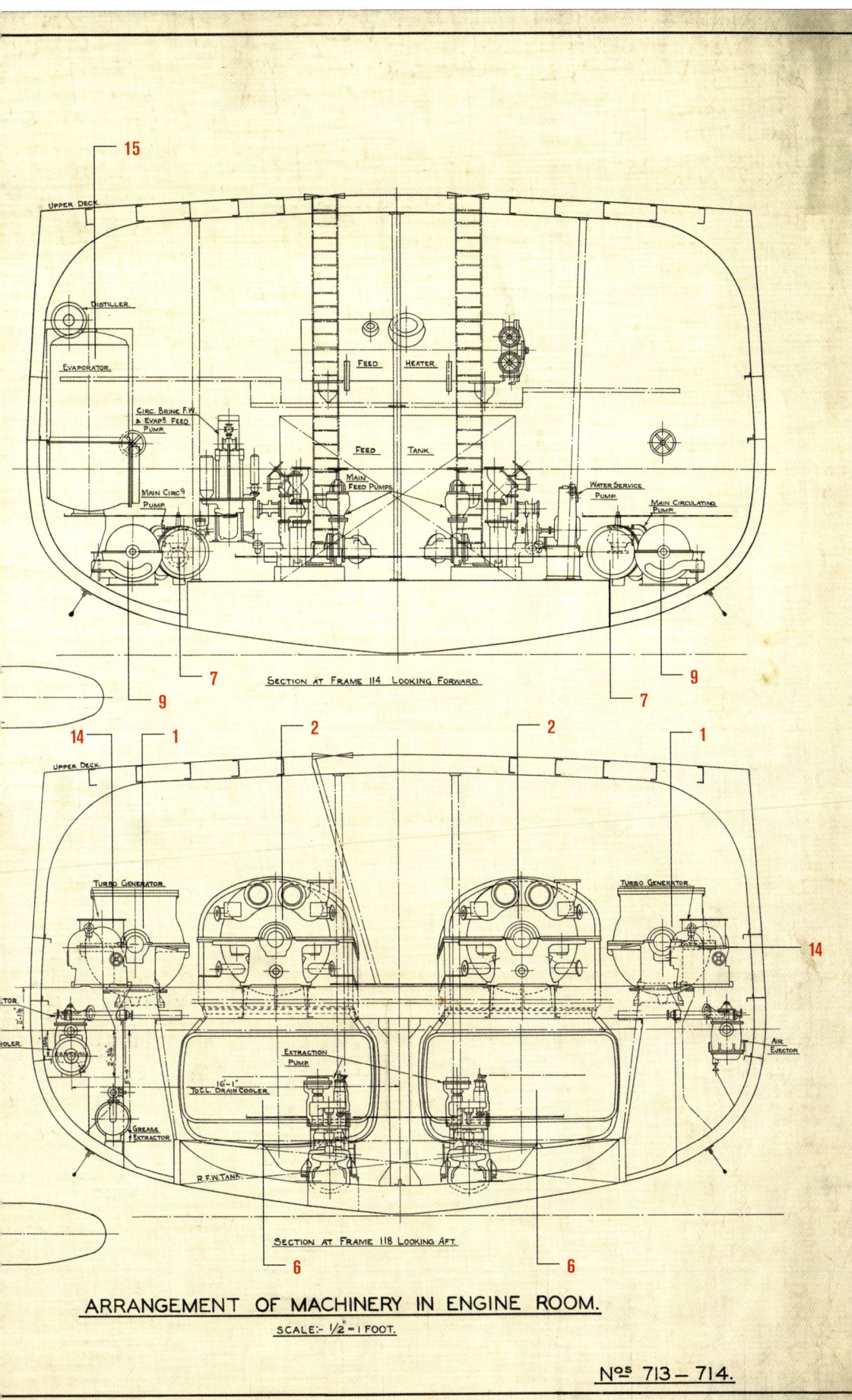

'TRIBAL' CLASS: ARRANGEMENT OF MACHINERY IN ENGINE ROOM
(Sheet 1)

Although the title suggests a single compartment, the gearing room was divided from the engine room by the water-tight bulkhead at Frame 130. Apart from the main machinery, these two spaces and the three boiler rooms contained the majority of the ship's principal auxiliary engines. The following key applies to both this drawing and that on pages 62–63. Note the table on page 63 lists the capacity and maker of the auxiliary machinery in the engine and gearing rooms. (M1810)

1. **The Parsons impulse/reaction HP turbines** were primarily of the reaction type but included an impulse first stage for general economy and low speed cruising. They were designed for a maximum power of 10,000shp at 3018rpm, the inlet steam pressure being 250psi.
2. **The Parsons LP turbines** included both reaction ahead and impulse astern stages. They were designed for a maximum ahead power of 12,000shp at 2162rpm.
3. **Steam inlet** to HP turbine.
4. **Steam exhaust** from HP turbine.
5. **Steam inlet** to LP turbine from HP turbine.
6. **The condensers**, slung below the LP turbines, each contained 8244 tubes with a total cooling surface of 15,085ft^2. This formed part of a 'closed feed system' in which the water in the condensers was pumped out by the extraction pump, passed through an air extractor and then returned to the boilers via the feed pumps and feed heaters. To maintain the water in the condenser at the required level, any surplus from the extraction pump could be diverted to the feed tank while any loss of water was corrected by supplying water directly from the feed tank to the condenser. Apart from a general loss of water in the system, variation in level was primarily caused by changes in boiler operation (loss on reducing speed and gain when increasing speed).
7. **The condenser inlet and outlet cooling water pipes.** There is no obvious indication of why the dog-leg in the port intake pipe is further aft than that to starboard.
8. **Double faced slide valves** to shut off the sea water inlets and outlets of the condenser during maintenance.
9. **The main circulating pumps** for the condensers consisted of an 'axial flow' impeller within the intake pipe driven by a small external steam turbine. The pump was only required at low speed since at moderate and higher speeds sufficient circulating water was provided by the ship's movement through the water (the impeller being allowed to spin freely).

Continued overleaf

'TRIBAL' CLASS: ARRANGEMENT OF MACHINERY IN ENGINE ROOM
(Sheet 2)

(M1887)

10. **The single reduction gear box** reduced the maximum speed of the turbines to 350rpm at the propeller shafts. The HP and LP pinions and the main wheel had 53, 74 and 457 teeth respectively. The teeth were AA (all-addendum) in which the diameter of the pinions was increased and that of the wheel reduced in order to balance the load bearing of the teeth (normally lower in the case of the pinion due to the way the teeth were machined). The term is a little misleading in that only the pinions were all-addendum (this being that part of the tooth outside the pitch circle diameter). The diameter of the main wheel was a fraction over 8ft.

11. **The hand wheels for the turbine turning gear**, provided for the rotation of the turbines when in harbour, with the steam supply shut off. The geared drive was connected to the end of the HP turbine shaft and was disconnected when not in use. Note that the turning gear would rotate both HP and LP turbines since these were linked by the gearbox.

12. **The turbo-hydraulic unit** supplying power for the after 4.7in gun mountings.

13. **The main turbine control hand wheels**. The two with horizontal axes are the ahead and astern wheels, the latter being the smaller of the two. The wheel with the vertical axis is the cruising control. The wheels were connected via rod gearing to steam regulating valves mounted on the top, fore end, of the LP turbines. Each group of valves was connected to a single steam pipe fed from a manifold on the after side of the forward ER bulkhead. The manifold served as a junction for the three pipes from the boilers (each having a shut-off valve on the ER side of the bulkhead).

14. **The 80kw turbo-generators,** manufactured by W H Allen of Bedford, were the ship's primary electricity supply engines. The driver was a single stage, 10,000rpm impulse turbine, with gear reduction to drive the generator at 1250rpm.

15. **The evaporator** boiled sea water, the resulting steam being passed through the condenser (positioned just aft of the evaporator) to provide fresh water for boiler feed and domestic purposes. The combined pump was three pumps (for brine, fresh water and feed water) driven by a single steam engine located on the port side of the fore bulkhead. This distillation plant could produce 50 tons of fresh water per day (the ship operating losses per day were estimated at maximum of 23 tons for the boilers and 10 tons for ship services).

16. **The Mitchell thrust bearings** transferred the thrust from the propeller shaft to the ship.

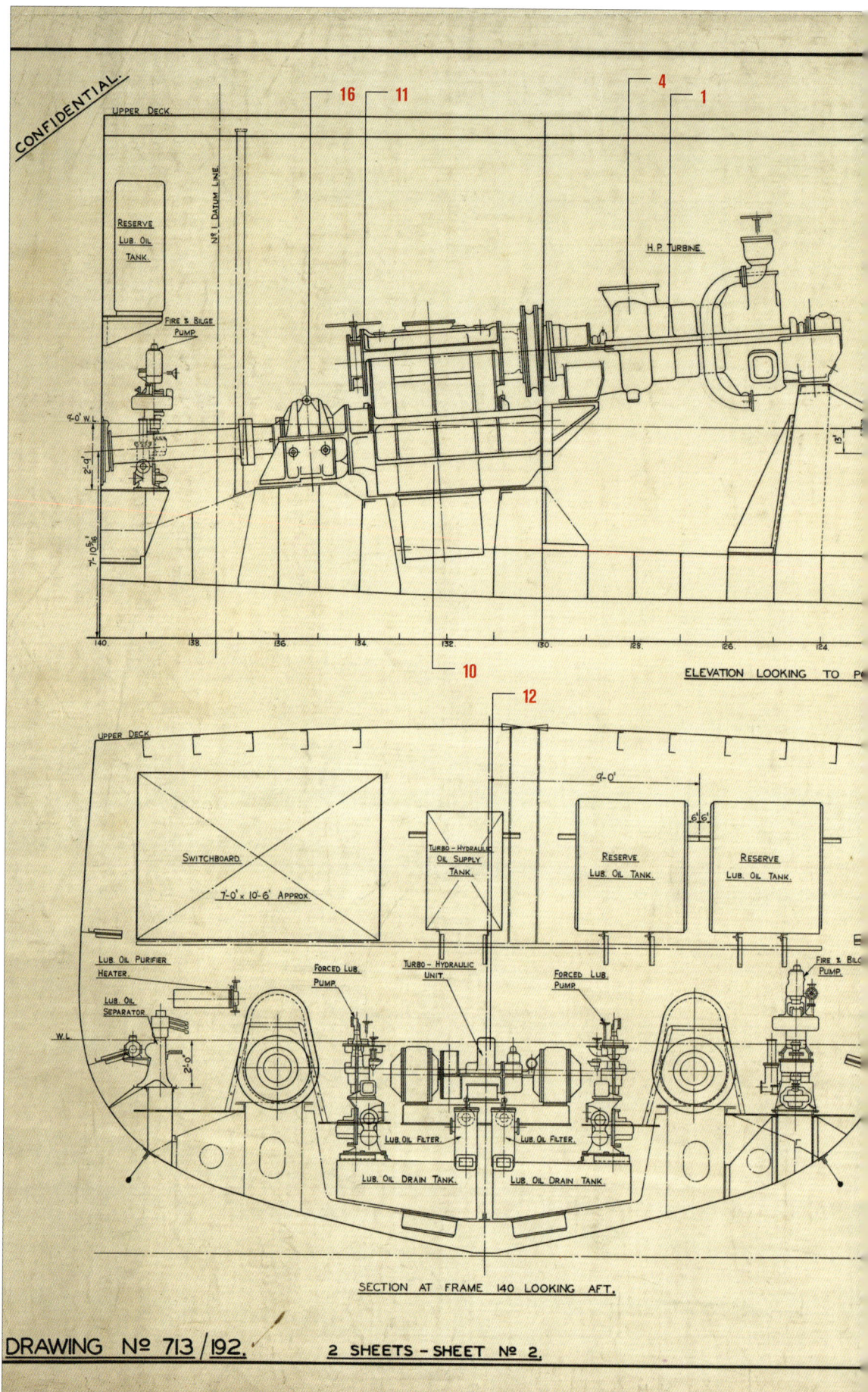

'TRIBAL' CLASS: ARRANGEMENT OF MACHINERY IN ENGINE ROOM

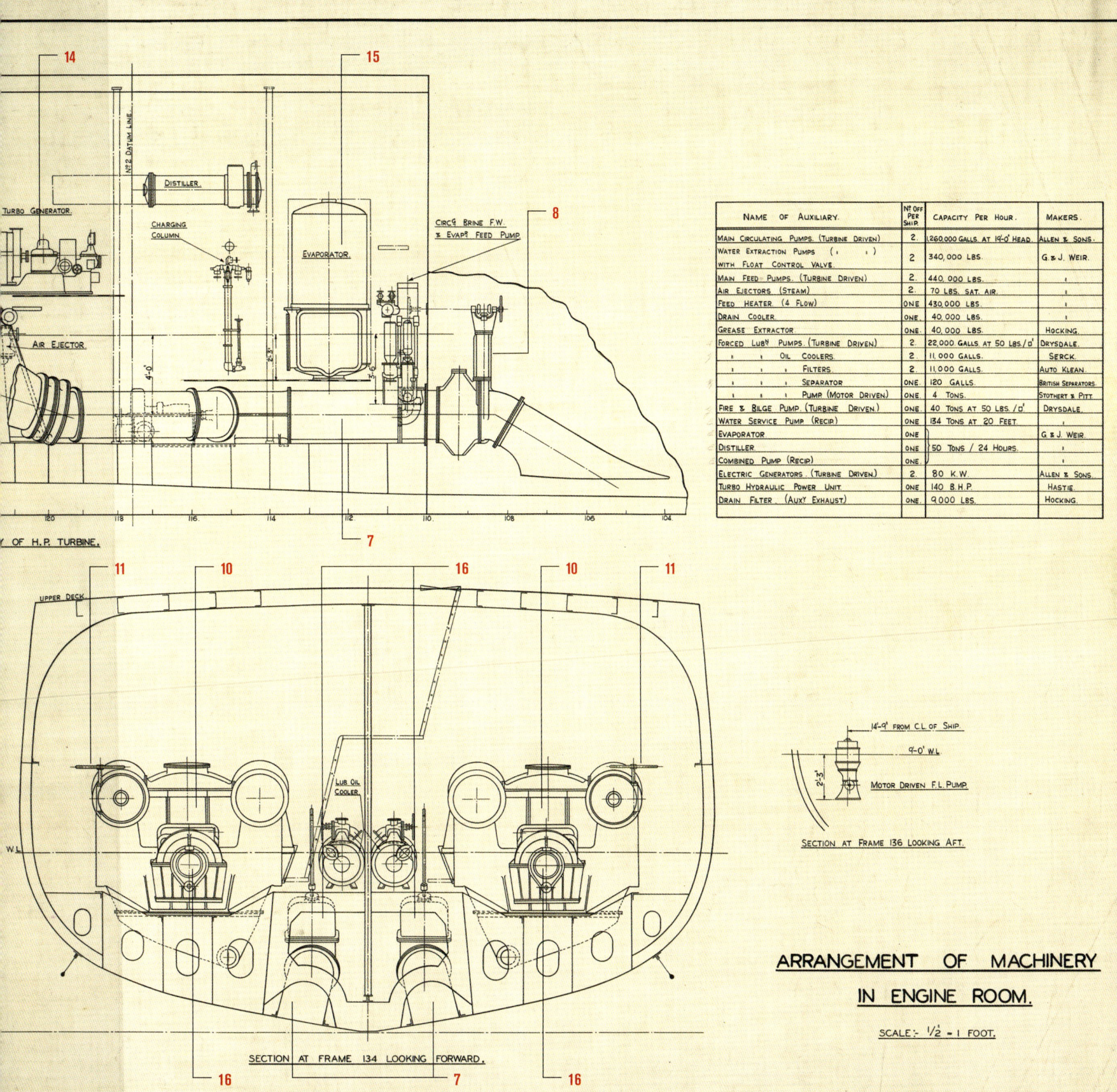

ARRANGEMENT OF MACHINERY IN ENGINE ROOM.

SCALE :- 1/2" = 1 FOOT.

Nos 713 & 714.

NAME OF AUXILIARY.	Nº OFF PER SHIP.	CAPACITY PER HOUR.	MAKERS.
MAIN CIRCULATING PUMPS. (TURBINE DRIVEN)	2	1,260,000 GALLS. AT 14'-0" HEAD.	ALLEN & SONS.
WATER EXTRACTION PUMPS (" ") WITH FLOAT CONTROL VALVE.	2	340,000 LBS.	G. & J. WEIR.
MAIN FEED PUMPS. (TURBINE DRIVEN)	2	440,000 LBS.	"
AIR EJECTORS (STEAM)	2	70 LBS. SAT. AIR.	"
FEED HEATER. (4 FLOW)	ONE	430,000 LBS.	"
DRAIN COOLER	ONE	40,000 LBS.	"
GREASE EXTRACTOR	ONE	40,000 LBS.	HOCKING.
FORCED LUBᴺ PUMPS. (TURBINE DRIVEN)	2	22,000 GALLS. AT 50 LBS./◻"	DRYSDALE.
" " OIL COOLERS	2	11,000 GALLS.	SERCK.
" " FILTERS	2	11,000 GALLS.	AUTO KLEAN.
" " SEPARATOR	ONE	120 GALLS.	BRITISH SEPARATORS.
" " PUMP (MOTOR DRIVEN.)	ONE	4 TONS.	STOTHERT & PITT.
FIRE & BILGE PUMP. (TURBINE DRIVEN.)	ONE	40 TONS AT 50 LBS./◻"	DRYSDALE.
WATER SERVICE PUMP (RECIP)	ONE	134 TONS AT 20 FEET.	"
EVAPORATOR	ONE		G. & J. WEIR.
DISTILLER	ONE	50 TONS / 24 HOURS.	"
COMBINED PUMP (RECIP)	ONE		"
ELECTRIC GENERATORS. (TURBINE DRIVEN.)	2	80 K.W.	ALLEN & SONS.
TURBO HYDRAULIC POWER UNIT	ONE	140 B.H.P.	HASTIE.
DRAIN FILTER (AUXᵞ EXHAUST)	ONE	9,000 LBS.	HOCKING.

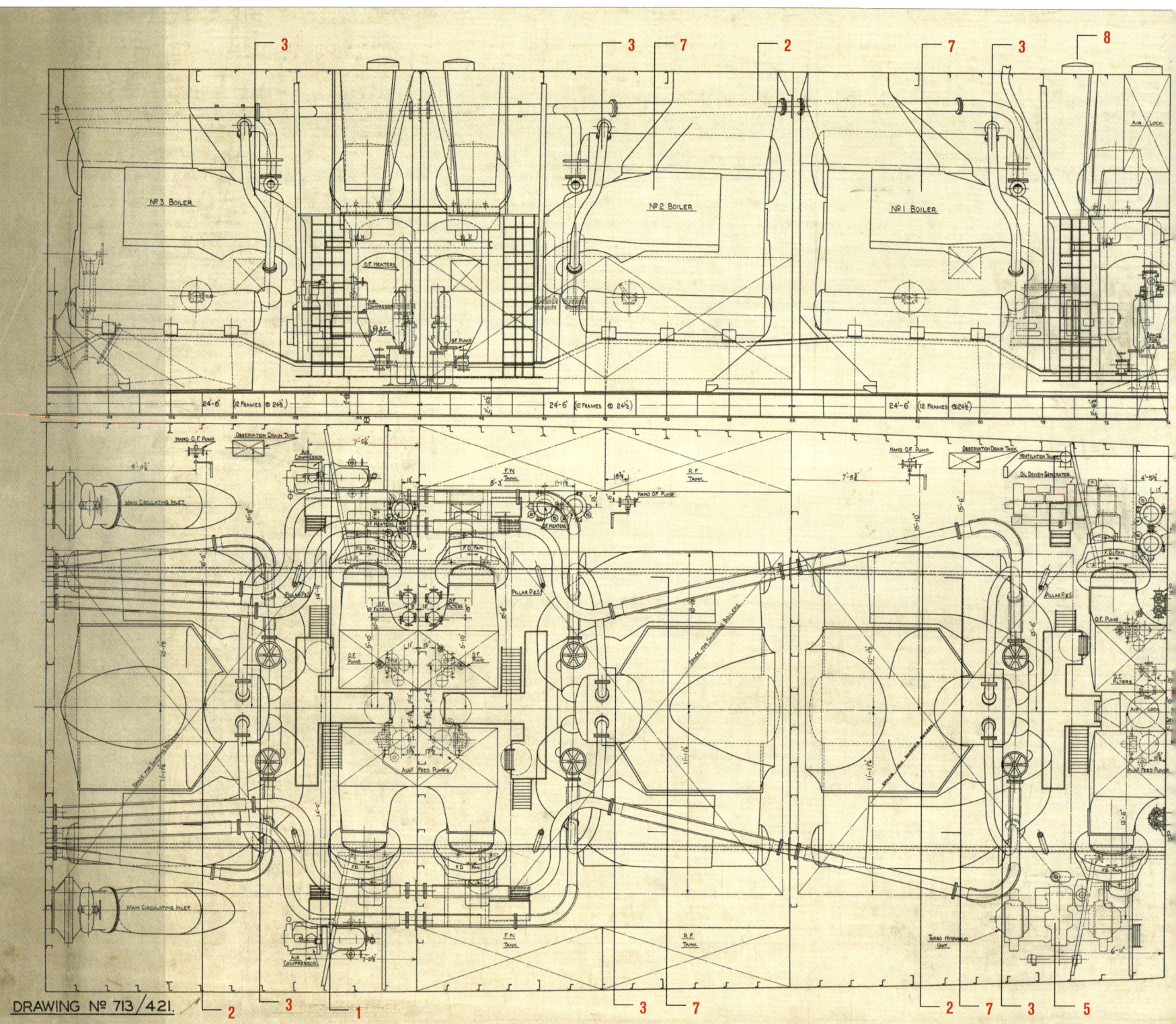

DRAWING No 713/421.

'TRIBAL' CLASS: ARRANGEMENT OF MACHINERY IN BOILER ROOMS

The Admiralty 3-drum boilers had a working pressure of 300psi, each having two superheaters and ten oil fuel sprayers (eight main and two of lower capacity for lighting-up). The heating surface for the main generator tubes in all three was 8550ft^2 but that for the superheaters in N°2 boiler was 1396ft^2 compared with 1410ft^2 in the other two. The latter appears to have resulted from a reduction in the volume of the furnace (938ft^3 compared with 950ft^3) although the reason for this variation has not come to light. The boiler auxiliaries in each room consisted of an OF pump, hand OF pump, auxiliary feed pump, two OF heaters and two OF filters. The OF and auxiliary feed pumps were driven by steam piston engines, unlike the majority of the pumps in the engine rooms where all but two (the water service and combined pump) were powered by turbines. Each boiler room did, however, have two turbo-driven 48in diameter forced-draught fans (manufactured by W H Allen). The air-locks, to avoid loss of forced-draught pressure, were located on the Upper Deck (below the 0.5in MG platform) for boiler rooms 2 and 3 and, in the case of boiler room 1, at its fore end immediately below the Upper Deck. Note that the boiler rooms 1 and 3 contain auxiliaries not directly related to boiler operation (identified below) and that, unlike the engine room plans, this includes the main steam pipes. (M1811)

'TRIBAL CLASS: ARRANGEMENT OF MACHINERY IN BOILER ROOMS

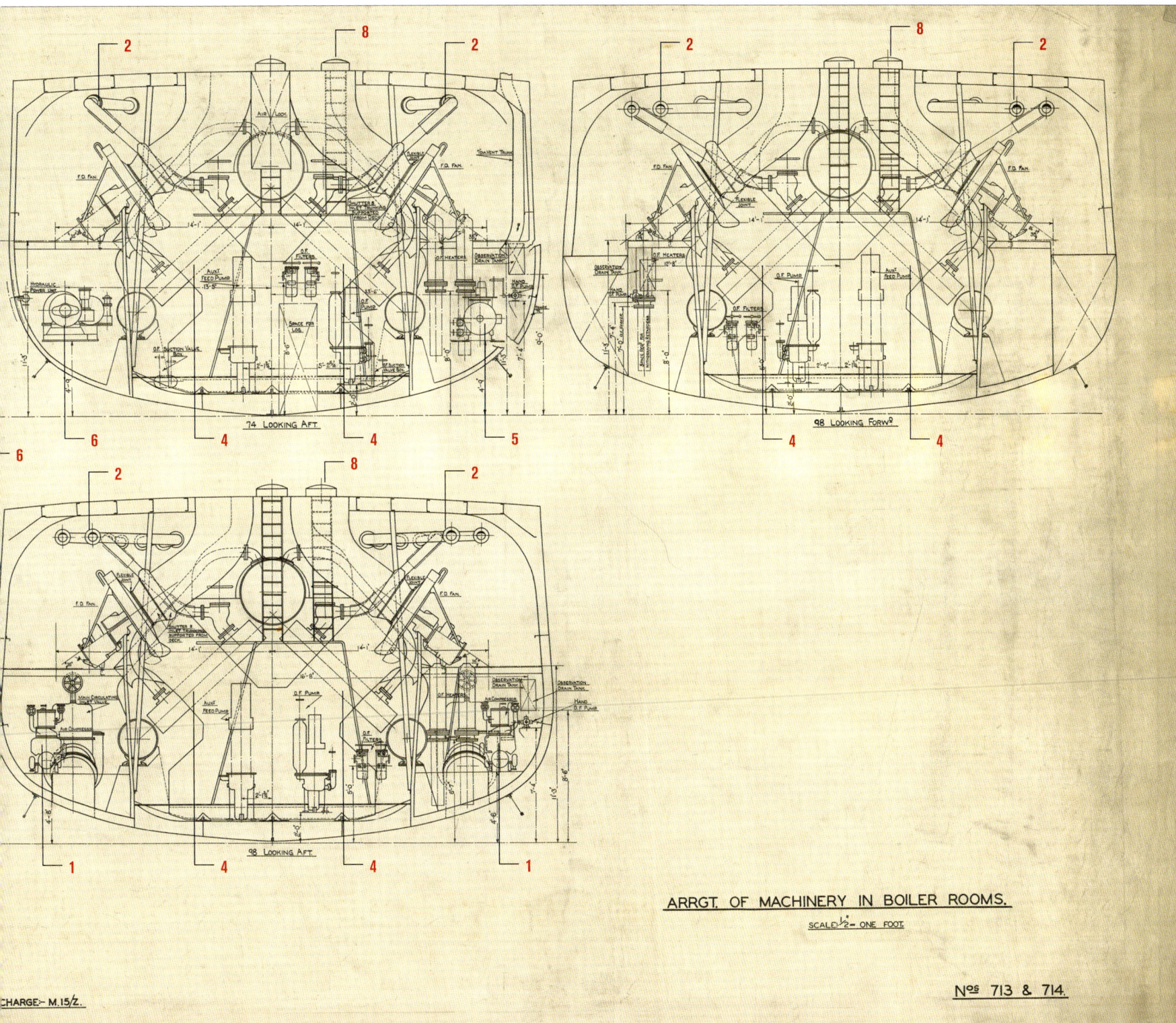

ARRGT. OF MACHINERY IN BOILER ROOMS.
SCALE ½" = ONE FOOT

Nos 713 & 714.

1. **The air compressors** were four stage compound HP/LP machines. The HP supply was used primarily for charging torpedoes, and supplying the recuperators of the 4.7in guns. The LP supply (provided from the HP side via a reducing valve) was used for clearing water from the boilers, checking condensers and water-tight compartments for leaks, pneumatic tools and for cleaning (including the exterior of boilers).
2. **The main steam pipes**, one on each side from each outlet of the boiler superheaters.
3. **The superheater steam supply pipes** connected the steam drums to the inlets of the superheater headers.
4. **The headers of the Admiralty superheaters** are represented by these diagonal rectangles (note that they pass through the hot-air duct).
5. **The turbo-hydraulic unit** suppling power for the forward 4.7in gun mountings.
6. **The 30kw Paxman-Ricardo 4cyl diesel driven generator** manufactured by Davey Paxman of Colchester. This engine served as back-up to the two main generators, in case of breakdown or servicing, and to provide essential services when the ship's main steam plant was not running.
7. **Hot-air ducts** to furnace space.
8. **Alternative access scuttles** to the boiler rooms for use when not operating under forced draught.

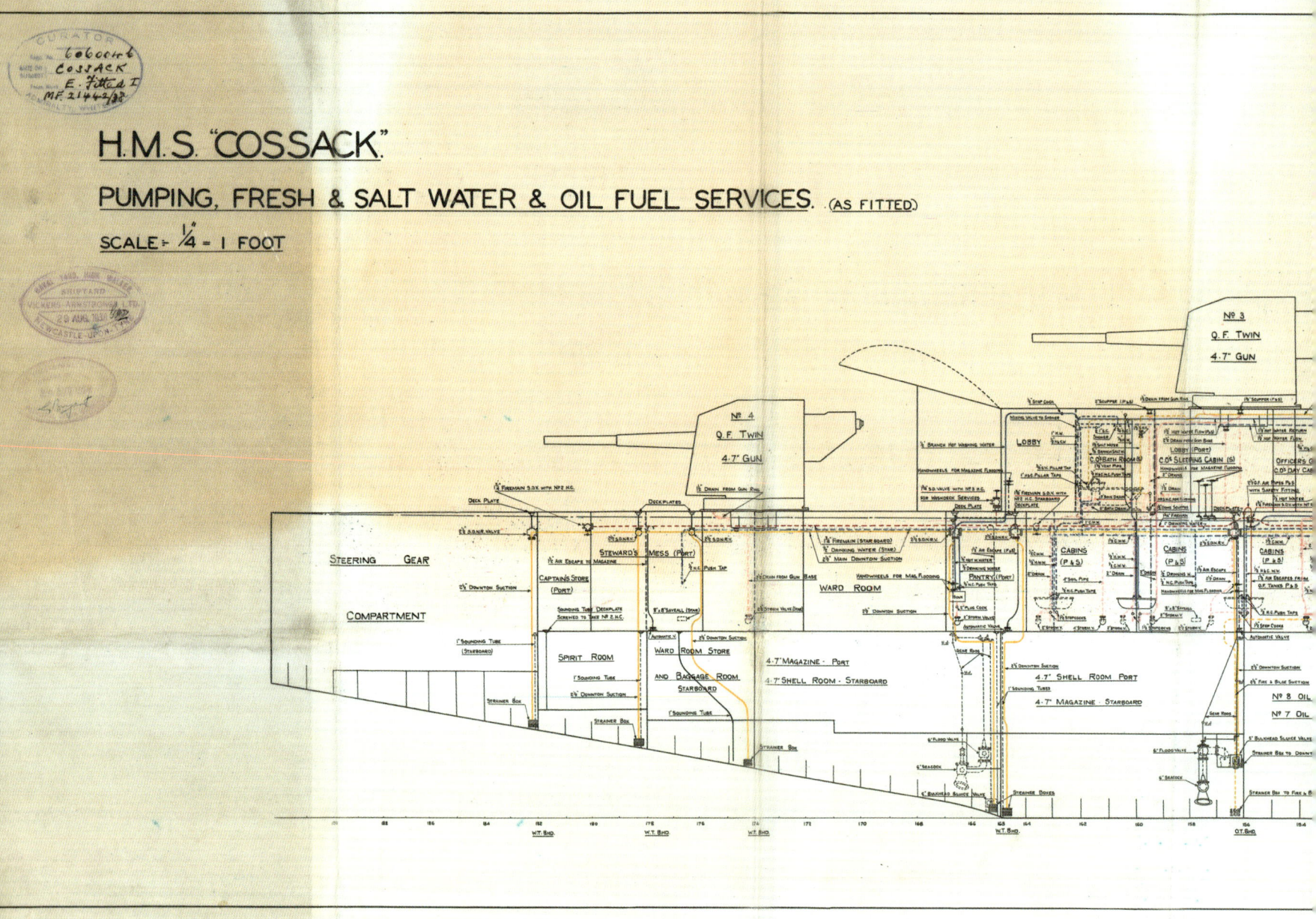

HMS *COSSACK*: WATER AND OIL FUEL SERVICES

This profile is spread over four pages while the accompanying plan views follow on pages 70–71. They provide a very detailed illustration of *Cossack*'s water and oil services, the interpretation of which is assisted by the colour coding of the pipes. Unfortunately, one of these colours (pink for the drains) has not aged well, although it is relatively easy to distinguish these from the fire main (red) with which they are most likely to be confused. There is also some limited damage to the fresh water pipes (blue) but not enough to cause serious difficulty. (M1816)

Salt water Services. The fire main ran the length of the ship and was supplied from the fire and bilge pump **(1)** in the gearing room. In addition to fire-fighting, it served for washing the anchor cables, boiler tubes and weather decks. It could also be employed for pumping out flood water and the bilges although its capacity was limited. There were two steam ejectors in each of the five machinery compartments which could deal with a substantial amount of flooding but they were extremely wasteful of fresh water. They were used in *Cossack* during the attempts to salvage her after she was torpedoed in 1941. They served reasonably well until it became necessary to shut down the boiler in use because the feed water had run out. Sea water could have been used but not without causing damage to the boiler and it was assumed the tug sent to tow her in would have a salvage pump. Unfortunately, this was not the case and some criticism was subsequently made that the boiler was not then restarted so the ejectors could be used. Interestingly, the *Cossack* was supplied with a 70-ton portable pump early in 1941 but managed to lose it about three or four months before she was herself lost! The main bilge suction was powered by a Downton hand pump **(2)**, with a capacity of 4.5 to 7 tons/hour, fitted on the Upper Deck forward of the after funnel. This ran the full length of the ship, just below the Upper Deck with down pipes leading to strainers (intended to stop debris blocking the pipes) at the bottoms of the main water-tight compartments (except for the oil fuel tanks). Salt water also served for flushing the toilets. This was supplied from gravity tanks **(3)**, one on the forward and one on the after superstructure, which were in turn supplied direct from the sea via a small electric pump **(4)** on the Lower Deck at Frames 64–65.

HMS COSSACK: WATER AND OIL FUEL SERVICES

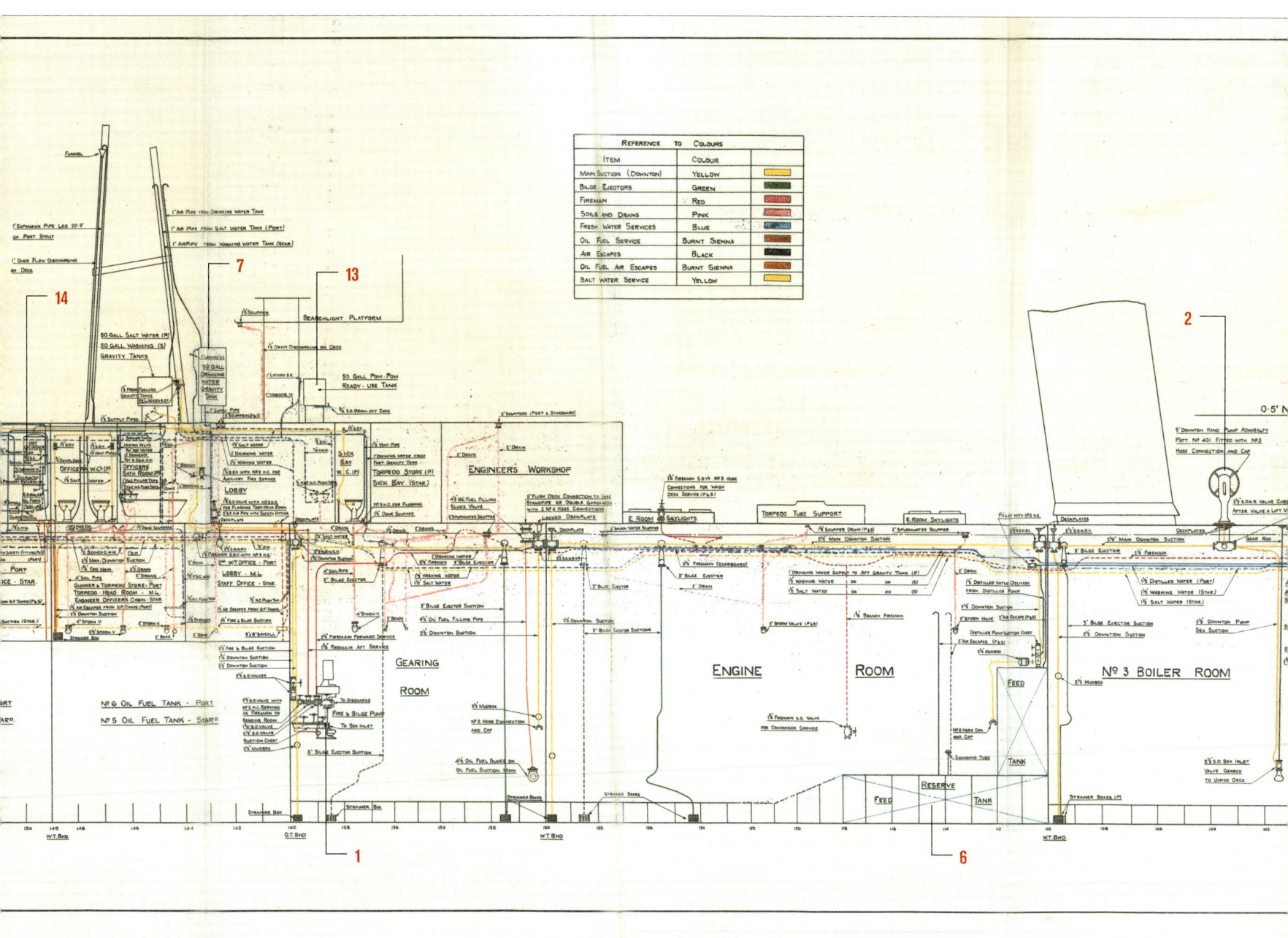

Fresh water services. Reserve feed water for the boilers was stored in three tanks, two in N°2 boiler room **(5)** and one in at the fore end of the engine room **(6)** – the latter also serving as the overflow tank for the main feed tank above it. Drinking water was supplied from gravity tanks **(7)** in the forward and after superstructure, these in turn being supplied from tanks **(8)** in the Hold forward via a small electric pump **(9)** on the Lower Deck at Frames 28–29. The tanks were normally filled from shore or water boat but could be topped up from the distillation plant in the engine room. Washing water was also supplied from fore and aft gravity tanks **(10)** these being supplied in turn from two tanks **(11)** in N°2 boiler room via a pump **(12)** fitted on top of the port tank. The washing water system also supplied a ready-use tank **(13)** for the cooling water of the pom-pom. Hot washing-water was provided from two hot water tanks **(14)** each heated by a small boiler, one set located in the seamen's galley, forward, and one in the officer's galley, aft.

Valve controls. Should a compartment in which a valve was located become inaccessible due to flooding or damage, the valve could be operated remotely from higher decks by hand wheels or from deck plates connected to the valves by gear-rods.

Air escapes and sounding tubes. Since a sealed vessel cannot be filled or emptied without an air escape, all tanks were fitted with air pipes. Tanks were also fitted with sounding tubes to allow for checking the level of their contents.

Oil fuel services. Oil tank filling was provided by stand-pipes that could be fitted to deck plates **(15)** on each side of the after end of the Forecastle Deck. These could fill any of the ship's tanks via the main oil fuel suction line. There was also a deck plate **(16)** on the port side for diesel oil filling but this supplied the fuel direct to the tank.

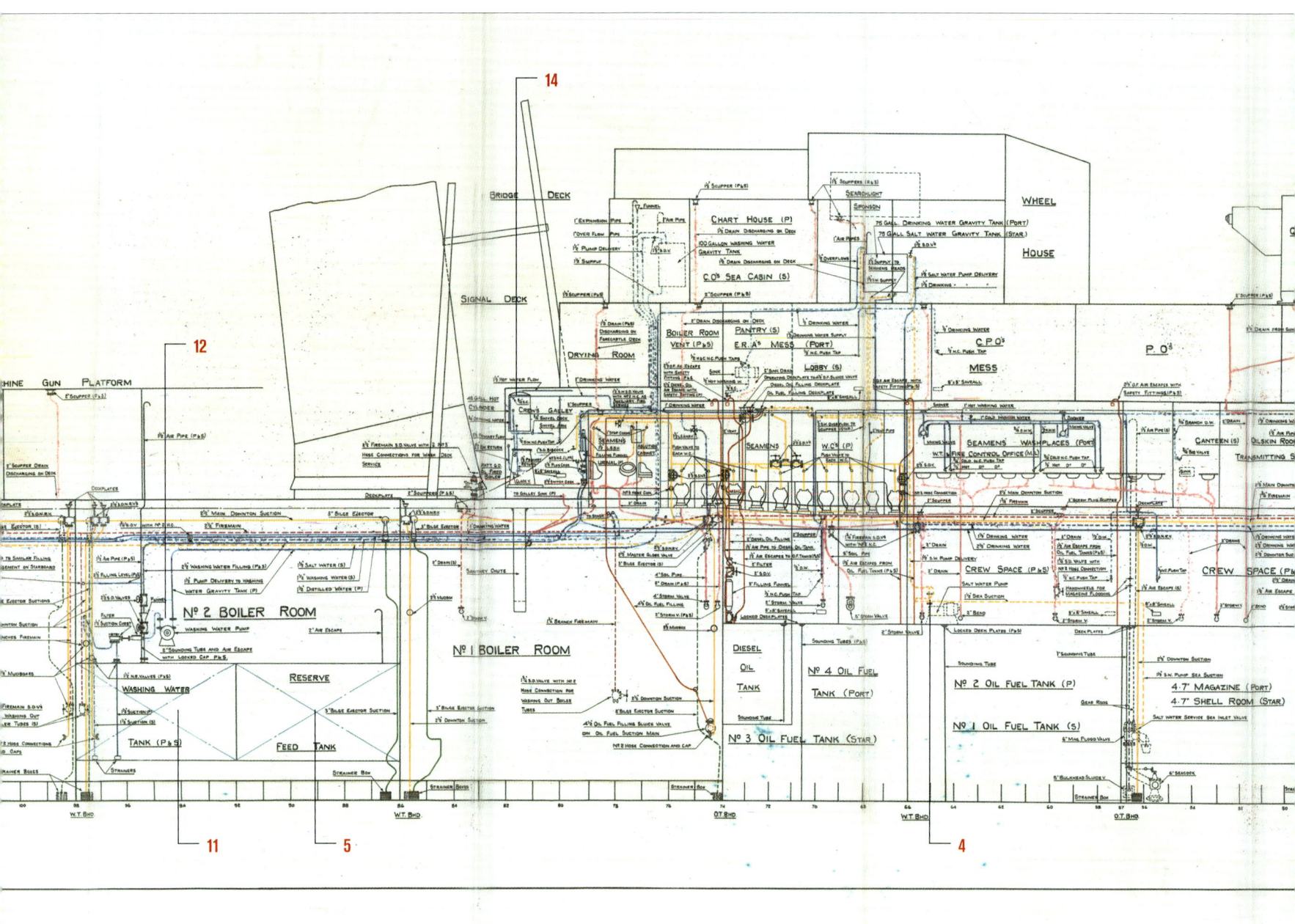

HMS *COSSACK*: WATER AND OIL FUEL SERVICES

Abbreviations
CWW	Cold Washing Water
DW	Drinking Water
HC	Hose Connection
HWW	Hot Washing Water
NC	Non Concussive (water push-tap)
SDNRV	Screw Down Non-Return Valve
SDV	Screw Down Valve
WTBHD	Water-Tight Bulkhead

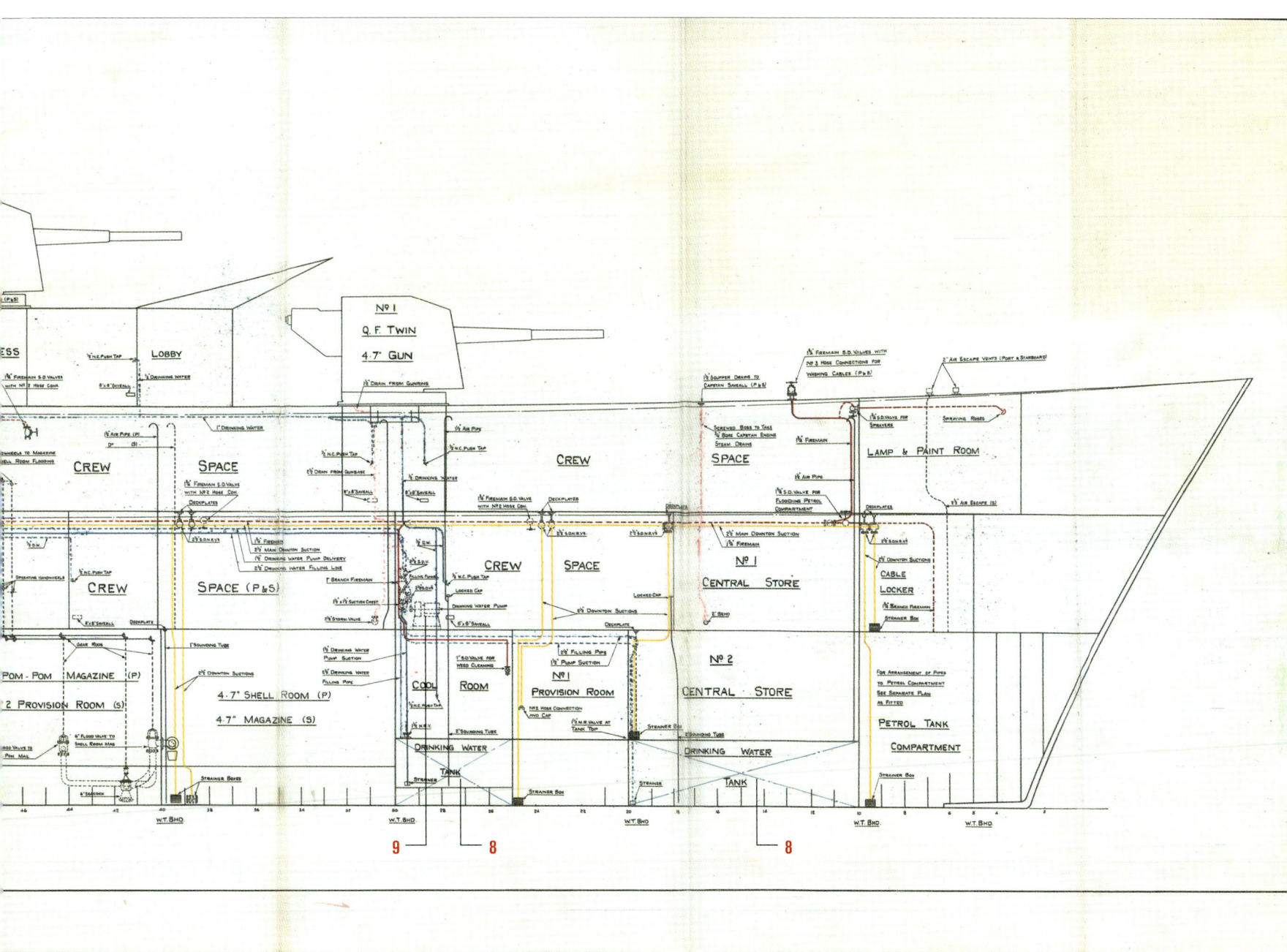

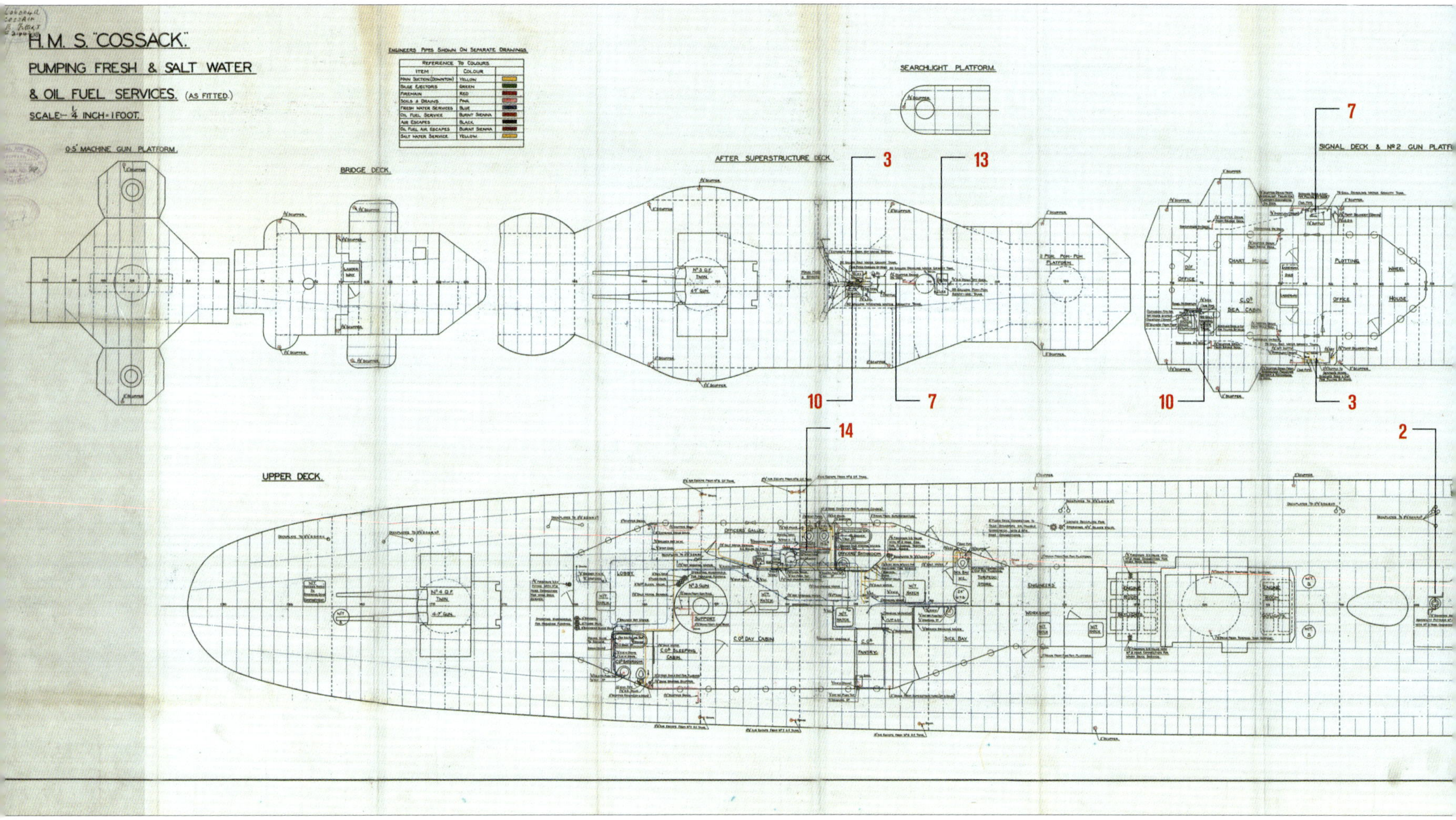
H.M.S. "COSSACK."
PUMPING FRESH & SALT WATER
& OIL FUEL SERVICES. (AS FITTED.)
SCALE:- 1/4 INCH - 1 FOOT.
ENGINEERS PIPES SHOWN ON SEPARATE DRAWINGS
REFERENCE TO COLOURS
ITEM | COLOUR
MAIN SUCTION (DOWNTON) | YELLOW
BILGE EJECTORS | GREEN
FIREMAIN | RED
SOILS & DRAINS | PINK
FRESH WATER SERVICES | BLUE
OIL FUEL SERVICE | BURNT SIENNA
AIR ESCAPES | BLACK
OIL FUEL AIR ESCAPES | BURNT SIENNA
SALT WATER SERVICE | YELLOW
0.5" MACHINE GUN PLATFORM.
BRIDGE DECK.
SEARCHLIGHT PLATFORM.
AFTER SUPERSTRUCTURE DECK.
SIGNAL DECK & Nº2 GUN PLATF
UPPER DECK.
3
13
7
10
7
10
3
14
2

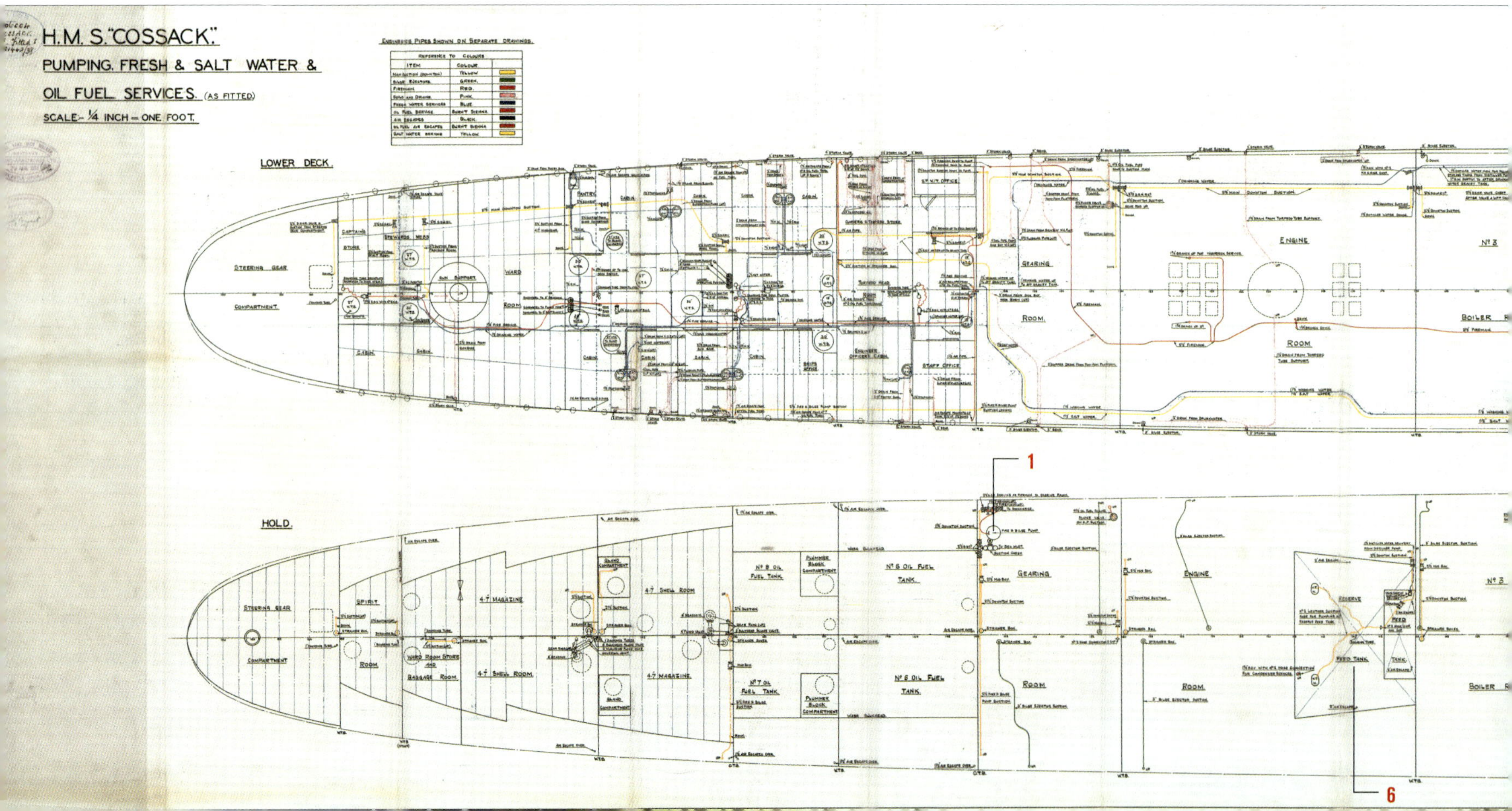
H.M.S. "COSSACK."
PUMPING, FRESH & SALT WATER &
OIL FUEL SERVICES. (AS FITTED)
SCALE:- 1/4 INCH - ONE FOOT.
ENGINEERS PIPES SHOWN ON SEPARATE DRAWINGS
LOWER DECK.
STEERING GEAR
COMPARTMENT
WARD
ROOM
GEARING
ROOM
ENGINE
ROOM
BOILER
HOLD.
4.7 MAGAZINE
4.7 SHELL ROOM
Nº 6 OIL FUEL TANK.
ENGINE
ROOM
1
6

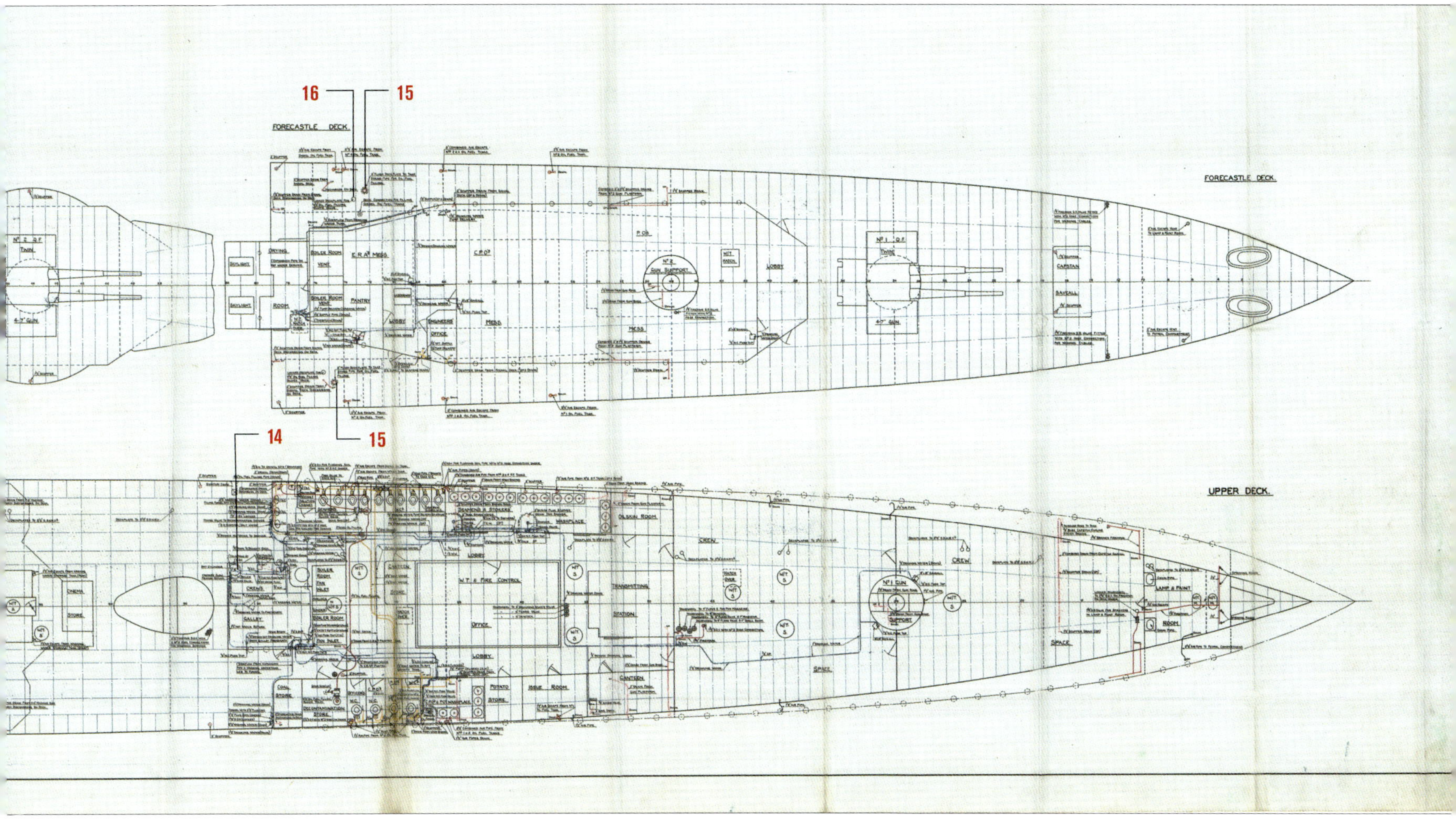

HMS COSSACK: WATER AND OIL FUEL SERVICES

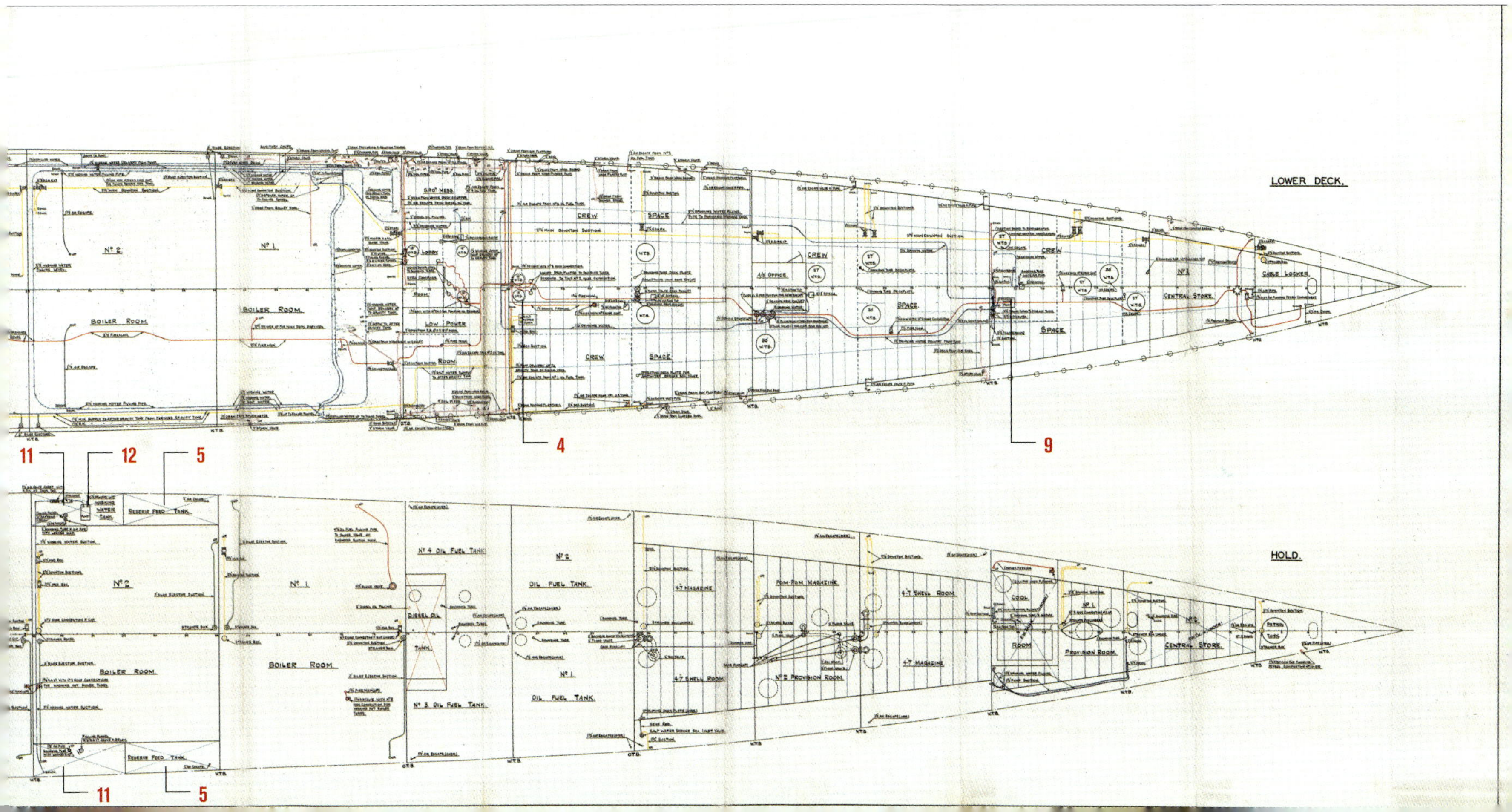

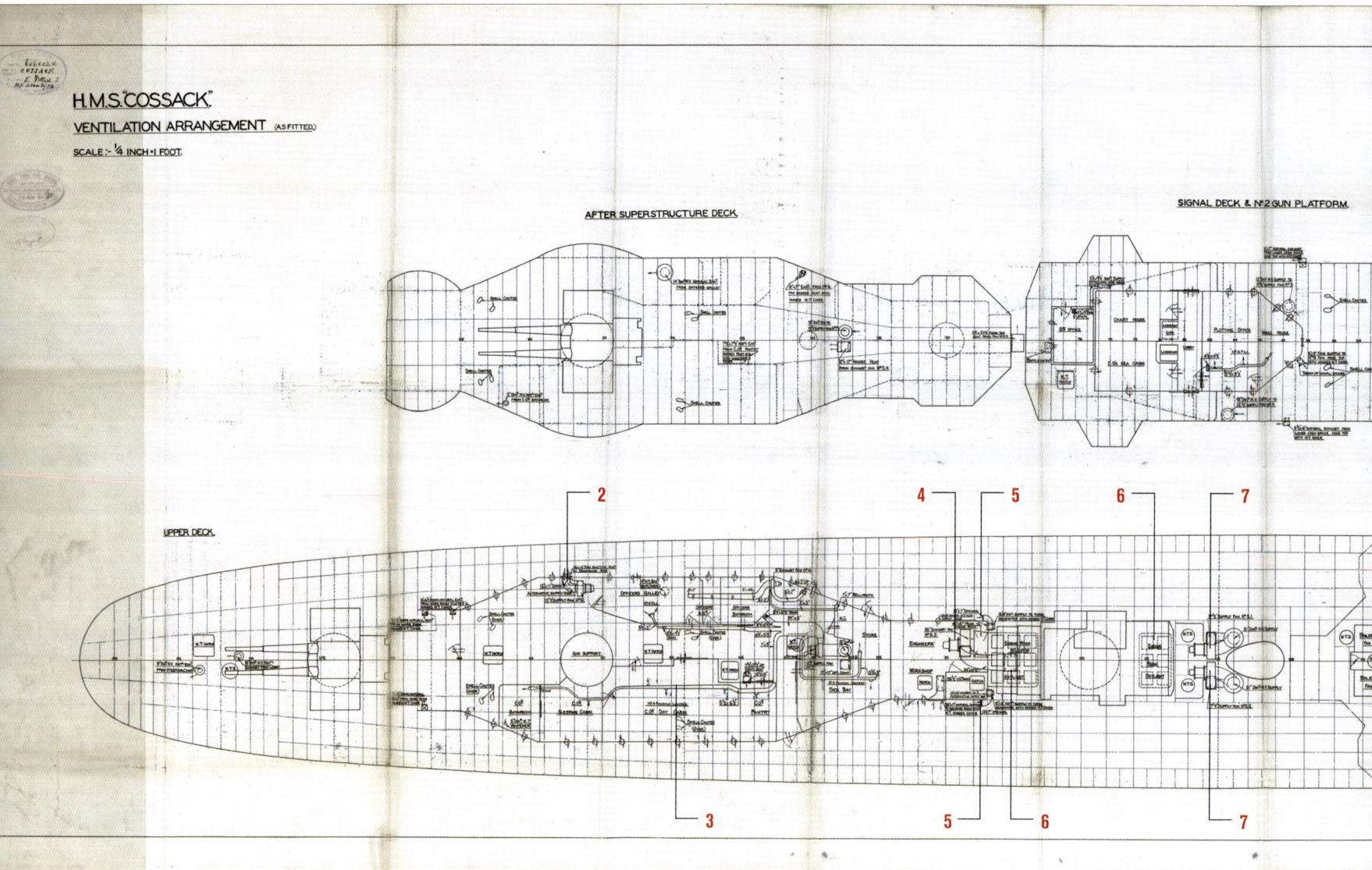

HMS *COSSACK*: VENTILATION ARRANGEMENT

The plans on these and following pages (top) cover the distribution of the ventilation trunks and electric fans but not the ventilation of the boiler rooms for which only the positions of the inlet trunks of the turbo fans are indicated. The plans also include the location of the lamps in the main machinery spaces and, to a limited extent, some of those in accommodation areas. Why these were added to the ventilation arrangement plans is unclear. The spaces and offices generally occupied by personnel have supply fans and natural exhaust except for galleys, bathrooms and toilets which have the reverse arrangement since they were intended to clear the air rather than supply it. The largest electric fans are provided for the engine room with two $17\tfrac{1}{2}$in supply fans at the fore end and a 20in exhaust fan at the after end. The gearing room also has a $17\tfrac{1}{2}$in exhaust fan but with a natural supply. The numbers of these four fans (1–4) are prefixed E for 'engine' while all the other fans have numbers in the sequence 1 to 7 for the $12\tfrac{1}{2}$in supply fans and 3 to 14 for the $7\tfrac{1}{2}$in and 5in fans. Oddly, there are numbers missing from these – 6 from the $12\tfrac{1}{2}$in sequence and 1, 2 and 4 from the $7\tfrac{1}{2}$in and 5in group (presumably the result of some change in the intended outfit?). The smaller fans were generally for exhaust apart from one $7\tfrac{1}{2}$in (supply to Main W/T and Fire Control Office and TS) and one 5in (supply to diesel generator in Nº1 boiler room). Weather deck intakes and exhausts were either mushroom top (primarily for fan supply), rectangular hooded vents (primarily for both fan and natural exhaust), rectangular mushroom top inlet and exhaust vent in the after sides of the fore deckhouse and a few trunks with rectangular, vertical water-tight covers. The only vents in the Hold are small pipes in the magazines, branched from the supply trunks in the decks above, and a fan supply and natural exhaust for the petrol tank compartment, forward. Any ventilation for the remaining compartments in the Hold relied on the opening of their access scuttles. The natural flow in this case could be enhanced in the case of the oil fuel tanks, magazines, shell rooms and stores by hoses fitted to connections on the supply trunks in the deck above – particularly useful if clearing fumes, stale air, etc. The arrows on the plans indicate supply (blue) and exhaust (red). Where both are shown it indicates the possibility of natural ventilation via doors, side scuttles, deck scuttles, etc, the direction of flow being largely dependent on the relative temperature difference between the interior and exterior of the ship. (M1837 and M1838).

HMS COSSACK: VENTILATION ARRANGEMENT

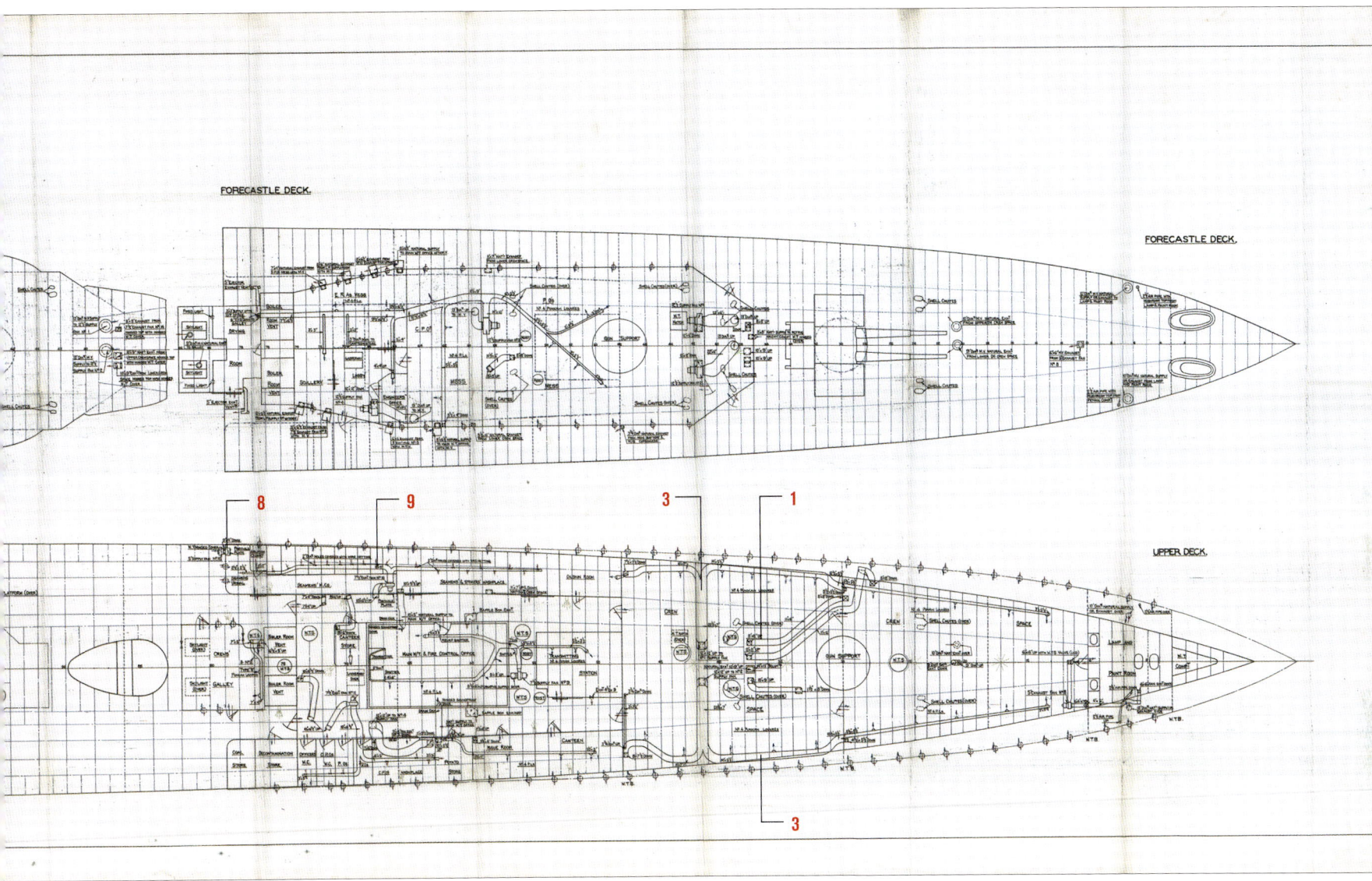

1. **Where the ventilation trunks pass through the decks** the 'up' or 'down' refers to the direction of the trunks as either to the compartment above or below and not to the direction of air flow.
2. **The 12½in supply fan** to the after, Lower Deck, accommodation areas could take its air from either inside or outside the after deckhouse via alternative hinged covers in its intake trunk.
3. **The supply trunks** reduced in section the further they were from their fan in order to maintain a steady air pressure. The half round extensions along their sides, with a blue supply arrow, are punkah louvres to control the strength and direction of output air.
4. **The 20in engine room exhaust fan.**
5. **Natural air supply** to the turbo-generators in the engine room.
6. **The engine room skylights** also served for natural ventilation.
7. **The 17½in engine room supply fans.**
8. **A 5in supply fan** for the diesel generator in N°1 boiler room.
9. **The exhaust trunks**, unlike the supply trunks, were fitted with holes covered with wire mesh to draw air from the compartments they were venting.
10. **The hoses** used to clear the Hold compartments are represented by blue dashed lines between the connections on the trunk and the access scuttles to the compartments below.
11. **The air supply trunks to the turbo-generators.**
12. **The supply trunk to the diesel generator** is mistakenly attributed to fan 5 (it is actually 12 – see deck above).
13. **The exhaust trunk array** fitted over the batteries in the low power room to clear any generated fumes.
14. **Vent trunks that passed through the Lower Deck** were fitted with water-tight shut valves to limit any flooding via the trunks in the event of damage.

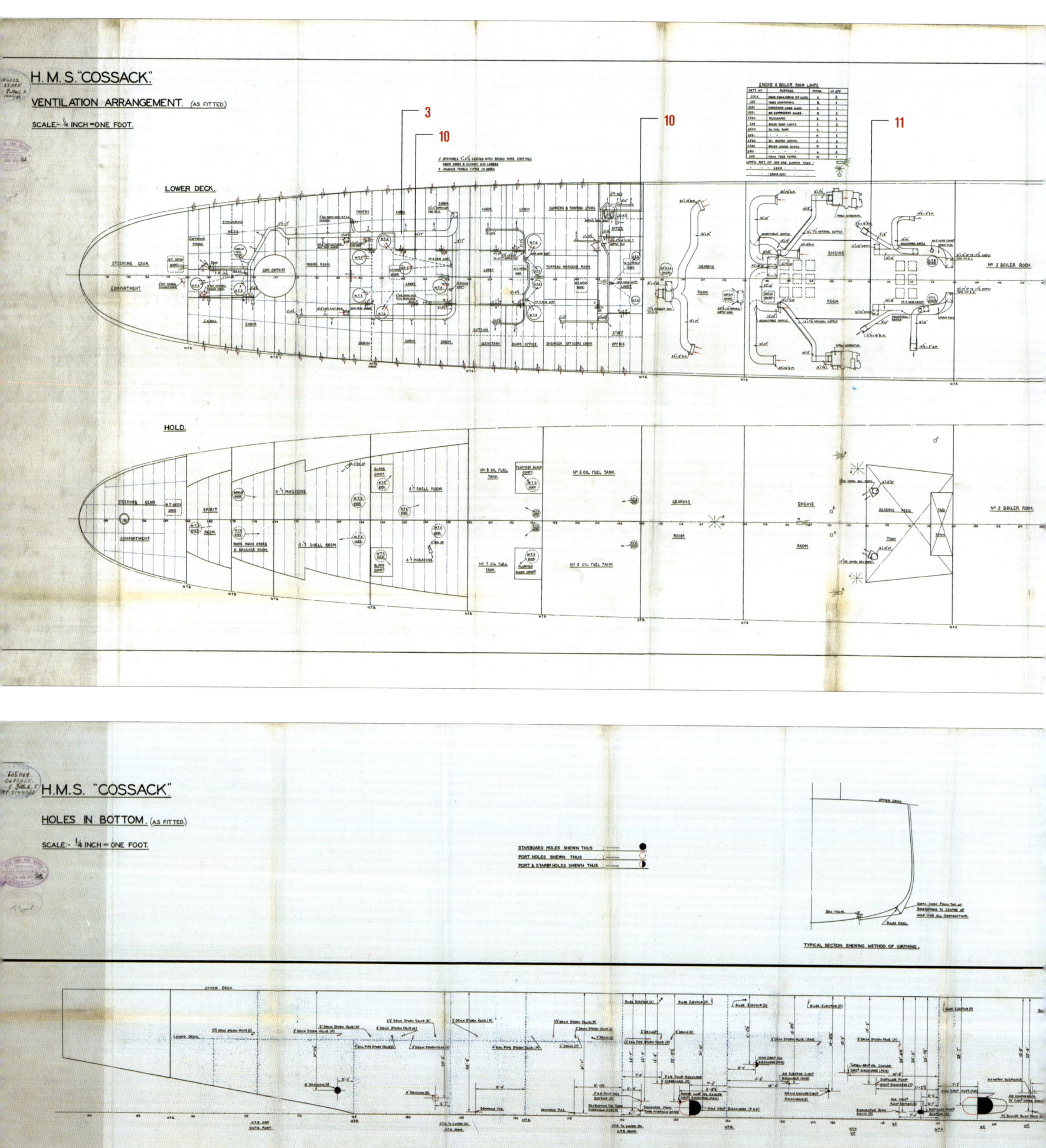

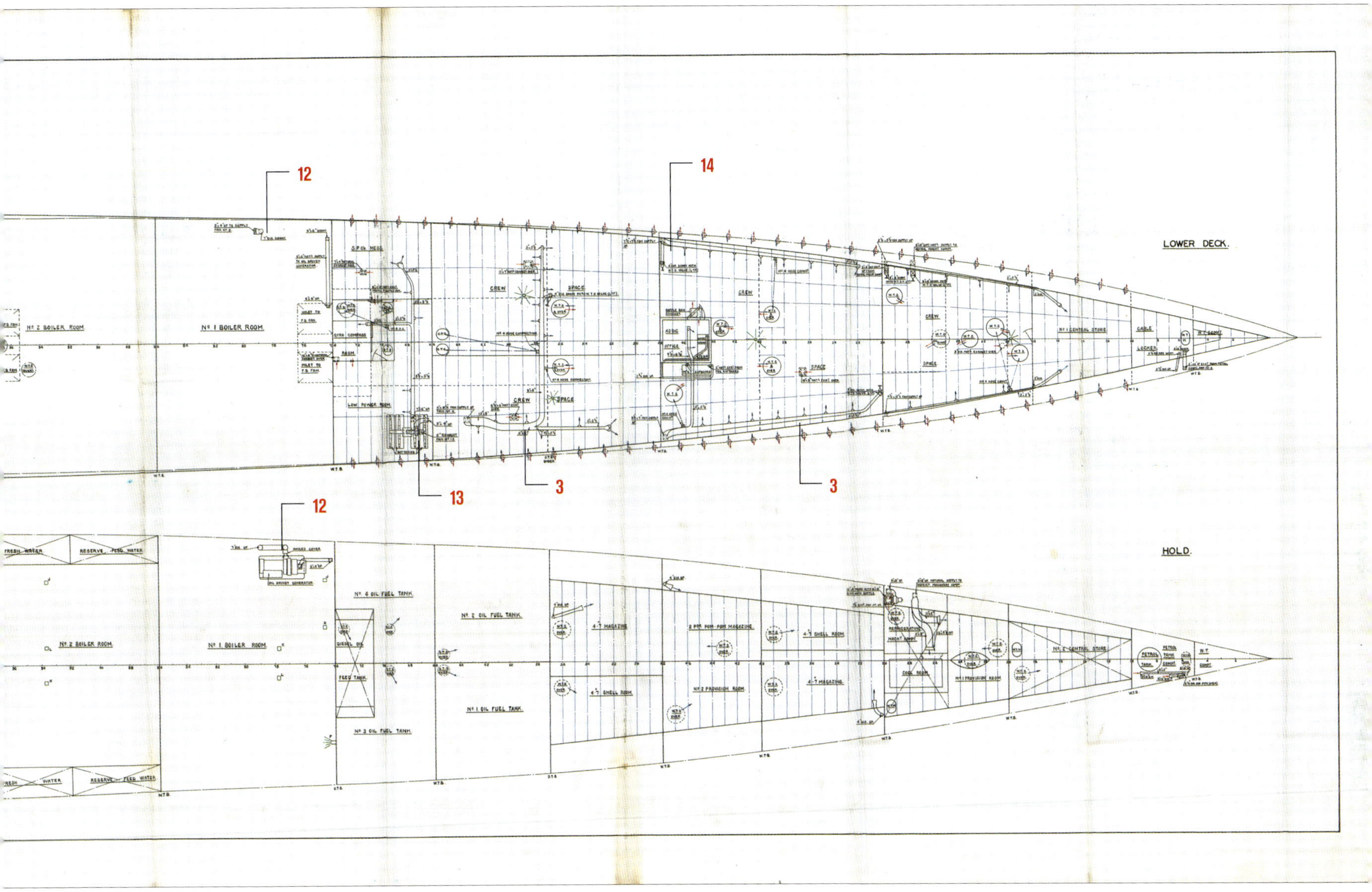

HMS *COSSACK*: HOLES IN BOTTOM

This plan provided a means of identifying openings in the ship's skin plating. The method of locating and measuring these positions vertically is neatly shown by the diagram at top centre while their position horizontally is simply measured from the nearest main water-tight bulkhead. The largest openings shown are those for the intakes and discharges of the main condensers, and that for the Asdic dome. The magazines were the only compartments fitted with flood valves, but other compartments could be flooded via the fire main, the exception in the case of the magazines resulting from the requirement for rapid flooding. There are various small sea connections for auxiliary machines dealing with salt water or using it for cooling purposes. The storm drains discharging just above the waterline mainly served scuppers on the Upper Deck and the bathroom and soil pipe drains. These were fitted with valves that closed the pipes if the sea level rose above their outlets. The drains direct from the scuppers at Forecastle Deck level or from platforms above this were not fitted with valves since, in the unlikely event of any back flooding, a limited amount of water would be discharged onto the weather decks. The drain holes close to the keel served to clear water from compartments when in dry dock. Other openings include the outlets of the bilge ejectors, just below the Upper Deck over the length of the machinery spaces, and that for the Chernikeef log just forward of Frame 75 near the keel line. (M1809)

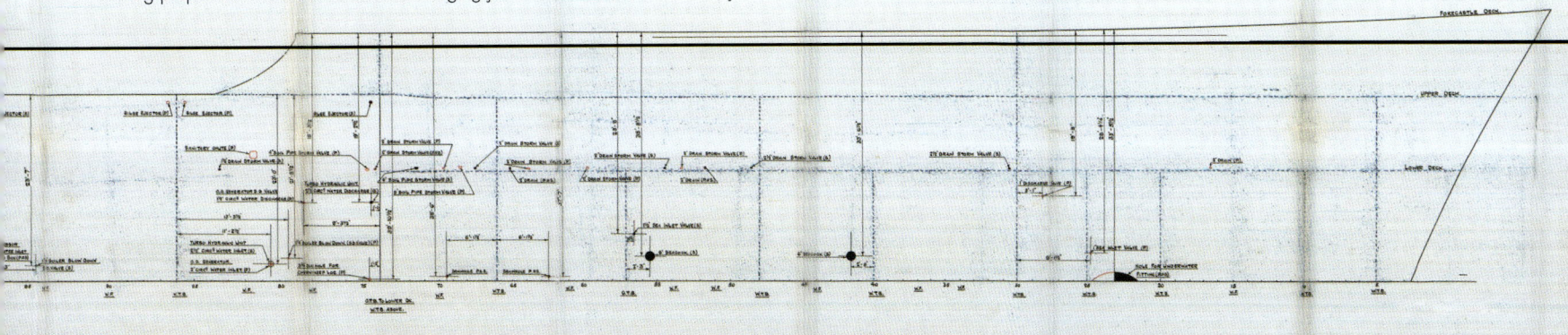

HMS *Ashanti*: TWIN BARREL STEAM CAPSTAN

This combined capstan and cable holder was the standard type employed in the majority of British destroyers from the 'D' class of the 1930 Programme onward. It consisted of a horizontal steam piston engine driving two vertical spindles via a worm and worm wheel drive. Above each worm wheel was the cable holder, for the anchor chains, and above that a capstan for working wire cables or hawsers. The worm wheel and cable holder were keyed to the drive shaft and rotated with it but the cable holder was driven by dogs around the base of the capstan barrel. The capstan could be moved vertically, and the dogs disengaged, using the hand wheel on the top of the capstan to raise the barrel via a screw thread at the top of the drive spindle. This left the cable holder free to rotate with its brake disengaged. This arrangement allowed the capstan to be operated independently of the cable holder and for the anchors to be let go by the freely rotating cable holder.
(M1813)

1. **The worm wheel.**
2. **The band brake** and brake drum of the cable holder.
3. **The cable holders.**
4. **The capstan barrels.**
5. **Capstan lifting hand wheels.**
6. **Threaded section at top of drive shaft** via which the capstan could be lifted clear of the cable holder. There is a threaded nut fixed to the inside of the hand wheel.
7. **Shaft keys** preventing the capstan and worm wheel rotating on their shaft.
8. **Casing of steam engine.**
9. **Steam engine operating handles.** That in the centre provided forward/reverse control; the second handle (which could be fitted to either side) controlled the steam supply and exhaust valves. These were removed and stowed when the machinery was not in use.
10. **Cable holder brake-operating wheels.**
11. **Worm and drive shaft from steam engine.**
12. **Steam engine cylinder heads.**
13. **Steam engine crank.**

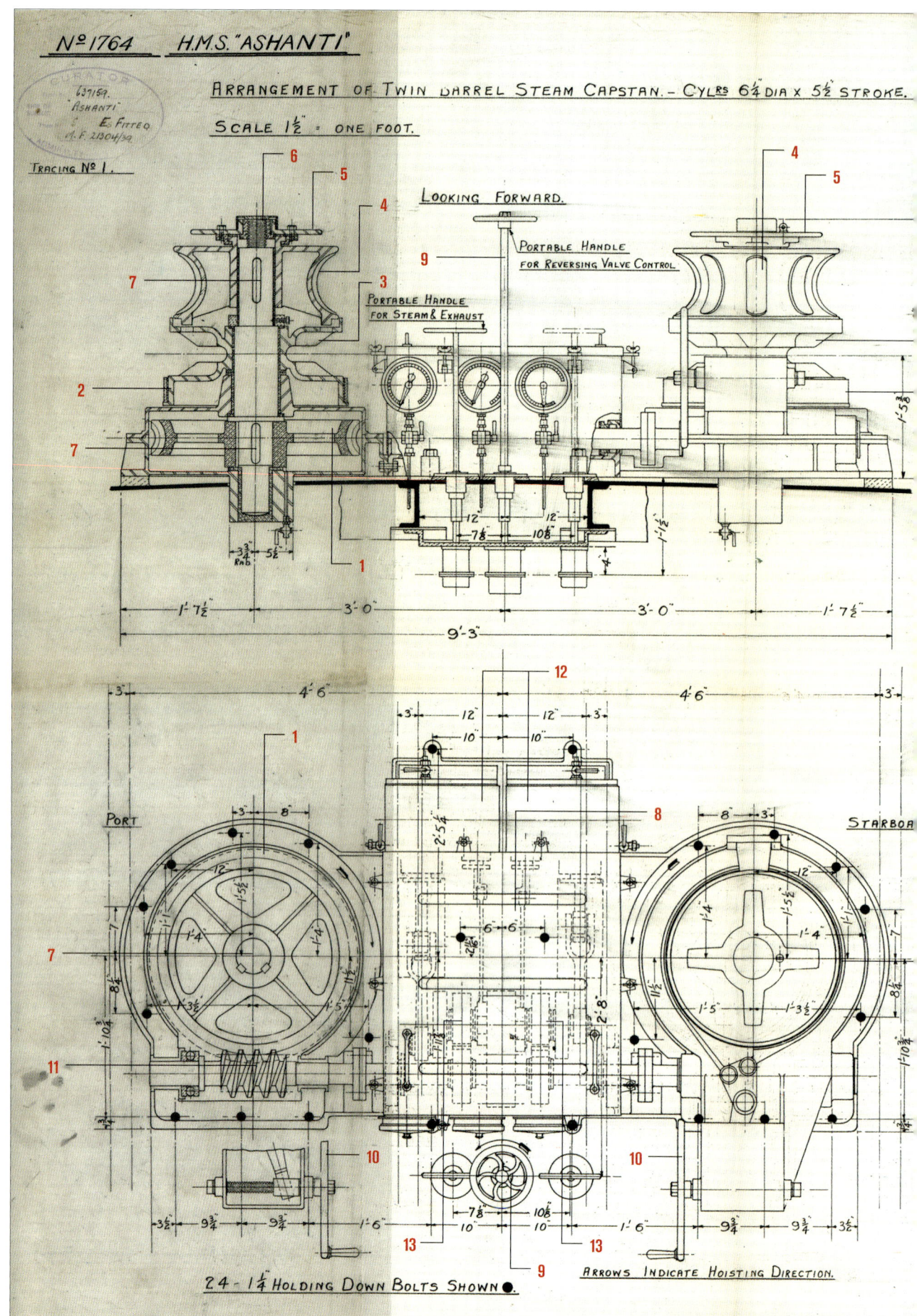

HMS ASHANTI: TWIN BARREL STEAM CAPSTAN

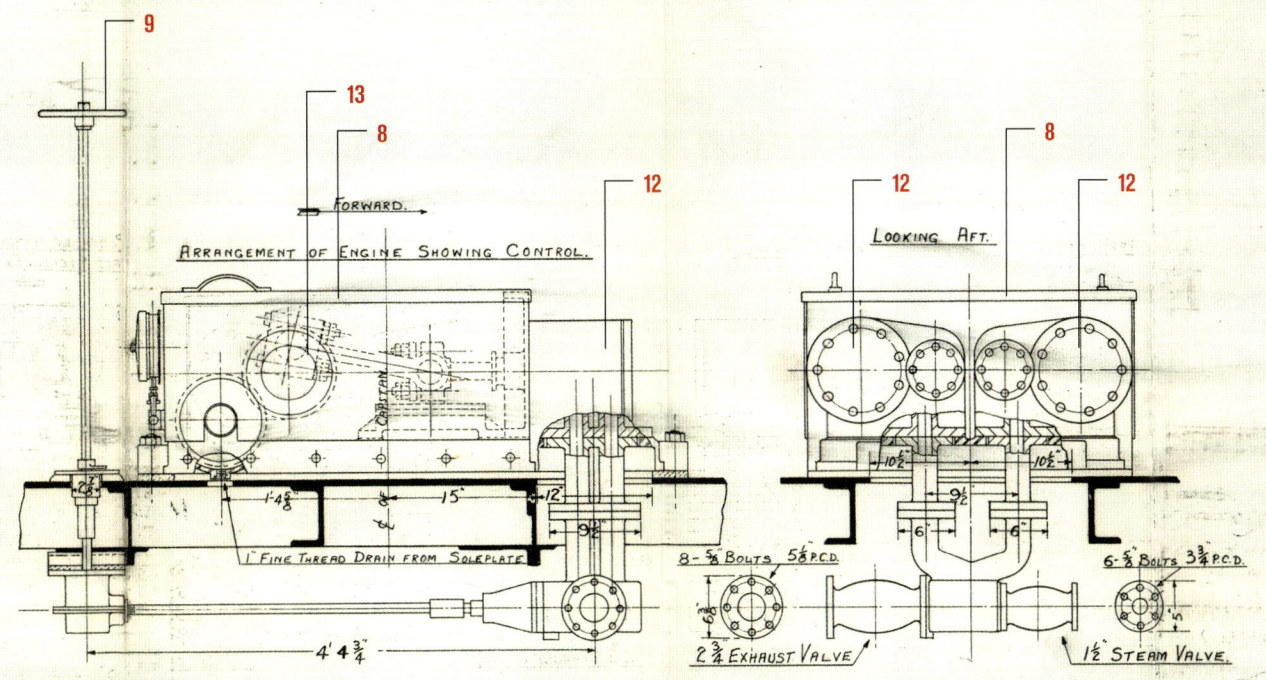

Thos. Reid & Sons (Paisley) Ltd, Paisley.

Arrangement of Engine Showing Control. — Looking Aft.

2¾" Exhaust Valve. — 1½" Steam Valve.

Cablelifter for 1⅜" Stud Link Cable
Warping Barrel 16" dia. for 4" circ. Wire Rope

Duty on Test:-
To Pull 13 Tons at 30 ft/min. from Cablelifter.
To Haul Slack Cable at 40 ft/min.
Steam Pressure 225 lbs/☐" at Cylinders.
Back Pressure 25 lbs/☐"
Boiler Pressure 300 lbs/☐"
Engine Speed 303 R.P.M. Full Load: 404 R.P.M. Slack Cable.
Engine & Gear to be Capable of Exerting a Pull = 24 Tons
Engine & Gear to be Incapable of Exerting a Pull Exceeding 29 Tons.

List of Materials.

Material	Components	Supplier
Cast Iron	Cylinders, Piston Valves, Piston Rings.	Henry & Galt, Paisley.
Cast Steel	Cablelifters, Capstan Barrels, Engine Soleplate, Worm Gearboxes & Brake Brackets, Control Brackets, Control Chest, Steam Branches, Capstan Hand Wheels.	Renton & Fisher, Bathgate.
Gunmetal	All Bushes, Glands, Compression Nuts, Eccentric Straps, Liners in Barrels, Reversing Valve & Chest, Mitres, Stop Valves.	Gray & Caldwell, Paisley.
Forged Steel	Capstan Spindles, Worm Shafts, Crankshaft, Crank Discs, Eccentrics, Pistons, Piston Rods, Piston Valve Rods, Connecting & Eccentric Rods, Brake Bands, Brake Levers, Brake Control Screws, Chain Redders, Spur Wheels, Collars.	Fife Forge Co. Ltd. Kirkcaldy.
Phos. Bronze	Worm Wheels.	Gray & Caldwell, Paisley.

Table of Weights.

	Tons.	Cwts.	Qrs.
Weight of Capstan	4	4	0
Weight of Spares	—	2	1
Total Weight	4	6	1

List of Spare Gear.

One Complete Set
- Brasses for Worm Shaft Bearing.
- Brasses for Worm Shaft Thrust Bearing.
- Brasses for Crank & Intermediate Shafts.
- Ball Thrust Bearing
- Brake Lining with Rivets Complete for one Brake.
- 1 Set Gland & Neck Bushes for Piston & Piston Valve Rods.
- 1 Connecting Rod Complete with Brasses & Bolts.
- Connecting Rod Brasses, Bolts, Nuts & Pin, Complete for one Rod in Addition to Above.
- 1 Eccentric Rod & Strap with Bolts, Nuts & Pin Complete.
- 1 Piston Rod with Slipper, Crosshead, Brasses, Bolts, Nuts & Pins Complete.
- 4 Piston Rings
- 1 Piston Valve Rod with Nuts Complete
- 2 Piston Valves
- 1 Control Valve
- 1 Complete Set Asbestos Packing for All Glands.
- Packing for Gland on Intermediate Shaft.
- 1 Set of Tools for Withdrawing Packing
- 1 Set of Tools for All Nuts, Mounted on Tool Rack.

HMS COSSACK: ENLARGED PROFILE AND SECTIONS, AS FITTED 1938

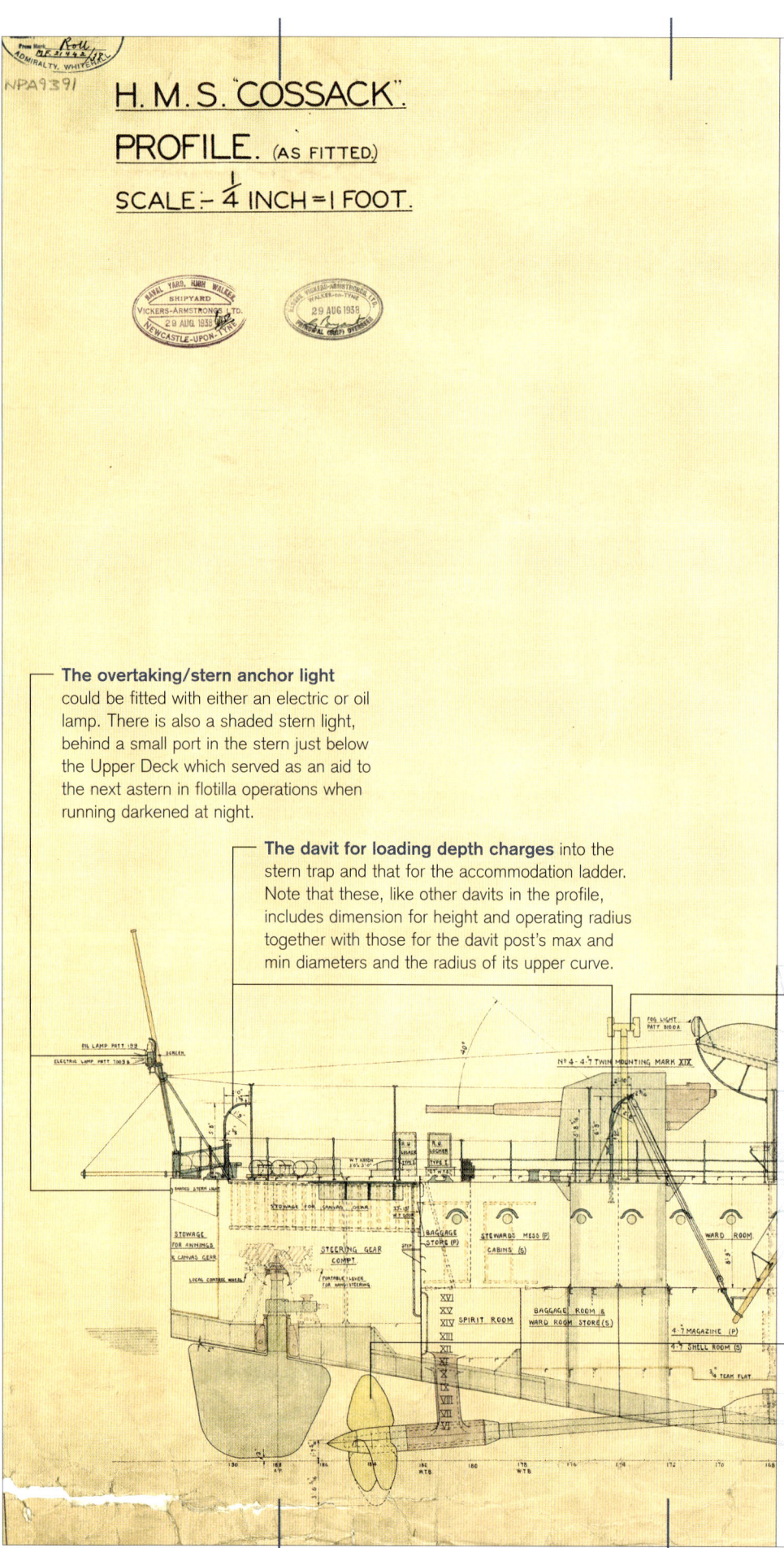

FRAME 188 **FRAME 172**

The overtaking/stern anchor light could be fitted with either an electric or oil lamp. There is also a shaded stern light, behind a small port in the stern just below the Upper Deck which served as an aid to the next astern in flotilla operations when running darkened at night.

The davit for loading depth charges into the stern trap and that for the accommodation ladder. Note that these, like other davits in the profile, includes dimension for height and operating radius together with those for the davit post's max and min diameters and the radius of its upper curve.

STERN TO FRAME 172

This detail of the main profile, and those on the following pages, are extracted from the as-fitted profile (M1801), shown in full in the gatefold (pages 35–38). They are accompanied by the relevant as-fitted sections for *Cossack* (M1806) plus two from the sections for *Mohawk* (M1843) in positions not covered by the *Cossack* set. In the latter case there would be little, if any, differences between the two ships, although the plans themselves differ, principally in the amount and clarity of the detail included.

Internal detail in the profile is shown as if the ship were cut down the centre, items to port being shown in dashed line while those which straddle the middle line are shown in full. This detail is, however, primarily concentrated on machinery and in other cases is mostly limited to doors, deck scuttles ladders and bulkheads. Above the weather decks dashed lines also serve to represent items to starboard that are hidden behind side screen, etc.

Along the keel line at least every other station (frames and bulkheads) is numbered. The majority of the main water-tight bulkheads extend from the keel to the Upper Deck but those at Frames 48, 30 and 10 extend to the Forecastle Deck and those at Frames 165 and 178 only to the Lower Deck. There is also a short bulkhead at Frame 25 between keel and the flat but this only served as a wt enclosure to one of the fresh water tanks. Note that the bulkhead at Frame 174 is not marked WTB although it is in the plan views. It is not in fact water-tight within N°3 4.7in magazine.

The funnel for the wardroom stove. As with all other stove funnels, the part above deck was portable since, in all but cooking stoves, it would only be required in cold weather. It was also necessary to remove these if they were in the way of any deck activity or in case of clearing for action.

The propellers, manufactured by Stones of Deptford, were three bladed, 10ft 3in in diameter and 13ft 1in pitch and had a blade area of 70ft^2 (expanded = total area of blades) and 59ft^2 (projected = total area of blades when viewed along axis of propeller).

STERN TO FRAME 172

SECTION AT FRAME 188, LOOKING AFT

The section of *Mohawk* is taken at the after perpendicular (the axis of the rudder stock) and, like all those that follow, shows the full width of the ship – standard for the as-fitted plans of destroyers and small ships and unlike those of larger ships which were normally limited to half sections.

SECTION AT FRAME 172, LOOKING AFT

This section looking toward the bulkhead at 174 Station passes through the wardroom and the shell rooms and magazine of Nº3 4.7in mounting. Note the arched opening in the bulkhead which gave access to the after section of the magazine – with the exception of the magazine space the bulkhead was water-tight.

The spaces around the steering gear were used for the storage of canvas, awnings, deck fittings, etc and some of the central stores. Visible here are a wood framed storage space to starboard, a bin for cowl vents to port and above that a shelf for rubber matting.

A shade across the back of the anchor light is represented by this rectangle. A similar rectangle is fitted near the heel of the ensign staff but its purpose is unclear as there is no evidence of a light being fitted in this position

The depth charge davit shown in broken line is the alternative position for that shown to starboard.

The towing slip – the actual slip is viewed side on.

The electric power units for the hydraulic steering gear.

A steel casting provided the main support and bearing for the rudder. It extended one frame space fore and aft of the rudder axis and between the 1st longitudinals to port and starboard.

The settees in the wardroom, one along the full length of the starboard side and a second wrapped around the cylindrical support of the 4.7in mounting above.

The ESSE Vista coal stove showing the full length of the funnel mentioned on the previous page. ESSE, the company that made the stove, was founded in 1854 and is still trading (2020).

This side view of the bottle racks for the 4.7in cartridges is about the only detail worthy of note in either this magazine or the shell room next to it.

The storage cupboards against the after bulkhead include one for pistols (at the top) and one for compasses, together with a bookcase and two telescope drawers. The cupboard to port has no designation so presumably served for general storage.

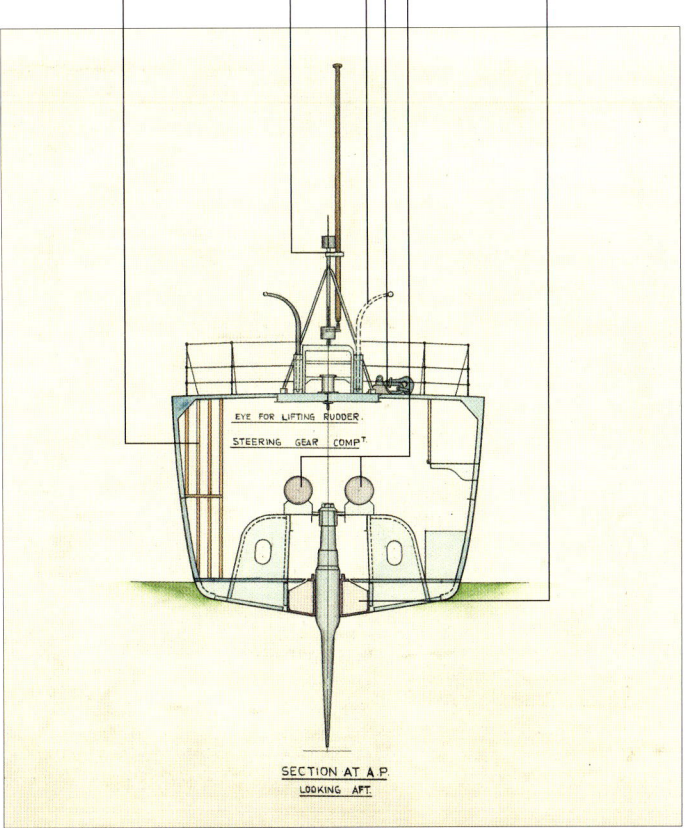

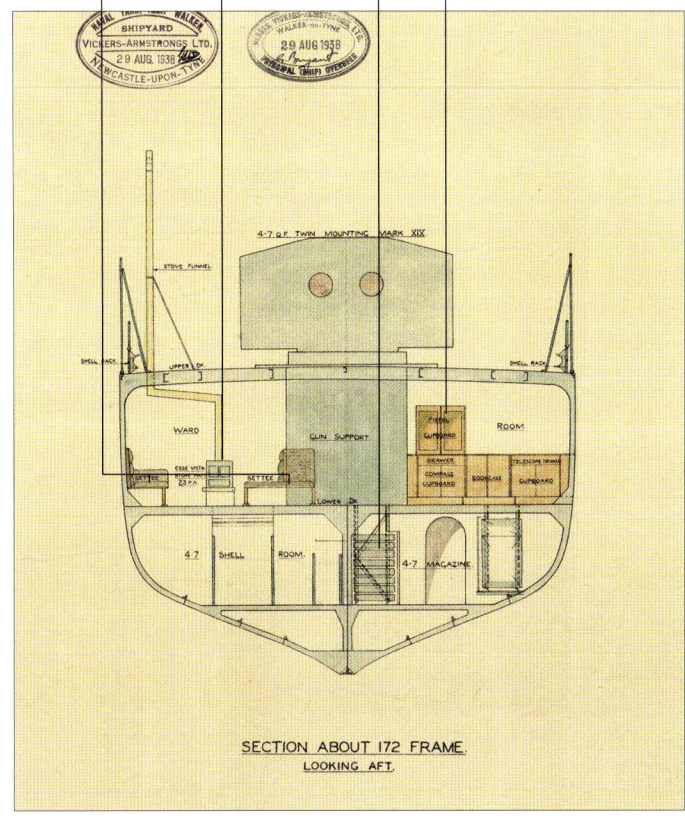

HMS COSSACK: ENLARGED PROFILE AND SECTIONS, AS FITTED 1938

FRAMES 172 TO 155

The twin 4.7in mounting was referred to at the design stage as HA/LA but its limited HA capability soon resulted in the mounting being regarded as primarily a LA weapon. The demand for improved AA self-defence for destroyers led to Nº3 4.7in mounting in the 'Tribal' class being replaced by a modern twin 4in HA/LA mounting. This gave the 'Tribal's some advantage over other pre-war destroyers, which were usually upgraded with a single 4in mounting of old design which had greater limits to its arcs of fire as a result of being positioned as a replacement for the after torpedo-tube mounting. The particulars of the twin 4in are given in the table on the following page.

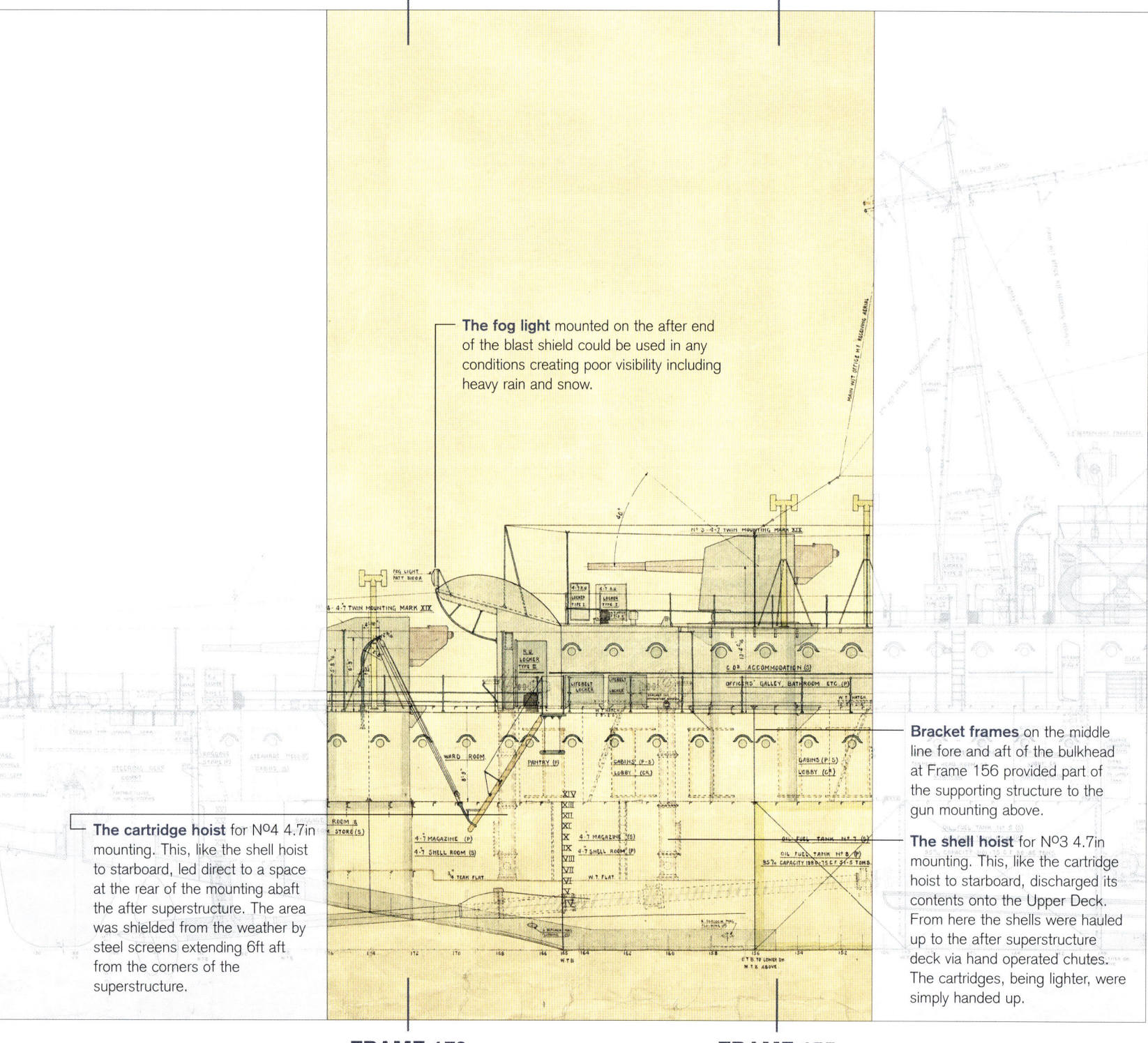

The fog light mounted on the after end of the blast shield could be used in any conditions creating poor visibility including heavy rain and snow.

The cartridge hoist for Nº4 4.7in mounting. This, like the shell hoist to starboard, led direct to a space at the rear of the mounting abaft the after superstructure. The area was shielded from the weather by steel screens extending 6ft aft from the corners of the superstructure.

Bracket frames on the middle line fore and aft of the bulkhead at Frame 156 provided part of the supporting structure to the gun mounting above.

The shell hoist for Nº3 4.7in mounting. This, like the cartridge hoist to starboard, discharged its contents onto the Upper Deck. From here the shells were hauled up to the after superstructure deck via hand operated chutes. The cartridges, being lighter, were simply handed up.

FRAME 172   **FRAME 155**

SECTION AT FRAME 155, LOOKING AFT

This section is one frame forward of the main bulkhead at 156 Station and shows the furniture at the after end of the cabins on the Lower Deck and the aftermost fuel oil tanks in the Hold. In the after superstructure there are cabin bulkheads at Frame 155 but these have been omitted in favour of a view of the spaces beyond them – the Captain's sleeping cabin to starboard and a lobby to port. Note that the Captain was the only officer provided with personal accommodation above the Lower Deck. The apparent centreline division between the Lower and Upper Decks is not a middle line bulkhead but a plate frame extending two frame spaces forward of the main bulkhead which, together with a matching frame aft of the bulkhead, provided additional support to the 4.7in mounting above. These fore and aft frames are shown in the profile (opposite) but not in the plan views.

4-inch/45cal QF/SA Mk XVI and XVI* Guns on Twin HA/LA Mk XIX CP Mounting

Weight of gun and BM:	2.01 tons (unloaded)
Weight of BM:	336lbs
Diameter of bore:	4in
Length of gun (incl breech-ring):	190.5in
Length of bore:	180in (45cal)
Length of rifling:	149.52in
Rifling:	32 grooves, uniform RH twist, 1 turn in 30cal
Weight of shell:	35lbs
Weight of charge:	9lbs (Cordite SC)
Total weight of fixed ammunition:	63lbs 8oz
Muzzle velocity:	2650fps
Maximum range at 45°:	19,850yds
Maximum height at 80°:	39,000ft
Weight of mounting (including guns):	16.55 tons
Working recoil:	15in
Elevation/depression:	+80°/-10°
Max rate of fire:	20rpg/min

Notes:
Figures above apply to the original hand-operated mounting. Later modifications, included power operation, resulted in increases in the weight of both the mounting and ammunition

A 10lbs 8oz flashless charge was also employed, the weight of the cartridge increasing in line with that of the charge.

The CO's sleeping cabin showing the end of his bedstead, an item unique to the Captain since other officers had bedberths (more commonly referred to as 'bunks') or, for the more senior officers (1st and 2nd Lieutenants and the senior engineer), bed settees to provide additional seating.

The 2nd Lieutenant's cabin showing his bed settee, wardrobes, wash basin and electric radiator. He also had a kneehole writing desk, a chest of drawers, a book rack, shelf space, a towel rail and a fan, which was essentially the basic outfit for all officers.

Steel oil-tight tubes passed through the after oil-fuel tanks to provide a passage for the ship's propeller shafts (the tubes are not shown in the profile). The bulkheads outboard of the tubes are non-watertight wash bulkheads to slow the flow of oil across the ship when rolling. The 2ft gap at the bottom of these bulkheads was, however, omitted over the length of the oil-tight vertical trunks that gave access the shaft plummer blocks in these compartments (see plan view on page 118).

The air intake in the side of the after superstructure for N°5, 12½in supply fan which ventilated the officer cabins on the Lower Deck between Frames 156 and 182.

The gunner's cabin showing his wardrobe, kneehole writing table and bedberth – the latter in section revealing three sliding storage trays in its base. The small, blue rectangle just inboard of the bedberth is an electric radiator. The shelf above the wardrobe accommodated a bookcase and a ledger rack which are not shown here but are in the plan view (page 114). Note that the cupboard for bedding is in the lobby outside this cabin.

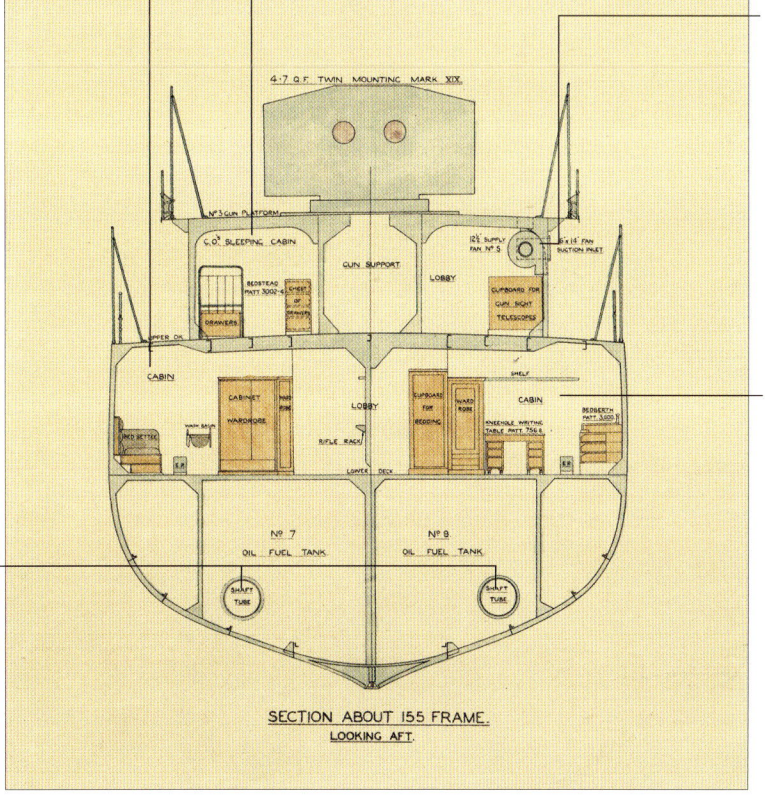

FRAMES 155 TO 138

The height of the mainmast above the 9ft lwl was approximately 68ft. Its primary function was to carry the after 18ft W/T yard, which in turn supported the after ends of the main W/T roof aerials and the vertically arranged receiving aerials of both the main and 2nd W/T offices. The aft end of the 2nd office W/T transmitting aerial was supported by a wire fitted to the mainmast just below the upper brace of the tripod. The aerials were insulated from their supporting rig, and from each other if two aerials occupied the same run of wire, by porcelain insulators (represented on the drawing by short dark lines with a small circle at each end). An example of the latter is the transmitting aerial of the 2nd W/T office which at its forward end is connected, via two insulators, to the after end of the auxiliary aerial of the main W/T office. The only other item of note on the mainmast is the gaff projecting aft at 45° to the horizontal with its heel just below the W/T yard. This served as an alternative position for the White Ensign which normally flew from the ensign staff at the after end of the Upper Deck. This alternative location was employed in peacetime in bad weather or during gunnery practice but in war it became the primary location for the ensign.

This spur, was fitted with a block for a flag halyard and was possibly a quick alternative to using the gaff for ceremonial purposes (flying the flags of visiting flag officers or dignitaries) or simply an alternative position from the foremast for signal flags.

This Jacob's ladder, shown in side-view, has it lower end fixed to a bar fitted between mainmast struts, just above the Type II ready-use locker. Access from the Superstructure Deck was provided by another Jacob's ladder at the port side of the bar (not shown). The main ladder terminates at the top of the struts. In *Mohawk*, and probably others of the class, the main ladder goes straight down to the deck.

Stove funnels for the ESSE Vista heating stove in the Captain's day cabin and, forward of that, for the cooking stove on the officers galley. Only the wardroom and the Captain were provided with ESSE stoves. The latter is located to starboard and that for the galley to port.

The 24in Searchlight Platform also provided the emergency steering and secondary fire control positions.

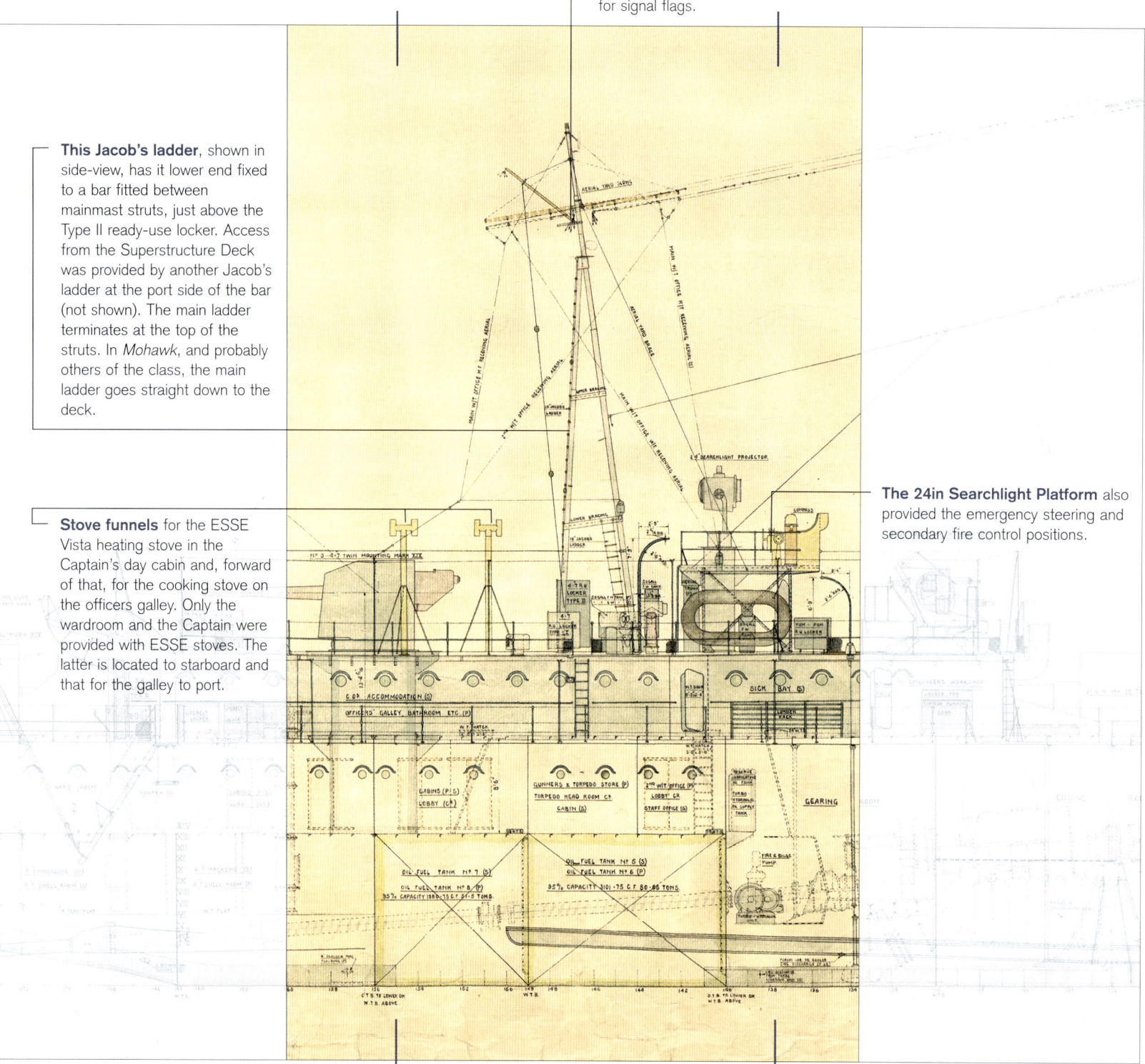

FRAME 155　　　　　　　　**FRAME 138**

FRAMES 155 TO 138

SECTION AT FRAME 138, LOOKING AFT

This section (shown in greater detail on page 82) is looking toward the after bulkhead of the gearing room from a position two frame spaces forward. The two lubricating oil drain tanks supplied oil to turbine-driven forced-lubrication pumps, one mounted on top of each tank. Via oil filters and coolers, these pumps supplied oil under pressure to the bearings of the turbines and reduction gears. The oil was then recycled back to the drain tank. Although there were cross connections between the pumps and tanks, they normally operated as independent units for each turbine group. There was also a small back-up forced-lubrication pump driven by an electric motor which started automatically if the turbine pumps stopped working. Auxiliary machines were lubricated by integral pumps or oil boxes and shaft bearings and thrust blocks simply ran in a bath of oil. These were maintained by regular checks on oil levels and topping-up as necessary.

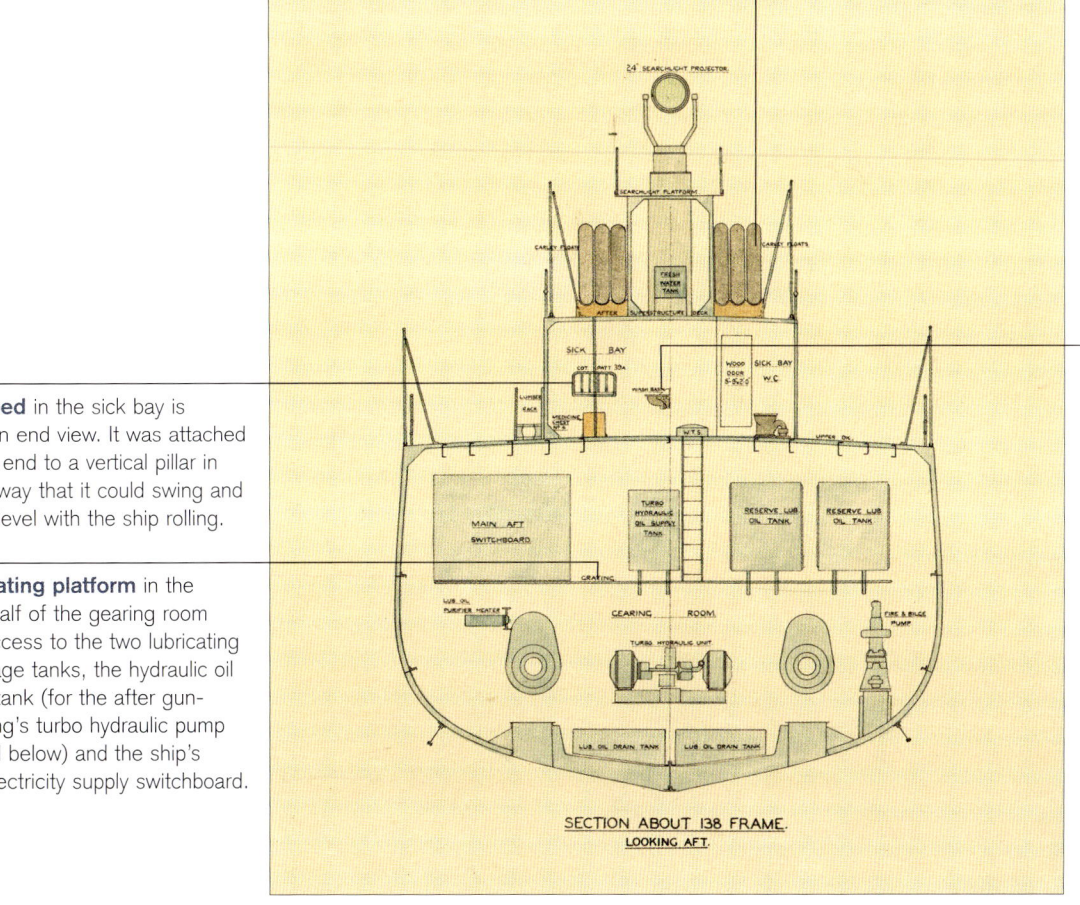

Pattern 20 Carley floats (10ft x 8ft with 15in diameter floats) of which eight were carried at the time of completion – six here, abreast the supports of the searchlight platform, and one on each side of the forward deckhouse below the wings of the Flag Deck.

This wash basin in the sick bay appears to be floating in space against a rather faint centre line but is in fact fitted to a middle line bulkhead between the Upper and Superstructure Decks.

A cot bed in the sick bay is shown in end view. It was attached at each end to a vertical pillar in such a way that it could swing and remain level with the ship rolling.

The grating platform in the upper half of the gearing room gave access to the two lubricating oil storage tanks, the hydraulic oil supply tank (for the after gun-mounting's turbo hydraulic pump situated below) and the ship's main electricity supply switchboard.

FRAMES 138 TO 118

Design consideration of blast from the after 4.7in guns, limited space and W/T range resulted in the not entirely ideal placing of the quad pom-pom mounting at the fore end of the after superstructure. Here it had reasonable arcs of fire on either beam but was restricted on forward and after bearings by the masts, rig and superstructure. Although developed in the mid 1930s, the quad was a modified version of the earlier eight-barrel mounting which was designed and developed over a lengthy period in the 1920s. In many ways it was out of date by the end of the 1930s but British development of new designs of close-range AA weapons was largely brought to a standstill by the outbreak of war. The gap was filled later by adopting mountings utilising the Swedish designed 40mm Bofors and the Swiss designed 20mm Oerlikon guns with mountings for the most part either designed in the US or UK. The pom-pom did nevertheless prove of value during 1939–45 and was subject to several improvements both in its design and in its fire control equipment. The particulars of the 2pdr gun and its quad mounting as they stood in 1939 are given in the table on the following page.

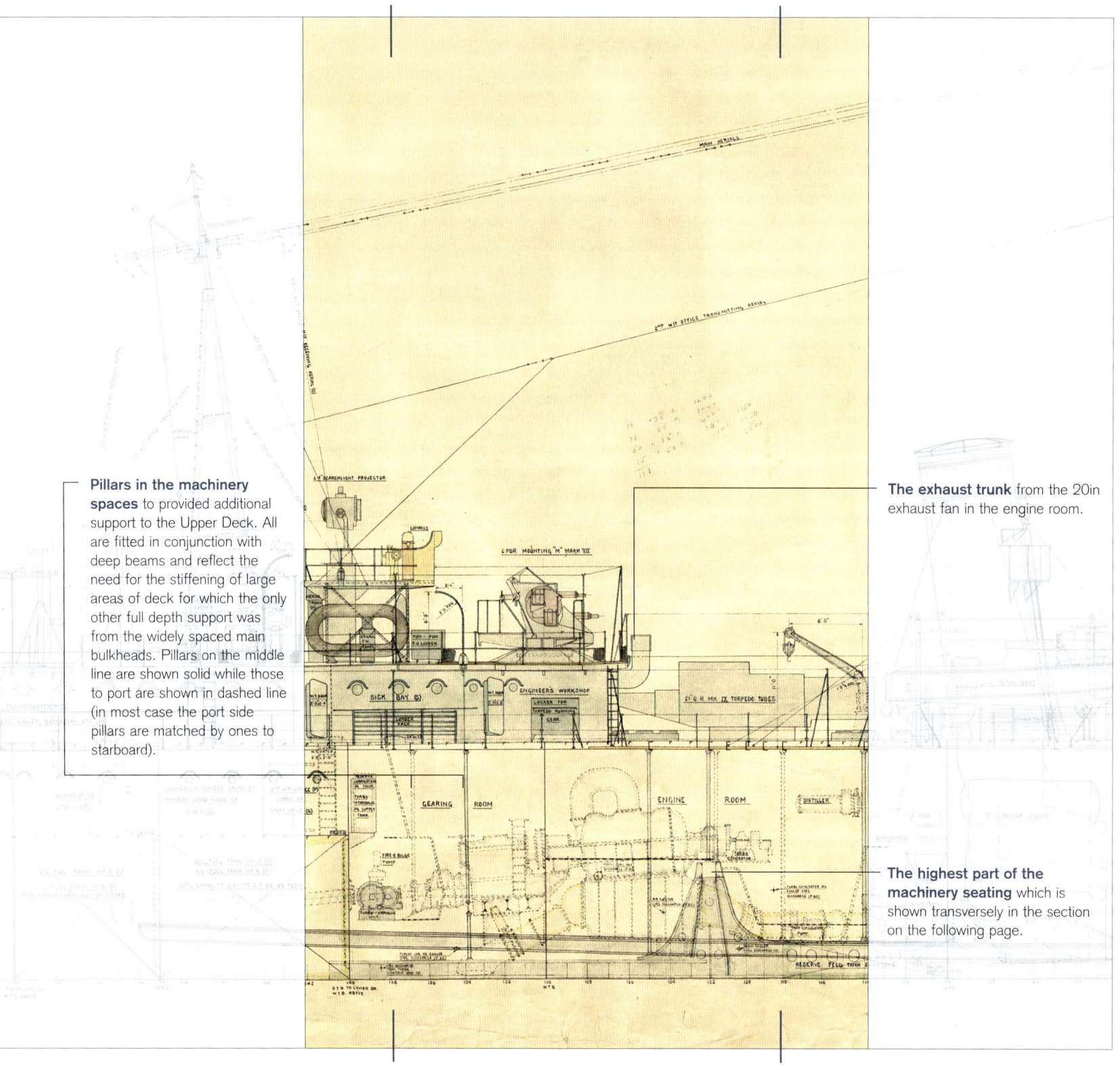

Pillars in the machinery spaces to provided additional support to the Upper Deck. All are fitted in conjunction with deep beams and reflect the need for the stiffening of large areas of deck for which the only other full depth support was from the widely spaced main bulkheads. Pillars on the middle line are shown solid while those to port are shown in dashed line (in most case the port side pillars are matched by ones to starboard).

The exhaust trunk from the 20in exhaust fan in the engine room.

The highest part of the machinery seating which is shown transversely in the section on the following page.

FRAME 138   **FRAME 118**

SECTION AT FRAME 118, LOOKING AFT

The transverse framing of the ship consisted primarily of 4in 'Z' bar frames joined to 3in x 2in angle bar deck beams by a flange bracket. To stiffen the hull form, deep frames were fitted at approximately 9ft–10ft intervals between bulkheads with occasional closer spacing where heavy weights were involved (the locations of the deep frames are indicated on the deck plating plans on pages 32–34, by the notation 'WF& deep beam' along the deck edge). Within the machinery spaces these were constructed of 7in channel bars (with a 2in reverse angle on the inboard side to form a 'T' section) joined to 10in channel bar deck beams by integral webs. The latter were constructed by splitting the 7in frames at the top and curving the inner section round to meet the lower edge of the beam, the space created being filled with a steel web. Deep webs also forming part of the machinery seating and were combined with the lower sections of the transverse framing throughout the machinery spaces. Every other beam within the machinery spaces, with some small exceptions, was reduced to a short section between the inner longitudinal deck girders (see section on page 86 showing beam at 97 Station); these were 3in x 2in angle apart from under the torpedo tubes where 10in channel was employed. The deep web frames fitted forward of the machinery were constructed of 7in channel bar frames and 6in channel bar deck beams. They did not have reverse angles on the frames. No deep frames were fitted abaft the machinery spaces but some positions both fore and aft, mainly under the gun mountings, had deep deck beams (some across the middle section only – see beam under Upper Deck in Frame 29, page 94) with web brackets but not deep frames. (The structural sections on pages 20–21 provide further detail on the dimensions and material of the framing.)

2pdr Pom-Pom Mk VIII Guns on Quadruple Mk VII Mounting

Weight of barrel:	125lbs
Diameter of bore:	40mm (1.575in)
Length of gun:	100.6in (115.6in with flame guard)
Length of bore:	62in (39.365cal)
Length of rifling:	54.84in
Rifling:	12 grooves, uniform RH twist, 1 turn in 30cal
Weight of shell:	1.836lb (HE), 2.375lbs (shot)
Weight of charge:	4.47oz
Total weight of fixed ammunition:	2.914lbs (HE), 3.434lbs (shot)
Muzzle velocity:	2300fps
Maximum effective range:	1700yds
Maximum height at 80o:	13,000ft
Weight of mounting (including guns):	8.575 tons (unloaded)
Working recoil:	7.5in
Elevation/depression:	+80°/-10°
Max rate of fire:	115rpg/min
Capacity of ammunition trays:	100 rounds each

Notes:

The mounting weight above applies to the original hand-operated mounting. Later modifications, including power operation, resulted in increases and variations in the weights of the mountings.

The weight given above for HE projectiles are for high velocity Mk I shell; later Marks and those fitted with tracer varied slightly in weight from these figures.

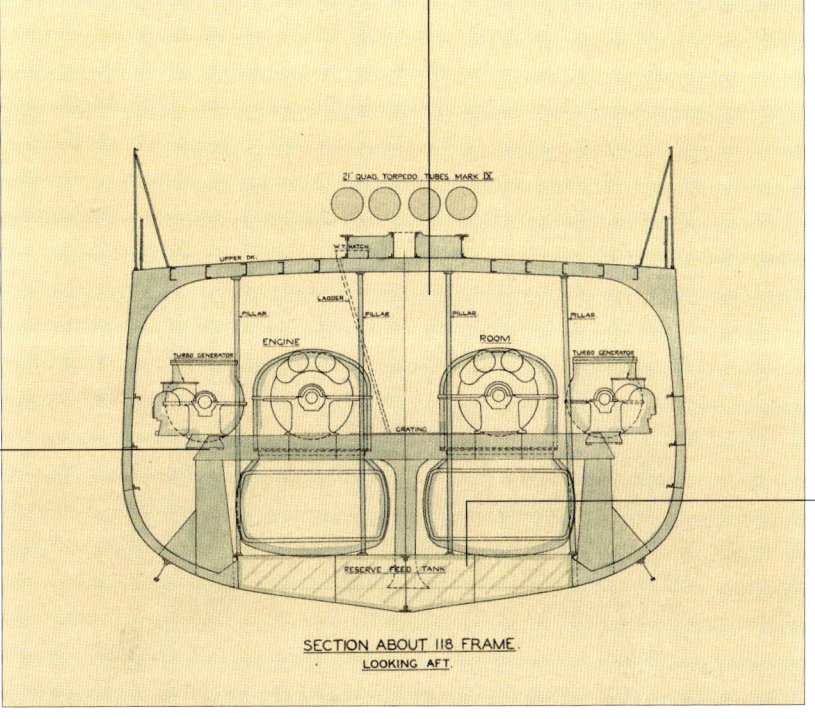

The machinery shown here can more clearly be viewed in the machinery section on page 81 which employs the same Frame number.

Part of the machinery seating, in this case supporting the forward turbine feet. These were arranged to allow the turbine casing to slide fore and aft to deal with heat expansion. The feet at the after end were firmly bolted down.

The reserve feed tank had a capacity of 25.63 tons but it is extremely unlikely that this was fully utilised given that it required some reserve capacity since it also served as the overflow tank for the main feed tank located immediately above it.

SECTION AT FRAME 98, LOOKING FORWARD

Station 98 is actually on the main bulkhead between Nº2 and Nº3 BRs but here the bulkhead has been omitted to show the after end of Nº2 BR. Above the Upper Deck the section is on Frame 98, passing through the middle of the 0.5in MG platform. The Vickers 0.5in MG, like the Vickers 0.303in MG, was a derivative of the Maxim MG which first appeared in the 1880s. Unlike its smaller calibre cousin, which enjoyed a very long and successful service with the British Army, it proved of limited value to the Navy in this configuration. The particulars of the quad 0.5in quad mounting are given in the accompanying table.

Vickers 0.5-inch Mk III Machine Guns on Quadruple Mk III mounting

Weight of gun:	56lbs (65.25lbs with water jacket full)
Diameter of bore:	0.5in
Length of gun:	52in
Length of bore:	31.11in (62.22cal)
Length of rifling:	54.84in
Rifling:	12 grooves, uniform RH twist, 1 turn in 30cal
Weight of bullet:	1.32oz
Total weight of fixed round:	2.9oz (approx)
Muzzle velocity:	2520fps (approx)
Maximum effective range:	800yds
Maximum height at 80°:	13,000ft
Weight of mounting:	1.309 tons
Recoil:	1.25in (approx.)
Elevation/depression:	+80°/-10°
Max rate of fire:	700rpg/min
Capacity of ammunition drums:	200 rounds each

Note:
Weight of mounting includes the guns (with water jackets filled) and ammunition drums.

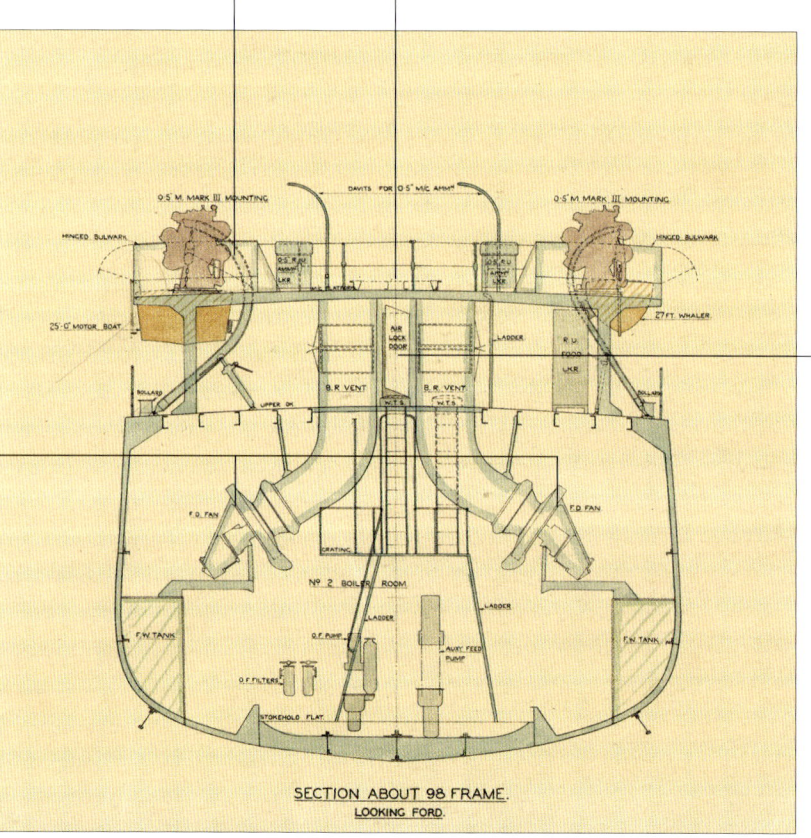

The davits on the port side are of the same design as those for the 27ft whaler on the starboard side but are more heavily constructed and of larger size to accommodate the greater weight and dimensions of the 25ft motor boat.

The circular base plate for the second quad pom-pom mounting that was never fitted despite an intention to do so

The air lock for both Nº2 and Nº3 BRs.

The forced draught turbo fans drew air from trunks above deck, in this case fitted under the 0.5in MG platform, to pressurize the BR. The pressure difference between stokehold and uptake drew air into the furnace through air ducts (which also served to heat the air).

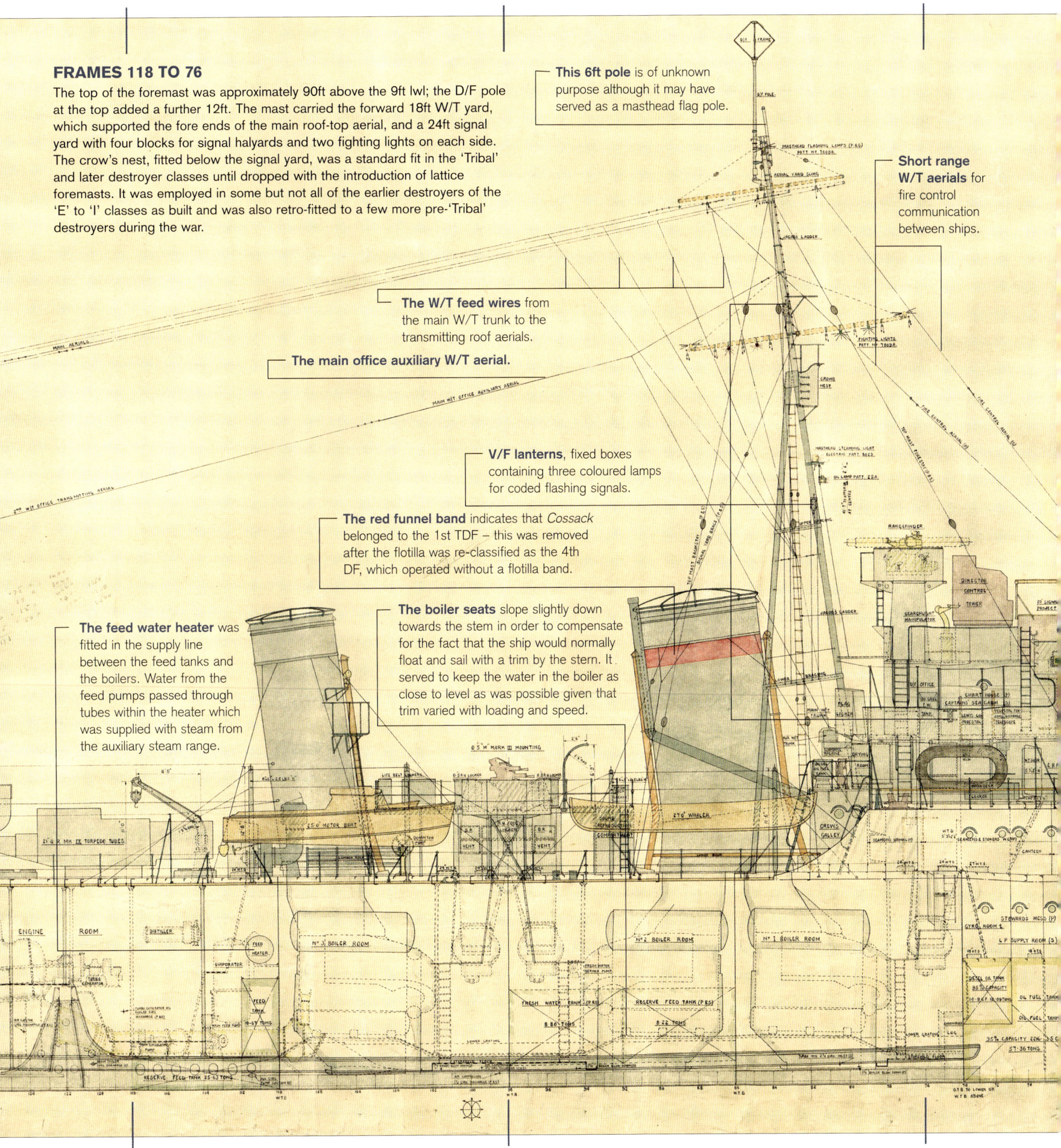

FRAMES 118 TO 76

The top of the foremast was approximately 90ft above the 9ft lwl; the D/F pole at the top added a further 12ft. The mast carried the forward 18ft W/T yard, which supported the fore ends of the main roof-top aerial, and a 24ft signal yard with four blocks for signal halyards and two fighting lights on each side. The crow's nest, fitted below the signal yard, was a standard fit in the 'Tribal' and later destroyer classes until dropped with the introduction of lattice foremasts. It was employed in some but not all of the earlier destroyers of the 'E' to 'I' classes as built and was also retro-fitted to a few more pre-'Tribal' destroyers during the war.

This 6ft pole is of unknown purpose although it may have served as a masthead flag pole.

Short range W/T aerials for fire control communication between ships.

The W/T feed wires from the main W/T trunk to the transmitting roof aerials.

The main office auxiliary W/T aerial.

V/F lanterns, fixed boxes containing three coloured lamps for coded flashing signals.

The red funnel band indicates that *Cossack* belonged to the 1st TDF – this was removed after the flotilla was re-classified as the 4th DF, which operated without a flotilla band.

The feed water heater was fitted in the supply line between the feed tanks and the boilers. Water from the feed pumps passed through tubes within the heater which was supplied with steam from the auxiliary steam range.

The boiler seats slope slightly down towards the stem in order to compensate for the fact that the ship would normally float and sail with a trim by the stern. It served to keep the water in the boiler as close to level as was possible given that trim varied with loading and speed.

FRAME 118   **FRAME 98**   **FRAME 76**

SECTION AT FRAME 76, LOOKING FORWARD

Looking toward the main bulkhead at 74 Station this view shows the main turbo fans and their supports, together with access to the stokehold floor and the two items of auxiliary machinery located in the BRs with no connection to boiler operation. The ventilation trunks have hinged flaps on their inboard faces at Forecastle Deck level. The space they open into is only accessible via a door from the drying room so it seems probable they provided air flow for that compartment. The space below this was a short passage between the BR vent trunks, only open at the fore end which gave access to the air lock for Nº1 BR via the scuttle in the Upper Deck.

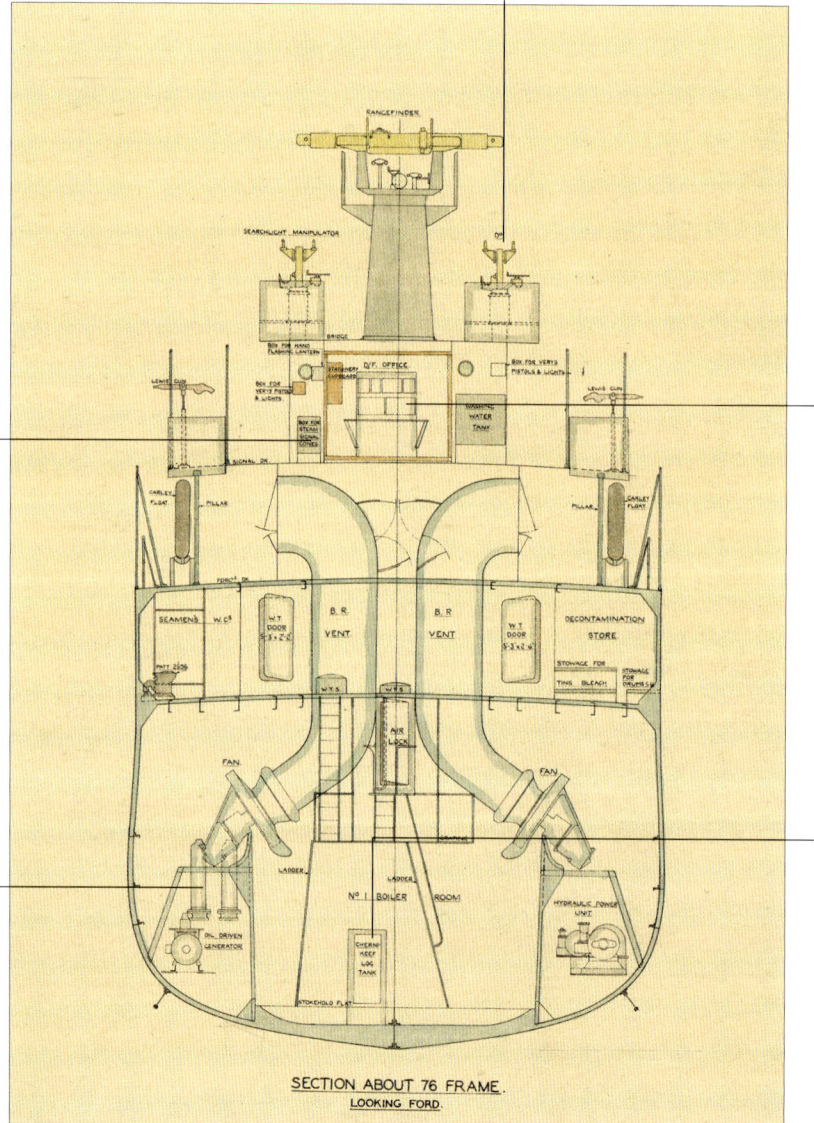

The searchlight sights remotely controlled the elevation and training of the 24in searchlight on the after superstructure.

The D/F office for the ship's FA2 set, which could operate in both MF and HF modes. Its frame aerial at the top of the foremast was either S16 or S17.

Box for steam signal cones. The cones indicated the ship's speed as either slow, moderate or fast. They were flown in combination with flag signals which defined the speed in knots.

Oil fuel heaters located against the fore bulkhead of No1 BR.

The tank for the Chernikeef log which consisted of an impeller mounted at the end of a stalk that could be lowered into the sea to measure the flow of water under the ship. This information was transferred electrically to instruments that recorded the speed and distance run. The tank contained the log and the mechanism for lowering and raising its stalk

FRAMES 76 TO 64

When the prototype 4.7in twin mounting was fitted in the destroyer *Hereward* she was also fitted with a modified bridge design in which the wheelhouse was placed forward of the bridge instead of under it. In part this was adopted to provide a higher position for the wheelhouse to give a clear view over the 4.7in mounting for the helmsman without raising the bridge as well. More importantly, since the helmsman rarely required a view ahead, the arrangement served to further limit the bridge height, in comparison with earlier destroyers, providing both a reduction in topweight and in silhouette, the latter to meet a general desire to limit a destroyer's target area and visibility. A similar bridge, which despite some misgivings about blast effects proved very popular, was also fitted in one of *Hereward*'s sisters, the *Hero*, and was adopted for all subsequent destroyers from the 'I' and 'Tribal' classes onward. It is worth noting that the bridge in the 'Tribal' class was about 2ft lower than that of the destroyers with the earlier bridge design while the increased height of the wheelhouse platform was only about 6in – in effect an overall reduction of 2ft 6in on the probable result if the wheelhouse had been fitted below the bridge.

The W/T trunks for the roof and auxiliary aerials.

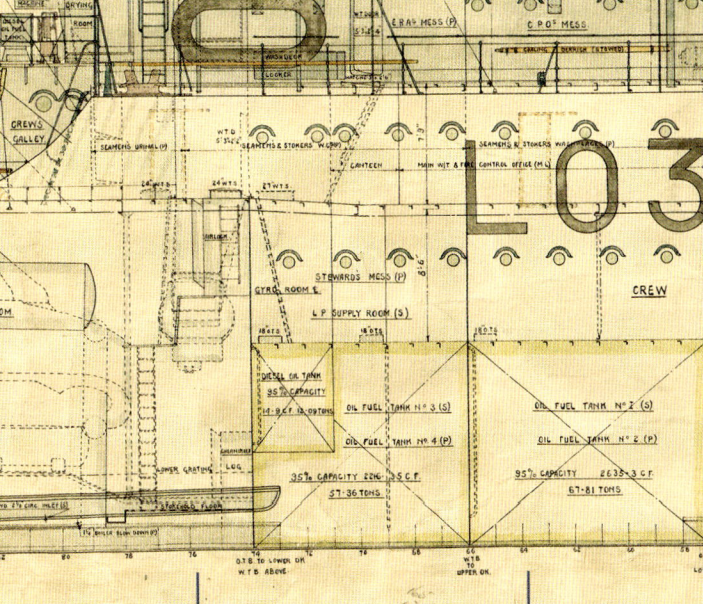

A 20in signalling projector, with a 6in signalling lantern and a semaphore forward of it, was provided on platforms projecting outboard from each side of the bridge. The platform supports served as weather screens for the sliding doors that gave access to the bridge structure.

The bridge chart table was fitted into a recess in the roof the wheelhouse. There is a 12in glass scuttle in the roof above it to provide light during the day and, without doubt, an electric light for night use.

W/T trunk for the fire-control aerials.

FRAME 76   **FRAME 64**

SECTION AT FRAME 64, LOOKING FORWARD

This view through the fore end of the bridge provides some detail of mess deck furniture, including the standard mess table with the stools and lockers that provided the seats. The CPOs' mess on the Forecastle Deck shows side views of these, complementing the end views in the Lower Deck crew spaces. Nº1 and 2 oil fuel tanks are, like the others, separated by a middle line oil-tight bulkhead (in the case of Nº3 and 4 oil tanks this bulkhead did not pass through the diesel oil tank). The wash deck bulkheads of the four forward tanks followed the pattern of those aft, including the 2ft gap in the plating at the bottom, except in not being arranged vertically,

The secondary Asdic control position located in a recess projecting into the upper part of the wheelhouse. The main control position was fitted in a silent cabinet on the Lower Deck between Frames 44 and 48.

Chart table recess, in the roof of the wheelhouse.

The view-plot trunk allowed officers on the bridge to look down at the ARL Mk VA plotting table located in the signal and plotting office below. The 'A' suffix indicated that the table was fitted with an Asdic attachment.

The door to the wheelhouse. The wheelhouse platform was about 3ft 8in high and was accessed via steps fitted just inside the door. The smaller door on the port side gave access to the space under the wheelhouse platform.

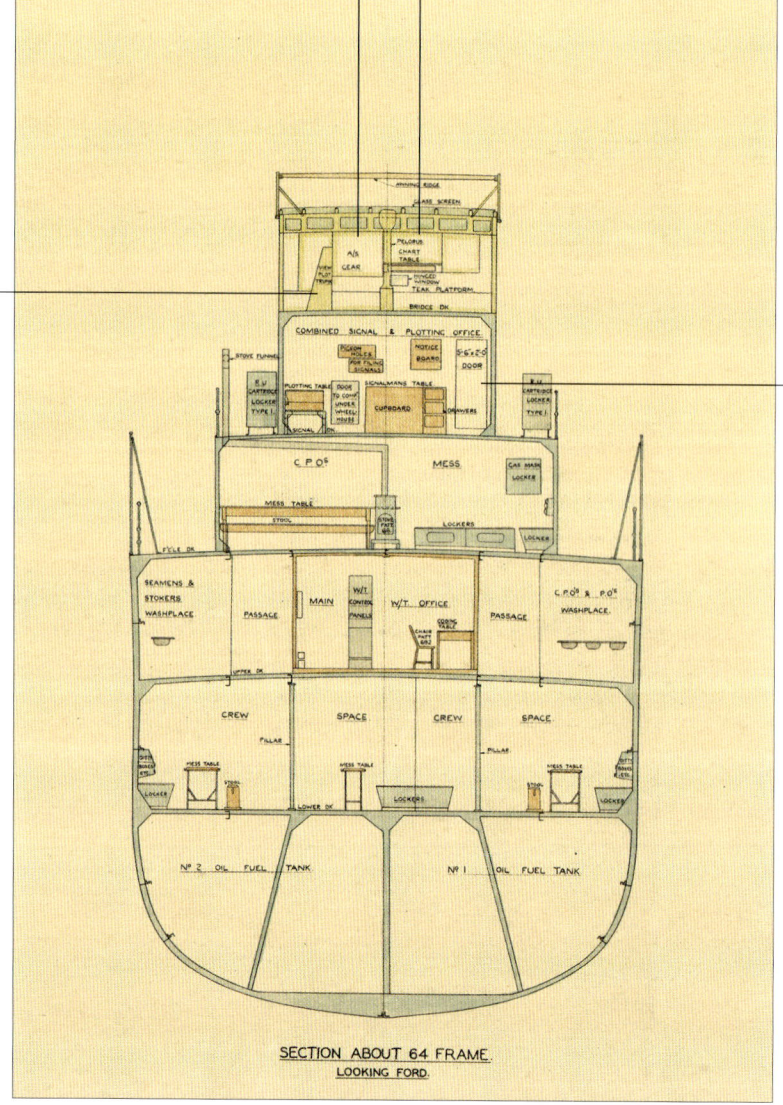

FRAMES 64 TO 46

The arrangement of guardrails was more complex than was usual in larger ships. Along the Forecastle and Upper Deck the basic version was three wire rails and fixed stanchions. Abreast the torpedo tubes the stanchions could be folded down to give a clear passage for firing, recovering or embarking and disembarking torpedoes. Abreast the 4.7in gun mountings the two lower rails were constructed of solid steel – the space below the middle rail being closed with wire catch-nets to stop ejected cartridge cases (or mishandled ammunition) from dropping over the side. In the profile the ends of the nets are shown as closely hatched dark patterns; these also coincide with the ends of the solid steel rails which are rendered in thicker lines than the wire rails. The section above the solid rails could be folded down to clear the arcs of fire of the guns. On the superstructure decks the same pattern as for those abreast the 4.7in guns was followed except that the lower steel rail was omitted and the stanchions were slightly shorter. The guardrails around the searchlight platform and the roof of the crew's galley were entirely constructed of solid steel. In *Cossack* and other ships of the class the wire netting was replaced by steel plate zarebas sometime during 1940–41.

The helmsman's window consisted of a vertically sliding glazed sash (20in high and 14in wide) with an exterior hinged cover.

This 11ft 6in coaling derrick served to embark the coal for the heating stoves in the mess decks, the Captain's day cabin and the wardroom. The coal bunker scuttle was located at the after end of the Forecastle Deck on the starboard side.

The ammunition hoists for forward guns discharged onto the deck below the mounting from whence they were passed up to the guns via a ramp (for the shell) and a hand-up (for the cartridges) in the same manner as that adopted for Nº3 mounting (see page 80).

FRAME 64

FRAME 46

SECTION AT FRAME 46, LOOKING FORWARD

To allow water run-off, the Forecastle, Upper and Superstructure Decks had a uniform camber generated by a curve based on a rise of 9ins on the middle line at the maximum width of the Upper Deck (35ft). Apart from the sheer at the fore end of the forecastle, these decks were horizontal along the middle line which, as the beam narrowed, created an upward curve along the deck edges towards the bow and stern. The Lower Deck and the flats in the Hold had no camber.

4.7-inch/45cal QF/SA Mk XII and XII* Guns on Twin Mk XIX CP Mounting

Weight of gun and BM:	3.245 tons (unloaded)
Weight of BM:	395lbs
Diameter of bore:	120mm (4.724in)
Length of gun (incl breech-ring):	224.08in
Length of bore:	212.58in (45cal)
Length of rifling:	179.2225in
Rifling:	38 grooves, uniform RH twist, 1 turn in 30cal
Weight of shell:	50lbs
Weight of charge:	11lbs 9oz (Cordite SC)
Weight of cartridge:	30lbs 5½oz
Muzzle velocity:	2650fps
Maximum range at 40°:	16,970yds
Weight of mounting (including guns):	25.49 tons
Working recoil:	26.5in
Elevation/depression:	+40°/-10°
Power training and elevation speed:	10°/sec (max)
Max rate of SA fire with power ramming:	12rpg/min

Notes:
The Mk XII and Mk XII* only differed in that the latter did not have a short step at the rear end of the 'A' tube.
The breech-ring could be fitted for either the left or right opening breech.
A 13lbs 2oz flashless charge (Cordite NFQ/S – re-designated post-war as NF/S) was also employed, initially only for star-shell. The weight of the star-shell cartridge increased in line with that of the charge.

- **The main ventilation trunks** for the mess spaces on the Upper Deck forward of 48 Bulkhead and those on the Lower Deck between Bulkheads 48 and 30.

- **The A/S office** was the main control position for the Asdic.

- **The No2 4.7in mounting.** Although it is shown at its full width, this section is actually 3ft 6in forward of the mounting's centre line. In other respects, it is an accurate representation of Frame 46 which, apart from the A/S office, is primarily occupied with mess spaces above the level of the Hold.

- **The base plates of the 4.7in mountings** required a level surface so were bolted down through a packing ring which eliminated the curve of the deck camber.

FRAMES 46 TO 29

The vertical keel, tinted in light grey, ran from the bulkhead at Frame 10 to the stern. Within the oil fuel tanks the vertical keel was integrated with the middle line bulkheads of those compartments, forming in effect their lower strake. This is indicated on the profile by continuing the light grey tint over the entire area of the bulkheads. The one-frame overlap of the keel plate at the ends of the oil tanks probably indicated the continuation of the angle bars at the top of the keel which did not continue further into the tanks. The lower strake of the bulkhead was 22in wide while the standard vertical keel was 20in wide. Other exceptions to the latter are the deepening of the keel around the steering gear and within the RFW tank and under the turbine supports in the engine room.

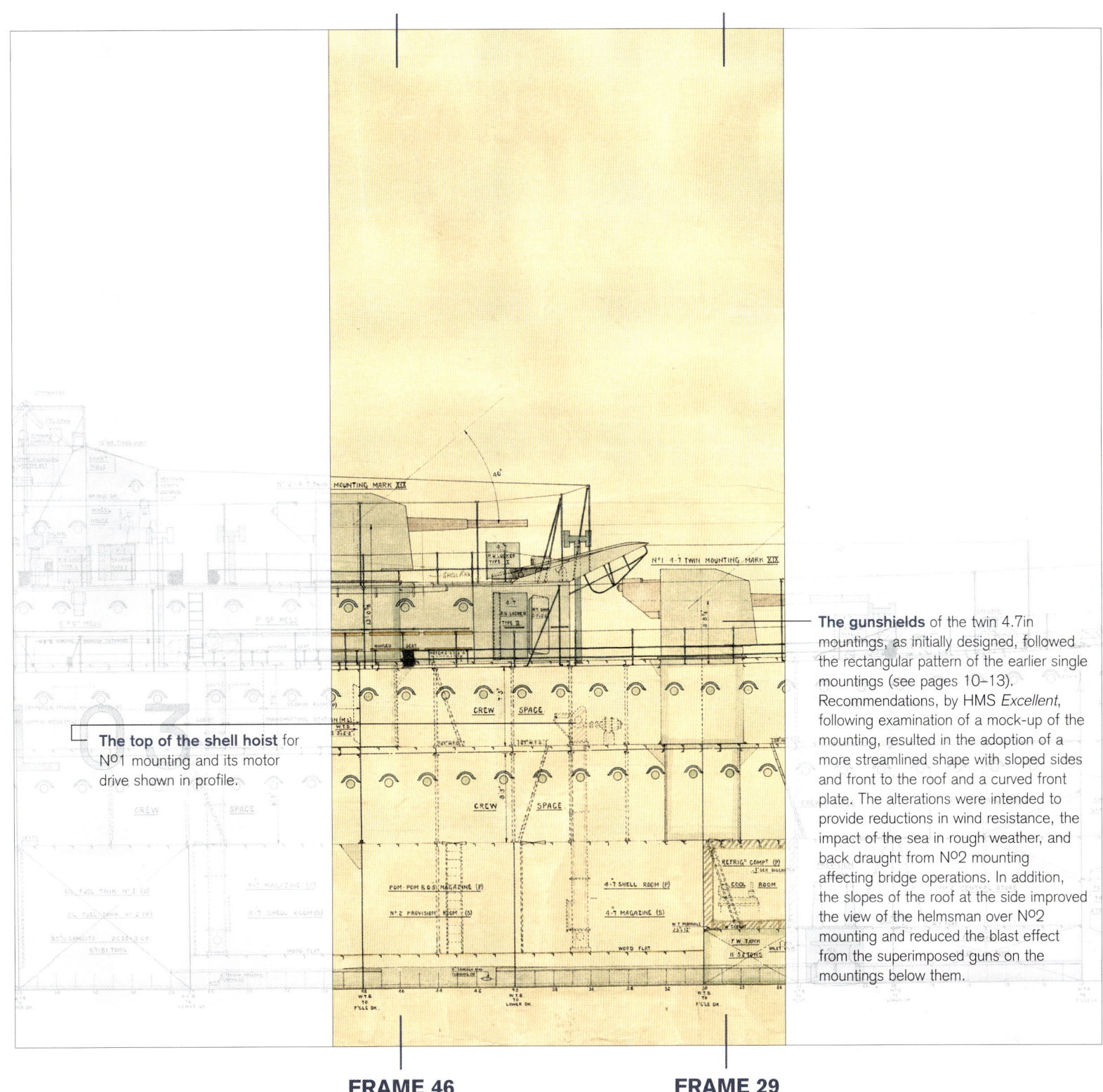

The top of the shell hoist for Nº1 mounting and its motor drive shown in profile.

The gunshields of the twin 4.7in mountings, as initially designed, followed the rectangular pattern of the earlier single mountings (see pages 10–13). Recommendations, by HMS *Excellent*, following examination of a mock-up of the mounting, resulted in the adoption of a more streamlined shape with sloped sides and front to the roof and a curved front plate. The alterations were intended to provide reductions in wind resistance, the impact of the sea in rough weather, and back draught from Nº2 mounting affecting bridge operations. In addition, the slopes of the roof at the side improved the view of the helmsman over Nº2 mounting and reduced the blast effect from the superimposed guns on the mountings below them.

FRAME 46   **FRAME 29**

SECTION AT FRAME 29, LOOKING FORWARD

This is the last of the forward sections provided in the as-fitted plans for *Cossack*. It is taken one frame space forward of the centre of the foremost 4.7in mounting. It serves to illustrate typical variations in the arrangement of deep beams to support the weight of the gun mountings. The primary support in this case is the tube between the Forecastle and Upper Decks and below that the bulkhead at 30 Station. Frame 29 has a deep beam below the forecastle from the support tube to the side of the ship where it is attached to the frames by web brackets. Below the Upper Deck there is a deep beam limited to the central section. These beams were designated as 'partial plate beams' as they were constructed from flat plates with angle bar edges rather than channel. At 28 Station 'full plate beams' were fitted, extending over the full width of the ship, the arrangement otherwise being the same as at 29 Station. Note that there is a middle line plate frame extending forward two frame spaces from 30 Bulkhead; that the beams under the Lower Deck for a distance of 4ft 6in on either side of the middle line are constructed of channel bar with a reverse angle at the top; and that the side frames are standard 4in 'Z' bar. This arrangement was mirrored in the two frames abaft Bulkhead 30.

SECTION AT FRAME 15, LOOKING FORWARD

This section of *Mohawk* again serves to add further information to the transverse arrangements in *Cossack* which were essential identical. The only crew space is that on the Upper Deck, the remaining internal spaces serving for storage.

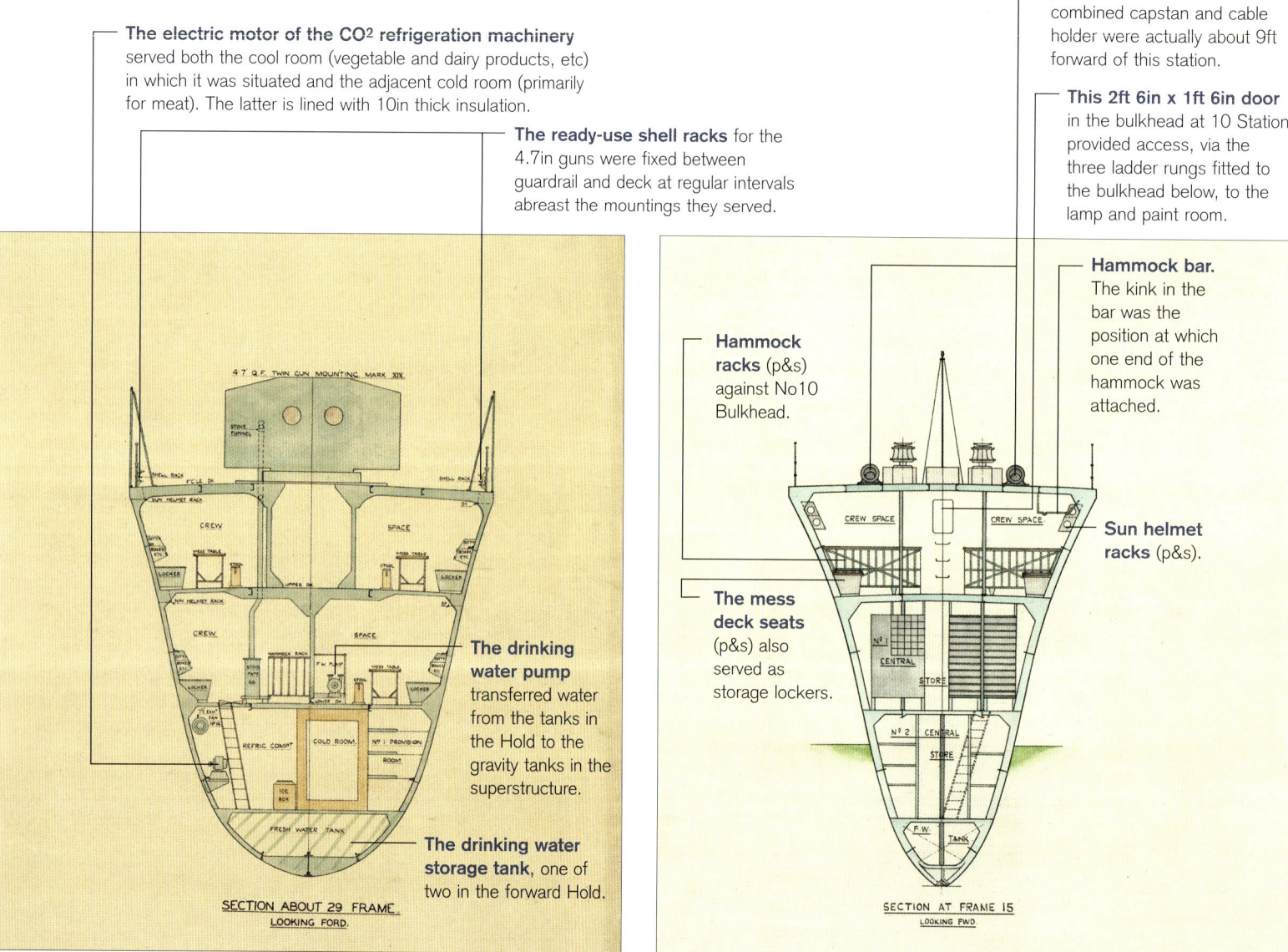

- **The electric motor of the CO_2 refrigeration machinery** served both the cool room (vegetable and dairy products, etc) in which it was situated and the adjacent cold room (primarily for meat). The latter is lined with 10in thick insulation.
- **The ready-use shell racks** for the 4.7in guns were fixed between guardrail and deck at regular intervals abreast the mountings they served.
- **The drinking water pump** transferred water from the tanks in the Hold to the gravity tanks in the superstructure.
- **The drinking water storage tank**, one of two in the forward Hold.
- **The tops of the anchor chain pipes** shown outboard of the combined capstan and cable holder were actually about 9ft forward of this station.
- **This 2ft 6in x 1ft 6in door** in the bulkhead at 10 Station provided access, via the three ladder rungs fitted to the bulkhead below, to the lamp and paint room.
- **Hammock bar.** The kink in the bar was the position at which one end of the hammock was attached.
- **Hammock racks** (p&s) against No10 Bulkhead.
- **Sun helmet racks** (p&s).
- **The mess deck seats** (p&s) also served as storage lockers.

FRAME 29 TO STEM

The 'Tribal' class were fitted with the Type 124 Asdic set, generally similar to the Type 121 of 1931 but with a much-improved range recorder. The A/S8 dome for this outfit was housed in a free flooding trunk (shaded pink in the profile) just forward of the bulkhead at 25 Station. Here it is shown retracted – when lowered it projected about 3ft 10in below the keel. The lowering mechanism consisted of two threaded shafts driven by an electric motor on top of the housing. When the dome was raised these shafts were housed within the two, tapered projections shown above the flat. The Asdic dome could only be used up to a speed of 21 knots and was automatically withdrawn if the ship's speed exceeded 24 knots.

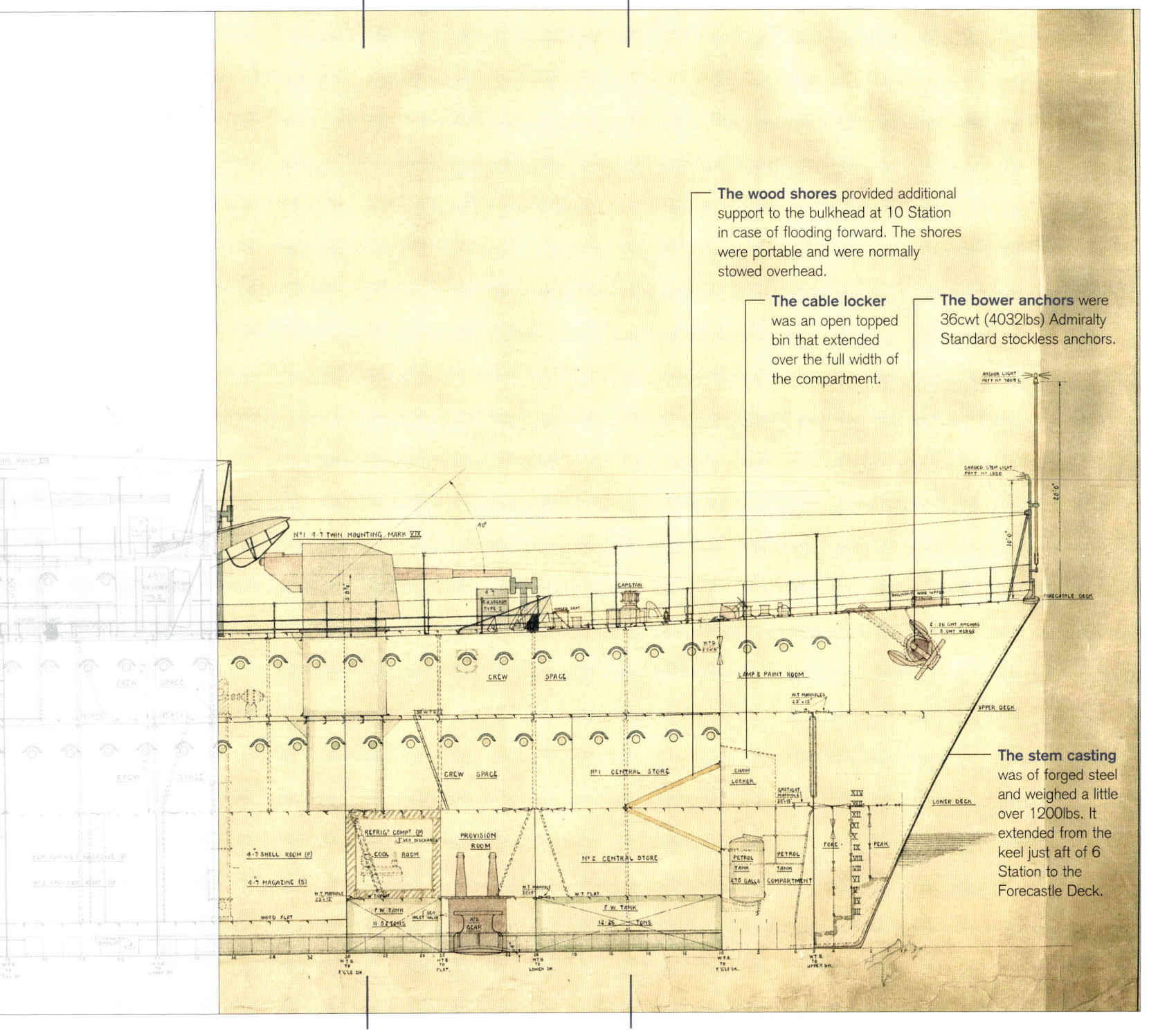

The wood shores provided additional support to the bulkhead at 10 Station in case of flooding forward. The shores were portable and were normally stowed overhead.

The cable locker was an open topped bin that extended over the full width of the compartment.

The bower anchors were 36cwt (4032lbs) Admiralty Standard stockless anchors.

The stem casting was of forged steel and weighed a little over 1200lbs. It extended from the keel just aft of 6 Station to the Forecastle Deck.

FRAME 29   **FRAME 15**

COMMUNICATIONS

PNEUMATIC TRANSMISSION OF MESSAGES

This means of transferring signal messages to and from the W/T offices and the plotting and signal office below the bridge became a standard fitting in British warships between the wars. The messages were placed in small cylindrical metal cases, loaded into brass tubes and then propelled to their destinations by compressed air. The process saved time and reduced the amount of human traffic that would have been involved in the transfer of messages by hand. The plan serves a secondary purpose in that it clearly identifies the main compartmentation of the ship. (M1821)

1. **The low-pressure air compressor** was driven by an electric motor. Note that both the 'WI' pipes are connected to the pump (there should not be a gap between the pump and the right-hand pipe).

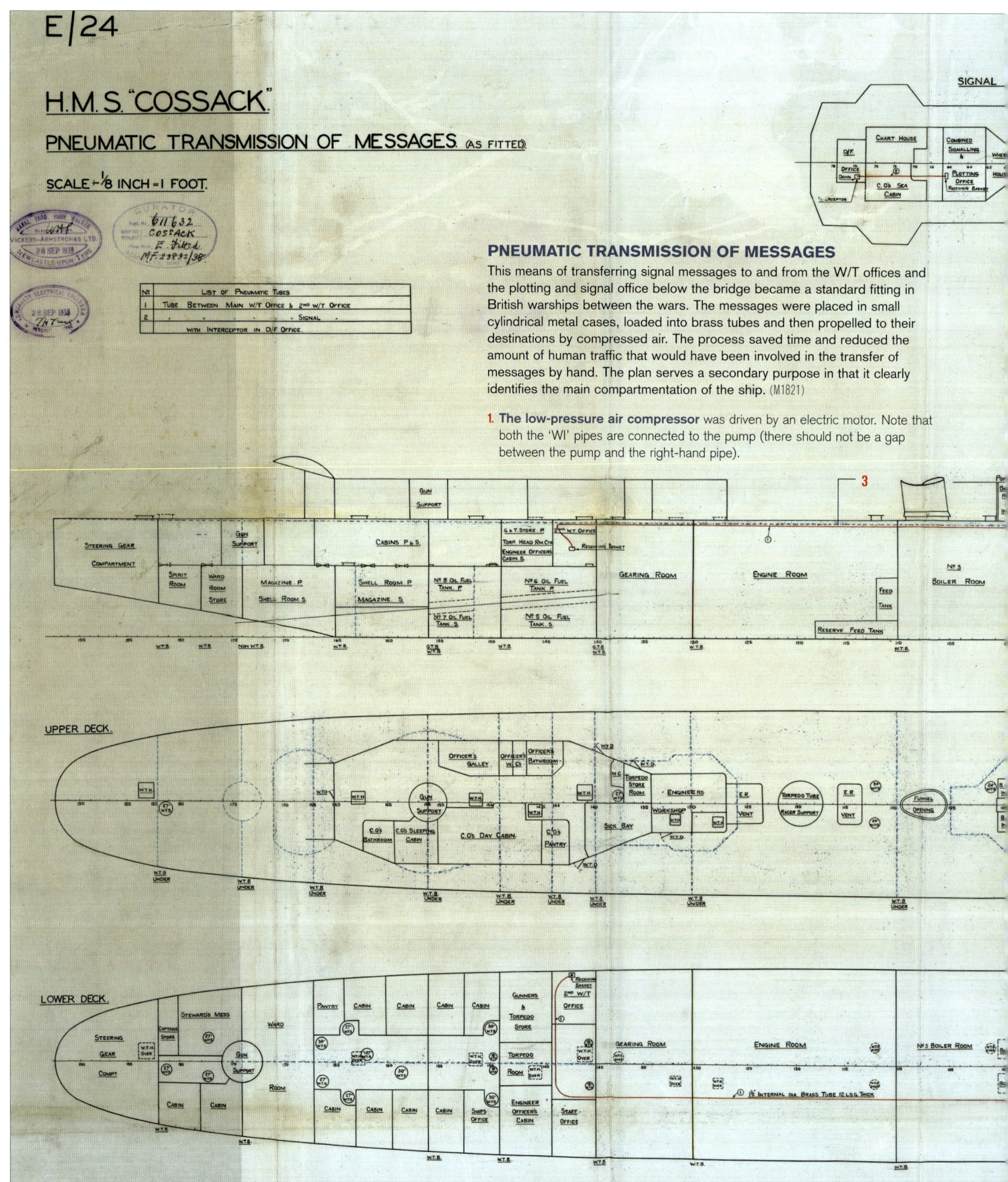

HMS COSSACK: PNEUMATIC TRANSMISSION OF MESSAGES, AS FITTED

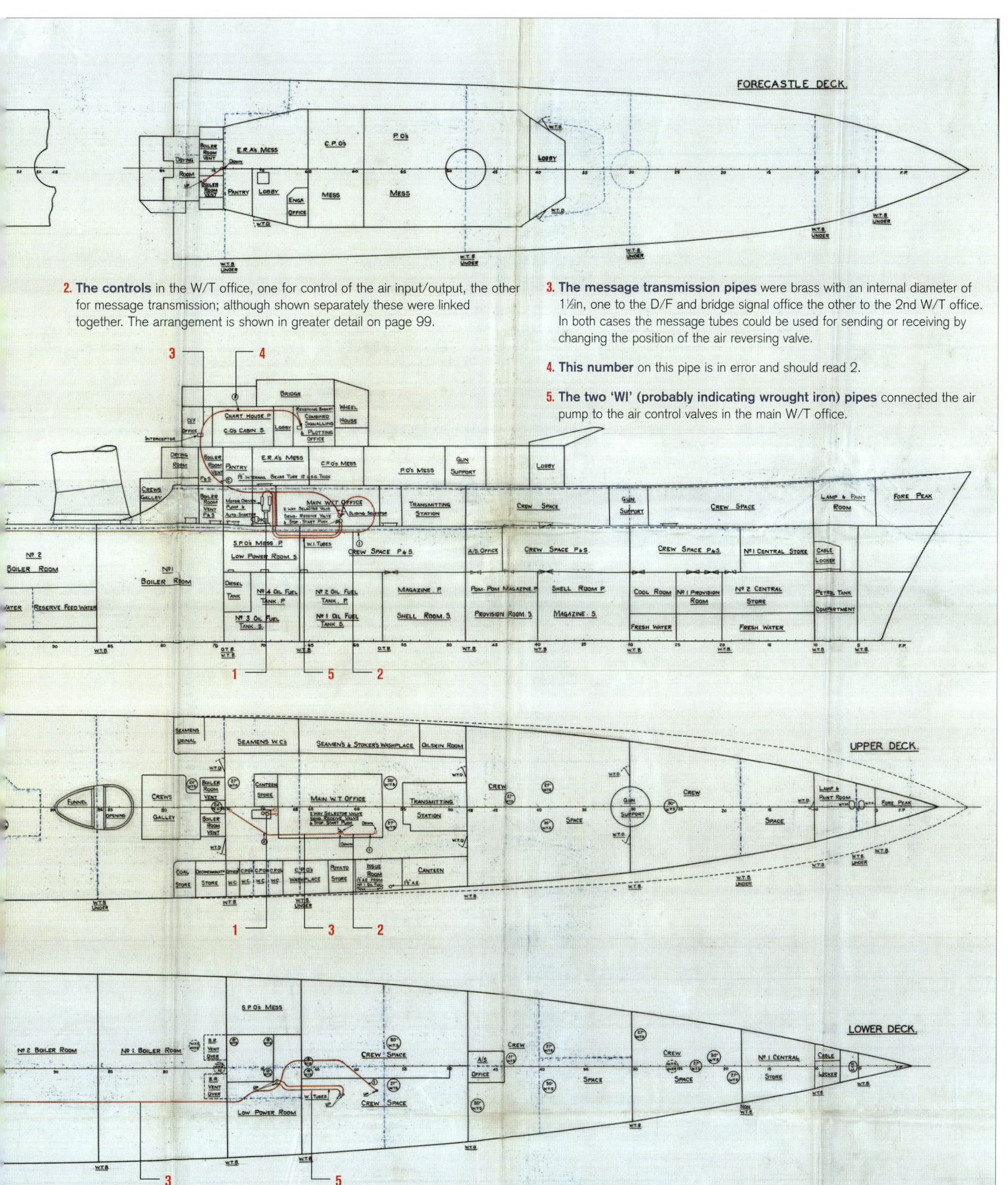

2. The controls in the W/T office, one for control of the air input/output, the other for message transmission; although shown separately these were linked together. The arrangement is shown in greater detail on page 99.

3. The message transmission pipes were brass with an internal diameter of 1½in, one to the D/F and bridge signal office the other to the 2nd W/T office. In both cases the message tubes could be used for sending or receiving by changing the position of the air reversing valve.

4. This number on this pipe is in error and should read 2.

5. The two 'WI' (probably indicating wrought iron) **pipes** connected the air pump to the air control valves in the main W/T office.

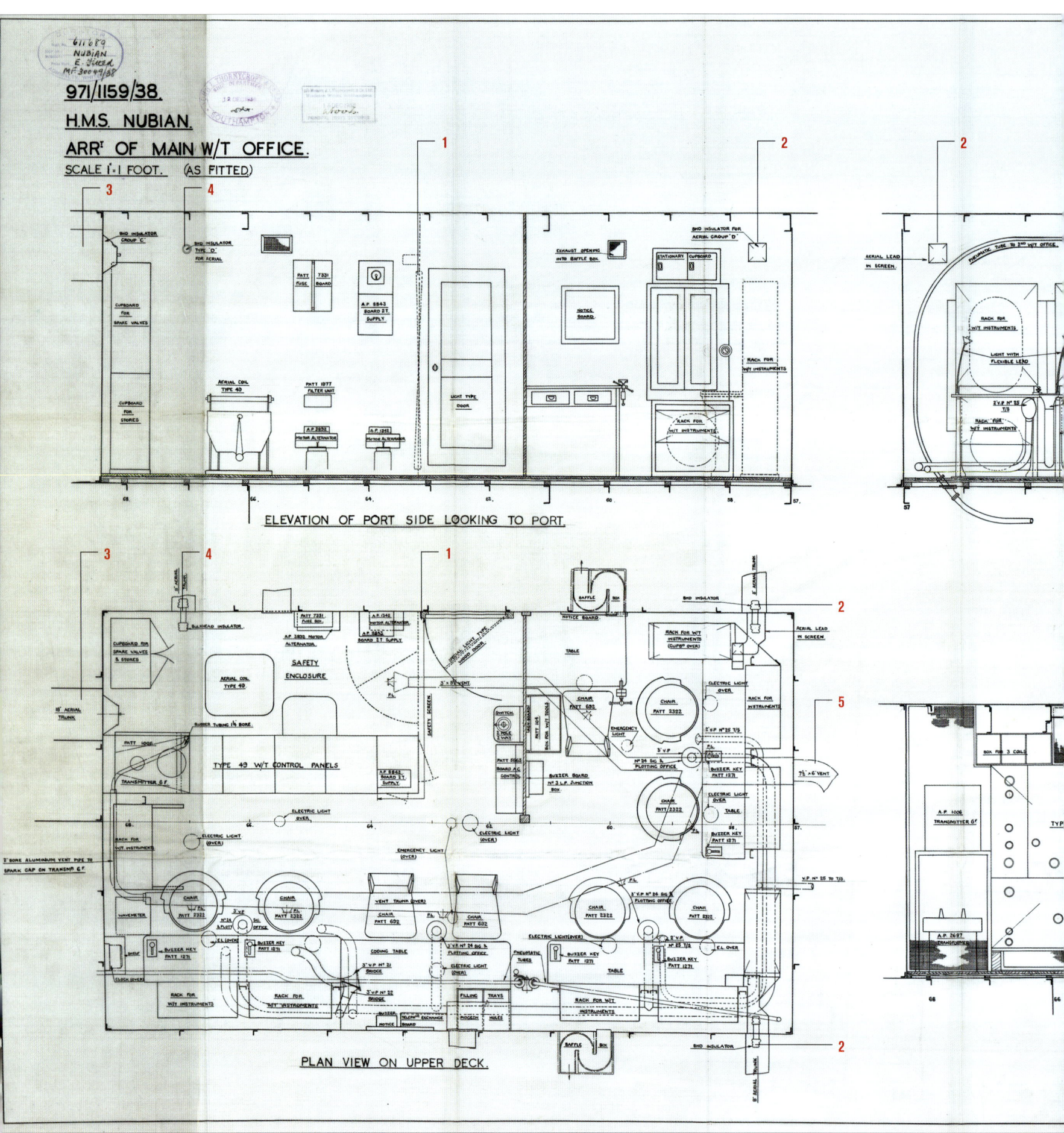

HMS NUBIAN, ARRANGEMENT OF MAIN W/T OFFICE

This, and the following drawing of the 2nd W/T office on pages 100–101, shows the standard arrangement of the W/T offices for all sixteen ships of the original 'Tribal' class. The main office contained a Type 49 and the 2nd office a Type 50 transmitter, both of which provided medium-power H/F for long range, medium-power M/F for medium range and low-power for short range communication. The main office also housed a Type 52HA, a low power H/F and M/F auxiliary set which served for both fleet wave and fire control communication. In addition, the ships of the class were provided with a Type 53, battery powered, portable set for ship-to-ship or ship-to-shore communication for boarding and landing parties. The operators for the Type 49, and the coding personnel, occupied the after end of the office and the operators for the Type 52 the fore end. The former had voice pipe communication with the bridge and the latter with the TS; both had voice pipe connection to the signal and plotting office. (M1818)

1. **A wire screen bulkhead** enclosed, for safety purposes, the high energy W/T power supply equipment. The entry gate to this area had a safety lock to prevent it being opened when the power was on.

2. **Trunks (p&s) for the fire control aerials.**

3. **Trunk for the aerial of the main Type 49 set.**

4. **Trunk for the auxiliary (fleet wave) aerial.**

5. **Ventilation trunk inlet.** The ventilation outlets were the sinuous pipes located in the baffle boxes (p&s) which served to suppress exterior noise.

6. **The operating valves for the pneumatic message tubes.** The lower valve served to change from send to receive and also controlled on/off for the air supply. The upper valve connected either the tube to the 2nd W/T office or that to the signal and plotting office. The sliding sleeves above the controls were the entry/exit points for the message cylinders.

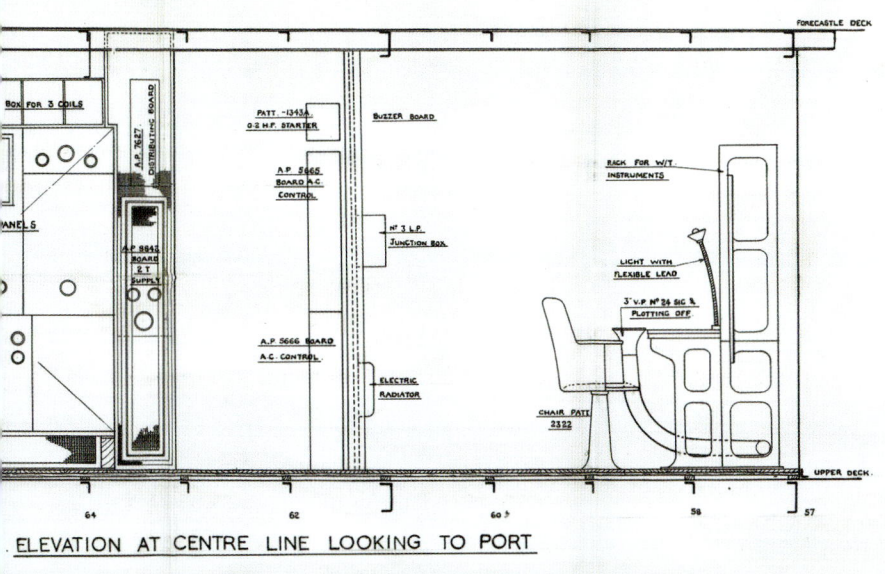

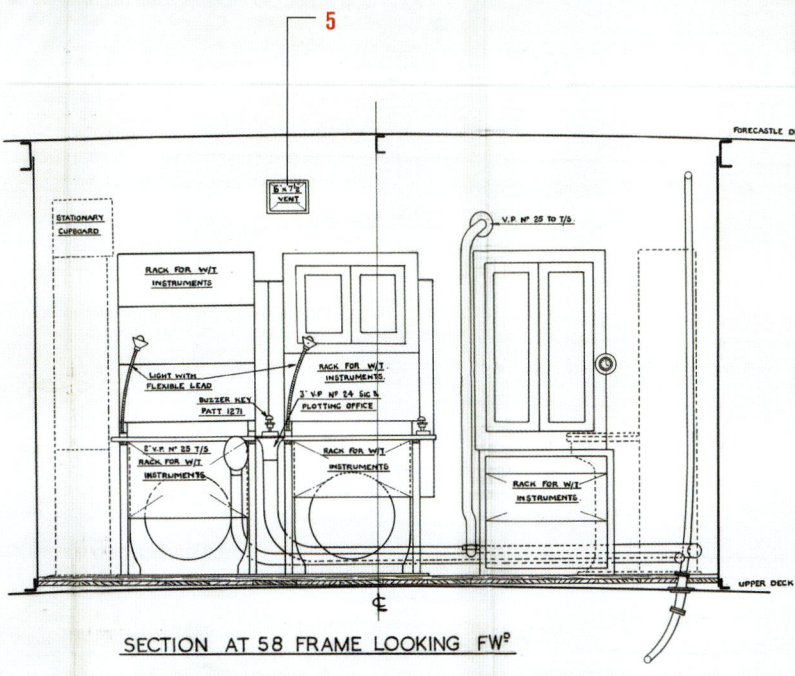

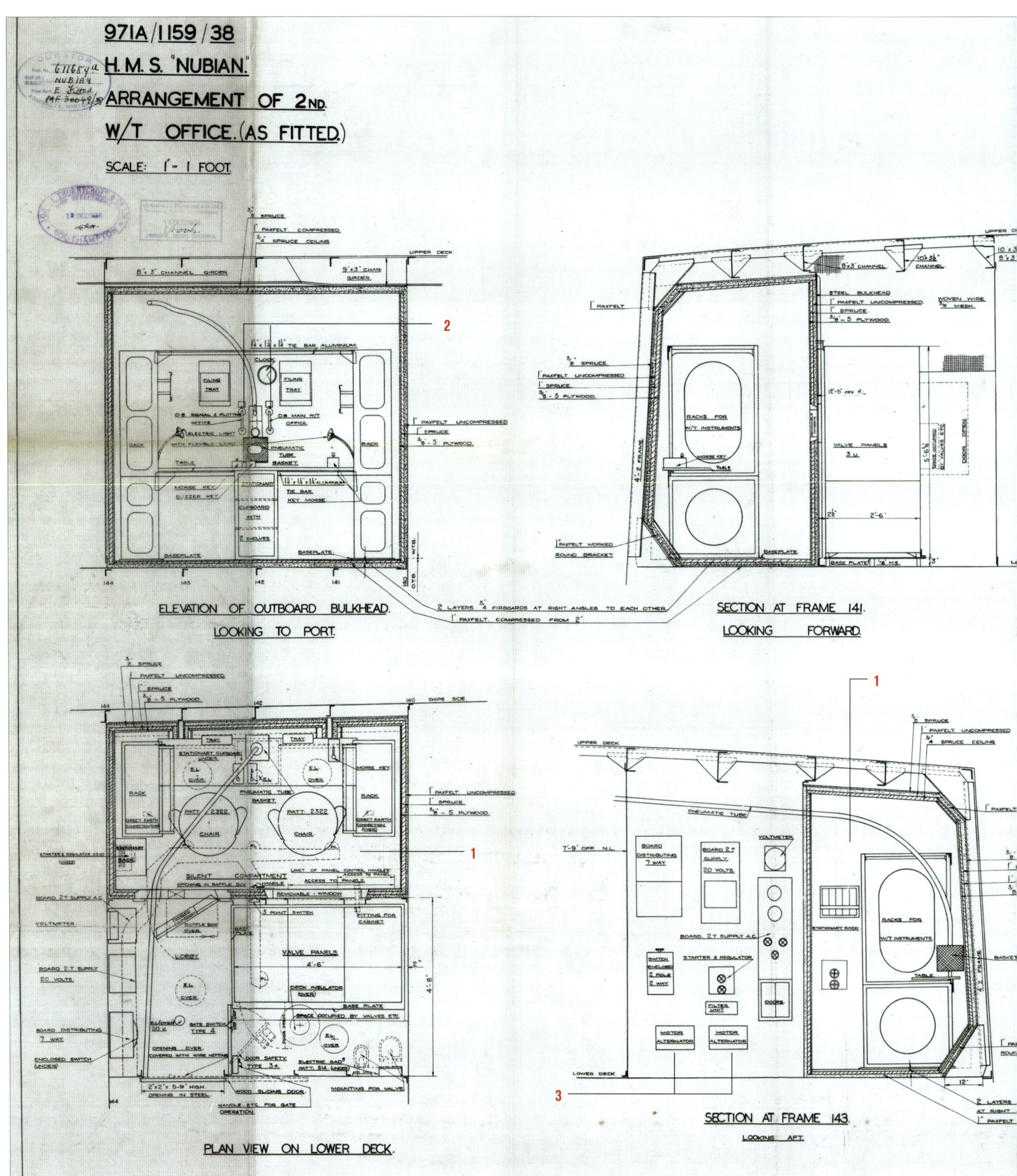

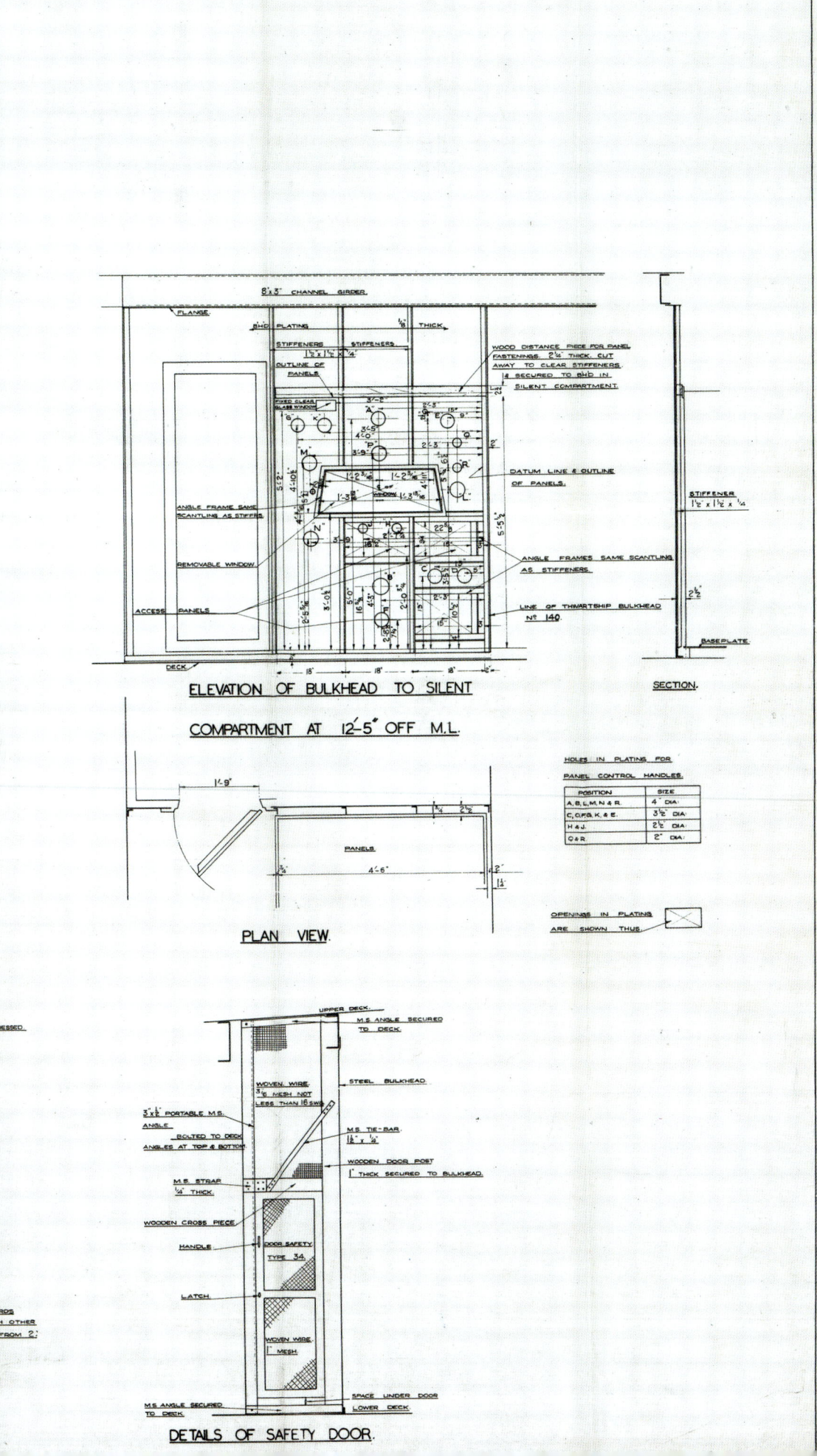

HMS *NUBIAN*, ARRANGEMENT OF 2ND W/T OFFICE

At the end of the 1930s the Admiralty instigated a major fleet W/T modernisation programme. As part of this programme it was decided in 1939 that the 'Tribal' class should have all their receiving sets and the aerial exchange outfit (a means of connecting any receiver to any of the ship's receiving aerials) replaced by all-wave receiver outfits. This plan was given 'A' priority but, considering the high demand for the manufacture and fitting of new W/T equipment throughout the fleet on the eve of war, it is probable that delays in installation were common. No information has come to light regarding when, or if, *Cossack*'s outfit was fully upgraded, which by early 1940 also included improvements for the Type 49 and 50 sets. (M1819)

1. The silent cabinet for the 2nd office was sound insulated by wood and felt panelling. Unlike the main office this was limited to the wireless operator space. In the main office sound insulation enclosed the entire compartment – not shown (except for the deck) in the drawing of *Nubian*'s main office but visible in *Cossack*'s deck plan on page 112 and in the section on page 90.

2. Telephones for communication with the main W/T office and the signal and plotting office.

3. Motor alternators supplied 20v ac power for powering the W/T outfit in both the 2nd and main offices. Back-up battery power was available if the main power supply failed.

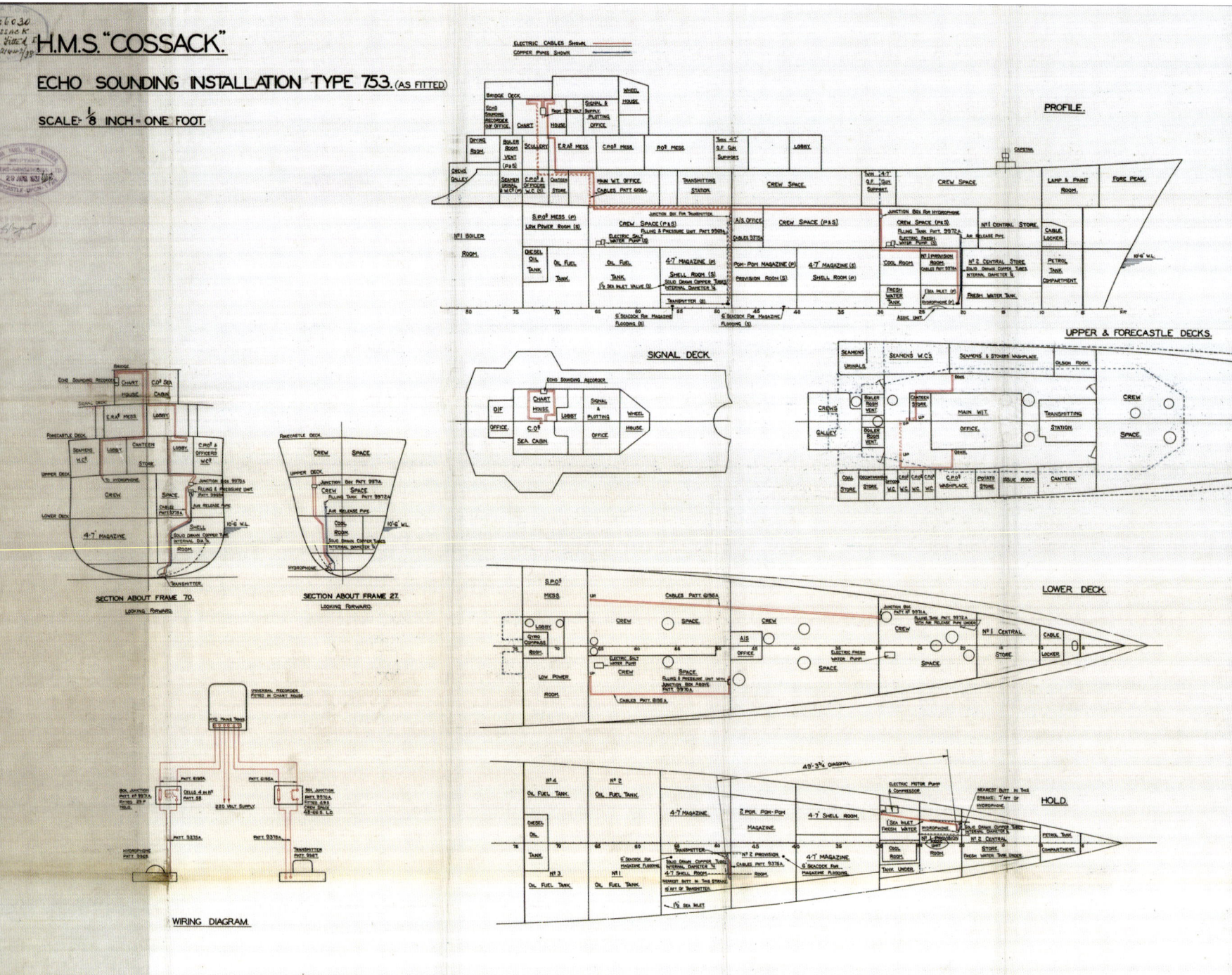

TYPE 753 ECHO SOUNDING INSTALLATION

The 'Tribal' class were among the first ships to be fitted with Type 753 echo sounding which superseded the Type 752. The new version differed only in that the audio receiver of Type 752, by which the operator could read off the depth on hearing the return echo, was replaced by a non-audio recorder which traced a depth record on a moving paper strip. The primary purpose was navigational, particularly in coastal waters, where the depths and surface variations of the sea floor could provide information relevant to the ship's position when used in conjunction with information from charts (or the knowledge of the navigating officer). The recorder was placed in the chart house and connected electrically to two small tanks in the Hold – one for the transmitter, which generated sound impulses, and one for the hydrophone which picked up the sound signal reflections from the seabed. The tanks were filled with water for signal continuity but were entirely inside the hull since the steel plating presented no impediment to transmission. They were positioned on opposite sides of the keel to avoid the possibility of direct signals between the tanks causing interference. The 'Tribal's were also fitted with a motor-driven Kelvin Mk IV sounding machine located on the starboard side of the roof of the crew's galley. The echo sounder was suitable for depths up to 140 fathoms and the sounding machine for depths up to 45 fathoms. (M1834)

THE 0.5-INCH MACHINE GUN PLATFORM AND FUNNELS

The 0.5in MG mountings were surrounded by 3ft 8in high bulwarks of which the top 2ft 3in could be folded down when the guns were in action. The inner ends of these bulwarks joined triangular brackets that extended a short distance inboard along the edge of the platform. Beyond these brackets, spurn waters served to stop water from rain or spray running onto the deck below and guided it to scuppers at the outer extremities of the MG positions. In the plan view the spurn waters are indicated by brown strips running just inboard of the edges of the platform. (M1805)

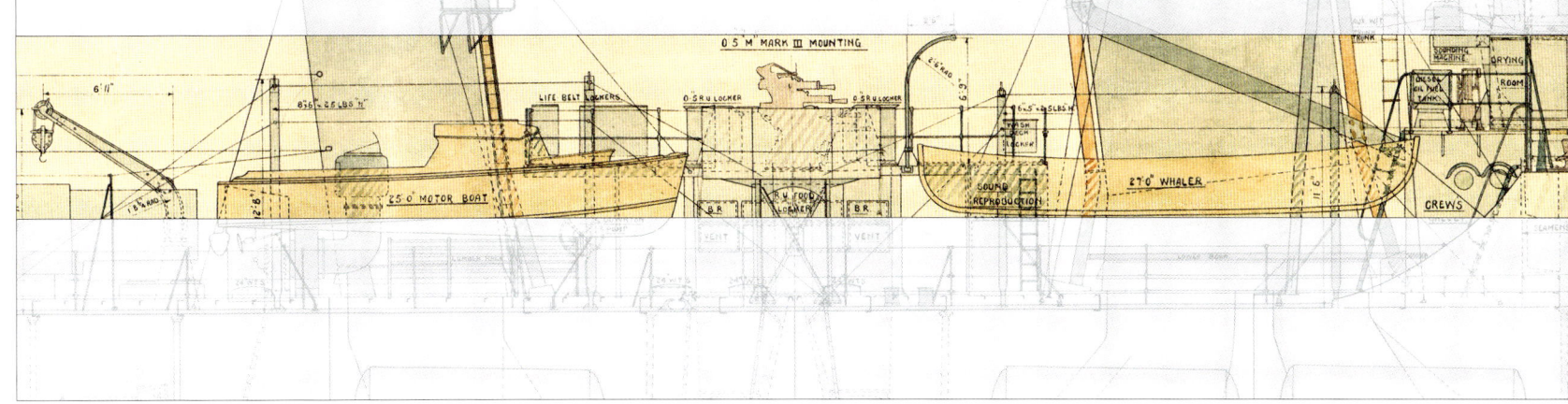

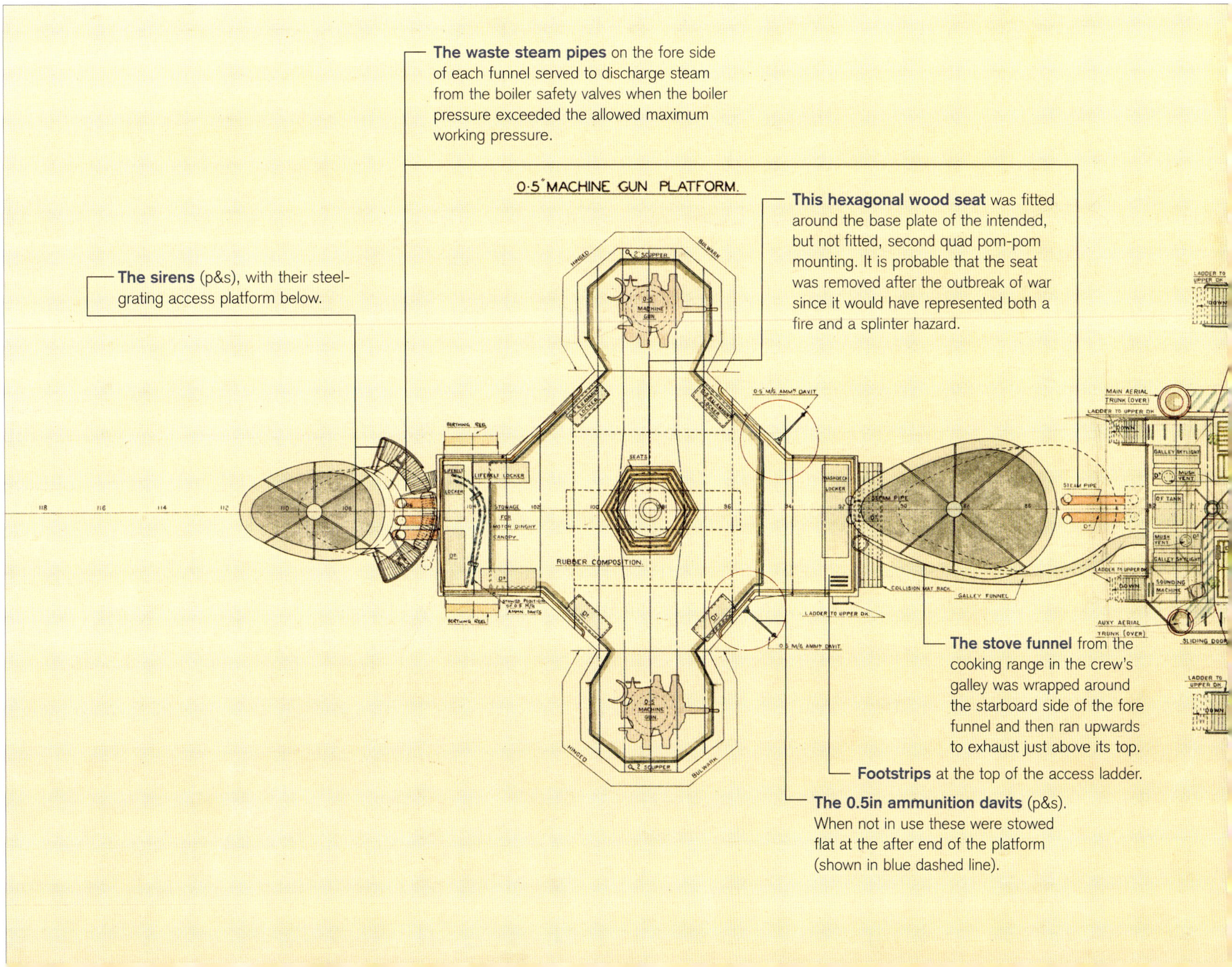

The waste steam pipes on the fore side of each funnel served to discharge steam from the boiler safety valves when the boiler pressure exceeded the allowed maximum working pressure.

This hexagonal wood seat was fitted around the base plate of the intended, but not fitted, second quad pom-pom mounting. It is probable that the seat was removed after the outbreak of war since it would have represented both a fire and a splinter hazard.

The sirens (p&s), with their steel-grating access platform below.

The stove funnel from the cooking range in the crew's galley was wrapped around the starboard side of the fore funnel and then ran upwards to exhaust just above its top.

Footstrips at the top of the access ladder.

The 0.5in ammunition davits (p&s). When not in use these were stowed flat at the after end of the platform (shown in blue dashed line).

SEARCHLIGHT PLATFORM AND AFTER CONTROL POSITION

As an emergency navigation position this platform was fitted with a steering wheel, magnetic compass, engine room telegraphs and voice pipes for communication with the engine room and the steering compartment. For gun control there were three voice pipes for communication with an after clock-position and shelves attached to the guardrails for a Mk VIII Dumaresq instrument. The after clock-position, located immediately below in the lobby to port of the sick bay, was provided with a Vickers range clock and a portable spotting table. All these instruments, including those for the control platform, were stored in the gunner's and torpedo store on the Lower Deck when not in use. The secondary fire control position was only intended to serve the after 4.7in gun mountings in divided control for which voice pipe communication was provided between the clock-position and the guns. (M805)

AFTER SUPERSTRUCTURE DECK

When *Cossack*'s Nº3 4.7in mounting was replaced by the twin 4in HA/LA mounting it was necessary to adapt the 4.7in HA fire control system to accommodate the ballistics of the 4in guns. This involved modifications to the FKC and the provision of a fuse conversion unit to align the 4in and 4.7in fuse settings. These changes could not be implemented quickly and initially *Cossack* was provided with a temporary system of HA control for the 4in mounting which provided a separate fuse transmitter and receiver in place of the conversion unit. This limited the long-range *controlled* HA fire to elevations above those for the 4.7in. Otherwise the mounting operated under local control. The final system was probably fitted in *Cossack* during 1941. The twin 4in was primarily intended as a defence against dive bombers but with the fire control system fully updated it could operate in conjunction with the 4.7in guns (up to their maximum elevation) in AA barrage fire. Apart from those lost, all the ships of the class were fitted with the twin 4in during 1940–41. No doubt the last of these refits also included the final HA control arrangements. (M1805)

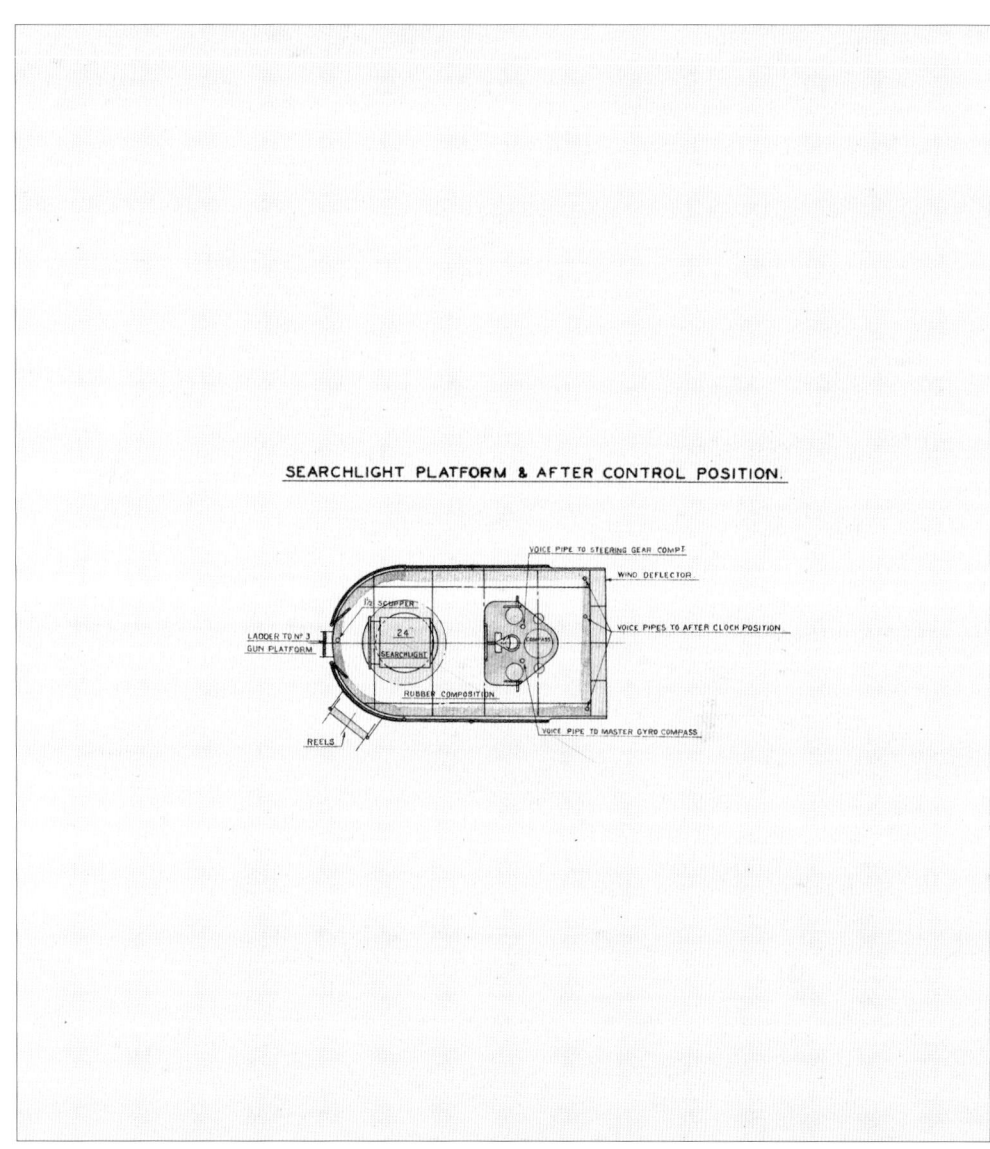

HMS COSSACK: ENLARGED DECKS, AS FITTED 1938

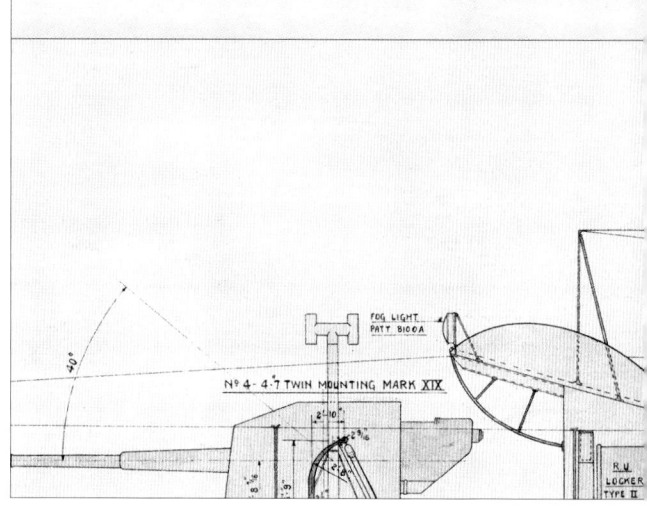

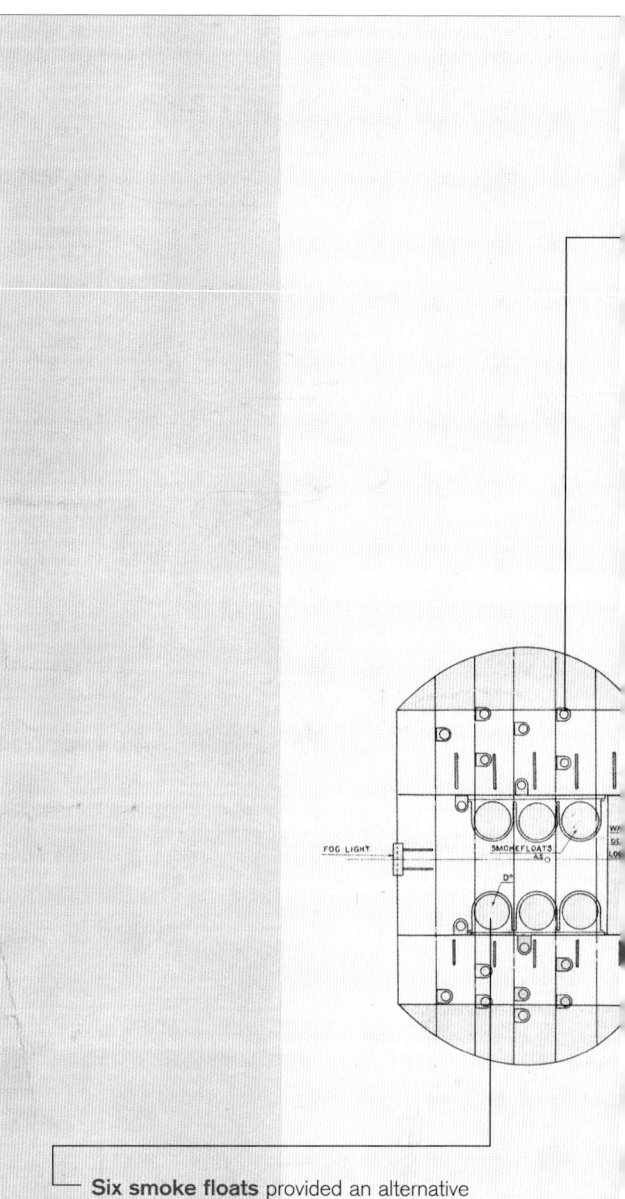

Six smoke floats provided an alternative and longer lasting means of generating a smoke screen than that provided by adjusting the boilers to produce dense funnel smoke. As the 'float' suggests, they were dropped over the side and produced dense white clouds by chemical reaction.

AFTER SUPERSTRUCTURE DECK

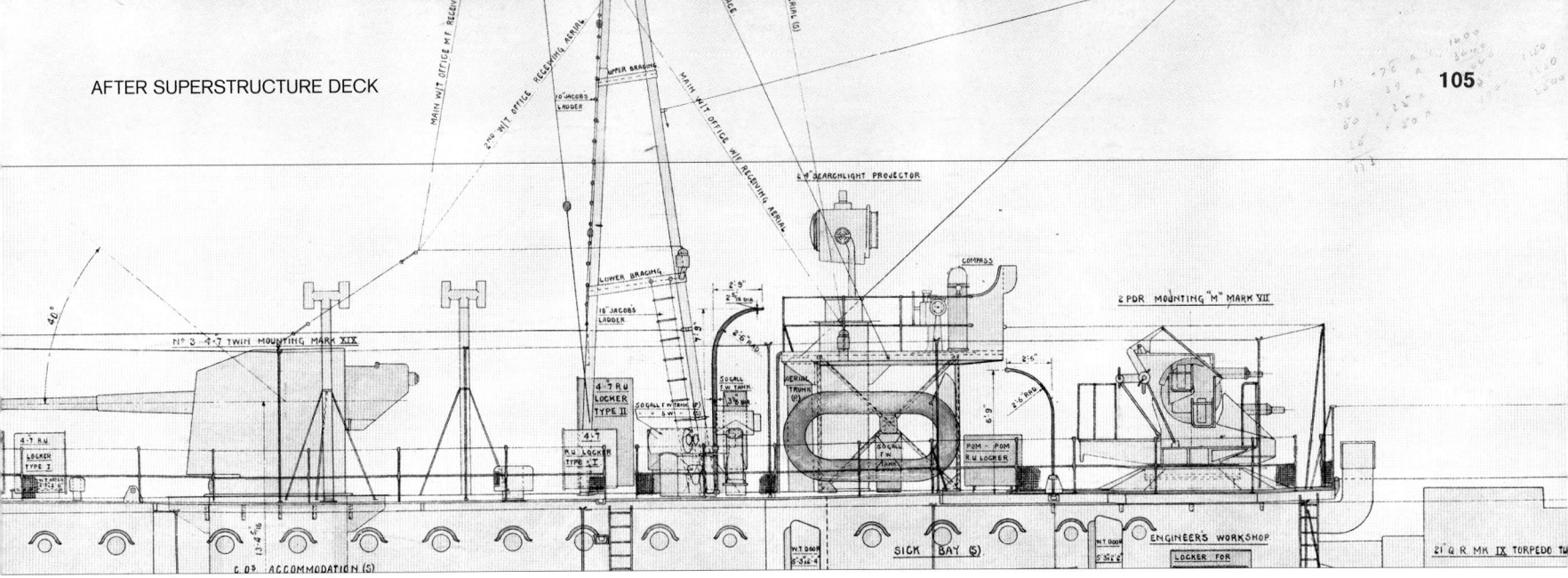

The ready-use shell racks located for the most part around the deck edges and on the blast-screen accommodated fifty 4.7in shell. A similar number was provided for mounting No 2 but mountings 1 and 4 had only forty each. Ready-use lockers (five for mountings 2 and 3, four for mountings 1 and 4) provided stowage for a similar number of cartridges. The original design requirement for ready-use 4.7in ammunition was 20 rpg. It is not clear why there was a 25 per cent increase for two of the mountings.

AFTER SUPERSTRUCTURE DECK & No 3 GUN PLATFORM.

Aerial trunk of the Type 50 set in the 2nd W/T office.

The support tube for the 24in searchlight.

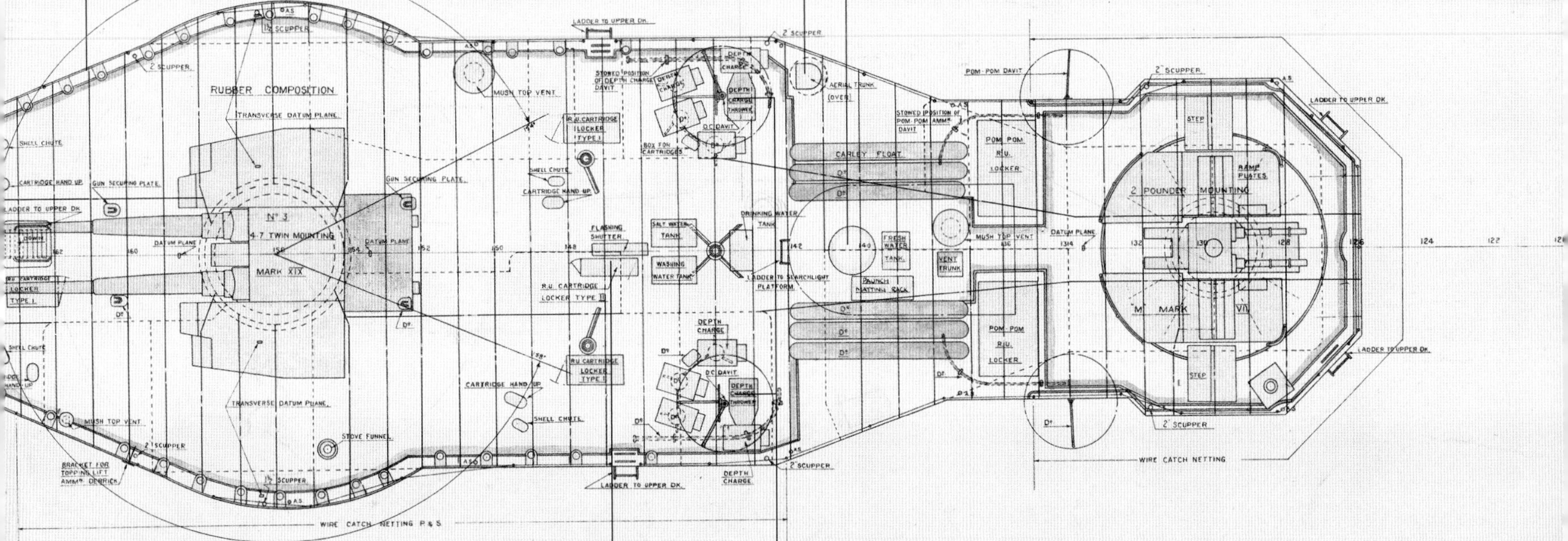

The depth charge throwers were each surrounded by stowage positions for three depth charges pre-fitted with the carriers required for them to be launched from the thrower.

The flashing shutter, shown here in its stowed position, could be fitted to the 24in searchlight for signalling purposes.

HMS COSSACK: ENLARGED DECKS, AS FITTED 1938

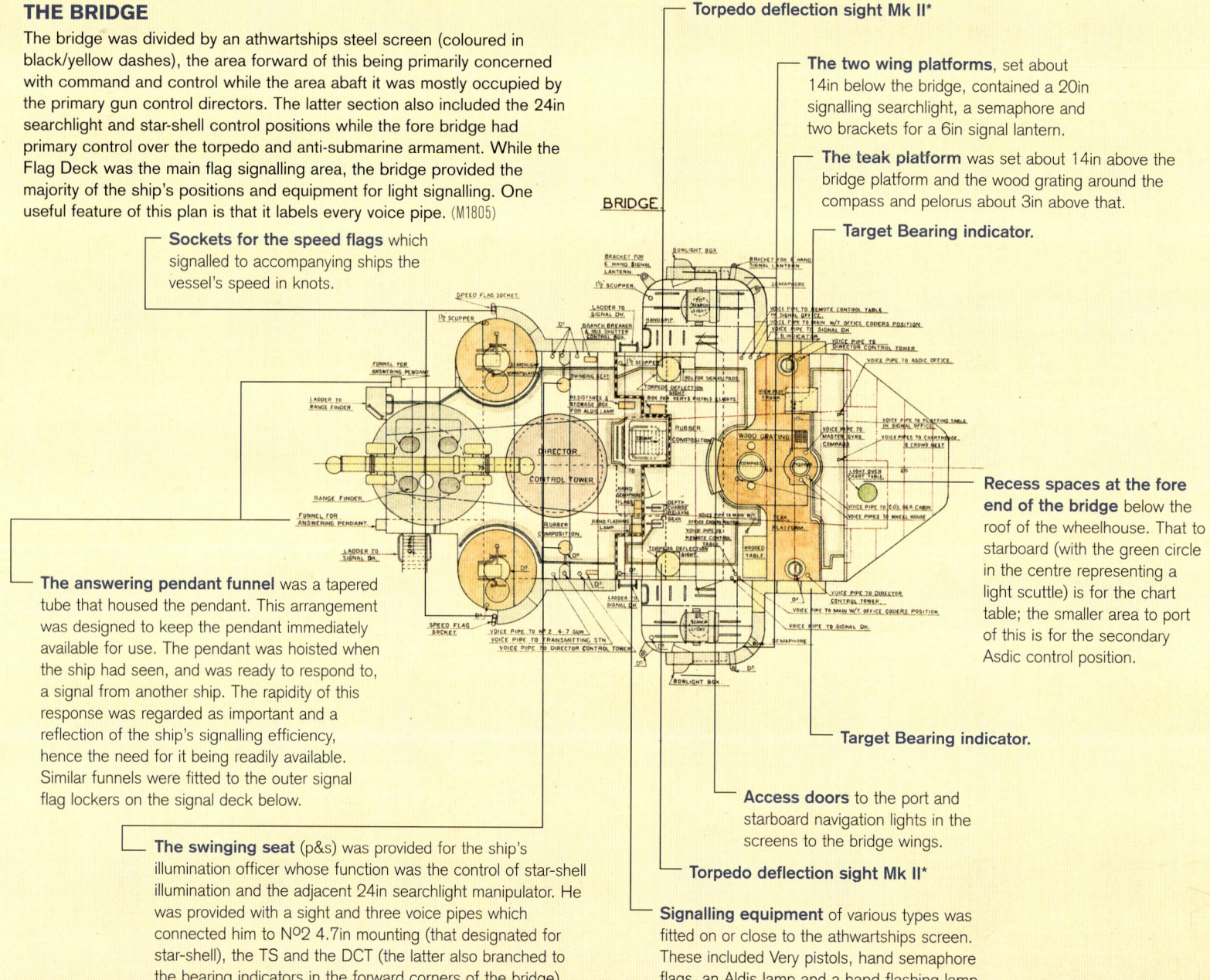

THE BRIDGE

The bridge was divided by an athwartships steel screen (coloured in black/yellow dashes), the area forward of this being primarily concerned with command and control while the area abaft it was mostly occupied by the primary gun control directors. The latter section also included the 24in searchlight and star-shell control positions while the fore bridge had primary control over the torpedo and anti-submarine armament. While the Flag Deck was the main flag signalling area, the bridge provided the majority of the ship's positions and equipment for light signalling. One useful feature of this plan is that it labels every voice pipe. (M1805)

- **Sockets for the speed flags** which signalled to accompanying ships the vessel's speed in knots.

- **The answering pendant funnel** was a tapered tube that housed the pendant. This arrangement was designed to keep the pendant immediately available for use. The pendant was hoisted when the ship had seen, and was ready to respond to, a signal from another ship. The rapidity of this response was regarded as important and a reflection of the ship's signalling efficiency, hence the need for it being readily available. Similar funnels were fitted to the outer signal flag lockers on the signal deck below.

- **The swinging seat** (p&s) was provided for the ship's illumination officer whose function was the control of star-shell illumination and the adjacent 24in searchlight manipulator. He was provided with a sight and three voice pipes which connected him to No2 4.7in mounting (that designated for star-shell), the TS and the DCT (the latter also branched to the bearing indicators in the forward corners of the bridge).

- **Torpedo deflection sight Mk II***

- **The two wing platforms**, set about 14in below the bridge, contained a 20in signalling searchlight, a semaphore and two brackets for a 6in signal lantern.

- **The teak platform** was set about 14in above the bridge platform and the wood grating around the compass and pelorus about 3in above that.

- **Target Bearing indicator.**

- **Recess spaces at the fore end of the bridge** below the roof of the wheelhouse. That to starboard (with the green circle in the centre representing a light scuttle) is for the chart table; the smaller area to port of this is for the secondary Asdic control position.

- **Target Bearing indicator.**

- **Access doors** to the port and starboard navigation lights in the screens to the bridge wings.

- **Torpedo deflection sight Mk II***

- **Signalling equipment** of various types was fitted on or close to the athwartships screen. These included Very pistols, hand semaphore flags, an Aldis lamp and a hand flashing lamp.

SIGNAL DECK AND BRIDGE

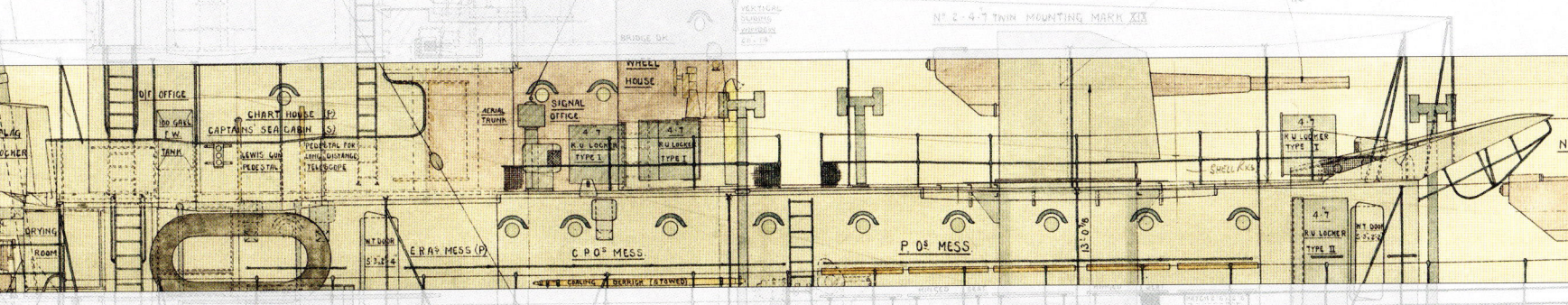

SIGNAL DECK AND Nº2 GUN PLATFORM

With the exception of Nº4 mounting, each 4.7in gun had a cartridge hand-up and a shell chute on each side of the deck both forward and abaft the mounting. This arrangement allowed the supply of ammunition to be switched to match the forward or after bearing the gun was trained on. At the after end of the Fag Deck there are four flag lockers and, to port and starboard, alternative positions, to those on the bridge, for the semaphore and hand signal lanterns. The latter location also provided stowage boxes for Aldis lamps and the (morse) keys to operate the yardarm and mast head flashing signal lights. (M1805)

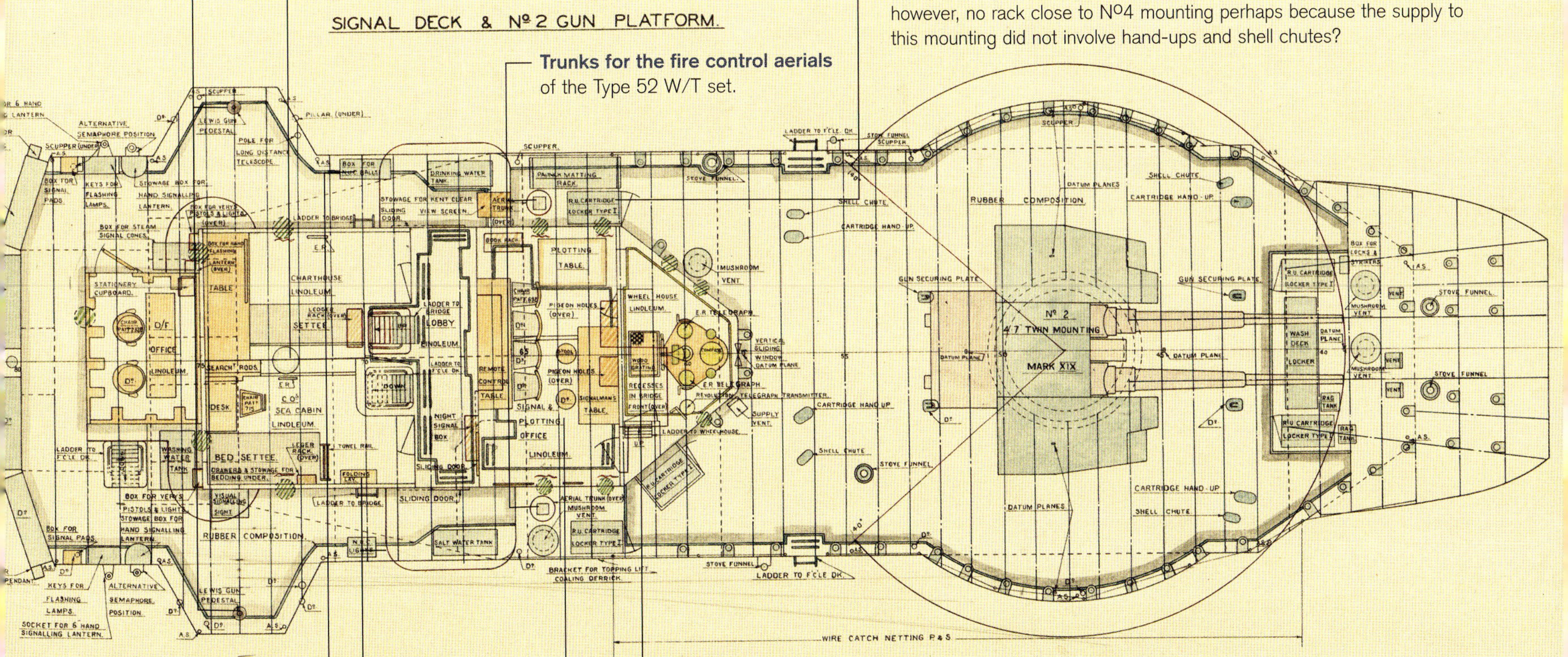

Lewis gun pedestals. These guns were originally omitted from the design due to lack of a suitable location. The wings of the Flag Deck were previously intended for pom-pom directors but these appear to have been dropped at the same time as the decision to delay the fitting of a second quad pom-pom mounting.

Support and cable/voice-pipe duct for the DCT.

Trunks for the fire control aerials of the Type 52 W/T set.

The paunch matting rack provided stowage for rope mats. Traditionally these mats were intended to provide protection from chaffing, particularly for yards and rigging during heavy weather. Given the location of this rack and two more (one on the after superstructure to starboard of the searchlight support – see page 105 – and another in the 'lobby and store' at the fore end of the forward superstructure – see page 109), it seems possible that in this case they were used primarily for some purpose related to the 4.7in ammunition supply. There is, however, no rack close to Nº4 mounting perhaps because the supply to this mounting did not involve hand-ups and shell chutes?

The signal and plotting office served the combined roles of signal distribution and maintenance of the ship's ARL automatic plotting table.

A folding lavatory (wash basin) in the Captain's sea cabin.

The NUC (not under control) signal stowage boxes – balls for daytime on the port side and lights for night, or low visibility, on the starboard side.

The wheelhouse contained the main steering wheel, a magnetic compass and port and starboard ER telegraphs. In addition, but not shown here, there were an engine revolution telegraph, a station keeping clock and a gyro compass repeat. Although provided with a window it was not under normal circumstances necessary for the helmsman to see where he was going since he was simply required to follow the course ordered from the bridge. For this his primary reference was the gyro repeat (or the magnetic compass if the gyro compass was disabled) not the view ahead.

HMS COSSACK: ENLARGED DECKS, AS FITTED 1938

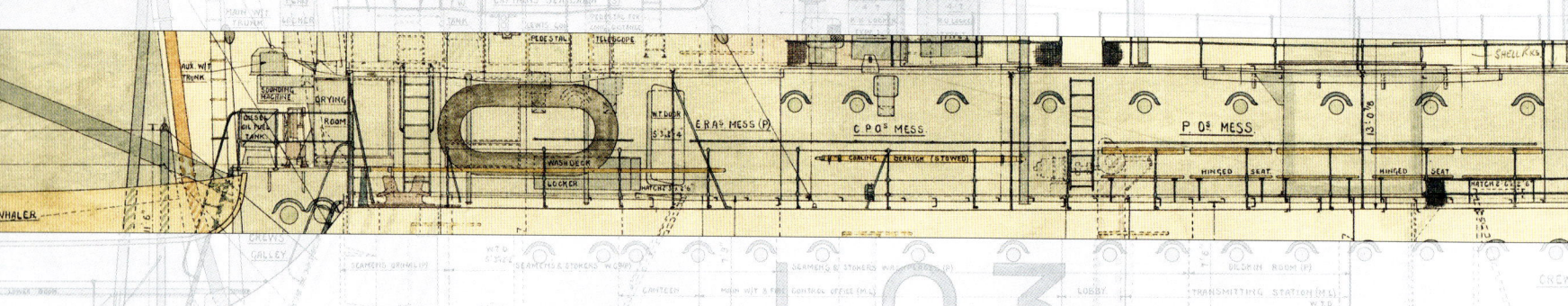

FORECASTLE DECK

The 'Tribal's and the 'I' class were the first British destroyers to be fitted with a breakwater on the forecastle. This derived from model trials in the test tank at Haslar in early 1936 to establish the sea-keeping advantages, if any, of the proposed modification of the bow form of the 'Tribal' design. It was concluded that the new bow was better since the increased flare served to throw water '… further off the ship's side'. The only exceptions occurred when the period of the ship coincided with that of the waves which resulted in heavy pitching and heavy seas being shipped over the bow. In this case there was only a slight difference between the bow forms but what difference there was still favoured the new bow. This resulted in testing the models with a breakwater. The results indicated that the flat middle section of the breakwater tended to cause water to break over N°1 mounting, although the deck abaft the breakwater was 'reasonably clear'. Some consideration was given to omitting the flat section and adopting a 'V' form but the breakwater ultimately adopted was the same as that first tried. The change to the 'V' form depended on Admiralty investigation of the effect on the position and working area for the capstan so it seems probably that the proposed change was not considered compatible with the capstan arrangement. (M805)

This diesel oil tank provided fuel for both the oil-fired stove and boiler in the crew's galley. There was a similar tank on the after superstructure for the stove and boiler in the officer's galley but it is not shown in the plans.

The aerial trunk for the feed from the Type 49 set in the main W/T office.

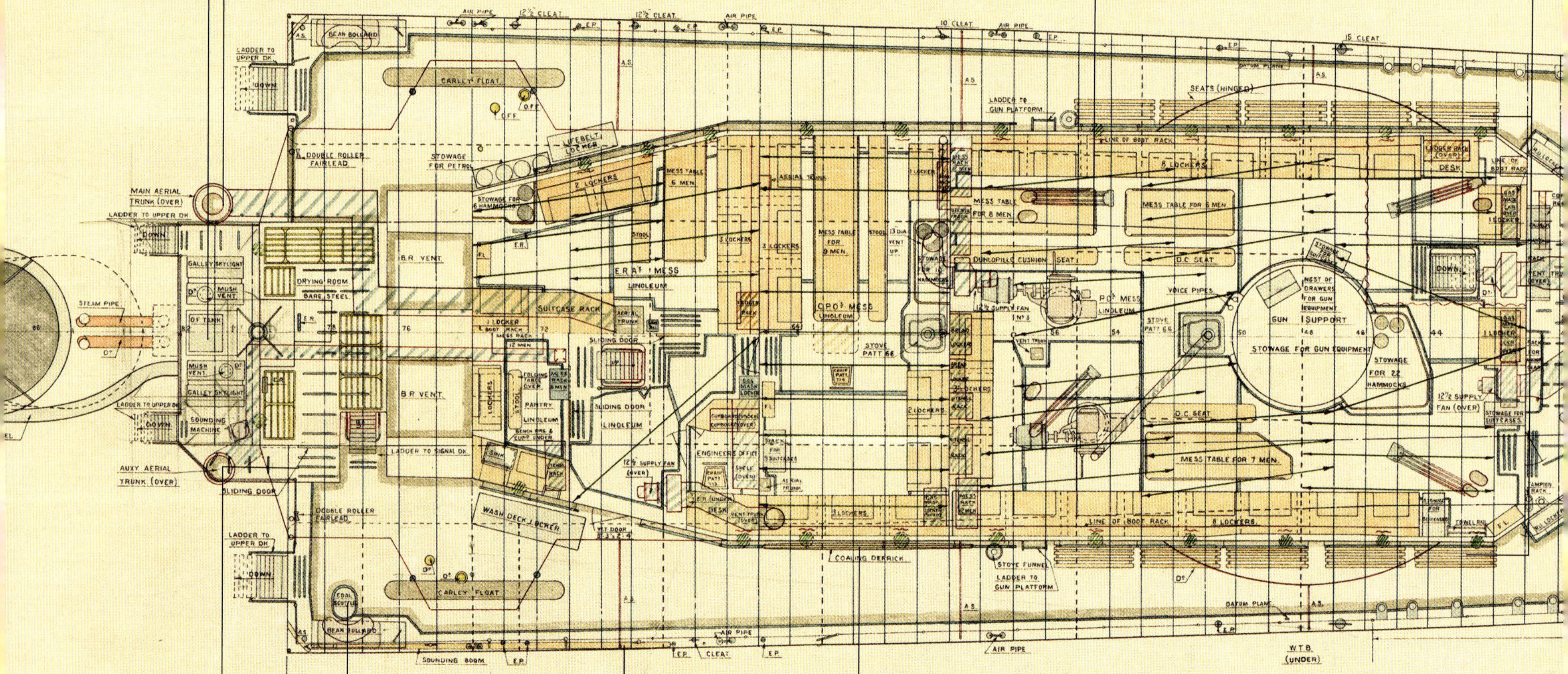

The forecastle superstructure was almost entirely occupied by accommodation for petty officers.

ERA^s MESS	CPO^s MESS	PO^s MESS
6 HAMMOCKS	9 HAMMOCKS - 1 HAMMOCK IN LOBBY	22 HAMMOCKS
6 SUNHELMETS	10 SUNHELMETS	22 SUNHELMETS
6 DITTY BOXES	10 DITTY BOXES	22 DITTY BOXES
6 LOCKERS	10 LOCKERS	21 LOCKERS
6 CAP BOXES	10 CAP BOXES	22 CAP BOXES

The coal scuttle for loading coal into the bunker below.

The auxiliary (fleet wave) aerial trunk for the Type 52 W/T set.

The 20ft sounding boom (stowed) for the Kelvin sounding machine fitted above the crew's galley.

The 11ft 6in coaling derrick stowed against the side of the superstructure.

FORECASTLE DECK

- **The wood seats** fitted along both sides of the superstructure could be folded up when not in use; in wartime they were removed entirely. Note that there are also two seats fitted forward of the breakwater.

- **The after hand-ups and shell chutes** for Nº1 mounting discharged ammunition into the 'store and lobby' at the fore end of the superstructure. Those on the fore side of the mounting discharged directly to the open deck as with all those for mountings 2 and 3. The openings in the deck were closed by hinged covers when not in use.

- **The sections of breakwater** that have crossed lines indicate removable sections for easy access to and from the fore end of the forecastle.

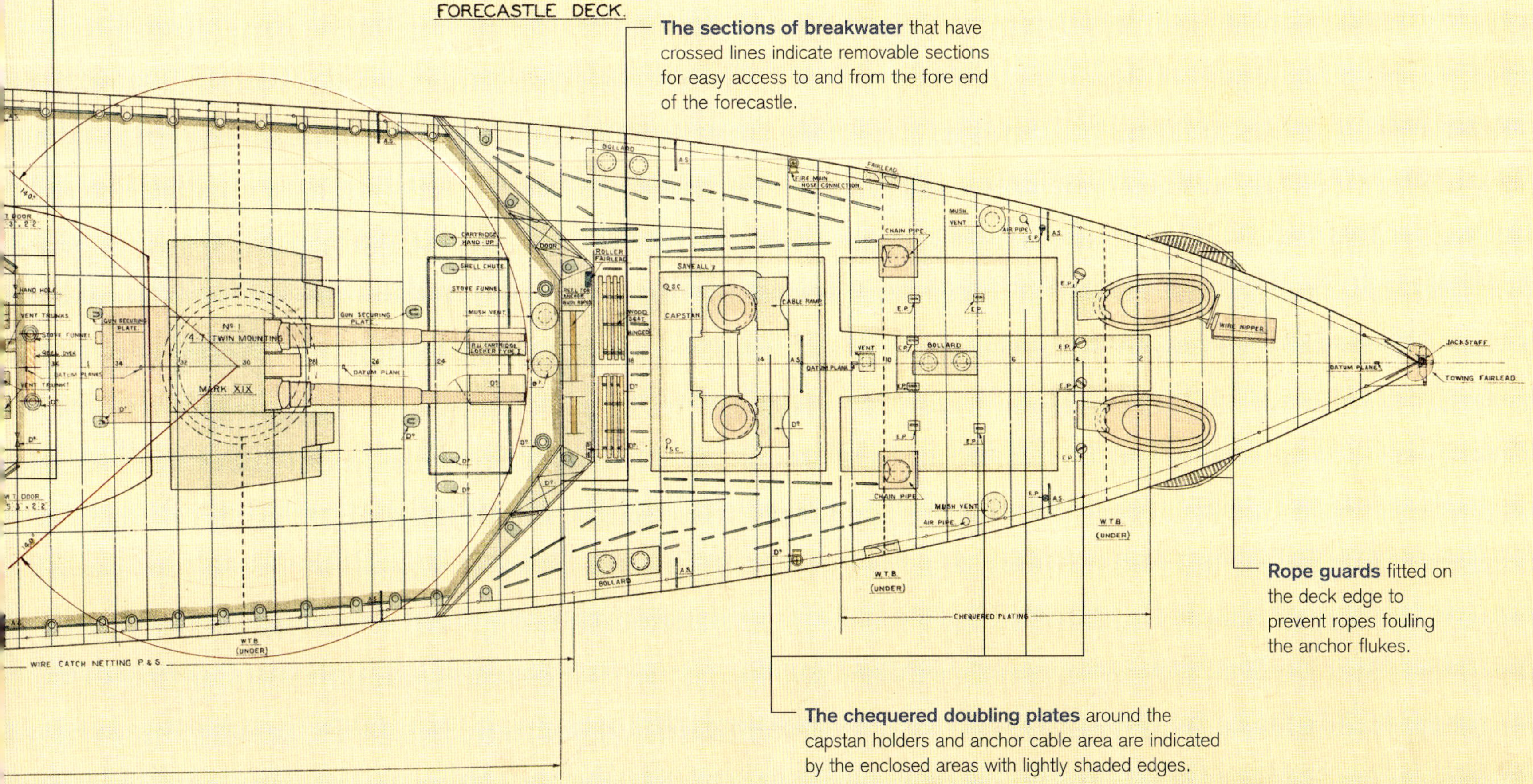

- **Rope guards** fitted on the deck edge to prevent ropes fouling the anchor flukes.

- **The chequered doubling plates** around the capstan holders and anchor cable area are indicated by the enclosed areas with lightly shaded edges.

HMS COSSACK: ENLARGED DECKS, AS FITTED 1938

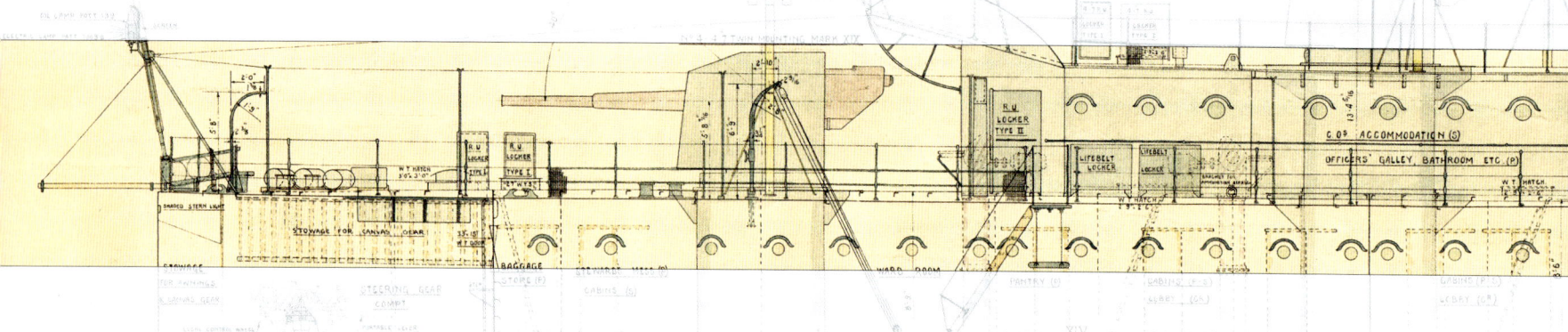

H.M.S. "COSSACK."
UPPER DECK. (AS FITTED.)
SCALE:- ¼ INCH = ONE FOOT.

UPPER DECK (AFT)

A cork-filled rubber composition for weather decks to replace the linoleum (Corticene) material normally fitted was tried in the destroyer *Fearless* and authorised for the 'I' class. It proved unsatisfactory for durability and did not provide sufficient foothold when washed down. The development of a sand-filled variant solved both problems and was adopted for the 'Tribal' class in 1937. The material – 'Aranbee', 'Semtex' and 'Supertex' – was manufactured respectively by Rowen and Boden, Dunlop and Northern British Rubber, and the colour, as specified by the Admiralty, was red/brown. Aranbee was fitted in

This cartridge hand-up is something of a mystery given that the after 4.7in mounting was supplied direct from the power hoists just abaft the after superstructure. The lobby below the hand-up does have access to No 3 magazine via a deck scuttle in the stewards' mess but there is no means by which shell could be supplied from abaft the mounting since, even if the cartridge hand-up was used there is no route from this to the shell room. Its only other possible use would seem to be speeding up the embarking procedure when taking on ammunition.

The accommodation ladder served to give easy access to the ship from boats alongside when in harbour. Two were provided with alternative locations at the stern or amidships (the latter shown in dashed line).

The side screen booms supported canvas awnings serving as sun-shades for the officers' accommodation.

The propeller guards extending outboard from the edge of the Upper Deck provided protection to the propeller blades against collision damage when coming alongside other ships or in harbour.

The depth charge rail carried three Type D charges which, together with the two DC throwers on the after superstructure provided for a five-charge pattern – one in the centre encircled by four at 90-degree intervals. There are three reloads for the rails which together with those on and around the DC thrower provided the peacetime outfit of 20 charges. In war this was increased to 30, the additions being stored in the Torpedo Head Room. The Type D weighed 440lbs and carried a charge of 300lbs of TNT or Amatol. The carriers for the DC thrower charges weighted about 100lbs.

Overhead fans, also known as sweeps, in the Captain's day cabin. A similar pair are fitted in the wardroom on the Lower Deck.

The red wavy lines indicate the positions of curtains hung across the side scuttles and sliding doors.

UPPER DECK

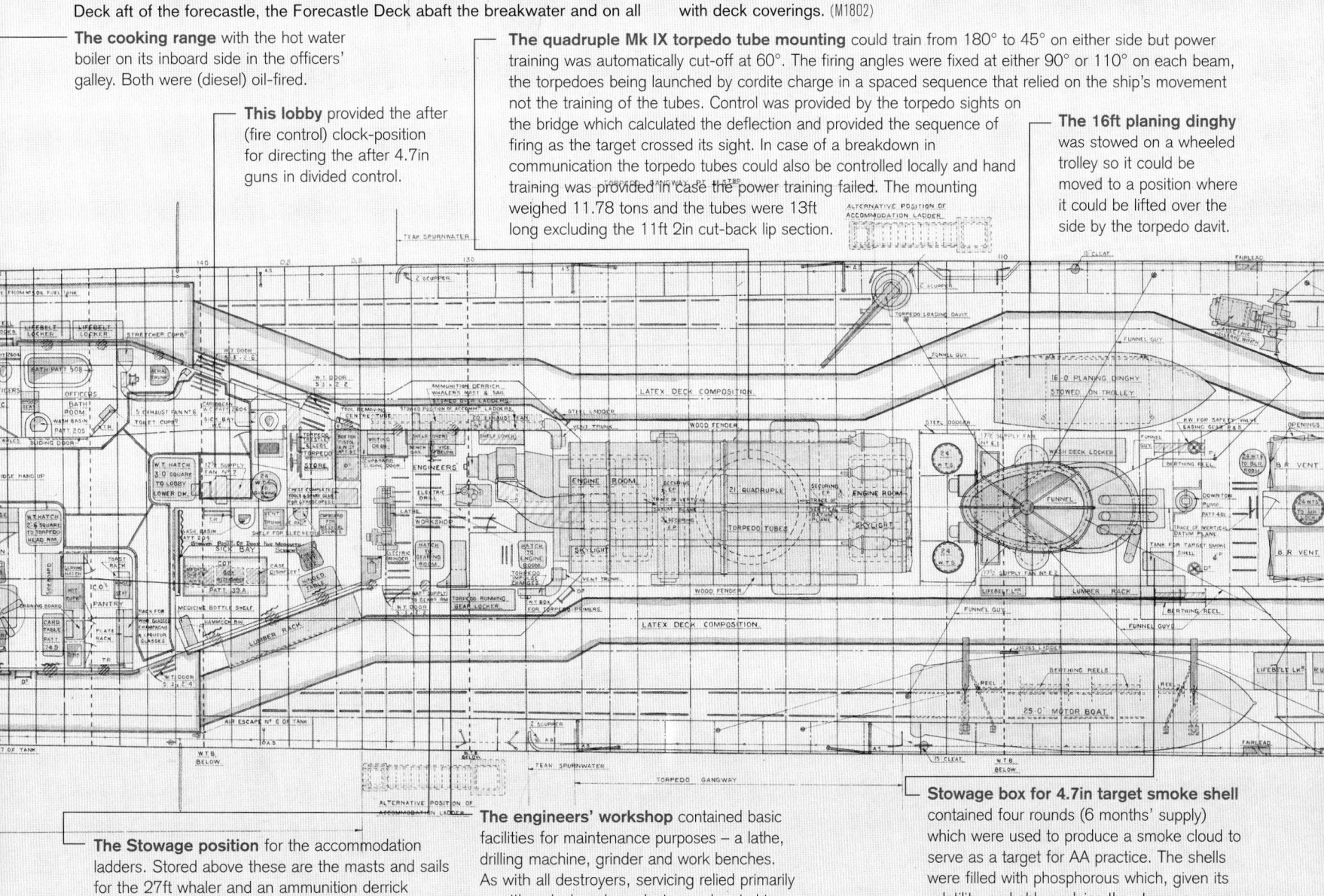

Cossack, *Afridi*, *Ashanti*, *Sikh* and *Zulu*, Semtex in *Bedouin*, *Eskimo*, *Gurkha*, *Maori*, *Mashona*, *Mohawk* and *Nubian* and Supertex in *Matabele*, *Punjabi*, *Somali* and *Tartar*. The composition subsequently became standard in British warships although it is unclear if all three continued to be used since the trade name 'Semtex' seems to have been used generally, implying that Dunlop became the sole or main supplier. Needless to say, it has nothing to do with the plastic explosive of the same name.

The deck plans for *Cossack* have the distinct advantage of identifying the areas of the new material as 'latex deck composition'. It is fitted on the Upper Deck aft of the forecastle, the Forecastle Deck abaft the breakwater and on all the superstructure decks and platforms. Corticene remained the deck covering internally being used in all the accommodation areas, offices and control positions and is identified in some places as 'linoleum'. Both the new compositions and Corticene had brass edge and division strips which are shown in the drawing as blue/grey lines. These serve to identify the outer limits of the material while bare deck can in many places be also identified by the fitting of foot strips. No edge strips are shown where the deck covering completely fills the space they occupy such as the officers' cabins and searchlight platform. Store rooms, galleys, wash places, etc were not fitted with deck coverings. (M1802)

The cooking range with the hot water boiler on its inboard side in the officers' galley. Both were (diesel) oil-fired.

This lobby provided the after (fire control) clock-position for directing the after 4.7in guns in divided control.

The quadruple Mk IX torpedo tube mounting could train from 180° to 45° on either side but power training was automatically cut-off at 60°. The firing angles were fixed at either 90° or 110° on each beam, the torpedoes being launched by cordite charge in a spaced sequence that relied on the ship's movement not the training of the tubes. Control was provided by the torpedo sights on the bridge which calculated the deflection and provided the sequence of firing as the target crossed its sight. In case of a breakdown in communication the torpedo tubes could also be controlled locally and hand training was provided in case the power training failed. The mounting weighed 11.78 tons and the tubes were 13ft long excluding the 11ft 2in cut-back lip section.

The 16ft planing dinghy was stowed on a wheeled trolley so it could be moved to a position where it could be lifted over the side by the torpedo davit.

The Stowage position for the accommodation ladders. Stored above these are the masts and sails for the 27ft whaler and an ammunition derrick (there are sockets for the heel of the latter p&s of the after superstructure just abaft Frame 160).

The engineers' workshop contained basic facilities for maintenance purposes – a lathe, drilling machine, grinder and work benches. As with all destroyers, servicing relied primarily on either dockyards or destroyer depot ships.

Stowage box for 4.7in target smoke shell contained four rounds (6 months' supply) which were used to produce a smoke cloud to serve as a target for AA practice. The shells were filled with phosphorous which, given its volatility, probably explains the stowage position on the Upper Deck.

HMS COSSACK: ENLARGED DECKS, AS FITTED 1938

UPPER DECK (FORWARD)

In all the plan views any items that are in the upper part of the compartment, stowed overhead or represent openings in the deck above are outlined in red. Where items extend from deck to deck head (such as ladders) the upper half is shown in red. In addition, overhead aerial trunks, ventilation trunks, boxes, shelves, stove funnels, etc are shaded with pale stripes. Beams and longitudinal girders under the decks are represented by lines broken at widely spaced intervals by short dashes, while bulkheads are represented by close dashed lines (except where the bulkhead is also above the deck in which case it is shown as a continuous line). Note that where intermediate beams under the Upper Deck have been restricted to the space between the inner longitudinal girders the short lines between the deck edge and the outer longitudinal girder represent the flange brackets at the tops of the frames. (M1802)

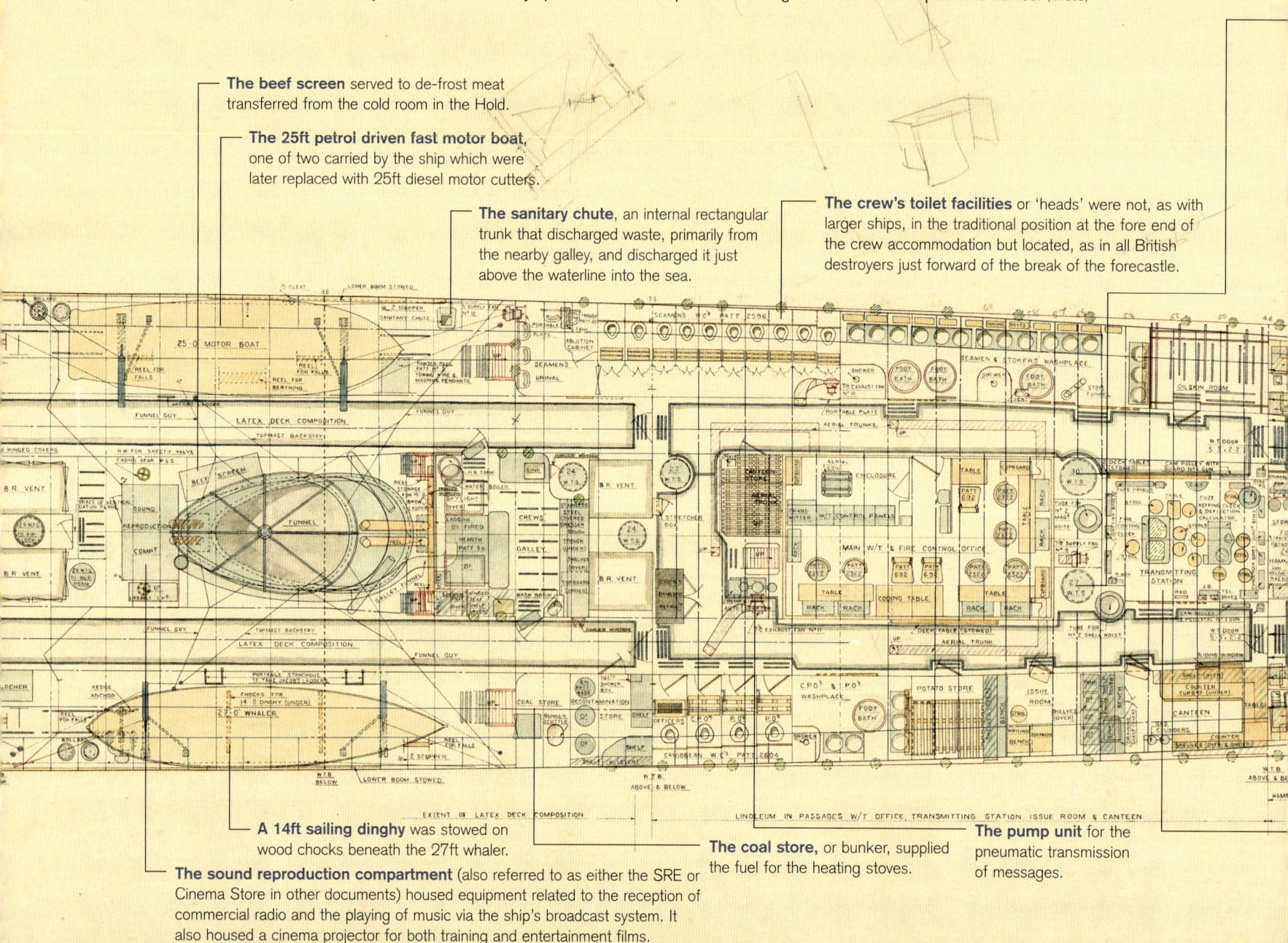

- **The beef screen** served to de-frost meat transferred from the cold room in the Hold.
- **The 25ft petrol driven fast motor boat**, one of two carried by the ship which were later replaced with 25ft diesel motor cutters.
- **The sanitary chute**, an internal rectangular trunk that discharged waste, primarily from the nearby galley, and discharged it just above the waterline into the sea.
- **The crew's toilet facilities** or 'heads' were not, as with larger ships, in the traditional position at the fore end of the crew accommodation but located, as in all British destroyers just forward of the break of the forecastle.
- **A 14ft sailing dinghy** was stowed on wood chocks beneath the 27ft whaler.
- **The sound reproduction compartment** (also referred to as either the SRE or Cinema Store in other documents) housed equipment related to the reception of commercial radio and the playing of music via the ship's broadcast system. It also housed a cinema projector for both training and entertainment films.
- **The coal store**, or bunker, supplied the fuel for the heating stoves.
- **The pump unit** for the pneumatic transmission of messages.

UPPER DECK

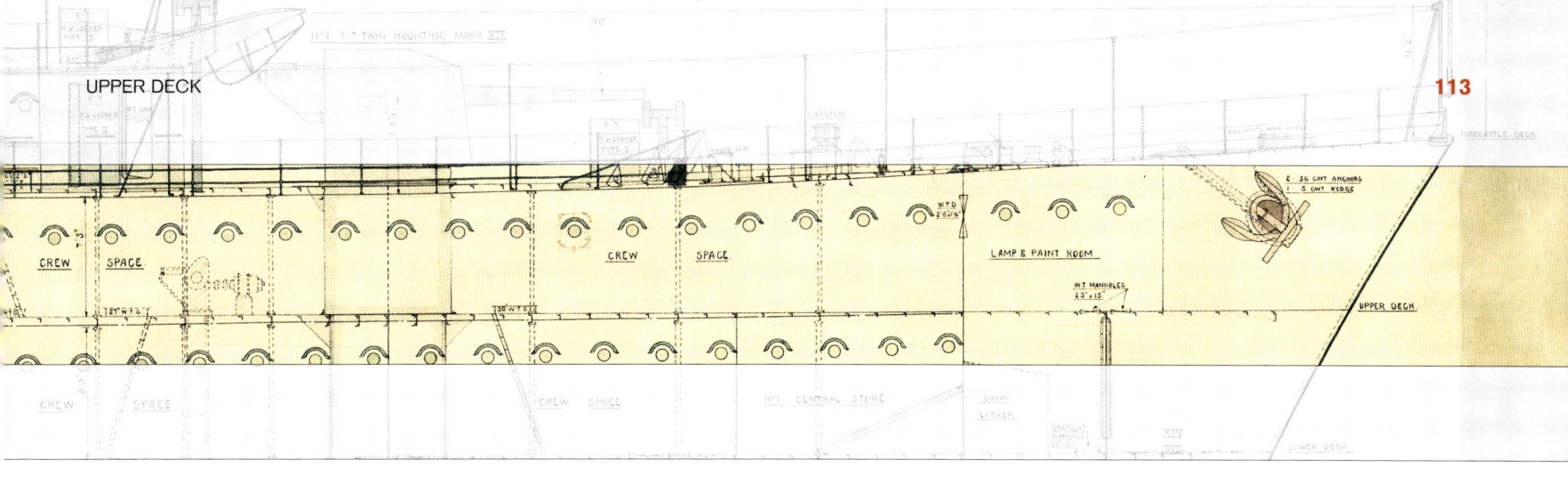

- **The circular water-tight scuttles** provided the primary means of access between decks. These were standard fittings in destroyers and smaller ships where rectangular hatches were limited in number and restricted to the Upper Deck and above. The sizes employed in *Cossack* and her sisters were 30in, 27in and 24in in diameter, the smaller of the three being used primarily for machinery spaces. Compartments that were not regularly accessed were provided with manholes (usually 23in x 15in) or, in the case of the fuel tanks, 18in diameter oil-tight scuttles.

- **The purpose of this ammunition hoist winch** is not entirely clear since it does not appear to be part of the primary supply arrangement, especially since this seems to be the only such item in the ship. It is possibly some aid to speed up the embarkation of ammunition.

- **The shell chutes** were fixed at an angle between the deck and deck head to supply shell transferred from the head of the power hoist to the guns of N°1, 2 and 3 mountings. The chute consisted of steel rods along which a sliding block shell carrier was hauled up via cable and pulley. The end of the cable was attached to a cross bar (shown at the top end of the chutes) which was pulled downward by hand to lift the shell up and through the opening in the deck above. Short troughs were provided as guides for the cartridges just below the hand-ups in the deck. Both the shell and cartridge chutes were stowed below the deck head when not in use. The film *In Which We Serve* (1942) has a few sequences showing both the hand and the power hoists in operation.

- **The lamp and paint room**, located remotely for safety reasons given the highly inflammable nature of the oil and paint it contained.

- **The Transmitting Station** showing the AFCC for LA control and, forward of it, the FKC for HA control. The GRU, at the port forward corner provided roll stabilisation for the FKC. The COS (change over switch), against the port side bulkhead, connected the system to either LA or HA control.

114   HMS COSSACK: ENLARGED DECKS, AS FITTED 1938

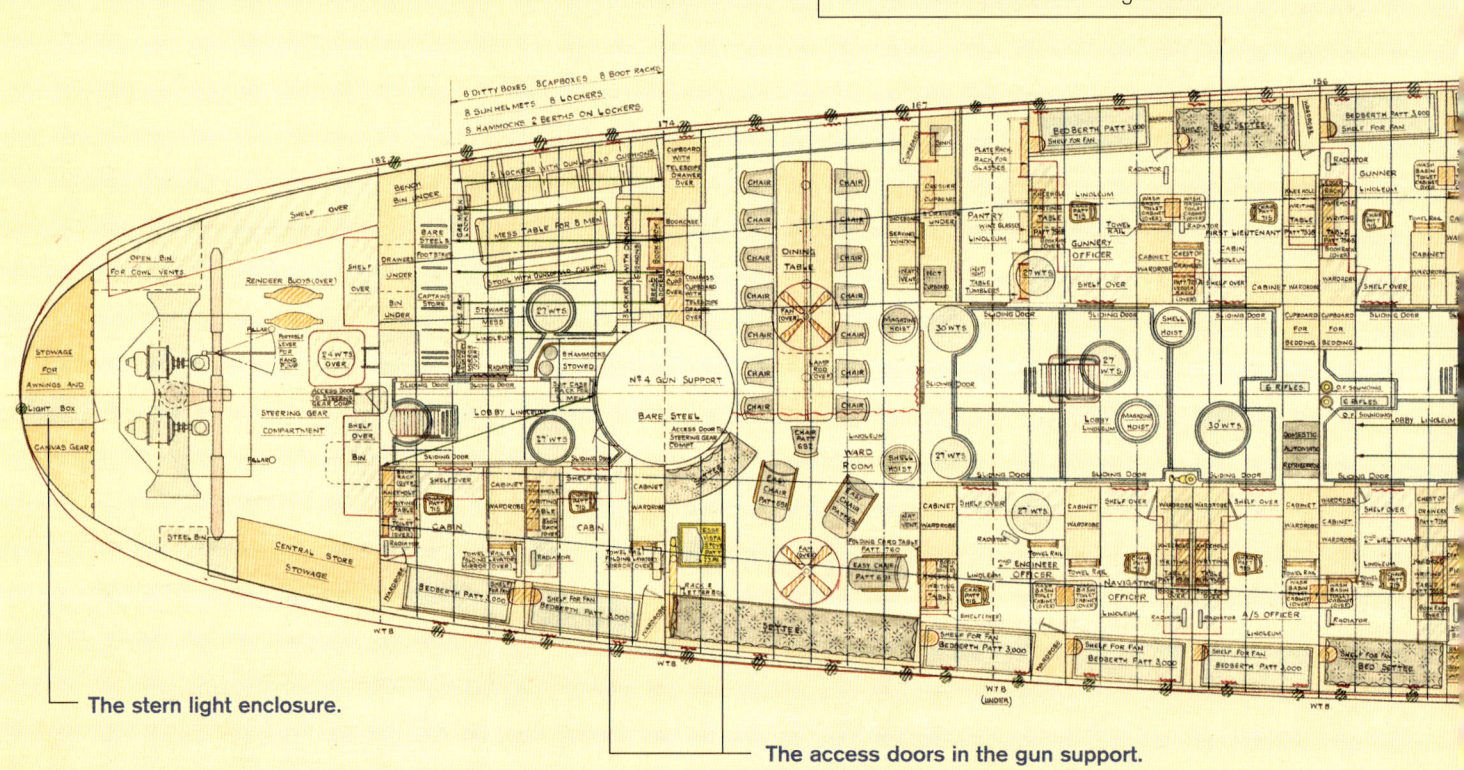

The officers' cabin lobby extended from the bulkhead at 149 Frame to the wardroom. Located in this area were a domestic refrigerator and four rifle racks accommodating six rifles each. There was another rifle rack (for 24 rifles) against the after bulkhead in the lobby between the staff office and the 2nd W/T office. Also located in the officers' lobby, but not shown here, were the handwheels to operate the flood valves for the after magazines.

The stern light enclosure.

The access doors in the gun support. Note that the door into the wardroom opens above a settee so it seem reasonable to assume that some method was available of ensuring that there was nobody sitting in that position before the door was opened.

LOWER DECK

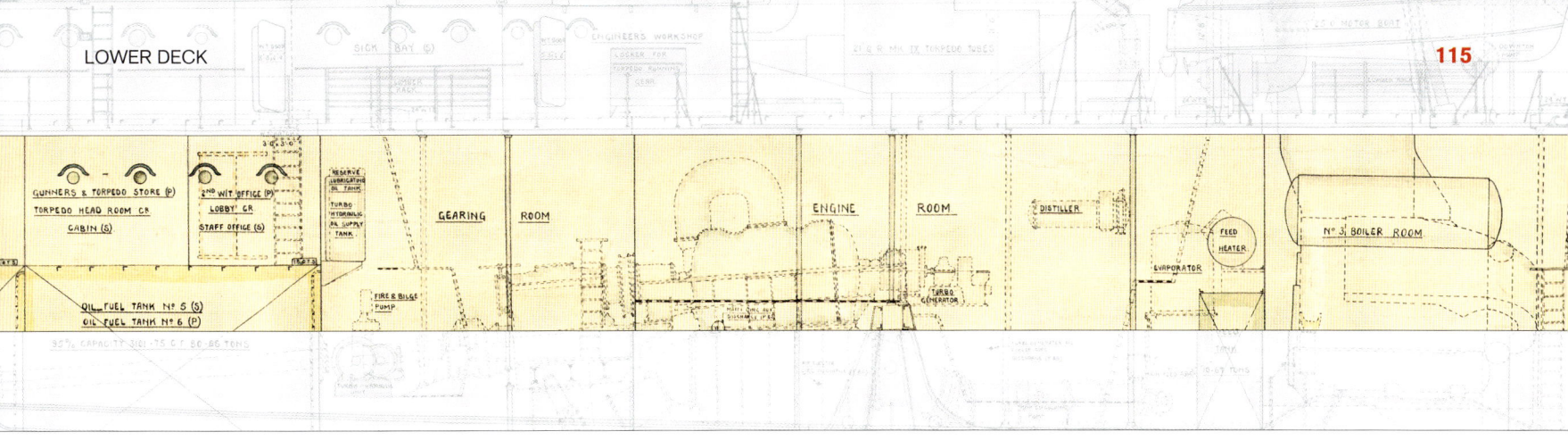

LOWER DECK (AFT)

The majority of the after section of the Lower Deck was occupied with officer accommodation. For the peacetime complement there were nine cabins, five for wardroom officers and three for warrant officers (gunner, 2nd engineer and schoolmaster). In addition, there were two cabins on the starboard side between the bulkheads at Frames 174 and 182 which provided for the additional officers required by the war complement. Opposite these spare cabins on the port side was the mess for the officer's stewards which accommodated eight men and their hammocks. There are, however, only six hammock berths, two stewards being bunked on top of the lockers on the port side and against the fore bulkhead. Access to forward areas for both the stewards and the additional officers was via the Upper Deck but given the risks involved in doing this in bad weather it seems likely that they then made their way to and from the wardroom through the access doors in No4 gun support. There was also supposed to be a hammock berth for a gunroom officer (presumably a midshipman since the only other gunroom officer was a sub-lieutenant and he was provided with a cabin) although no such officer was posted to *Cossack* on completion. There were actually four hammock berths available, three at the fore end of the officer cabin lobby and one in the lobby between the stewards' mess and the spare cabins but only stowage for two hammocks (at for end of the lobby). Presumably these were provided to cover any future demand for additional accommodation. Note that the engineer commander's cabin is forward of the bulkhead at Frame 149 so he did not have direct access to the lobby and the wardroom abaft that bulkhead. (M1803)

The side stringers ran the length of the machinery spaces. The method of construction employed where they crossed both the deep and standard frames is shown in greater detail on page 21.

The two 80kw turbo generators in the engine room supplied the ship's 220-volt dc ring main.

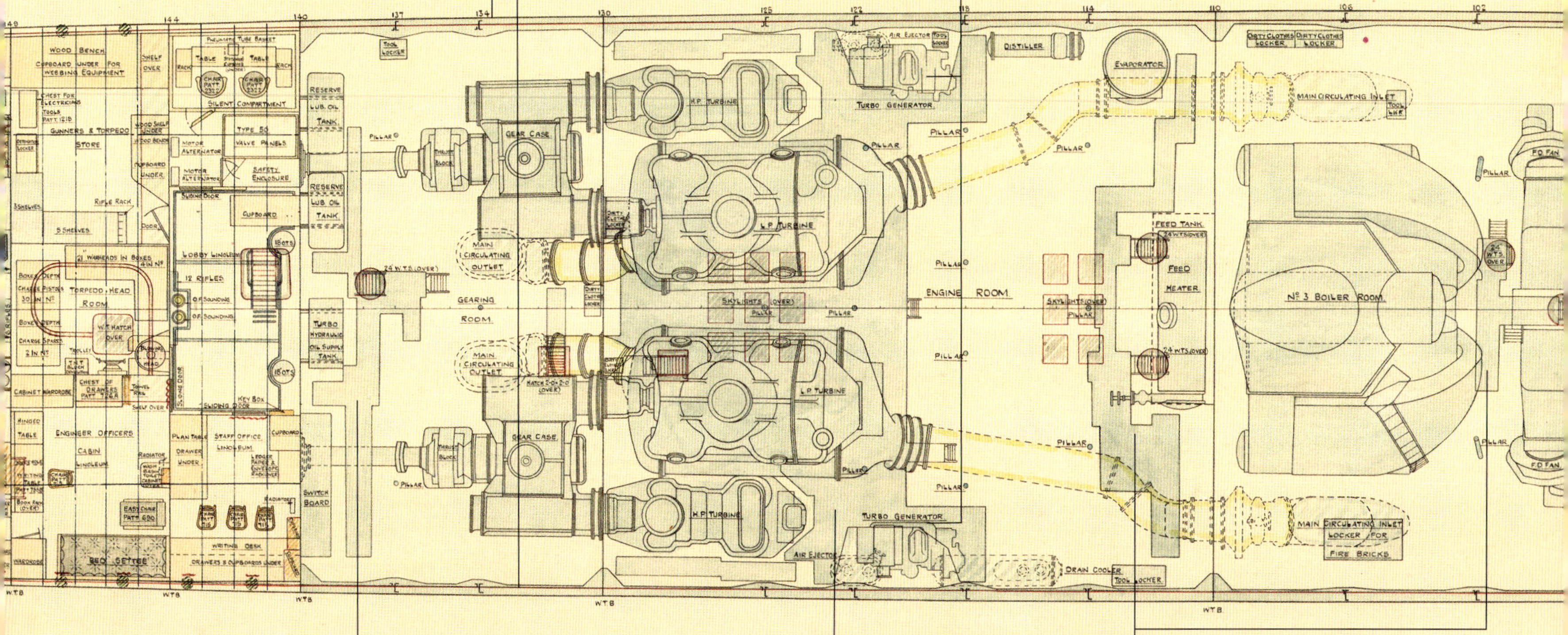

The upper level grating platforms in the machinery spaces, shaded, like the machinery, in light grey/green.

HMS COSSACK: ENLARGED DECKS, AS FITTED 1938

LOWER DECK (FORWARD)

The forward section of the Lower Deck, together with the fore end of the Upper Deck provided all the mess spaces for the ship's seamen and stokers. The CPOs, POs and ERAs were all accommodated on the Forecastle Deck, except for the steward POs who were provided with a mess between Frames 66 and 77 on the port side of the Lower Deck. The contents of the messes (storage boxes, shelves, racks and hammock stowage etc), are listed along the sides of the decks. The numbers of these items relate to the full war complement of 187 men (10 more than in peacetime). The figures given for the POs, etc do not align with the approved numbers (53 in war and 48 in peace) since they total only 43. (M1803)

The low power room contained the forward (secondary) HP switch board and the main LP switch board together with the majority of the ship's low power generators. These were driven by dc motors powered by the ship's 220-volt ring main to produce low power dc or ac supplies, motor generators (M/G) and motor alternators (M/A) respectively. The main M/G units are the two 4kw machines in the middle of the room which provided 22-volt dc for telephones, fire control, firing circuits, bells and buzzers etc. The other four units in the room are M/A to supply ac power for the W/T, fire control instruments, the pom-pom mounting and the gyro roll unit. The batteries in the starboard corner were permanently connected to the LP switchboard to assisted in maintaining a stabilised dc low power supply and to serve as a back-up should the mains power fail. Note that there were also local M/As in the main and 2nd W/T offices.

The location of hammock berths are indicated by these green lines with an arrow at each end. The ends of the hammock lines were tied to steel bars fixed to the deck beams or bulkheads.

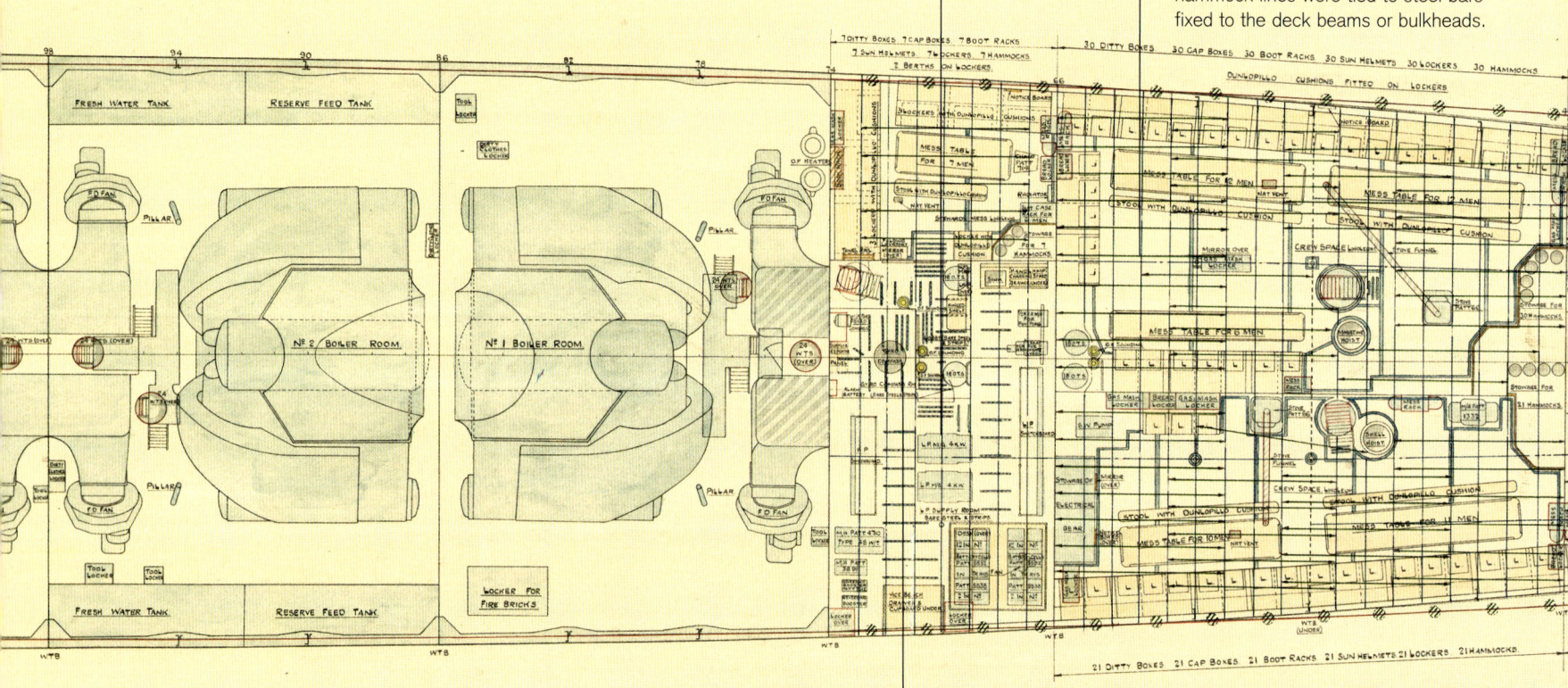

The gyro compass with, in the after port corner of the compartment, its M/A power supply.

LOWER DECK

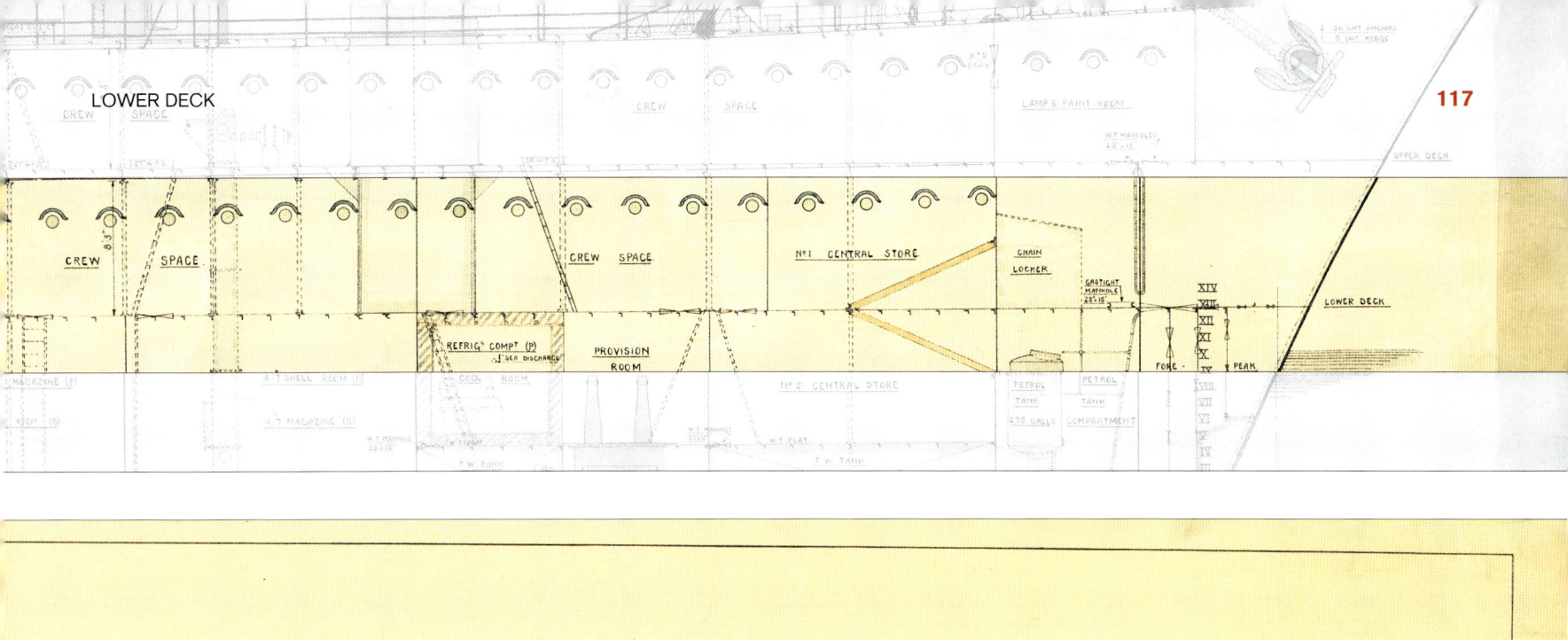

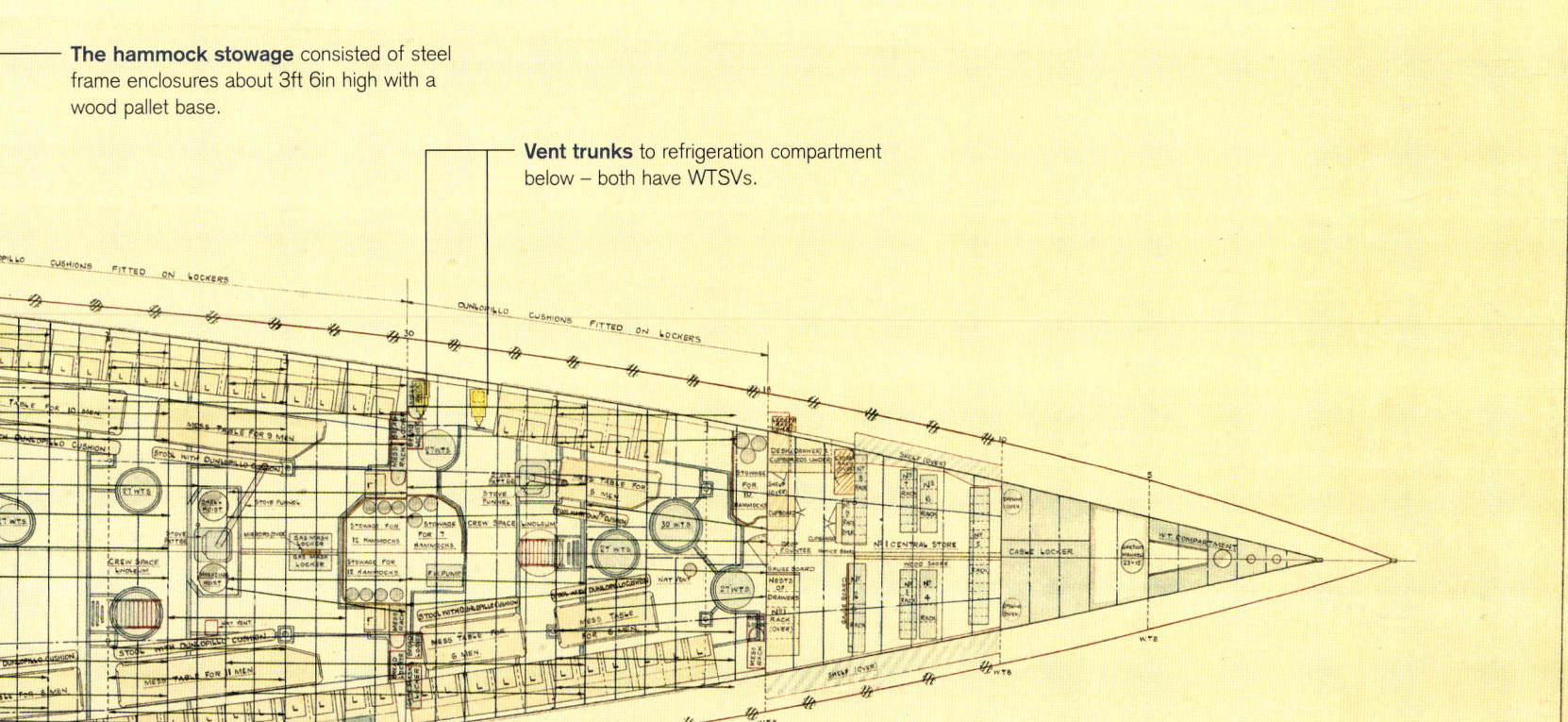

The hammock stowage consisted of steel frame enclosures about 3ft 6in high with a wood pallet base.

Vent trunks to refrigeration compartment below – both have WTSVs.

The A/S office was the primary control position for the Asdic and had direct voice communication with the bridge. The position controlled the training of the Asdic dome and (like the secondary control position on the bridge) was provided with a range recorder and distance finder. The office was a 'silent cabinet' as evidenced by the all-round sound insulation.

HMS COSSACK: ENLARGED DECKS, AS FITTED 1938

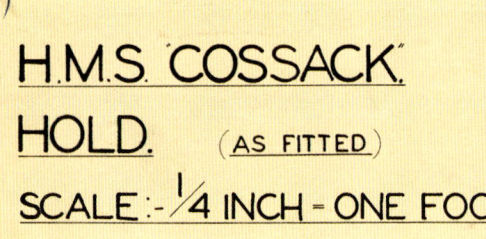

H.M.S. COSSACK.
HOLD. (AS FITTED)
SCALE :- ¼ INCH = ONE FOOT.

HOLD (AFT)

The flats in the Hold were mostly non-water-tight teak platforms mounted on steel beams. Non-water-tight steel flats were fitted in the steering compartment and within the machinery spaces. The only water-tight flats were fitted to the tops of the drinking water supply tanks forward (Frames 10–20 and 25–30) and in No 3 magazine and shell room. The compartment below the latter was occupied by the propeller shafts and was made water-tight in case of flooding resulting from a failure of the shaft stuffing boxes (also referred to as glands). (M1804)

CONTENTS OF 4.7" SHELL ROOM (165–174)	№
SHELLS Q.F 4.7" S.A.P.	380
SHELLS Q.F 4.7" H.E.D.A.	20
SHELLS Q.F 4.7" H.E.T.F.	100
SHELLS Q.F 4.7" H.A PRACTICE	26
SHELLS Q.F 4.7" L.A PRACTICE	80
BOXES FUZES Nº 198	6
BOXES FUZES Nº 230	5
BOXES UNDER WATER EXPLODING SIGNALS	2
BOXES CARTRIDGE SIGNALS 1"	3
BOX FIREWORKS	1
BOX SIGNAL ROCKETS 1LB	1
AMMUNITION WHIPS	
THERMOMETER MAX. & MIN.	1
SHELL BAGS	40
BOXES FUZES Nº 206	6
DRILL CARTRIDGES	10
DUMMY SHELLS	10

CONTENTS OF 4
Q.F. 4.7" CARTRIDGES
BOX CARTRIDGE IMPUL
DEPTH CHARGE PRIMER
HYGROMETER & THERM
IGNITERS IN TANK

The hydraulic steering gear was powered by two William Janney variable-delivery pumping units each driven by a 20bhp electric motor. Both pumps were normally used but the steering gear cylinders could be operated by one. An alternative hand pump was provided in case the electric power failed – the portable hand lever for this is shown in its working position extending forward of the port pump unit. The rudder area was 53ft² and had a maximum working angle of 35° p&s at which angle the ships of the class took 3min 20sec to turn a full 360° and 1min 40sec to turn 180° with an initial speed of 33 knots (this slowed substantially during the turn). The tactical diameter under the same conditions was about 900yds.

The plummer block compartments were deep oil-tight trunks passing through the after oil fuel tanks to provide for access from the Lower Deck for maintenance of the shaft plummer blocks.

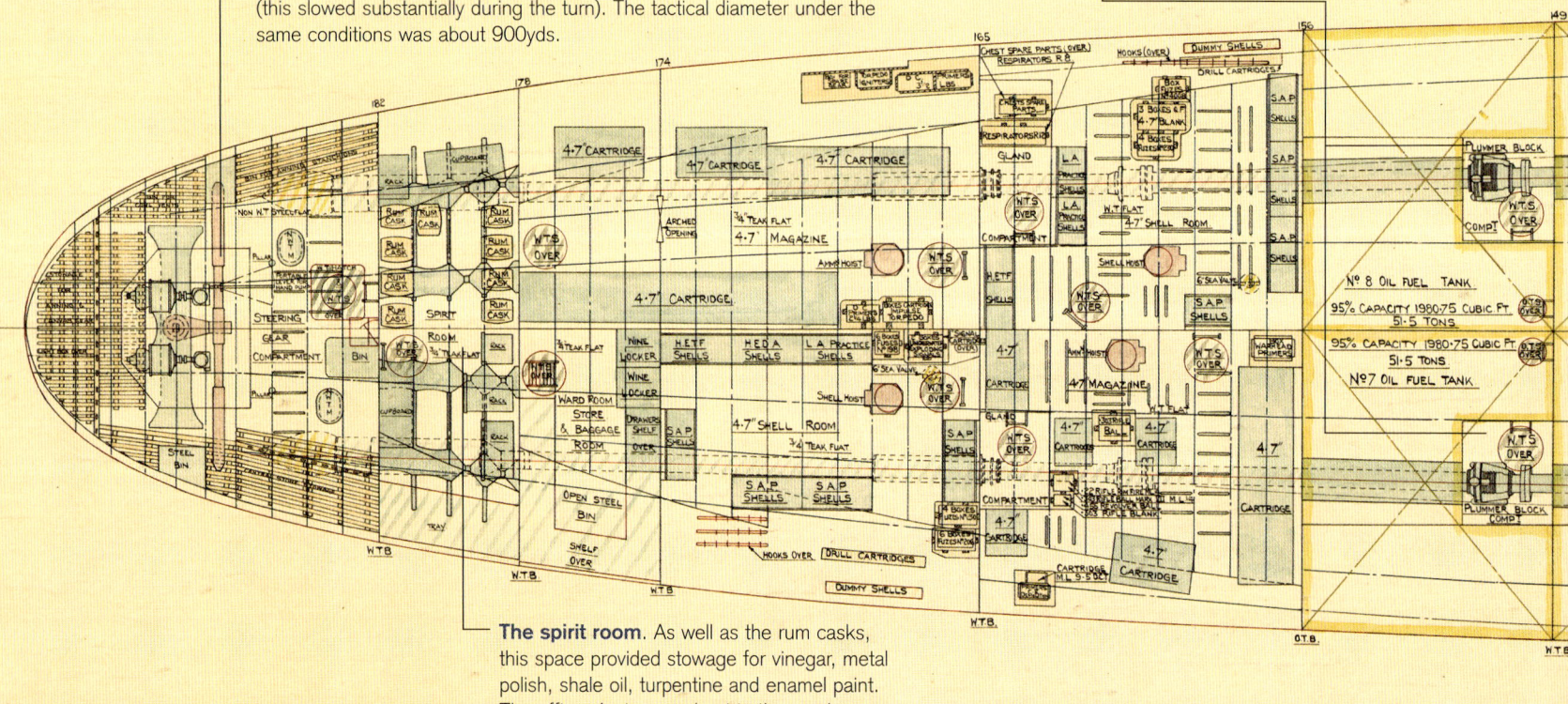

The spirit room. As well as the rum casks, this space provided stowage for vinegar, metal polish, shale oil, turpentine and enamel paint. The officers' wine was kept in the wardroom store just forward this compartment. Note that although the spirit room has a teak flat the drawings shows the frame structure beneath it.

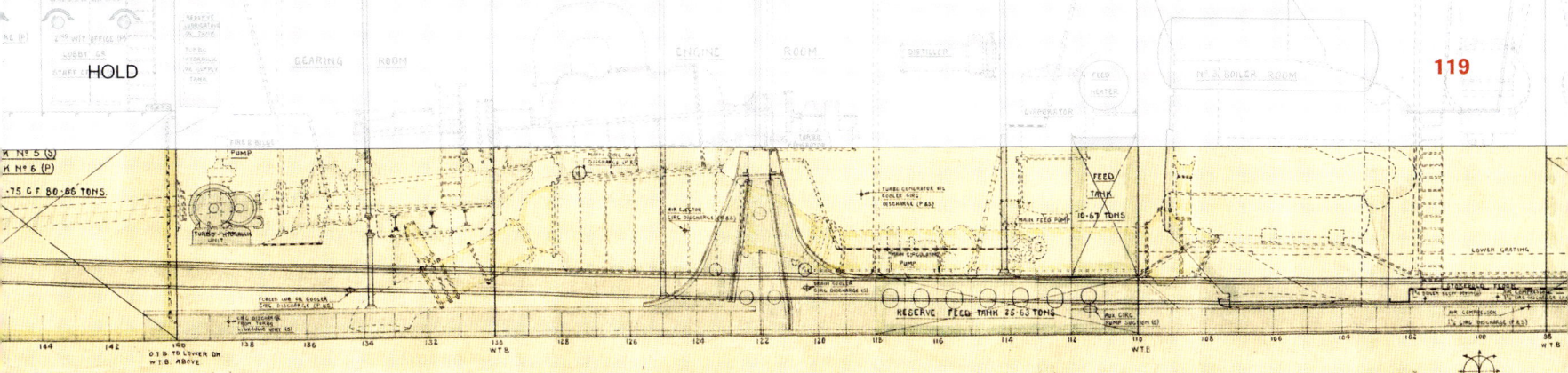

(165 – 178)	Nº
	4
	2
	2

CONTENTS OF 4·7" SHELL ROOM (156 – 165)	Nº
SHELLS Q.F. 4·7" S.A.P.	380
SHELLS Q.F. 4·7" H.E.D.A.	20
SHELLS Q.F. 4·7" H.E.T.F.	100
SHELLS Q.F. 4·7" H.A. PRACTICE	26
SHELLS Q.F. 4·7" L.A. PRACTICE	80
BOXES Q.F. 4·7" BLANK	3
BOXES FUZES Nº 198	6
BOXES FUZES Nº 230	5
BOXES FUZES Nº 400	8
BOXES FUZES Nº 206	6
BOXES ANTIGAS RESPIRATORS R 12	2
BOXES ANTIGAS RESPIRATORS R 8	2
CHEST OF SPARE PARTS	2
SHELL BAGS	40
BOXES TUBE VENT T.I.T	2
DRILL CARTRIDGES	10
DUMMY SHELLS	10
BOX ANTIGAS SPARES	1

CONTENTS OF 4·7" MAGAZINE (156 – 165)	Nº
Q.F. 4·7" CARTRIDGES 500 ROUNDS	
BOX ·303" RIFLE BALL MK. VII	43
BOX ·455" REVOLVER BALL	4
BOX ·303 RIFLE BLANK	3
BOX ·22" RIFLE RIM FIRE M.L. ¼	3
BOX WARHEAD PRIMERS 4LBS 4½ OZS C.E.	1
BOX C.E. " DEMOLITION	1
BOX CARTRIDGE ML 9·5 D.C.T	2
BOX ·303" RIFLE BALL MK VII M.L. ¼	3
HYGROMETER & THERMOMETER	

CONTENTS OF 4·7" SHELL ROOM (48 – 57)	Nº
SHELLS Q.F. 4·7" S.A.P.	380
SHELLS Q.F. 4·7" H.E.D.A.	20
SHELLS Q.F. 4·7" H.E.T.F.	100
SHELLS Q.F. 4·7" H.A. PRACTICE	26
SHELLS Q.F. 4·7" L.A. PRACTICE	80
SHELLS Q.F. 4·7" STAR	50
BOXES FUZES Nº 198	9
" " Nº 230	5
AMMUNITION WHIPS	
THERMOMETER MAX & MIN	1
PORTABLE STOOL	
SHELL BAGS	40
BOXES FUZES Nº 400	4
BOXES FUZES Nº 206	9
BOXES GRENADES	2
SAFETY BELT	1
DRILL CARTRIDGES	10
DUMMY SHELLS	10

The propeller shafts are indicated in broken line and pale shading to denote that they are hidden either within these tubes or below the flats. The same method is used for the sea valves under the flats.

The machinery foundations were constructed as extensions to the frames and longitudinals of the hull structure.

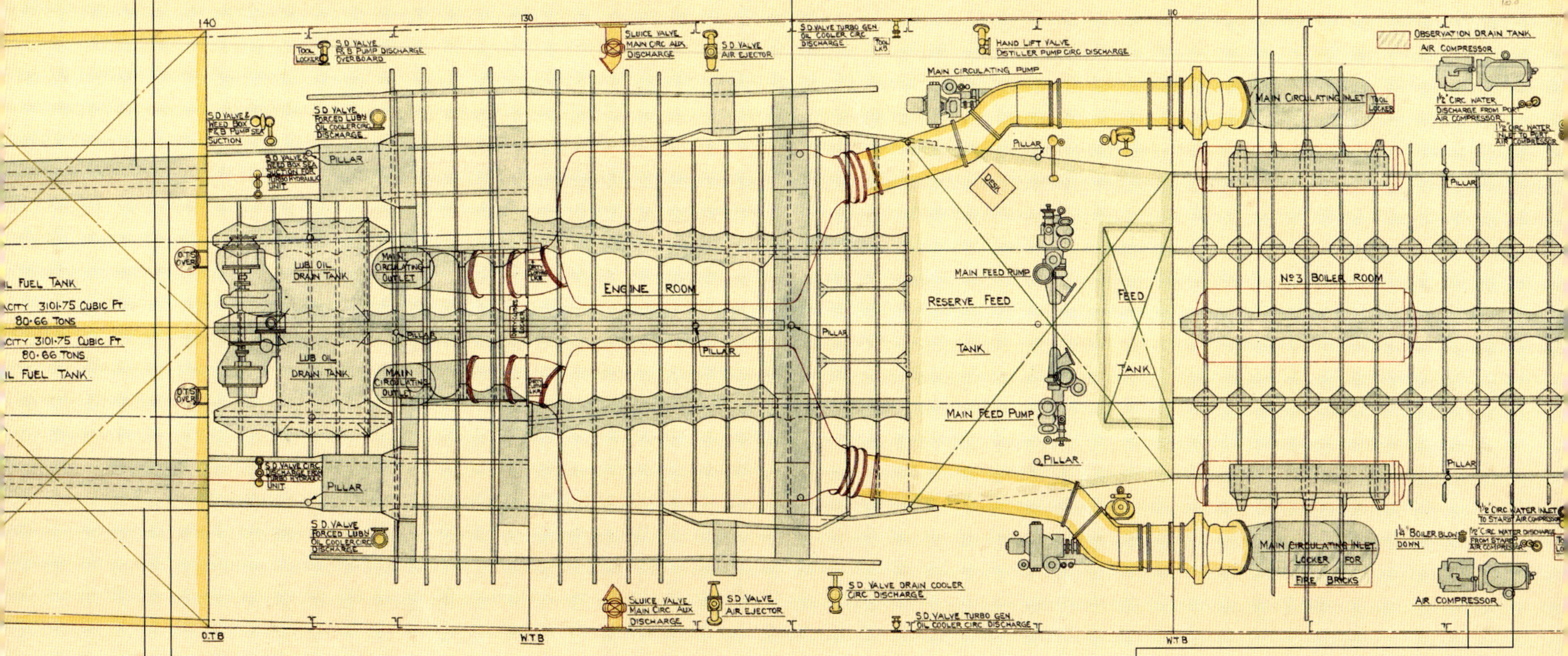

The wash bulkheads in the port and starboard oil fuel tanks are represented by these lines.

The Reavell TC6 air compressors could each deliver 17.5ft^3 of air at a pressure of 3500psi in 60 min.

HMS COSSACK: ENLARGED DECKS, AS FITTED 1938

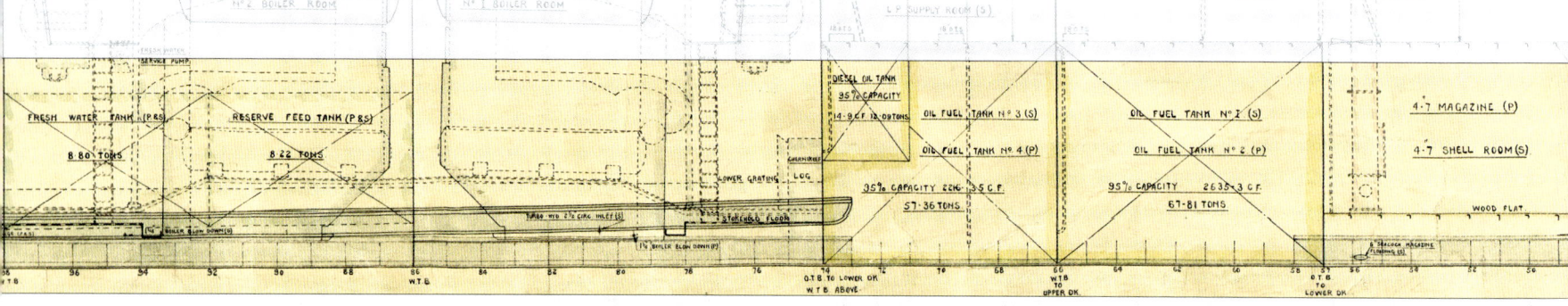

Contents of 4·7" Magazine (48 – 57)	No
G F 4·7" Cartridges 503 Rounds	
" " Star Cartridges 56 Rounds	
Boxes 2 Pdr Sub-Calibre C 102 Mk. II	19
Hygrometer & Thermometer	
Safety Belt	1
Handing Stool (Portable)	1

Contents of 2 Pdr. Pom Pom Magazine (40-48)	No
Boxes "M" Pom-Pom C 190 Mk. I	258
Boxes Pom-Pom Practice	12
Boxes A S A C5 Mk XI (·5 MG Ammunition)	15
Boxes A S A H24 Mk. I (" ")	54
Hygrometer & Thermometer	
Ammunition Whips	
Portable Stool	
Hooks for Portable Lamps	2

Contents of 4·7" Shell Room (30 – 40)	No
Shells Q F 4·7" S A P	380
Shells Q F 4·7" H E D A	20
Shells Q F 4·7" H E T F	100
Shells Q F 4·7" L A Practice	80
Shells Q F 4·7" H A Practice	26
Boxes Fuzes No 198 or 206	6
Boxes Fuzes No 230	5
Boxes Fuzes No 400	4
Ammunition Whips	
Thermometer Max & Min	1
Portable Stool	
Shell Bags	40
Safety Belt	1
Drill Cartridges	10
Dummy Shells	10

Contents of 4·7" Magazine	No
G F 4·7" Cartridges 500 Rounds	
Boxes ·303" Lewis Ball Mk VII	
" " Tracer	
Carriers Mag Lewis	
·303" Vickers Ball Mk VII	
·303" Vickers Machine Gun Belts	
Line Throwing Rifle	
Hygrometer & Thermometer	
Safety Belts	
Handing Stool (Portable)	
Box ·303" Ballistite Cartridges	

The location of web frames is indicated but not that of the standard 'Z' frames.

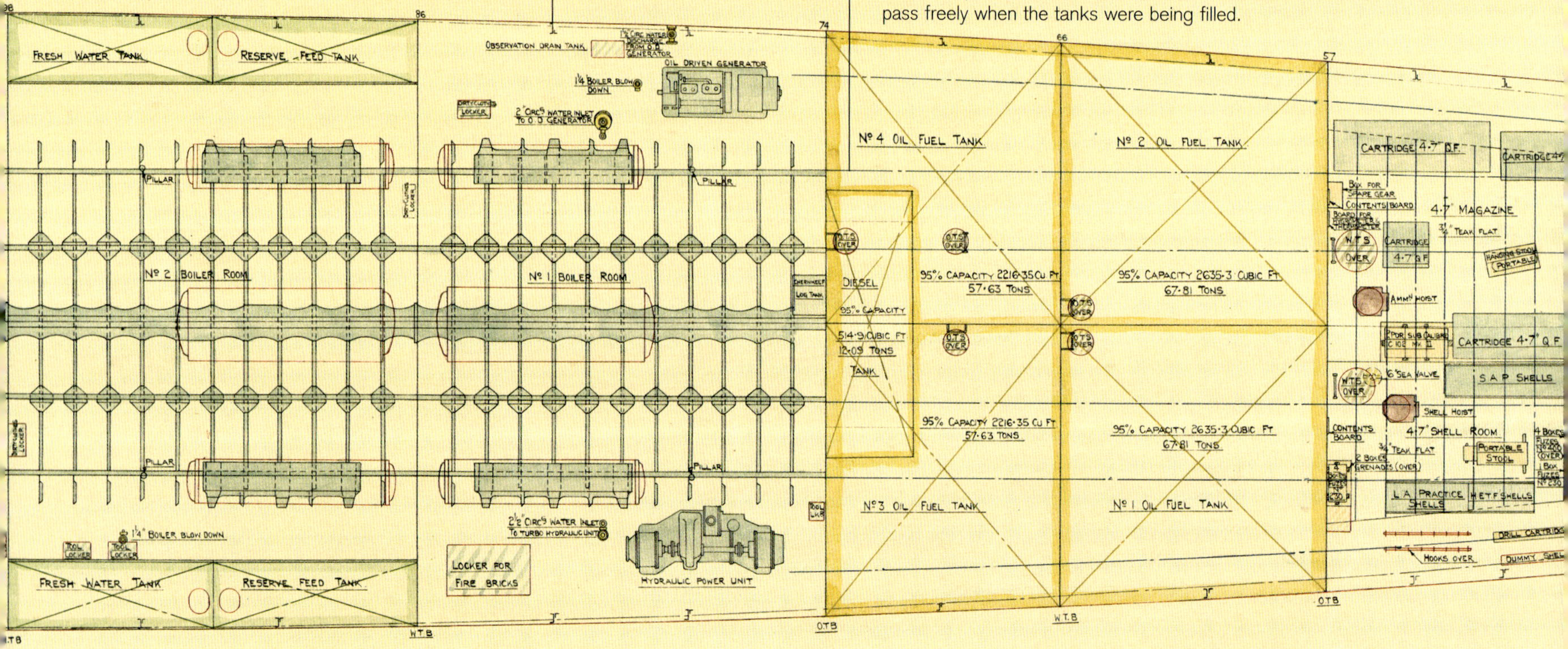

The line of the 2nd longitudinals is also the location of the heels of the wash bulkheads within the oil fuel tanks, noting that only the stiffeners of this bulkhead were actually fixed to the longitudinals since the bulkhead plating ended 2ft above it. The top edge of the bulkheads is not shown except for a faint line just inboard of the outer limits of the diesel fuel tank. The tops of the wash bulkheads (except where they served as part of the diesel tank) had 6in diameter holes to allow air to pass freely when the tanks were being filled.

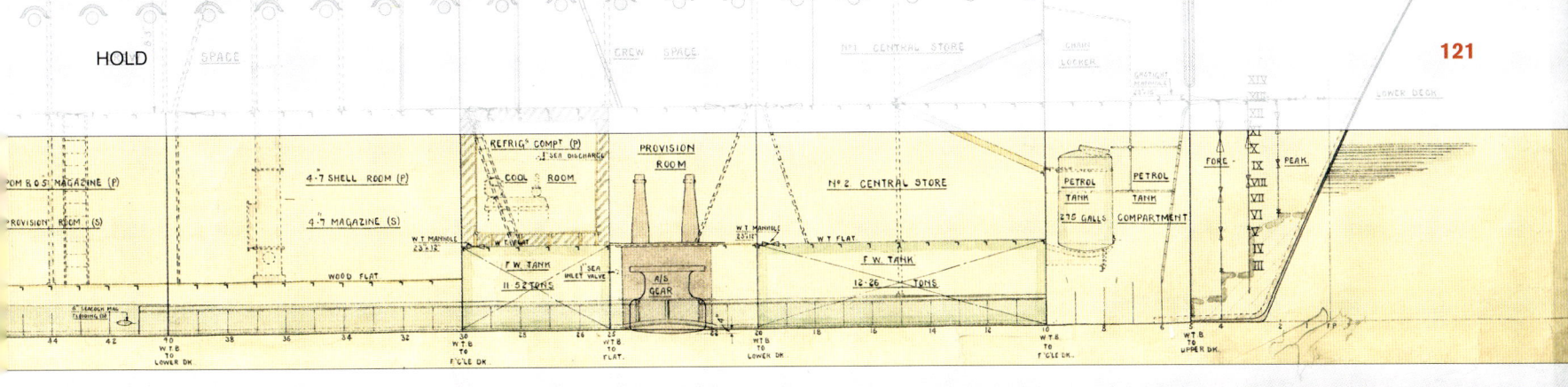

No	Capacities of O.F Tanks Calculated	Gross Capacity Gallons	Tons	95% Capacity Gallons	Tons
17	No 1 Tank Starbd	17132	71·38	16275	67·81
5	No 2 Port	17132	71·38	16275	67·81
12	No 3 Starbd	14558	60·66	13830	57·63
10	No 4 Port	14558	60·66	13830	57·63
14	No 5 Starbd	20376	84·90	19357	80·66
1	No 6 Port	20376	84·90	19357	80·66
1	No 7 Starbd	13009	54·20	12359	51·50
1	No 8 Port	13009	54·20	12359	51·50
	Diesel Centre	3385	12·72	3216	12·09

Capacities of F.W Tanks			
Tank	Frames	Gallons	Tons
F.W Tank Centre	10–20	2743	12·26
F.W Tank Centre	25–30	2578	11·52
Reserve Feed Tank Port	86–92	1839	8·22
Reserve Feed Tank Starbd	86–92	1839	8·22
F.W Tank Port	92–98	1970	8·80
F.W Tank Starbd	92–98	1970	8·80
Feed Tank Centre	110–112	2388	10·67
Reserve Feed Tank Centre	110–118	5734	25·63
Daily Storage Tank (Frd Starbd)		100	·45
Daily Storage Tank (Frd Port)		75	·34
Daily Storage Tank (Aft Starbd)		50	·22
Daily Storage Tank (Aft Centre)		50	·22
Cooling Water for Pom-Pom (Aft Centre)		50	·22

HOLD (FORWARD)

While the plans cover the arrangement of the hull structure fairly well, they provide little information with regard to the bulkheads. The as-fitted plans only indicate their positions and not their supports except for a few boundary angles in the profile. In general these were constructed mainly of 5lbs (⅛in) mild steel plates, 5ft wide and supported by vertical stiffeners spaced about 2ft apart. Those within the machinery spaces, which had no deck support, had a lower strake of 6lbs and 6in x 3in x 3in channel bar stiffeners. That between the engine and gearing rooms was also connected to the gear cases and the supports of the after turbine feet. The bulkheads at the ends of the machinery spaces (74 and 140) were 7lbs and stiffened with 3in x 1.5in x 1.5in channel bars below the Lower Deck and 5lbs with 3in x 2in angle bars above the Lower Deck. Beyond the machinery compartments the bulkheads were 4lbs with a 5lbs (6lbs at 66 and 147) lower strake, and 4in x 2in x 2in 'Z' bar stiffeners with the exception of the steering compartment bulkhead at Frame 182, which was constructed entirely of 10lbs plating, and that at Frame 178 which was of 8lbs plating. The constructional sections (pages 20–21) give a clearer idea of the general form of bulkhead construction as they show some of the longitudinal bulkheads (and the oil fuel tank wash bulkheads) while the drawing of the damage to *Eskimo* is helpful in showing the arrangement of stiffeners on bulkheads 140 and 149. (M1804)

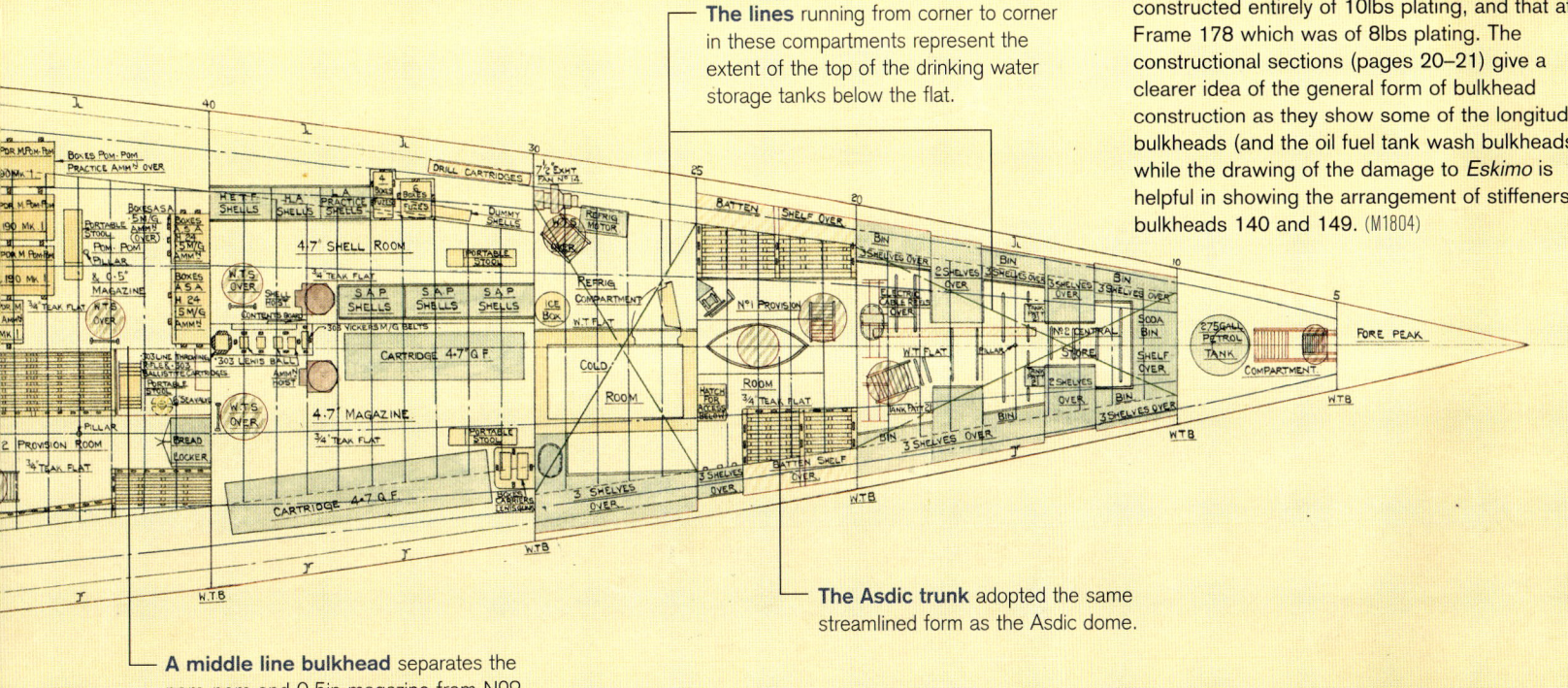

The daily storage tanks listed in this table refers to the fresh-water gravity tanks fitted on the forward and after superstructures.

The lines running from corner to corner in these compartments represent the extent of the top of the drinking water storage tanks below the flat.

The Asdic trunk adopted the same streamlined form as the Asdic dome.

A middle line bulkhead separates the pom-pom and 0.5in magazine from No 2 provision room, an item not entirely clear since its line is faint and appears to be a continuation of the centre line.

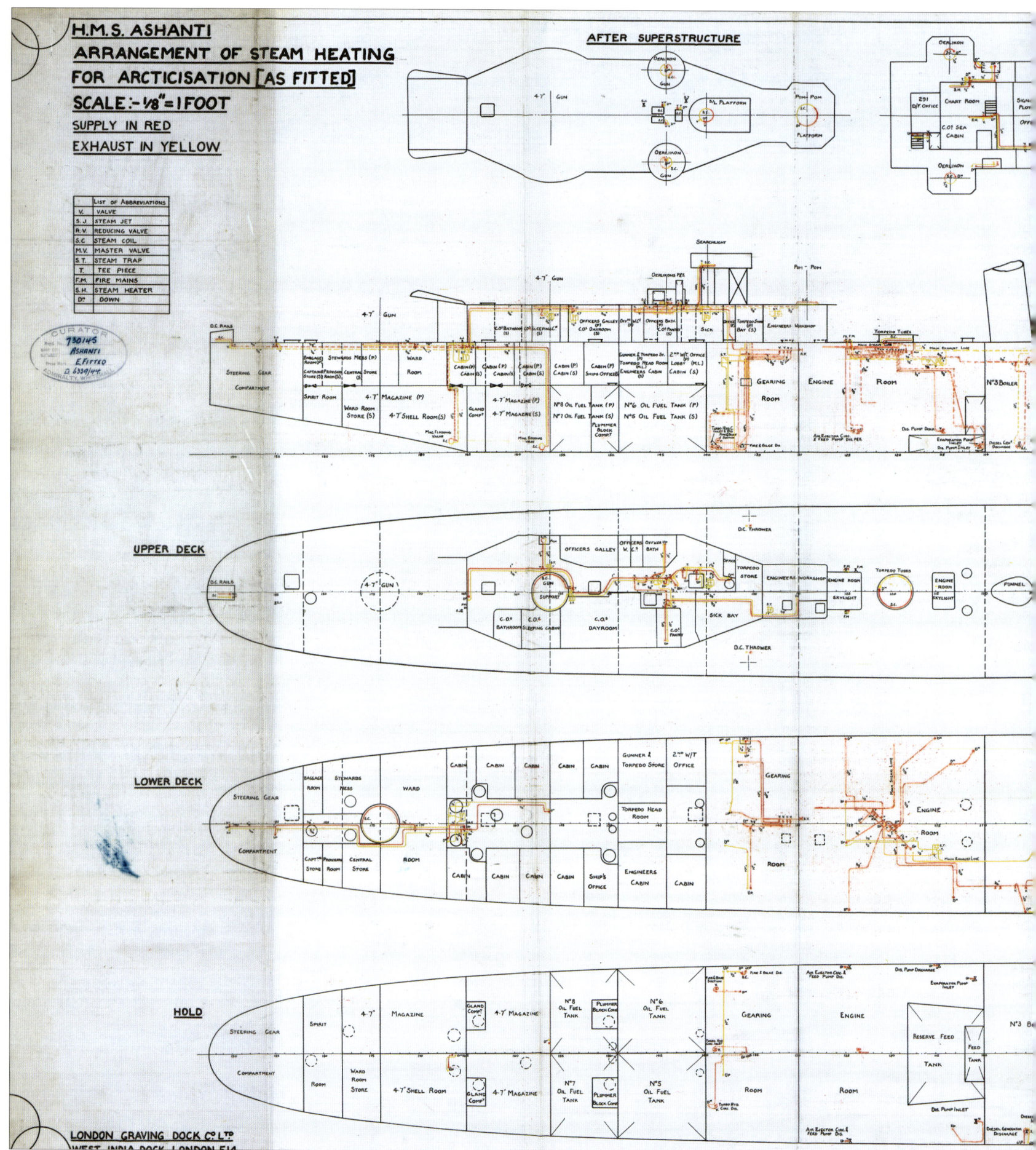

HMS ASHANTI: ARRANGEMENT OF STEAM HEATING FOR ARCTICISATION, AS FITTED

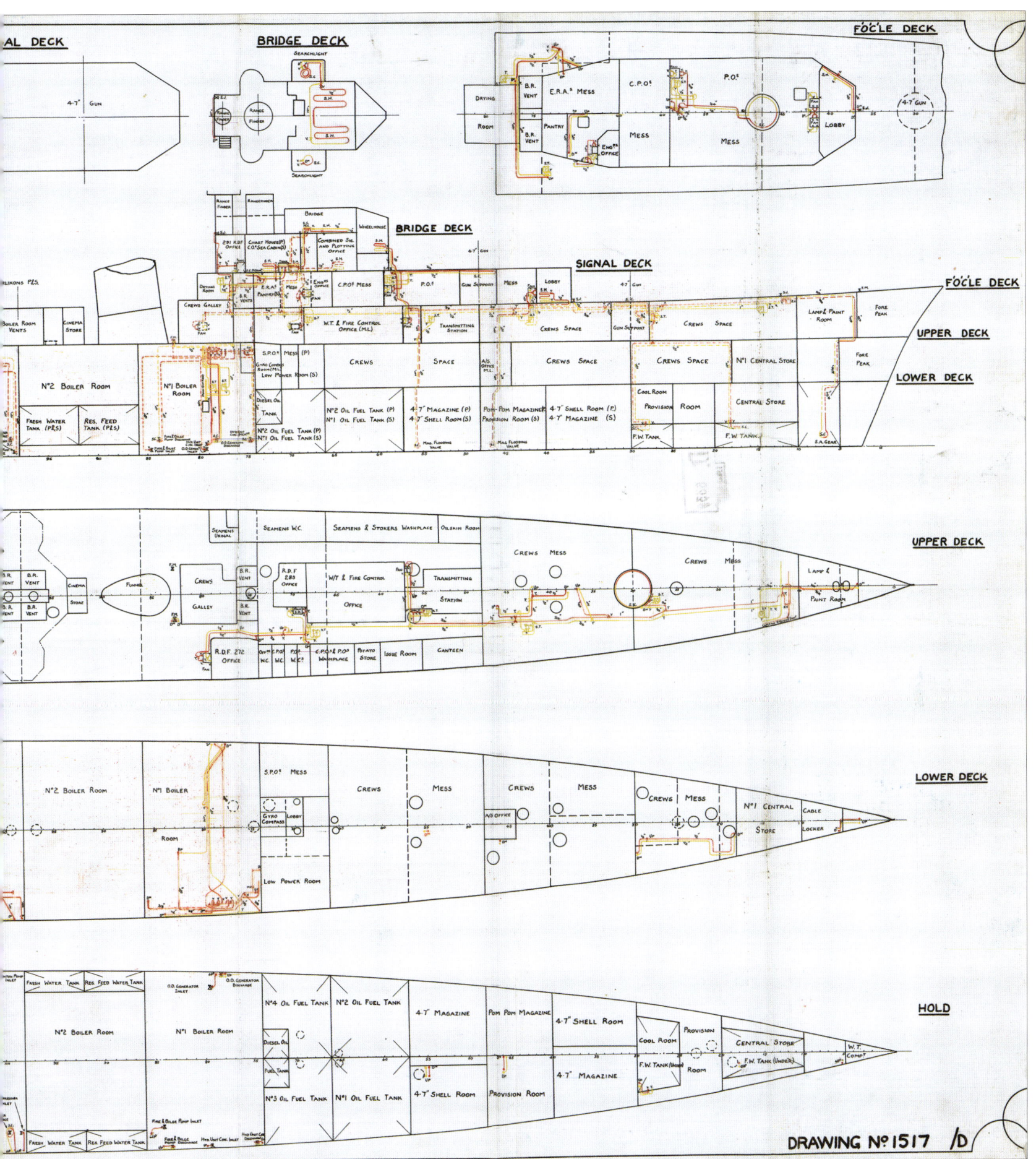

Drawing No. 1517/D

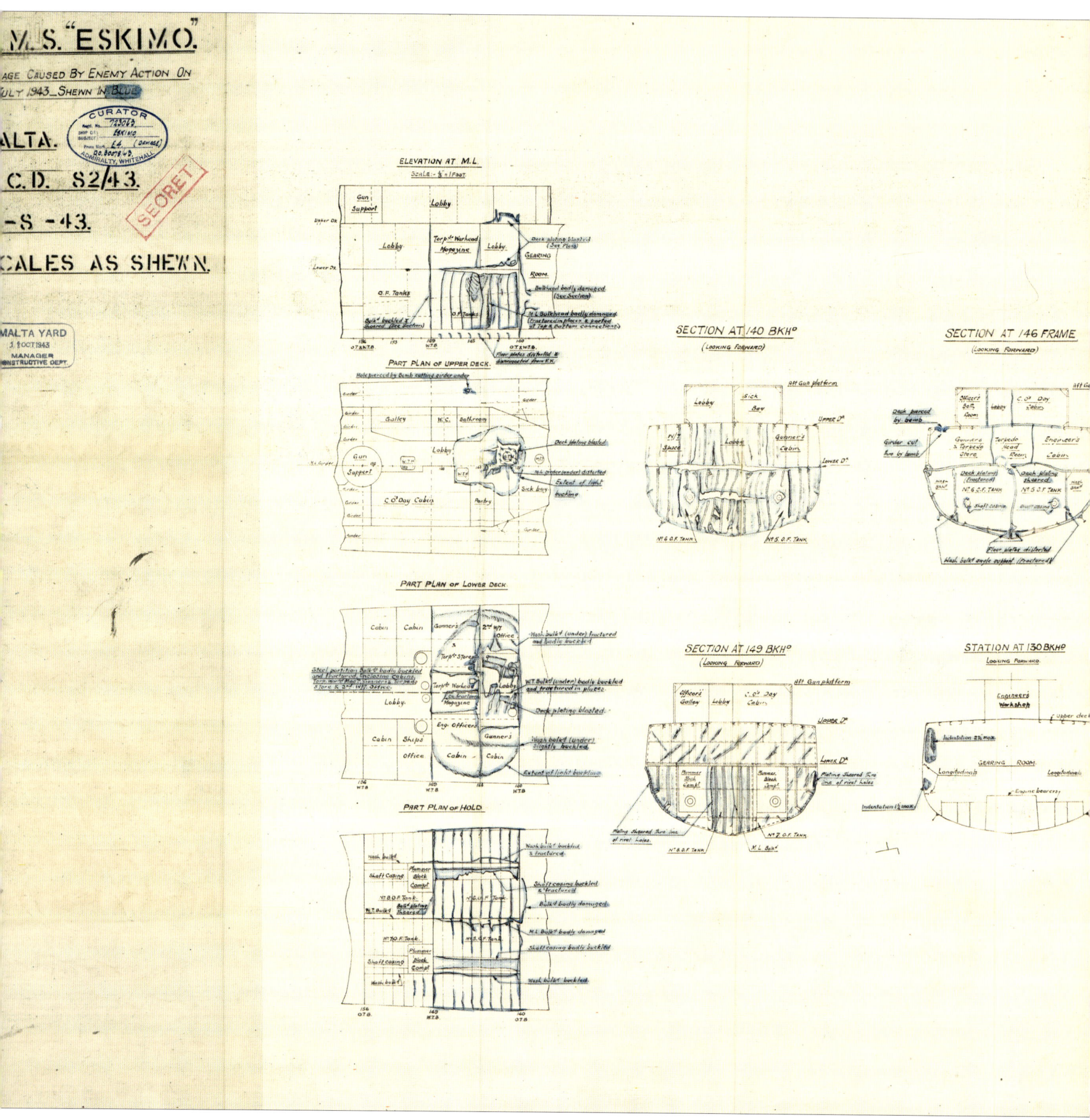

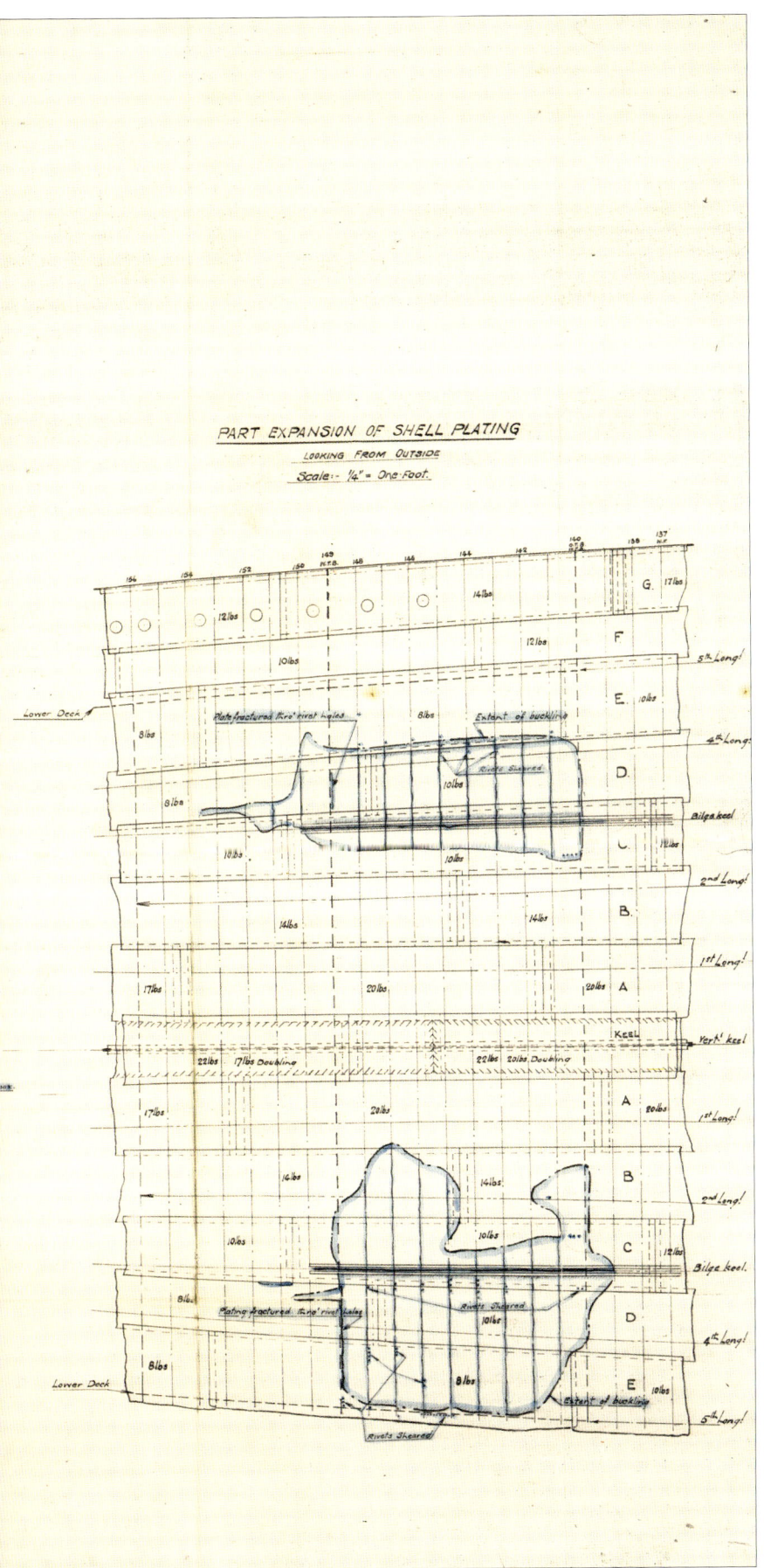

HMS *ASHANTI* ARCTICISATION (previous pages)

Service in arctic waters in winter often involved serious problems due to the build-up of ice and snow on decks and superstructure, which could seriously comprise a ship's stability and the operation of the armament and other shipboard equipment. In addition, the efficiency of the crew was affected by low temperatures and the fatigue resulting from the effort of clearing ice and snow. Plans to improve this situation, by fitting additional heating and insulation, were taken relatively early in the war and were included in the list of alterations for the 'Tribal' class approved up to November 1942. As usual these changes took some time to implement and generally awaited the next convenient refit/repair. In the case of the 'Tribal's it is probable that only the four survivors of the original class *Ashanti*, *Eskimo*, *Nubian* and *Tartar* were fitted for arctic service and then not until 1943–44. This plan shows the arrangement of the steam heating pipes fitted in *Ashanti* while refitting in London during July–September 1943. It does not show the origin of the steam supply but presumably this came off the auxiliary machinery steam-line. The system provided heating to the gun and torpedo tube mountings; the depth charge rail and throwers; water tanks; flood, intake and discharge valves in the bottom; and for personnel in both their operational positions and accommodation spaces. There are also a number of steam jet hose connections on the decks for clearing ice and snow from the upper works. (M1835)

DAMAGE TO HMS *ESKIMO*, 1943

In the early morning of 12 July 1943 while proceeding at 20kts to Augusta, Sicily the *Eskimo* was attacked by dive-bombers 3 miles S by E of Cape Murro di Porco. She was near missed by two bombs, one forward and one aft, and hit by a third close to the port side of the Upper Deck abreast the mainmast. The 250kg bomb passed though the Lower Deck and exploded in the fore end of No 6 oil-fuel tank causing severe disruption to the surrounding bulkheads and decks and extensive damage to the gearing room. Splits in the skin plating rapidly flooded No 5 and 6 fuel tanks, the plummer block compartments, gearing room and the Lower Deck compartments between Frames 140 and 149. The bomb also started an oil-fuel fire but this was extinguished 40 minutes later. The hydraulic pump machinery for the after 4.7in mounting was wrecked, as were the fire control circuits, reducing the after mountings to local control and, in the case of the 4.7in, manual operation. Other problems, including a bent port propeller shaft and damage to the forced lubrication system, brought the ship to a standstill. She was towed to Malta by *Tartar*, where temporary repairs were carried out during July–August and then returned home to be fully repaired at Immingham between September 1943 and April 1944. The accompanying drawing was produced by Malta Dockyard as part of their report on the damage to the ship.

It is notable that although 75 per cent of the original 16 'Tribal's were lost, an even larger number were damaged and survived. The one weapon where survival was rare was the torpedo. Six 'Tribal's were lost to torpedoes, two from destroyers, three from submarines and *Bedouin* from an aircraft (although in the latter case after being disabled by gunfire). The lone survivor was *Eskimo*, whose hull from No 1 gun forward was destroyed by a torpedo during the 2nd Battle of Narvik on 13 April 1940; luckily this extensive damage did not explode the forward magazine or compromise the integrity of her surviving structure. Damage was more frequent than loss where bomb damage was concerned since near misses were more common than hits. Ships of the class survived a total of fourteen damaging bomb attacks of which only three involved direct hits while the majority of the remainder only caused superficial damage. There were five losses from bombs of which two were due to close near misses. Gun actions were rare and, with a few exceptions such as the 2nd battle of Narvik, rarely produced major damage. Only the *Sikh* was sunk solely by shell fire (from shore batteries at Tobruk), and the *Bedouin* (as mentioned above) in part by shell damage. No 'Tribal's were lost to mines although two (*Cossack* and *Zulu*) suffered shock damage from acoustic mines. Despite the misgivings of the Admiralty about increased target size and general vulnerability the 'Tribal's do not appear to have been any more liable to loss than smaller destroyers. The 'J' and 'K' class that followed the 'Tribal's also suffered 75 per cent losses. The earlier 'A' to 'I' flotillas averaged about 50 per cent but this probably reflects that fact that many of these vessels were withdrawn from fleet operations, mainly to serve as Atlantic escorts, as new war-built destroyers entered service. The destroyers that joined the fleet from 1940 onward had a shorter war and steadily improving circumstances which resulted in a progressive reduction in losses from class to class. (M1836)

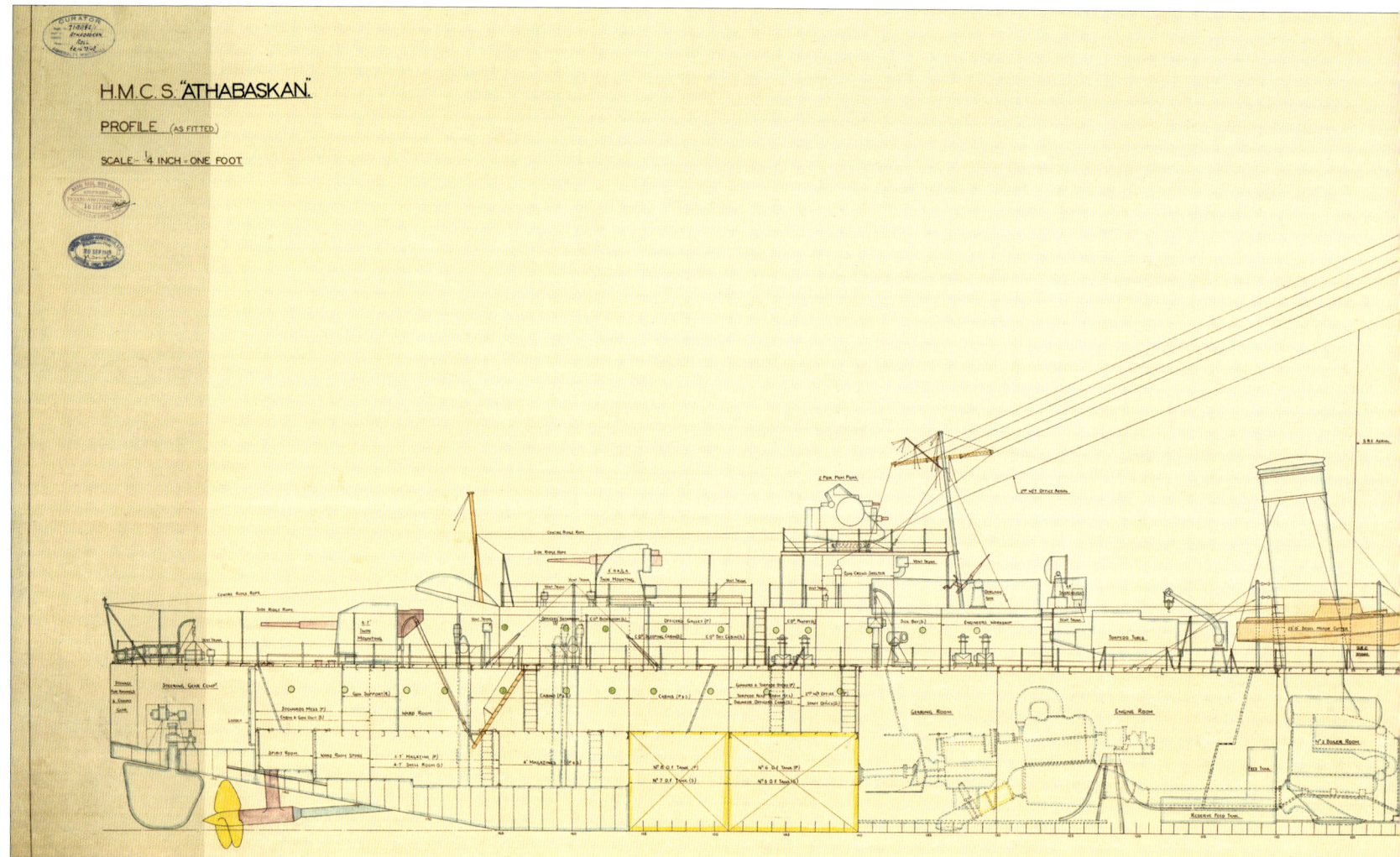

HMCS ATHABASKAN PROFILE, AS FITTED 1943

Despite the stamps carrying a September 1943 date the *Athabaskan* was completed in this configuration in February 1943. Unlike the Australian ships, which were built to the original design (with approved changes), the Canadian vessels incorporated modifications to the design to meet specific Canadian requirements in relation to hull strength, stability and habitability. In part these resulted from strength problems arising with some of the RN 'Tribal's in heavy weather during the winter of 1940–41. Working of the hull caused leaks which contaminated the reserve feed water tank in the engine room and the fresh-water storage tanks forward. In addition, the keel and garboard strakes were corrugated between Frames 25 and 40. As a result stiffening was fitted to the bottom plating abreast the keel forward and to the bottom plating and Upper Deck amidships. This was incorporated in the Canadian ships as built. Additional requirements were a 1ft increase in beam to 37ft 6in and heating of accommodation and machinery areas to cope with the winter weather in Canada. The latter consisted of a steam heating pipe system supplied by and auxiliary boiler in Nº1 boiler room and the substitution of a pressurised plumbing system in place of gravity tanks since these were prone to freezing. Other changes made to the design up to the end of 1940 included:

1. A 44in searchlight in place of the 24in.
2. Updating of the quad Mk IX torpedo tube mounting to Mk IX* (a minor improvement on the original that had already been adopted for RAN ships).
3. Electro-hydraulic pumps for the main armament in place of the turbo-hydraulic units in the RN 'Tribal's. This had already been adopted in the 'J', 'K' and 'N' class destroyers. There were three pump units, one for each 4.7in mounting but those for the forward mountings were cross connected so they could supply either mounting.
4. Increasing the electricity power supply by fitting two 200kw turbo generators and two 60kw oil driven generators in place of the two 80kw and single 30kw units in the RN ships. This provided for the increased demand created by the installation of the electro-hydraulic pumps, the 44in searchlight and general increases in demand resulting from wartime additions such as radar.
5. Relocation of the quad pom-pom to a raised platform aft of the searchlight platform where it enjoyed a much-improved arc of fire, especially on after bearings.
6. Larger main diesel fuel tank giving a 95 per cent capacity of 29 tons. The tank was deeper than in the RN ships and extended to the full depth of the oil fuel compartments. The loss in oil fuel capacity was mostly made up by the increased beam but the 95 per cent oil fuel capacity was slightly less than in the RN ships at 509 tons.
7. To prevent contamination by sea water through leaks in the bottom, the reserve feed tank in the engine room was moved to a position 18in above the bottom. Note that the profile of *Athabaskan* designates this tank as the overflow feed tank and not as a reserve feed tank as in the RN ships although in both cases they served both functions.

Apart from the above, which were specific to the RCN ships, the following modifications, decided upon for the RN 'Tribal's up to the end of 1942, were also adopted in the four RCN ships constructed by Armstrongs:

1. Twin 4in mounting substituted for Nº3 4.7in together with necessary changes to magazine stowage and to fire control system.
2. Fitting of six single 20mm Oerlikons, three each side – in the wings of the Flag Deck, in place of quad 0.5in MG mountings and in place of the DC thrower on the after superstructure (the thrower was moved down to the Upper Deck). By the end of 1942 the allocated outfit was modified to provide twin power

HMCS ATHABASKAN: PROFILE, AS FITTED 1943

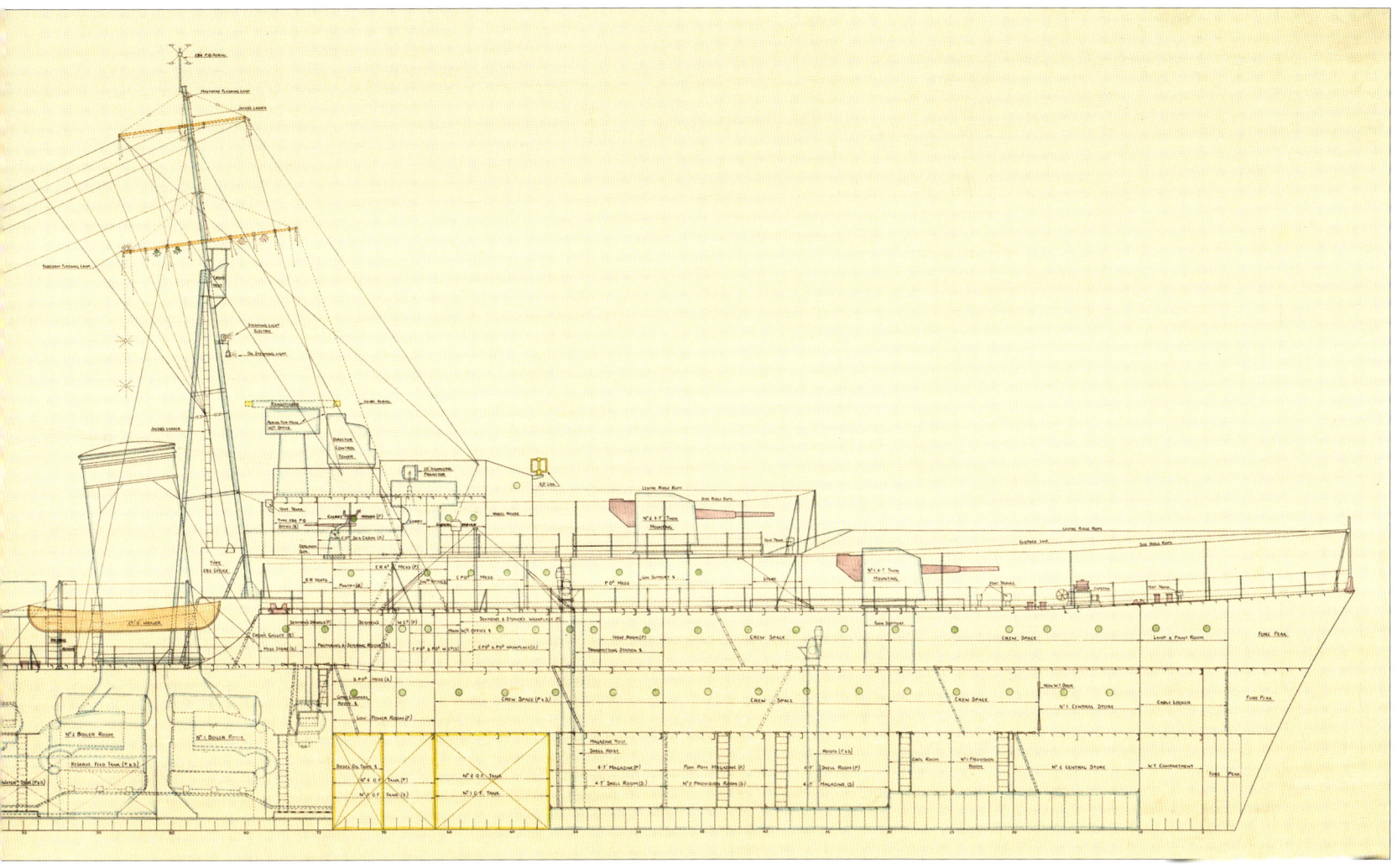

operated 20mm in the fore and after positions and this was later modified to a uniform six twin 20mm. However, changes were often delayed by shortages of both equipment and time so mixed arrangements, including combinations of 0.5in MG and single 20mm and single and twin 20mm, were common. *Athabaskan*, as shown above, was completed with six single Oerlikons but these were replaced by twins while she was under repair at Devonport in August–November 1943.

3. Fitting of windshield to rangefinder/director which was re-designated Mk III(W). The last of the Armstrong built RCN ships to complete, *Haida* and *Huron*, had a modified fire-control system in which the destroyer DCT was omitted and the rangefinder/director updated to MkIII(W). The latter was adopted in the first two RCN ships built in Canada.
4. Fitting of radar Type 286PQ and Type 285 and IFF Mk III. The aerial for the former is shown above at the foremast head but that for the Type 285 has been omitted even though it had been installed by January 1943. The Type 285 office can be seen at the base of the foremast above the crew's galley. Sometime between completion and mid-1943 *Athabaskan* was fitted with a Type 271 with its aerial lantern located between the pom-pom and searchlight platforms. It is also possible that she had the Type 286 replaced with Type 291 at this time. Unlike her sisters, she was not fitted with a lattice mainmast for HF/DF but during her August–November refit and repair she received the standard late war lattice foremast with HF/DF FH4 aerial on the fore topmast and Type 293 radar with its aerial on the foremast platform. At the same time the Type 271 and 286 (or 291?) were removed.
5. Depth charge outfit increased from 30 to 46. Note that *Athabaskan* has a six-charge rail at the stern and more reloads for the DC thrower than were originally provided.
6. Height of after funnel reduced by 4ft. Note that the profile of *Athabaskan* does not include this alteration although it was applied to that ship before completion.
7. Replacement of mainmast by a short pole to carry the W/T yard.
8. Zarebas fitted in place of wire netting abreast 4.7in gun mountings.
9. Ensign staff fitted at after end of after superstructure.

The first two Canadian built 'Tribal's, *Micmac* and *Nootka* completed shortly after the war and incorporated the latest modifications applied to the earlier RCN ships. In addition, *Nootka* was fitted with two twin 40mm mountings in place of the quad pom-pom. The next pair, *Cayuga* and the second *Athabaskan*, completed in 1947–48 with a uniform main armament of four twin 4in mountings, a Mk VI director and a close-range armament of two twin and four single 40mm Bofors. During the late 1940s the remaining RCN ships had the forward 4.7in mountings (with the exception of *Haida*) replaced with twin 4in mountings and the after 4.7in mounting with Squid anti-submarine mortars (also fitted to *Athabaskan* and *Cayuga* in place of a twin 4in). An exception was *Micmac* which retained the two after 4in mountings and had her forward 4.7in mountings replaced by a Squid mortar on the forecastle and a quad 40mm mountings on No2 gun deck. During the same period the 20mm guns in all ships were gradually supplanted by single 40mm Bofors mountings. In the early 1950s all the RCN ships were converted to A/S destroyers with a generally uniform configuration: two twin 4in forward, a twin US 3in AA mount on the after superstructure and four single 40mm. Two squid mountings were fitted aft and the radar, W/T and sonar equipment updated. All, except the two ships with Mk VI directors, were fitted with a US Mk 63 fire control system.

The ships of the RAN also followed the general pattern of modifications applied to the RN 'Tribal's during the war but unlike the RCN ships were little changed post-war. In the early 1950s the *Arunta* and *Warramunga* had the after 4.7in mounting replaced by a Squid A/S mortar and their quad pom-pom by a twin 40mm. The *Bataan* only had the latter alteration. (M1839)

SOURCES

NATIONAL MARITIME MUSEUM (BRASS FOUNDRY, WOOLWICH ARSENAL)
Tribal Class Ships Covers 541, 541A
Canadian Tribal Class (British Built) Ships Covers 629, 629A.
Tribal Class Specification Book

THE NATIONAL ARCHIVES (KEW)
HMS Cossack Ship's Logs, 1938–39. ADM53/102010-015, ADM53/108114-125
New Construction Programme for Cruisers. ADM1/8828
'V' class Leader building Programme. ADM1/9376
HMS Afridi Ship's Book. ADM136/19
Report on Damage to Cossack, April 1940. ADM267/98
Report on Loss of Cossack, 1941. ADM267/93
Operations in Relation to Convoy HG75 and Loss of Cossack. ADM199/1197
Appropriation of Torpedoes, Torpedo Tubes, etc. ADM186/545
Progress in Naval Gunnery, 1939. ADM239/137
List of HM Ships Showing their Armaments, April 1938. ADM186/179
Drill Book for 4.7in Mk XII and XII* Guns on CP Mk XIX Mounting. ADM186/348
Handbook for 4.7in Mk XII and XII* Guns on CP Mk XIX Mounting. ADM234/192
Confidential Admiralty Fleet Orders (CAFOs), various entries 1937–1943. ADM182 series

OFFICIAL ADMIRALTY PUBLICATIONS (HMSO)
Machinery Handbook (BR 77)
Naval Marine Engineering Practice, 1955 (BR 2007)
Director Handbook, Part 12, 1937 (BR912[12])
Torpedo Control Pocket Book, 1951
Handbook on Naval Ammunition, 1935 (OU5463)
Admiralty Handbook on Ammunition, 1945 (BR 932)
Naval Electrical Pocket Book, 1933 and 1953. (BR 157)
Manual of Seamanship, Vol 1, 1937 and 1951
Manual of Seamanship, Vol 2, 1932 and 1951
Handbook of Wireless Telegraphy, Vol 1, 1938 (BR 229)
Admiralty Navigation Manual, Vol 1, 1938

BIBLIOGRAPHY
Brice, Martin H, *The Tribals* (Ian Allan, 1971)
Campbell, John, *Naval Weapons of World War Two* (Conway Maritime Press, 1985)
English, John, *Afridi to Nizam* (World Ship Society, 2001)
Hodges, Peter, *Tribal Class Destroyers* (Almark Publications, 1971)
Lenton, H T, *British Fleet and Escort Destroyers*, Vol 1 (Macdonald, 1970)
Newton, R N, *Practical Construction of Warships* (Longmans, 1957)

ORIGINAL PLANS USED IN THIS BOOK

'TRIBAL' CLASS DESIGN, NOVEMBER 1935
Profile	M1797
Superstructure, Forecastle and Upper Deck	M1796
Lower Deck and Hold	M1795
Sheer Drawing	M1792
Sections	M1798
Constructional Sections	M1791
Fly to Sheer Drawing, March 1936	M1793
Proposed Re-arrangement of After End, 1936	M1800

HMS COSSACK (General Arrangements, As Fitted August 1938)
Profile	M1801
Forecastle Deck, Bridges, etc	M1805
Upper Deck	M1802
Lower Deck	M1803
Hold	M1804
Sections	M1806

HMCS HAIDA (General Arrangements, As Fitted October 1943)
Sketch of Rig	M1820

HMS MOHAWK (General Arrangements, As Fitted October 1938)
Profile	M1840
Upper, Forecastle and Bridge Decks	M1842
Lower Deck and Hold	M1841
Sections	M1843

DETAIL DRAWINGS
HMS *Cossack*: Bullet Proof Plating, As Fitted	M1831
'Tribal' Class: Weather Deck Fittings, 1937	M1832
Fly to Weather Deck Fittings, December 1937	M1833
HMS *Nubian*: Arrangement of Petrol System, As Fitted 1938	M1812
HMS *Ashanti*: Expansion of Shell, Upper and Forecastle Deck Plating, As Fitted	M1807
HMS *Cossack*: Upper and Forecastle Decks Plating, As Fitted	M1808
General Arrangement of 4.7-inch Twin Mk XIX CP Mounting	S5725
HMS *Cossack*: Stowage of 2pdr Pom-Pom and 0.5-inch Magazine, As Fitted	M1827
HMS *Cossack*: Stowage of Nº3 4.7-inch Shell Room, As Fitted	M1826
HMS *Cossack*: Stowage of Nº3 4.7-inch Magazine, As Fitted	M1825
HMS *Cossack*: Torpedo Head Room and Torpedo Store Room, As Fitted	M1828
HMS *Ashanti*: Stowage of 4-inch Magazine (Port), As Fitted 1941	M1829
HMS *Ashanti*: Stowage of 4-inch Magazine (Starboard), As Fitted 1941	M1830
'Tribal' Class: Arrangements of Machinery In Engine Room (Sheet 1)	M1810
'Tribal' Class: Arrangements of Machinery In Engine Room (Sheet 2)	M1887
'Tribal' Class: Arrangements of Machinery In Boiler Rooms	M1811
HMS *Cossack*: Fresh & Salt Water and Oil Fuel Services, As Fitted – Profile	M1816
HMS *Cossack*: Fresh & Salt Water and Oil Fuel Services, As Fitted – Upper Decks	M1815
HMS *Cossack*: Fresh & Salt Water and Oil Fuel Services, As Fitted – Lower Decks	M1814
HMS *Cossack*: Ventilation Arrangement, As Fitted – Upper Decks	M1838
HMS *Cossack*: Ventilation Arrangement, As Fitted – Lower Decks	M1837
HMS *Cossack*: Holes in Bottom, As Fitted	M1809
HMS *Ashanti*: Twin Barrel Steam Capstan	M1813
HMS *Cossack*: Pneumatic Transmission of Messages, As Fitted	M1821
HMS *Nubian*: Arrangement of Main W/T Office, As Fitted	M1818
HMS *Nubian*: Arrangement of 2nd W/T Office, As Fitted	M1819
HMS *Cossack*: Echo Sounding Installation Type 753, As Fitted	M1834
HMS *Ashanti*: Arrangement of Steam Heating for Arcticisation, As Fitted	M1835
HMS *Eskimo*: Damage Caused by Enemy Action on 12 July 1943	M1836
HMCS *Athabaskan*, Profile, As Fitted	M1839

National Maritime Museum ship plans Exact scale colour prints of ship plans can be purchased online from **http://prints.rmg.co.uk** or please contact **pictures@rmg.co.uk** for scanning services.